Red Gadiantons

What the Prophets Have Taught about the Communist Secret Combination that Threatens Mankind

Zack Strong

This book is dedicated to the ancient Nephite prophet Moroni who relayed to mankind the Lord's commandment to "awake to a sense of your awful situation, because of this secret combination which shall be among you" (Ether 8:24), and who bore such a powerful witness against Satan's secret societies and ruthless conspiracies. May we be like him and stand boldly against Babylon and wickedness in high places and *never* deny the Christ (Moroni 1:3).

A special thank you to Kylie Malchus and her sister Jessica Malchus who did such a brilliant job bringing to life my vision for this book's cover art. Their amazingly professional work exceeded my wildest expectations. Please support these two remarkable Latter-day Saint women. Visit Kylie's Amazon profile at the link below. She has written several books, including the wonderful work *End Feminism; Save the World*, and spends much of her time producing art for patrons, often in collaboration with her likewise talented sister Jess. Again, a *huge* thank you to Kylie and Jessica Malchus for creating such a visually stunning cover for this book!

Visit Kylie Malchus's Amazon page here:
https://www.amazon.com/Kylie-Malchus/e/B00L6A7QE6/ref=sr_ntt_srch_lnk_1?qid=1527829328&sr=8-1

Contents

Introduction

"Let's get one thing straight at the very beginning. International communism is the self-avowed enemy of every loyal American. It has declared war against us and fully intends to win. The war in which we are engaged is total. Although its main battlefields are psychological, political and economic, it also encompasses revolution, violence, terror and limited military skirmishes. If we should lose this war, the conquering enemy's wrath against our people and our institutions will result in one of the greatest blood-baths of all history. Call it a "cold war" if it makes you feel better, but our freedom and our very lives are the stakes of this contest." – President Ezra Taft Benson, An Enemy Hath Done This, 165.

No Latter-day Saint living in tune with the Spirit and in harmony with the teachings of modern prophets can be confused regarding the identity of the enemy that lurks in "secret chambers" (D&C 38:13; 28) and seeks "to overthrow the freedom of all lands" (Ether 8:25). The Lord's servants have painstakingly identified our greatest enemy – the church of the Devil or synagogue of Satan – as the murderous communist conspiracy. Few subjects have drawn forth such emphatic, repeated, and ominous warnings from our prophets as secret combinations and the mortal threat they pose to man's agency and the progress of the Church.

It is the aim and design of this book to present the history of secret combinations as found in the holy scriptures and to document what our modern seers have revealed regarding the identity, tactics, goals, and catastrophic success of the modern conspiracies in our midst. I hope to impress upon you – as the Spirit and our beloved prophets have impressed upon me – that communism is *the* secret combination foreseen by Moroni and the most powerful and threatening of all the Devil's mechanisms for enslaving mankind.

The world has reached a critical crossroad. Latter-day Saints are faced with a myriad of difficult challenges and decisions. However, few have more sweeping and lasting impact for ourselves and the human family as the decision to stand with or against Babylon. The collective world has taken a stand for, and has entered into an alliance with, Babylon and the kingdom of the Adversary. Sadly, many Saints have also rejected – knowingly or inadvertently – the Gospel light in favor of Satan's deceptively decorated darkness. Many have fallen into forbidden paths because of the organized deception promulgated by the "servants of Satan" lurking throughout our society (D&C 10:5).

In 1986, President Ezra Taft Benson cautioned the Saints in this manner:

> "We live in a day of great challenge. We live in that time of which the Lord spoke when he said, "Peace shall be taken from the earth, and the devil shall have power over his own dominion." (D&C 1:35.) We live in that day which John the Revelator foresaw when "the dragon was wroth with the woman, and went to make war with the remnant of her seed, which keep the commandments of God, and have the testimony of Jesus Christ." (Rev. 12:17.) The dragon is Satan; the woman represents the Church of Jesus Christ. Satan is waging war against the members of the Church who have testimonies and are trying to keep the commandments. And while many of our members are remaining faithful and strong, some are wavering. Some are falling. Some are fulfilling John's prophecy that in the war with Satan, some Saints would be overcome. (See Rev. 13:7.)" (President Ezra Taft Benson, "The Power of the Word," General Conference, April, 1986).

In the years since President Benson uttered this warning, the world has spiraled out-of-control at an increased velocity. Satan's war against the Kingdom of God continues. Tragically, casualties are mounting because many of us have not taken the time to learn about our enemy. Because we do not understand Satan's strategies and the secret combinations he uses to direct his malicious assault, we have been caught flatfooted and ill prepared.

This book will help the Saints identify the enemy, his lies, his tactics, and his aims, and, thus, will arm them with power to resist and reject the cunning lies. With this essential knowledge, you will be able to more effectively defend your family and fortify them against all the raging tempests of darkness wreaking so much havoc on our society. The Adversary is waging open and covert, blatant and disguised war against the essential pillars of human happiness – faith, family and Freedom. If you arm yourself with the light of truth and the sword of the Spirit, you will plainly see the enemy for what he is – regardless of his clever disguises and deceptive labels – and will vanquish him every time he hurls a fiery dart at you or your loved ones.

Chapter 1

Our Imperative Duty

A frequently quoted verse of latter-day scripture states:

> "For there are many yet on the earth among all sects, parties, and denominations, who are blinded by the subtle craftiness of men, whereby they lie in wait to deceive, and who are only kept from the truth because they know not where to find it" (D&C 123:12).

With rare exceptions, we quote this verse and move on without discussing the connecting verses or the context that elicited such a declaration from the Prophet Joseph Smith. We likewise completely ignore the Prophet's proposed solution to the problem of mankind's being kept in darkness by men who "lie in wait to deceive."

Numerous verses in *Doctrine and Covenants* section 123 are adjoined with hyphens, making the meaning of one incomplete without the other. Verse twelve just cited is one such verse. It is adjoined to the former and subsequent verses. We would profit greatly from exploring these connected verses to learn more about our duty as Saints in relation to our brothers and sisters of the world who sit in suffocating darkness and who do not know where to find the truth that we enjoy.

Preceding verse twelve, we find the dear Prophet imploring the Saints to "gather" facts, lists, and names of the Saints' persecutors and oppressors (v. 1-9). These facts, he said, should be published "to all the world," including to "heads of government" (v. 6). He referred to the "diabolical rascality and nefarious and murderous impositions" heaped upon the Saints (v. 5) and requested they be published "in all their dark and hellish hue" (v. 6).

These malevolent deeds to be published included "the most damning hand of murder, tyranny, and oppression, supported and urged on and upheld by the influence of that spirit which hath so strongly riveted the creeds of the fathers, who have inherited lies, upon the hearts of the children, and filled the world with confusion, and has been growing stronger and stronger, and is now the very mainspring of all corruption, and the whole earth groans under the weight of its iniquity" (v. 7).

To notify the world of this gross wickedness was then, and is now, "an imperative duty that we owe to all the rising generation, and to all the pure in heart" (v. 11). This last verse is attached to verse twelve which informs us that there are many people who are kept from the truth because they know not where to find it. With this context in mind, the Prophet's following instructions, adjoined to and immediately following verse twelve, take on a far greater significance. He wrote:

> "Therefore, that we should waste and wear out our lives in bringing to light all the hidden things of darkness, wherein we know them; and they are truly manifest from heaven—
>
> "These should then be attended to with great earnestness" (v. 13-14).

It is highly significant to my mind that in response to the mass deception of humanity perpetrated by Satan's henchmen who "lie in wait to deceive," the Prophet's suggested course of action – the "imperative duty" we owe to mankind – is to "waste and wear out our lives in bringing to light all the hidden things of darkness." Have *you* worn out *your* life in exposing the things of darkness and the works of the Devil?

Joseph Smith the Seer gave us a warning regarding this counsel to expose Satan's "hidden works of darkness." Said he:

> "Let no man count them as small things; for there is much which lieth in futurity, pertaining to the saints, which depends upon these things. . . .
>
> "Therefore, dearly beloved brethren, let us cheerfully do all things that lie in our power" (v. 15, 17).

It is not a "small thing" to fight Satan's kingdom. It is not a secondary responsibility. It is an "imperative duty." It is one of the "weightier matters of the law" (Matthew 23:23). Indeed, "there is much . . . which depends upon these things" for ourselves and for the rising generation.

I ask again, not by way of condemnation, but by way of encouragement, what have *you* done to "bring to light the hidden things of darkness"? Have *you* worn out *your* life in obedience to these directives? Let us be faithful to the Prophet Joseph Smith's wishes and fight Satan with all the power of our spirits, and with every talent and resource at our disposal.

Some Latter-day Saints feel it is not the duty of a Christian to contend against the Adversary. Some think it improper to speak badly of anyone, even Satan and his hate-filled minions. They would rather tolerate Babylon and have a cordial relationship with Beelzebub than make the unpopular stand against the Prince of Darkness.

And even among those who *do* recognize the need to actively resist Satan's kingdom there are many who are too scared to act or who sit by waiting for the Church to lead the way by creating a regimented program to fight against evil and defend our rights and our God-inspired Constitution. Yet, the verses just noted make it abundantly clear that our duty is to drag into the light all of Satan's evil deeds and expose their diabolical character.

Additionally, we have the following scriptures to encourage us in our lofty task. In a famous revelation given through the Prophet Joseph Smith, the Lord commanded:

> "Contend against no church, save it be the church of the devil" (D&C 18:20).

Against this evil church, this "synagogue of Satan" (Revelation 2:9; 3:9), we are to fight with "the sword of the Spirit" (D&C 27:18), which the Apostle Paul informed us "is the word of God" (Ephesians 6:17). This sword, or the word of God, "is quick and powerful" and "shall divide asunder all the cunning and the snares and the wiles of the devil"

4

(Helaman 3:29). We are to *actively* wage war against Satan with the Lord's Spirit as our Excalibur. We are the Lord's shock troops – His Praetorian Guard tasked with defending His latter-day Kingdom against Satan's relentless machinations.

In Paul's famous "armor of righteousness" epistle, he tells the Saints that they need their armor – including the "sword of the Spirit," an offensive weapon – in order to wage war against evil in high places. Said he:

> "For we wrestle not against flesh and blood, but against principalities, against powers, against the rulers of the darkness of this world, against spiritual wickedness in high places" (Ephesians 6:11-17).

Fighting against the "rulers of the darkness of this world" is the very purpose we are instructed to don our armor and wield the sword of the Lord's Spirit! No true Saint can escape his duty to vigorously contend against "spiritual wickedness in high places." Satan's principalities grossly outnumber our own at the present time, yet *we* have the Lord's power. "If God be for us, who can be against us?" (Romans 8:31)

As will be quoted in more detail later, President Ezra Taft Benson taught the Saints that it is their solemn responsibility to be involved in the war against Satan; yes, even in the so-called "political" realm. In other words, we are to be engaged in the paramount issue of defending Freedom and human agency. In his brilliant April 1965 General Conference address "Not Commanded in All Things," he stated:

> "And now as to the last neutralizer that the devil uses most effectively—it is simply this: "Don't do anything in the fight for freedom until the Church sets up its own specific program to save the Constitution." This brings us right back to the scripture I opened with today—to those slothful servants who will not do anything until they are "compelled in all things." Maybe the Lord will never set up a specific church program for the purpose of saving the Constitution. Perhaps if he set one up at this time it

might split the Church asunder, and perhaps he does not want that to happen yet for not all the wheat and tares are fully ripe (D&C 86:7).

"The Prophet Joseph Smith declared it will be the elders of Israel who will step forward to help save the Constitution, not the Church. And have we elders been warned? Yes, we have. And have we elders been given the guide lines? Yes indeed, we have. And besides, if the Church should ever inaugurate a program, who do you think would be in the forefront to get it moving? It would not be those who were sitting on the sidelines prior to that time or those who were appeasing the enemy. It would be those choice spirits who, not waiting to be "commanded in all things" (D&C 58:26) used their own free will, the counsel of the prophets, and the Spirit of the Lord as guidelines and who entered the battle "in a good cause" and brought to pass much righteousness in freedom's cause. . . .

"Brethren, if we had done our homework and were faithful, we could step forward at this time and help save this country. The fact that most of us are unprepared to do it is an indictment we will have to bear. The longer we wait, the heavier the chains, the deeper the blood, the more the persecution, and the less we can carry out our God-given mandate and worldwide mission. The war in heaven is raging on earth today. Are you being neutralized in the battle?"[1]

Powerful words and piercing questions from a spiritual giant! We would do well to look ourselves in the mirror and ask: "Am I being neutralized in the battle for Freedom? Am I sitting on the sidelines? Am I too afraid to stand up against the Devil and oppose Babylon? What am *I* doing to further the Lord's plan of agency and Liberty?"

---

[1] President Ezra Taft Benson, "Not Commanded in All Things," Conference Report, April, 1965, 121-125, http://scriptures.byu.edu/#:t585:p401.

Latter-day Saints have been blessed with the light of the Restored Gospel. It is our duty and challenge to take the Lord's light to the world, to inform mankind of error, to proclaim truth, to stand as witnesses of the Savior Jesus Christ, and to stand on our watchtower day and night warning, teaching, beckoning, and inspiring. We have been saved to come to earth in these last days of tribulation for this very purpose.

Speaking prophetically of the last days, the Lord told the prophet Isaiah:

> "I have set watchmen upon thy walls, O Jerusalem, which shall never hold their peace day nor night: ye that make mention of the Lord, keep not silence,
>
> "And give him no rest, till he establish, and till he make Jerusalem a praise in the earth" (Isaiah 62:6-7).

To the modern Twelve Apostles, the Lord has given a like charge:

> "Contend thou, therefore, morning by morning; and day after day let thy warning voice go forth; and when the night cometh let not the inhabitants of the earth slumber, because of thy speech" (D&C 112:5).

And to each person who has received the warnings from these inspired watchmen on the walls of latter-day Zion, the charge is the same – to warn our neighbor. The Lord has instructed:

> "Behold, I sent you out to testify and warn the people, and it becometh every man who hath been warned to warn his neighbor" (D&C 88:81).

The book you are holding in your hands, or viewing on your electronic device, is a book of warning. I have spent my life pouring over the words, warnings, and instructions of the very watchmen Isaiah foresaw – the men called by our Lord in our day to deliver His word to the human family. Many years ago, I felt that the injunction to waste and wear out my life in bringing to light the hidden things of the Adversary was my life's mission. I have tried, as imperfectly as my efforts may have been, to share my vibrant and sincere testimony of the truth and of my Lord Jesus Christ. I love Him and I want to serve Him by defending truth and opposing falsehood and wickedness wherever possible.

One of the greatest truths I have learned for myself is that Satan operates through conspiracies, most often called "secret combinations" in the scriptures. I have learned that these secret conspiracies are alive today and that they seek to destroy the Freedom of *all* lands and to subjugate humanity under the iron yoke of bondage. Our modern prophets have identified the most threatening of these secret societies as the communist conspiracy. They have compared the communist conspiracy to the Gadianton Robbers of Nephite times. Because of these stunning comparisons, I have chosen the name "Red Gadiantons" to describe the modern communist conspirators who, like the ancient Gadiantons, have united with Satan in his war against Christ and against the Freedom of the world.

My heart and soul have been touched profoundly by the warning voice of prophets such as President Ezra Taft Benson, President David O. McKay, President J. Reuben Clark, Jr., President Marion G. Romney, President John Taylor, Elder Bruce R. McConkie, Elder Hans Verlan Andersen, and others. These watchmen identified the threats that exist in our midst and at length, over many decades, preached against them with the scorching sword of the Spirit. This book is an attempt to follow in their tradition of warning and instructing the Saints of the Church regarding Satan's greatest threats to our spiritual wellbeing, our families, our happiness, and our precious Liberty.

Some Latter-day Saints recoil at the mention of secret combinations. They think it is an unsavory topic and prefer to talk about "happy" subjects like hope and faith. They avoid what they wrongly call "contention" at every turn. Yet, this is a misguided and dangerous mindset. It is not in harmony with the scriptures nor the teachings of modern prophets. Enoch, Elijah, Jonah, Abinadi, Alma, Samuel the Lamanite, and other prophets were sent *into* the fray, not away from it. It is our duty, armed with the Spirit, to advance against the enemy and dismantle his kingdom piece by piece, preparing the way for the return of the true King, Jesus Christ.

Alma the younger explained that one of the reasons the Lord would reveal *The Book of Mormon* record in the last days was to, referring to the Jaredites, "bring forth out of darkness unto light all their secret works and their abominations." According to Alma, the Lord said: "I will bring to light all their secrets and abominations, unto every nation that shall hereafter possess the land." Alma then confirmed that "thus far the word of God has been fulfilled; yeah, their secret abominations have been brought out of darkness and made known unto us" (Alma 37:25-26).

As explained by the prophet Alma, the Lord has decreed that all peoples whom He brings to this land shall know about the secret combinations and works of darkness of past nations who lived here. This is *imperative* if Alma's instructions to Helaman, and, by proxy to us, are to be fulfilled. Alma instructed Helaman to "teach [the people] an everlasting hatred against sin and iniquity" (Alma 37:32). This would not be possible if we remained ignorant of sin and iniquity and the secret societies which facilitate so much of the world's wickedness.

Not only must we have a knowledge of sin, but President Brigham Young taught that we must study evil:

> "We should not only study good, and its effects upon our race, but also evil, and its consequences."[2]

What President Young recommended is a far cry from burying our heads in the sand because we think secret combinations and politics are contentious or dark topics. It is our *duty* – as acknowledged by Alma, Brigham Young, and other inspired leaders – to study Lucifer's ways and understand the devastating consequences they bring upon humanity. We

---

[2] President Brigham Young, *Journal of Discourses*, Vol. 2, 93-94, February 6, 1853, http://jod.mrm.org/2/90.

are to study and preach against them as fervently as Nephi did from his garden tower (see Helaman 7 and 8).

Elder Hans Verlan Andersen explained why it is so vital to have a working knowledge of sin and evil. He wrote:

> "The scriptures contain numerous statements concerning Satan and evil which we are under obligation to study and learn if we obey the commandment to "live by every word which proceedeth forth out of the mouth of God." (D&C 98:11) Since God is omniscient, he knows evil as well as good and if we are going to become "as gods knowing good and evil," we must be instructed in both. A failure to learn about Satan's plan for man here on earth would be fatal to the full exercise of free agency. The reason for this lies in the fact that in the final analysis, free agency is the opportunity to choose between good and evil. But in order to intelligently make such a choice one must understand the alternatives – both of them. To the extent that one is ignorant of these alternatives, to that same extent he has not made a complete choice. Until a person understands Satan's plan he can never be certain he does not believe in it and is not helping to carry it out."[3]

What a powerful statement! If we do not understand Satan's plan, how do we know we aren't following it, at least in some respects? If we do not understand the principles of communism, for instance, how indeed can we say we are not promoting or supporting communism? Similarly, if we do not understand the principles of Liberty, how can we claim to be defenders of Freedom? If we want to be fully righteous, we must first become fully informed.

This book is designed to part the veil and reveal Satan's coordinated plan to destroy our Father's children. We will study the tactics of the Adversary

---

[3] Hans Verlan Andersen, *The Great and Abominable Church of the Devil* (1972), 23.

and expose the major players and key philosophies involved. By acquainting ourselves with Lucifer's communistic agenda, we empower ourselves to notice it at work, resist its advances, and intelligently warn others of the danger.

The world squabbles about whether it is the Jews, the Jesuits, the Chinese, the bankers, the New Agers, the Americans, the Bilderbergers, etc., who pull the strings in modern day secret combinations. Yet, our prophets have been kind enough to not only answer the question "Who is the man behind the curtain?" but have expounded the matter in some detail over many decades.

My heart aches for those not of our faith who do not have access to the scriptures and to the words of our latter-day prophets. Yet, I feel an even greater sense of pity — and, at times, indignation — for those Latter-day Saints who *do* have access to latter-day scriptures and the words of the prophets, but do not use them or heed them.

Many members of the Church are almost criminally ignorant of the revelations and teachings of the prophets regarding secret combinations, politics, and related issues. It is my sincere wish that this book will help break the ice for some of my fellow Saints that we all may become one in our worship of the Savior and in the building up of Zion. I bear my witness that it is never too late to reverse course, learn new truths, and recommit ourselves to God's Gospel. If we may have been less than stalwart in times past, we yet have the chance to arm ourselves with the sword of truth and join the fight.

Now, a few words about the "official" or "unofficial" nature of the quotes I share in this book, and the commentary that I provide. I want to make it abundantly clear that I do not pretend to declare Church doctrine. My book is *not* an official publication of the Church. Yes, I fully believe that the quotes I share represent the Church's position relative to communism and secret combinations, but I hold no keys, no position of authority, and have no assignment from the president of the Church by which I can authoritatively declare doctrine.

Declaring doctrine is the sole job of the president of the Church and I defer to him. My words, therefore, should not be taken as an official statement of the Church, though I *have* included within this text many such official declarations from past first presidencies and presidents of the Church which one would do well to heed.

It is my only desire, and I have made the attempt with all the sincerity of my soul, to provide an accurate interpretation of the Church's position relative to communism in particular and secret combinations in general. I have a burning testimony of the truthfulness of the core argument I present (namely, that communism is of Satan and constitutes *the* secret combination foretold anciently), but I have no authority or keys whereby I can state such as "doctrine." You are left totally free to decide for yourself regarding the accuracy of the positions I have taken. If what I have presented is not accurate, "judge ye" (2 Nephi 33:11). You are under no obligation to accept doctrine from my mouth.

That being stated, Elder John A. Widtsoe offered this illuminating comment regarding statements from Church leaders. Said he:

> "The history of the restored Church is evidence that counsel given by the Prophet and President of the Church has always been found to be for the best good of the people. They who follow their own inclinations in opposition to the light that comes from the head of the Lord's Priesthood on earth are never gainers thereby. To argue whether this or that utterance is official and therefore should not be obeyed, is at best a futile exercise."[4]

If "this or that" statement transmitted in this book is not "official," you may judge for yourself. I have tried to diligently pull together quotes which, to my best understanding, represent the common attitude and mind of the General Authorities as expressed in their talks and writings

---

[4] Jerreld L. Newquist, ed., *Prophets, Principles and National Survival* (Salt Lake City, Utah: Publishers Press, 1977), 8.

over the course of this entire dispensation. But you are free to choose for yourself.

President Joseph Fielding Smith once wrote:

> "When one of the brethren stands before a congregation of the people today, and the inspiration of the Lord is upon him, he speaks that which the Lord would have him speak. It is just as much scripture as anything you will find written in any of these records. . . .
>
> "The word of the Lord, as spoken by other servants at the general conference and stake conferences, or wherever they may be when they speak that which the Lord has put into their mouths, is just as much the word of the Lord as the writings and the words of other prophets in other dispensations."[5]

Whether the individual utterances recorded in this work were or were not spoken by inspiration, is your duty and privilege to discern. An inspired declaration can only be understood when the hearer or reader possesses the same Spirit by which it was uttered (D&C 50:17-22). Thus, we are called to actively seek the Spirit and to be instructed from on high. And we had better be very careful that we do not wrongly judge in this matter (Moroni 7:18), for the apostles I've quoted just may be speaking the very word of our Master and Lord.

In your individual quest for certainty and spiritual confirmation of the statements cited hereafter, I encourage you to remember Elder Widtsoe's remark that it is normally a "futile exercise" to nitpick and make lists of "official" and "unofficial" statements. Remember that those who reject the prophets' counsel "are never gainers thereby." Yet, you have your agency and may accept or reject them as you see fit and as the Spirit directs you.

---

[5] President Joseph Fielding Smith, *Doctrines of Salvation*, Vol. 1 (Salt Lake City, Utah: Bookcraft, 1954), 186.

It should be recalled that prophets have not only a right, but a sacred duty, to speak on matters of political, cultural, social, or economic importance. Some Saints are uncomfortable when a prophet speaks on politics or social issues. They want the prophet to mind his business or just stick to "religious" topics. And some even believe Church leaders have no legal right to speak about politics at all, erroneously citing "separation of church and state" as justification for their view. To such, I quote several statements on this vital subject.

President Brigham Young famously taught:

> "I defy any man on earth to point out the path a Prophet of God should walk in, or point out his duty, and just how far he must go, in dictating temporal or spiritual things. Temporal and spiritual things are inseparably connected, and ever will be."[6]

The scriptural record, as well as the history of the latter-day Church, illustrate that temporal and spiritual matters are "inseparably connected, and ever will be" (see also D&C 29:31-34). A prophet, therefore, may speak on any subject as directed by the Lord – and the Saints are under obligation to accept his teachings as if from the Lord's own mouth (D&C 1:38).

Another time, President Young said:

> "The brethren have been talking about temporal things. We cannot talk about spiritual things without connecting with them temporal things, neither can we talk about temporal things without connecting spiritual things with them. They are inseparably connected. . . .
>
> ". . . We, as Latter-day Saints, really expect, look for, and we will not be satisfied with anything short of being governed and

---

[6] President Brigham Young, *Journal of Discourses*, Vol. 10, 364, November 6, 1864, http://jod.mrm.org/10/358.

controled by the word of the Lord in all of our acts, both spiritual and temporal. If we do not live for this, we do not live to be one with Christ. . . .

"When we talk of politics we are one. The world complain of us with regard to our politics, and enquire, "Are there any Democrats here? Are there any Republicans here?" We do not care who rules; we are satisfied with God, who setteth up one man, and casteth down another."[7]

As Latter-day Saints, we ought to be concerned with principles, not parties; ideals, not individuals. We cannot afford to be swept up in a cult of personality or to cling tribally to one or another political party or social movement. We must take the Lord's revealed word – most importantly the modern instructions delivered by His prophets – as our standard and *never* compromise regardless of the circumstances, the popularity of such instructions, or the tide of prevailing opinion.

In practical terms, this means that if the revealed principles of God dictate that we reject one bad political candidate even if the opposing candidate might be worse, it is our duty to reject him, and come what may. Likewise, if the prophets tell us to reject communism, to do so is our duty regardless of persecution. And again, if the prophets tell us to uphold the U.S. Constitution, we must do so in the same spirit we would do family history, give Priesthood blessings, or hold family home evening.

A third quotation from President Young is noteworthy:

"Whenever there is a disposition manifested in any of the members of this church to question the right of the President of the whole church to direct in all things, you see manifested the

---

[7] President Brigham Young, *Journal of Discourses*, Vol. 10, 329, June, 1864, http://jod.mrm.org/10/328.

evidences of apostasy—of a spirit which, if encouraged, will lead to separation from the church and final destruction."[8]

Truly, it is the spirit of apostasy that inspires men and women in this Church to pick and choose which prophetic utterances they will heed. It is pride which prompts us to say we know more than the prophets when the prophets lift up their voices to instruct the Saints. The best policy has always been to follow the prophet for, as our primary hymn states, "he knows the way."

Fourthly, President Brigham Young gave this profound observation:

> "When we see a religion, and one which is claimed to be the religion of Christ, and it will not govern men in their politics, it is a very poor religion, it is very feeble, very taint in its effects, hardly perceptible in the life of a person. The religion that the Lord has revealed from heaven unites the hearts of the people, and when they gather together, no matter where they are from, they are of one heart and one mind."[9]

Every aspect of an individual's life ought to be altered, transformed, and elevated by the Gospel of the Lord Jesus Christ. A religion that does not instruct its adherents in the principles of politics, social relations, and so forth, is incomplete and "feeble."

The Saints of God should feel honored that the Lord cares enough about them to give them counsel regarding their politics and day-to-day activities. True it is that we must not be commanded in all things, but it is equally true that all our actions must accord with revealed principles and stay within the prescribed boundaries of proper behavior outlined by the Lord. The same God who created the earth and upholds the universe has

---

[8] President Brigham Young, *Journal of Discourses*, Vol. 11, 136, August, 1865, http://jod.mrm.org/11/129.

[9] President Brigham Young, *Journal of Discourses*, Vol, 14, 159, June 4, 1871, http://jod.mrm.org/14/156.

16

the inherent right to instruct us in any aspect of our lives He feels necessary. It is our privilege to be so led.

President Joseph F. Smith, speaking of then President of the Church John Taylor, said:

> "He is placed over the people for the purpose of leading them in the way of truth and righteousness, and it is his business to look after the temporal—if you chose to make any distinction between the temporal and spiritual—as well as the spiritual things. And President Taylor has as much right to direct the people in temporal things as he has in spiritual things. We ought to acknowledge that right, and ought to do it freely and cheerfully, because we should see that it is right. We are under no compulsion to do so if we do not see that it is right; but at the same time it is a correct principle, and every Latter-day Saint ought to have intelligence enough to know that this is the best thing for him to do—to be united, to be one with his brethren."[10]

When prophets speak on temporal matters, we should listen to them as "freely and cheerfully" as we would their General Conference addresses on subjects like faith, hope, and charity. Of course, as President Smith pointed out, each Saint is free to choose for himself. But if we as a people are to be one – a Zion society – we must become one even in politics and issues related to the free will and agency of mankind.

Lastly, in a 1959 *Church News* piece, Elder Mark E. Petersen stated:

> "There are people in the Church who sometimes complain because some of their leaders, either bishops or stake presidents, or even occasionally one of the General Authorities, gives advice on practical, everyday, temporal matters.

---

[10] President Joseph F. Smith, *Journal of Discourses*, Vol. 25, 251, July 18, 1884, http://jod.mrm.org/25/244.

"There are some who suppose that the direction of the Church leaders should be limited to spiritual matters and never touch the practical things in life.

"They forget that all through the centuries the prophets of ancient times gave practical advice, even on political and other current questions. They did it as the prophets of God. They did it as the servants of God trying to guide and direct the people into paths of safety. There were some who objected anciently to this kind of advice, but in spite of objections the prophets gave it – the people could follow it or reject it as they liked, but the advice was there."[11]

As in ancient times, so today. The prophets have spoken frequently on politics and have expounded political principles applicable in all ages and for all succeeding generations. We can accept or reject their words, but there they sit beckoning, warning, and lighting the correct path. Do we have the courage to stand with the Lord's servants in *all* things?

I pray that we will not be like the prideful and unrighteous in olden days who raised objections when the Lord's servants spoke on controversial topics and when they warned of threats to their societies, such as when Alma, Helaman, and Nephi warned of the Gadianton infestation among the Nephites. May we instead humble ourselves, heed our modern prophets' warnings and counsel, and sustain the men our Savior has chosen to preside over His Church.

President Ezra Taft Benson pleaded with the Saints to listen to the warnings of the Lord's watchmen in these last days. He declared:

"As watchmen on the tower of Zion, it is our obligation and right as leaders to speak out against current evils—evils that strike at

---

[11] Newquist, ed., *Prophets, Principles and National Survival*, 19.

the very foundation of all we hold dear as the true church of Christ and as members of Christian nations."[12]

The greatest evil our leaders have spoken out against is the communist conspiracy and its allied philosophies. As you will discover, not only did President Benson speak of communism and international conspiracy, but many prophets and apostles have done so since the founding of the Church. It is their "right as leaders" to raise the warning voice and it is our duty and privilege as members of the Lord's Church to heed their inspired messages – messages designed to inform and protect us.

A much earlier first presidency rhetorically asked the Saints:

> "Brethren, when will you be wise, and follow in the precepts of wisdom? Must you first be destroyed and wasted away like unto the Nephites, or will you hearken unto counsel in time to save yourselves and your families, your flocks and your herds from destruction?"[13]

The Book of Mormon declares that it was the Satanic secret society of Gadianton that ultimately destroyed the Nephite nation. Their prophets had warned of this demonic cabal but their words were rejected. Will it be the same with the United States and the American People? Will we be destroyed by the enemies of Freedom identified by our modern prophets, or will we heed these clear warnings and move to oppose Satan's advancing kingdom?

I bear my testimony that Jesus is the Christ, our Lord and Master. He is the Lord of lords and King of kings. His Kingdom has been established on earth

---

[12] President Ezra Taft Benson, "Watchman, Warn the Wicked," *Ensign*, July, 1973, https://www.lds.org/ensign/1973/07/watchman-warn-the-wicked?lang=eng.

[13] First Presidency, "Eleventh General Epistle," April 10, 1854, in James R. Clark, ed., *Messages of the First Presidency*, Vol., 2, (Salt Lake City, Utah: Bookcraft, 1965), 132.

again through The Church of Jesus Christ of Latter-day Saints. I am proud to belong to that marvelous organization.

I sincerely desire that this book will be a great aid and resource to Church members who want to know what the prophets have taught about the threats to our society – including the grave threat of communism – and who wish to know more about secret combinations from a scriptural and LDS point of view. I hope that the reader may feel inspired to come to Christ and openly declare that he is on the Lord's side.

Let me share few words of autobiographical interest before turning my full attention to the scriptures and the prophets. I have spent many years studying these topics, with a special emphasis on communism. At age twelve, the Holy Spirit touched my heart in a profound way and confirmed to my soul the truth that communism is *not* dead and that the Soviet Union never "fell." I learned that the USSR faked its demise in order to fool the West and lull us into a false sense of security in preparation for delivering what it assumes will be a death blow when the moment is right. That profound witness changed my life and I bear my testimony of that truth and am happy that my secular study has further confirmed what the Spirit revealed to me on that hallowed occasion.

My early studies were greatly aided by my time serving a mission for the Church in Moscow, Russia from 2006-2008 and by learning the Russian language. These studies have only intensified since that time and I have become even more involved in the political field and in teaching and spreading ideas.

In January 2018, I self-published my first book titled *A Century of Red*. That book details the origins, history, and legacy of the communist conspiracy, with an emphasis on its occult nature. I have also written many articles, run my own website and Facebook pages, and ran for Congress in Utah's third district under the Independent American Party banner in 2014.[14] I have tried my best to expose the "hidden things of darkness" because I know that it is an "imperative duty" to do so.

Furthermore, I cherish the U.S. Constitution, which I declare was inspired by the Lord and is a sacred document as holy as the holy scriptures. I'm a dyed in the wool American and a thorough Jeffersonian in my principles. I honor our Founding Fathers who were, according to the revelations of the Lord, "wise men" whom God "raised up" for the purpose of establishing a free Republic and instituting the Constitution based upon Biblical principles (D&C 101:77-80). As Latter-day Saints, we *must* defend the U.S. Constitution from its enemies, chief among whom are the communist conspirators who understand that the Constitution is a major bulwark against their despotism.

To close this opening chapter, I express great appreciation for your willingness to pick up this book and give it the time of day. I invite you, as you read, to pray to know for yourself the truthfulness of the quotations I have presented. I pray that you will catch the vision and understand the urgency with which we must fight Satan's kingdom.

I am wonderfully flawed and my efforts no doubt have been less than perfect, but I have tried with all my heart, mind, and soul to wake people up, teach correct principles, spread truth, and denounce Satan's evil combinations which war against our faith, families, and Freedom. No matter the cost, I will continue to raise the warning voice, because to do so is our "imperative duty." If this book helps anyone in the fulfillment of this duty, I will consider it a great success. May the Lord Jesus Christ bless you with wisdom so that you in turn can defend your family against the Devil's secret combinations which hide in our midst today and threaten the entire overthrow of our once great society.

---

[14] I'm happy to report that despite being illegally barred front the debates by the state of Utah even though I was officially on the ballot, I took third because of the generous votes of those almost 3,200 people who still love Liberty and understand the corruption of both the Republican and Democratic Parties. For more about the principles of the Independent American Party, see their website: https://www.independentamericanparty.org.

Chapter 2

Satanic Secret Societies

in the Scriptures

In the New World in 52 B.C., a contentious election gave rise to a murderous secret society – an elitist sect known as the Gadianton Robbers. The members of this conspiracy were bound together with Satanic blood oaths and united in their hatred of God's people and their lust for political power. This clique resolved to subvert society, undermine faith in God, degrade the culture, corrupt the law, capture the economy, assassinate the opposition, and, finally, place its members in key positions in the government, thus dominating and controlling the Nephite nation.

This Satanic secret society ultimately caused the entire destruction of the Nephite People. As the evidence will demonstrate, a secret society patterned off of this Gadianton cabal exists today and is working feverishly toward the same goal of total dominion not only over the American People, but the whole of mankind.

The ancient Nephite People were united, for a time, in a self-governing republic where rule of law and individual rights held sway. The Nephite system allowed the People to vote for judges to administer their laws for the good of society. In 52 B.C., the chief judge – a righteous man named Pahoran – died in office, thus necessitating a popular election to select a new leader. Per custom, the Nephites often elected one of the judge's sons to fill the vacant position. In this instance, three of Pahoran's sons campaigned for the judgeship.

The names of the men in the running were Pahoran, Paanchi, and Pacumeni. The scriptural account tells us that "Pahoran was appointed by the voice of the people to be chief judge and a governor over the people of Nephi" (Helaman 1:5). Acknowledging his defeat, Pacumeni "did unite with the voice of the people" (Helaman 1:6). Paanchi, however, was not as humble as his brother. We read:

> "But behold, Paanchi, and that part of the people that were desirous that he should be their governor, was exceedingly wroth; therefore, he was about to flatter away those people to rise up in rebellion against their brethren" (Helaman 1:7).

Clinging tenaciously to their inspired system of law and order, as well as their God-given duty to choose their representatives, the Nephite People put an end to Paanchi's machinations before they could lead to civil war. The scripture tells us "he was taken, and was tried according to the voice of the people, and condemned unto death; for he had raised up in rebellion and sought to destroy the liberty of the people" (Helaman 1:8). Perhaps, in a different time and a different place, this would have been the end to the story. Unfortunately, this was only the genesis of a development that changed the course of Nephite history.

The inspired account informs us:

> "Now when those people who were desirous that [Paanchi] should be their governor saw that he was condemned unto death, therefore they were angry, and behold, they sent forth one Kishkumen, even to the judgement-seat of Pahoran, and murdered Pahoran as he sat upon the judgement-seat" (Helaman 1:9).

After the murder, the assassin named Kishkumen:

> "went unto those that sent him, and they entered into a covenant, yea, swearing by their everlasting Maker, that they would tell no man that Kishkumen had murdered Pahoran. . . .
>
> "And Kishkumen and his band, who had covenanted with him, did mingle themselves among the people, in a manner that they all could not be found" (Helaman 1:11-12).

Thus, with the assassination of the chief Nephite leader, and with a blasphemous oath sworn in the name of God to conceal the murderer, the conspiratorial sect later to be known as the Gadianton Robbers was born. Let us analyze what we have learned so far about the goals, organization, and tactics of this secret society.

First, it is significant that this murderous secret combination was born during a combative election; and not just any election, but a national election for the highest office in the land. This fact immediately tells us that the conspiracy was politically motivated, sought political power, and was willing to go to great lengths to manipulate events in their favor.

There is a short-sighted tendency today to look to organized crime families or street gangs as the secret combinations prophesied to exist during our day. While the conspiracy routinely uses organized crime to fulfill its purposes, we must always remember that secret societies exist to bring about changes in politics. By controlling the course of politics, a secret society wields great power over the destiny – political, economic, cultural, and religious – of any nation. Thus, the first thing to underscore is that the Gadiantons' chief goal was to manipulate or capture the mechanisms of government.

Next, it is significant to understand the basic organization of this society. The Gadianton sect was a *secret* society. They did not want to be known and thus "mingled" among the People to avoid detection. To enforce their code of secrecy, these elitists swore oaths to one another in the name of God. Because the Savior Jesus Christ has ordered us to "swear not at all; neither by heaven, for it is God's throne" (3 Nephi 12:34; Matthew 5:34), we can assume that the Gadiantons' oath was of a Satanic nature. This is in fact confirmed by additional scriptures which will be discussed later. The key takeaway is that the Gadianton cabal was composed of elite families which operated in secret and used deception as their chief tool. This secrecy was enforced by Satanic oaths keeping the members in check and ensuring their loyalty to the aims of the Brotherhood.

Finally, to carry out their objective of manipulating politics, the Gadiantons employed murder as their defining method of operation. As will be discussed in some detail throughout this book, the Gadiantons constituted a murder cult and killed everyone from politicians to prophets to laymen to defectors. They assassinated leaders in public and silenced holy men in private. They started wars and fomented revolutions. With dagger in hand, the conspirators murdered their way to prominence and power. They are men who "love death" (Proverbs 8:36) and who "made a covenant with death" and hell (Isaiah 28:15).

As will be noted, once the Gadiantons had seized power, they often used the guise of law to convict righteous people and dissenters of fictitious crimes during public show trials, thereby putting them to death "legally." Whether with the sanction of corrupt judges and laws or in the shadows, forever and always these Satanic conspirators murdered and employed the threat of death to get their way and carry out their dark agenda.

As the Gadianton society laid low after the assassination of Pahoran, the Nephites elected Pacumeni to fill the judgement-seat. In 51 B.C., a short war erupted as the Nephites' arch enemies, their kinsmen the Lamanites, invaded and conquered the capital city of Zarahemla. Pacumeni was killed in the struggle, leaving the judgement-seat vacant once more. In 50 B.C., when order was restored following the Nephite victory over the Lamanites, a prophet of God named Helaman was elected to be the new chief judge. At this stage, the Gadiantons silently maneuvered into position to reenact the assassination drama and seize the government.

The scriptures tell us that among the band "there was one Gadianton, who was exceedingly expert in many words, and also in his craft, to carry on the secret work of murder and of robbery; therefore he became the leader of the band of Kishkumen" (Helaman 2:4). From this man, the conspiracy derives its infamous name.

The reader will note that Gadianton is described as a great orator, a man of flattery, a common thief, and a cunning murderer. The Gadianton Society came to embody these very characteristics, and more especially murder. We should also remember that Kishkumen, the assassin and nominal founder of the group, was a man skilled in trickery and disguises, and "was upheld by his band, who had entered into a covenant that no one should know his wickedness" (Helaman 2:3). Thus, the Gadianton Robbers adopted the traits of their homicidal and scheming founders.

Under Gadianton's shrewd leadership, the organization became disciplined and harnessed their collective influence and talents towards destroying Helaman and conquering the government. We read:

> "Therefore [Gadianton] did flatter them, and also Kishkumen, that if they would place him in the judgment-seat he would grant unto those who belonged to his band that they should be placed in power and authority among the people; therefore Kishkumen sought to destroy Helaman" (Helaman 2:5).

During a secret planning meeting where details of the assassination were hammered out, one of Helaman's servants was in attendance. We are not told how except that it was "through disguise" (Helaman 2:6), but this servant had uncovered the existence of the Gadiantons and infiltrated their ranks. At the meeting, the servant learned of the plot to murder Helaman. Unfortunately for the conspiracy, this man remained faithful to Helaman and the government and played a key role in delaying the Gadiantons' plans.

We are told that:

> "as [Kishkumen] went forth towards the judgement-seat to destroy Helaman. . . .

> "[the servant] met Kishkumen, and he gave unto him a sign; therefore Kishkumen made known unto him the object of his desire, desiring that he would conduct him to the judgement-seat that he might murder Helaman.

> "And when the servant of Helaman had known all the heart of Kishkumen, and how that it was his object to murder, and also

that it was the object of all those who belonged to his band to murder, and to rob, and to gain power, (and this was their secret plan, and their combination) the servant of Helaman said unto Kishkumen: Let us go forth unto the judgement-seat.

". . . but behold, the servant of Helaman, as they were going unto the judgement-seat, did stab Kishkumen even to the heart, that he fell dead without a groan. And he ran and told Helaman all the things which he had seen, and heard, and done" (Helaman 2:6-9).

Upon being informed of the existence of this murder cult, Helaman moved quickly to eradicate them. He "did send forth to take this band of robbers and secret murderers, that they might be executed according to the law" (Helaman 2:10).

Tragically for the Nephite nation, Gadianton suspected that they had been detected when Kishkumen did not return as scheduled. We read that "he feared lest that he should be destroyed; therefore he caused that his band should follow him. And they took their flight out of the land, by a secret way, into the wilderness" (Helaman 2:11). Helaman's faithful servant earned the Nephites a brief reprieve, but, within one generation, the Gadianton cabal would regroup and strike again.

During the years that followed, the Gadianton sect remained underground and operated from the shadows, carefully avoiding detection by the authorities. However, their pernicious influence was felt throughout both Nephite and Lamanite society. Without knowing it, the People became infected by this insidious virus and soon began showing the contagion's hideous signs and scars.

We are told that in 49 B.C. "a little pride" could be seen in the People's conduct (Helaman 3:1). "Pride goeth before destruction, and an haughty spirit before a fall." (Proverbs 16:18). However, on the whole, the Nephites remained a good People and the Lord blessed them with "exceedingly great prosperity" so much so "that even the high priests and the teachers [of the Church] were themselves astonished beyond measure" (Helaman 3:24-25). Yet, by 41 B.C. that "little pride" had blossomed and the Nephites are described as being "lifted up in pride" (Helaman 3:34). One short year later, we read of "the exceedingly great pride which had gotten into the hearts of the people" (Helaman 3:36).

From that point on, the Nephites became wicked and materialistic, weak and apathetic, and even changed their once just and worthy laws to better accommodate their self-serving and corrupt natures (Helaman 4:20-25). In this condition, war again broke out between the Nephites and Lamanites in 35 B.C. Significantly, it seems the war occurred in no small part because of the secret society of Gadianton. We are told that "this great loss of the Nephites, and the great slaughter which was among them, would not have happened had it not been for their wickedness and their abomination which was among them" (Helaman 4:11).

The term abomination generally denotes especially loathsome wickedness amounting to idol worship. However, the word is also associated in more than one place with the Gadianton conspiracy and secret combinations in general, such as when Moroni wrote to us and chided: "Yea, why do ye build up your secret abominations to get gain . . . ?" (Mormon 8:40); or when Alma used variations of the phrases "secret abominations," "secrets and abominations," and "secret murders and abominations" ten separate times in Alma chapter 37, a chapter devoted largely to warning about secret combinations. I believe the Gadianton Order is what is being implied in Helaman 4:11 by the word "abomination."

At any rate, the text had previously stated that in 43 B.C. "there was continual peace established in the land, all save it were the secret combinations which Gadianton the robber had established in the more settled parts of the land, which at that time were not known unto those who were at the head of government; therefore they were not destroyed out of the land" (Helaman 3:23).

Is it a coincidence that the Gadianton sect became established in the cities at the same time the People became prideful and materialistic? Is it a coincidence that Gadiantonism gripped Nephite hearts just before "many dissensions in the church" sprang up and "dissenters . . . went up from the Nephites unto the Lamanites" and urged them to war (Helaman 4:1-5)? Is it a coincidence that societal infiltration by the Gadiantons occurred at the very time the Nephites began changing their laws? Is it a coincidence that the prophet, in hindsight, explained that an "abomination" was among the Nephites which was primarily responsible for bringing this awful situation upon them?

So bad were the circumstances caused by the Gadiantons and the pride of the People that "the church had begun to dwindle; and they began to disbelieve in the spirit of prophecy and in the spirit of revelation; and the judgments of God did stare them in the face" (Helaman 4:23). Because they embraced wicked ways, the Nephites became "weak" and "the Spirit of the Lord did no more preserve them" (Helaman 4:24). All of this had befallen the Nephites "in the space of not many years" (Helaman 4:26) – years which, not coincidentally, coincided with the establishment and building up of the Gadianton secret society.

Silently and incrementally the Gadianton Robbers subverted society, orchestrated changes in the law, corrupted the People's faith, and helped instigate a devastating war. A mere twenty-four years after the failed assassination attempt on Helaman drove them underground, the Gadiantons had become so entrenched and so strong that they were ready to make their presence felt.

In 26 B.C., the chief judge Cezoram "was murdered by an unknown hand as he sat upon the judgement-seat. And it came to pass that in the same year, that his son, who had been appointed by the people in his stead, was also murdered" (Helaman 6:15). These back-to-back assassinations of the chief magistrate had a corrosive and disillusioning effect upon the People, for we read in the immediate aftermath that "the people began to grow exceedingly wicked again" (Helaman 6:16).

The Nephites became so wicked that many of them began to unite with the Gadianton Robbers. But it is important to note that the *Gadiantons* were the carriers of this caustic contagion. This wickedness spread from *them* to the rest of society. The fruit of wickedness did not grow spontaneously – its seeds had been carefully planted by the Gadianton conspirators years previous. In confirmation of this fact, we read that the Nephites:

> "began to set their hearts upon their riches; yea, they began to seek to get gain that they might be lifted up one above another; therefore they began to commit secret murders, and to rob and to plunder, that they might get gain.

> "And now behold, those murderers and plunderers were a band who had been formed by Kishkumen and Gadianton. And now it had come to pass that there were many even among the Nephites, of Gadianton's band. But behold, they were more numerous among the more wicked part of the Lamanites. And they were called Gadianton's robbers and murderers.

> "And it was they who did murder the chief judge Cezoram, and his son, while in the judgement-seat" (Helaman 6:17-20).

Yes, the Nephite People became prideful and engaged in a wide range of criminality, but the Gadianton secret society was the impetus. *They* were the murderers and plunderers. *They* were the assassins and political shakers. *They* encouraged whoredoms and vice. *They* instigated violence and promoted organized crime. *They* initiated the People into Satan's wicked oaths and covenants.

The account continues and describes crucial details about the inner workings and motives of this secret clique:

> "Satan did stir up the hearts of the more part of the Nephites, insomuch that they did unite with those bands of robbers, and did enter into their covenants and their oaths, that they would protect and preserve one another in whatsoever difficult circumstances they should be placed, that they should not suffer for their murders, and their plunderings, and their stealings.

"And it came to pass that they did have their signs, yea, their secret signs, and their secret words; and this that they might distinguish a brother who had entered into the covenant, that whatsoever wickedness his brother should do he should not be injured by his brother, nor by those who did belong to his band, who had taken this covenant.

"And thus they might murder, and plunder, and steal, and commit whoredoms and all manner of wickedness, contrary to the laws of their country and also the laws of their God.

"And whosoever of those who belonged to their band should reveal unto the world of their wickedness and their abominations, should be tried, not according to the laws of their country, but according to the laws of their wickedness, which had been given by Gadianton and Kishkumen" (Helaman 6:21-24).

These verses are highly revealing. We are informed that Gadianton did much more than preside over a shadowy Brotherhood of criminals. Rather, Gadianton created a secret system of government – endowed with the full range of power over life and death granted to legitimate governments – that ruled its members with an iron fist. This shadow government operated by means of blood oaths and Satanic covenants. It was cloaked in ritual and occult symbolism remarkably similar to those found in modern Freemasonry.

These oaths served a dual purpose: First, the oaths cast a cloak of secrecy over the entire society and allowed its members to commit any crime with impunity; and second, they constituted a threat to anyone with cold feet who might seek to leave the group and inform the authorities. Anyone who dared "reveal unto the world of their wickedness and their abominations" was taken and tried "according to the laws . . . which had been given by Gadianton and Kishkumen." In a word, the leaders of the clique kept the underlings in line with blackmail and death threats.

A society guarded by "secret signs," "secret words," and laws permitting wickedness appeals to carnal man. Such guarantees of protection no matter one's behavior embolden people in committing wickedness and in satisfying every lust of the flesh without worry of punishment. The prophet Alma explained this tendency when he taught:

> "Now, if there was no law given – if a man murdered he should die – would he be afraid he would die if he should murder?
>
> "And also, if there was no law given against sin men would not be afraid to sin" (Alma 42:19-20).

The Gadianton Order gave no laws prohibiting sin, but, rather, *encouraged* murder, sexual perversion, lying, theft, and every other sin so long as it did not injure or impede the society's power or progress. This hedonistic "do what thou wilt" philosophy governed the Gadiantons as it did the anti-Christ Korihor and all apostate groups, secret societies, and leaders throughout history.

Of this Devilish "do what thou wilt" philosophy, President James E. Faust said:

> "We please the devil when we argue that all roads lead to heaven and that, therefore, it does not matter which road we take, because we will all end up in God's presence. And he is no doubt pleased when we contend that we are all God's children; therefore, it makes no difference to which church a person belongs, because we are all working for the same place.
>
> "This man-made philosophy – for such it is – sounds good, but the scriptures do not support it. I assure each of you that the road to God's presence is not that easy. It is strait and narrow."[15]

---

[15] James E. Faust, *Finding Light in a Dark World* (Salt Lake City, Utah: Deseret Book Company, 1995), 76.

One of the core ideologies emanating from ancient times states that sin is a myth, that there are no otherworldly consequences for one's actions, that judgement day will never come, and that God's laws are oppressive and restrictive. Satan teaches the following to his supporters:

> "And behold, others he flattereth away, and telleth them there is no hell; and he saith unto them: I am no devil, for there is none – and thus he whispereth in their ears, until he grasps them with his awful chains, from whence there is no deliverance" (2 Nephi 28:22).

While the nature of their oaths manifest that the ancient Gadiantons clearly acknowledged the existence of God, and the reality of beings from the spirit world, Satan's conspirators then and now deny that he is an evil being. They see him as Lucifer, the light bearer. Lucifer promotes himself as a benevolent being who is here to teach, uplift, and emancipate mankind from the chains of Christian superstition. Just as he told Eve in the Garden that he is her brother, so, too, does Satan tell his followers that he is their advocate, their brother, their friend, and a spiritual master to help them evolve and become like the gods.

When Satan appeared to the anti-Christ Korihor, these were his contradictory instructions and teachings. Korihor recounted:

> "But behold, the devil hath deceived me; for he appeared unto me in the form of an angel, and said unto me: Go and reclaim this people, for they have all gone astray after an unknown God. And he said unto me: There is no God; yea, and he taught me that which I should say" (Alma 30:53).

It is fascinating that Satan appeared as an angel, which likely means he appeared surrounded by light and power. He apparently represented himself as an advanced being or heavenly messenger. He taught Korihor that the Nephite People – who were Christians – had gone astray after an "unknown God." Korihor was told to "reclaim" them, which implies bringing them to the worship of a god that Satan would have represented as the true god – a god in opposition to the "unknown God" who was Jesus Christ. Yet, at the same time, Satan – parading in angelic disguise – taught that there was no god and told Korihor to teach carnal things that eventually led many people to commit whoredoms (Alma 30:17-18).

In studying both ancient and modern occultism, Satanism, Theosophy, Witchcraft, and today's New Age movement, I am struck at how remarkably similar their doctrines are to what Satan revealed to Korihor. And just as Satan personally appeared as an angel, many contemporary occult teachings have even been transmitted to modern anti-Christs by supernatural beings posing as advanced men and "Ascended Masters of Wisdom." The leader of these Masters of Wisdom is a figure called Lord Maitreya, known by other names in various cultures, such as "the Christ" to Christian occultists, "the Messiah" to Jewish Kabbalists, Krishna to Hindus, the Imam Mahdi to Muslims, and so forth.

These Masters of Wisdom have taught many pupils who subsequently became internationally influential. Such individuals include Helena Blavatsky, Annie Besant, and Alice Bailey, the three leading figures in the modern occult movement known as Theosophy which kick started the New Age movement and has a heavy influence in the United Nations.

These "angelic" Masters taught Blavatsky, Bailey, and their fellows that modern society has gone astray and that they must be reclaimed and brought to worship correctly, which constitutes worshipping an ecumenical god – a force that permeates the universe. In some traditions, such as Theosophy, the adherents outright admit that their god is Lucifer – but they of course maintain that he is a benevolent being of light and love who stands in opposition to the "cruel" and "intolerant" god known as Jehovah.

For instance, Helena Blavatsky, in her influential tome *The Secret Doctrine*, wrote:

> "The appellation of Sa'tan . . . "an adversary" . . . belongs by right to the first and cruellest *"adversary of all the other gods"* –

Jehovah, not to the Serpent, which spoke only words of sympathy and wisdom."[16]

Again, she penned this remarkable admission:

"The devil is now called Darkness by the Church, whereas, in the Bible he is called the "Son of God" (see Job), the bright star of the early morning, Lucifer (see Isaiah). There is a whole philosophy of dogmatic craft in the reason why the first Archangel, who sprang from the depths of Chaos, was called Lux (Lucifer), the "Luminous Son of the Morning," or manvantaric Dawn. He was transformed by the Church into Lucifer or Satan, because he is higher and older than Jehovah, and had to be sacrificed to the new dogma."[17]

Numerous such statements lauding Lucifer can be found littering the writings of modern occultists, New Agers, communists, and their ilk. Just as God is the same yesterday, today, and forever, so, too, is Satan the same yesterday, today, and forever. His game plan never changes. He uses the same methods and tactics to deceive, destroy, and subjugate mankind. He appears as an angel of light, tells his followers he is a benevolent being and a fellow servant on the path to enlightenment, and preaches that there is no Devil, no sin, and no hell. From day one in the Garden of Eden, this has been Lucifer's method of operations on planet earth.

At this point, a step back is in order. Was Gadianton the real originator of the oaths and covenants mentioned above, and of the libertine ideology that characterized the conspirators? True, he formulated the rules of the Gadianton society and disciplined his co-conspirators, but where did the overarching plot come from? The scriptures give us the answer:

---

[16] Helena Blavatsky, *The Secret Doctrine*, Vol. 2 (1888; Alhambra, California: The Cunningham Press, facsimile reprint, 1982), 387.

[17] Blavatsky, *The Secret Doctrine*, 70-71.

"Now behold, those secret oaths and covenants . . . were put into the heart of Gadianton by that same being who did entice our first parents to partake of the forbidden fruit –

"Yea, that same being who did plot with Cain, that if he would murder his brother Abel it should not be known unto the world. And he did plot with Cain and his followers from that time forth. . . .

"Yea, it is that same being who put it into the heart of Gadianton to still carry on the work of darkness, and of secret murder; and he has brought it forth from the beginning of man even down to this time.

"And behold, it is he who is the author of all sin. And behold, he doth carry on his works of darkness and secret murder, and doth hand down their plots, and their oaths, and their covenants, and their plans of awful wickedness, from generation to generation according as he can get hold upon the hearts of the children of men" (Helaman 6:25-30).

In these verses, the core truth of all conspiracy is revealed. The great secret behind conspiracy is that *the plotters are Luciferians*. It is a Luciferian cabal – *not* an atheist, Jewish, Jesuit, Islamic, U.S., or Russian conspiracy.

The golden thread that binds the international conspirators together today is the same one that bound the Gadianton Robbers together; namely, their belief in, worship of, and oaths sworn to Satan. In other words, the conspirators are *knowing* Satanists who covenant with the Father of Lies to do his bidding and carry forth his plans for the destruction and enslavement of mankind.

The schemers may pose as Jesuits or Hindus or atheists, but these are disguises meant to deflect suspicion from their real religious creed. Their true allegiance is to the Luciferian doctrine as expounded in secret combinations. The political manifestation of this religious creed is inevitably communistic.

This conspiracy is a generational conspiracy that has existed – in a stunningly consistent form – in nearly every age, from the time of Cain to the present. Because of modern technology, it is international in scope and exists in every nation. A pagan network now spans the globe and wields almost exclusive power in high places.

The conspiracy is designed to conquer the globe and use the power and wealth of the world to usher in the reign of the Anti-Christ and a one-world occult religion. The plotters will not establish Catholicism, Islam, or Judaism as the world religion, nor will the Catholic Church or the Rabbinical councils lead the movement. Rather, an ecumenical form of occultic, pagan Devil worship will be foisted upon mankind. It will be a hodgepodge of "do what thou wilt" doctrines. All roads will lead to Lucifer and the Adversary will be enthroned as the god of this world. And make no mistake; it is Satan's overarching goal to be the sole ruler of this world and to usurp the crown from Christ.

In *The Pearl of Great Price*, the establishment of a Satanic covenant between Cain and Lucifer is explained. The experience begins with these lines:

> "And Cain loved Satan more than God. And Satan commanded him, saying: Make an offering unto the Lord" (Moses 5:18).

This statement makes it clear that Cain knew Satan. Satan evidently appeared to Cain. It is my assumption that he appeared as an "angel of light" (2 Corinthians 11:13-14) as he did when seducing and instructing the anti-Christ Korihor (Alma 30:53), and as his followers do when they pose as Masters of Wisdom. Satan no doubt played the role of mentor, told Cain that he was his brother, flattered Cain that he would look after and protect him, taught him the lie that "whatsoever a man did was no crime" (Alma 30:17), and turned his heart against God's laws, which would have been made to appear oppressive and restrictive.

Significantly, Satan taught Cain the art of deception. Notice that the Devil does not command Cain to make an offering to *him*. Rather, Lucifer instructs Cain to make an offering "unto the Lord." We know from the Prophet Joseph Smith that Cain held the Priesthood and was authorized to make sacrifices, and that he was most likely a high priest in the Church before his fall from grace.[18] Thus, Satan wanted his servant Cain to infiltrate the Lord's Church from within. Cain was taught to keep up appearances and continue officiating in ordinances and sacraments while in reality his heart was dark and he was secretly serving Lucifer. He was Christian in name only. He was a wolf in sheep's clothing.

President Brigham Young gave this insight into Cain's motivations and confirmed that Cain did not sin ignorantly, but made a conscious choice to serve Satan in order to get power and gain:

> "Cain conversed with his God every day, and knew all about the plan of creating this earth, for his father told him. But, for the want of humility, and through jealousy, and an anxiety to possess the kingdom, and to have the whole of it under his own control, and not allow anybody else the right to say one word, what did he do? He killed his brother."[19]

Please note that it is for power and control of "the kingdom" that Cain murdered Abel. And all of this was done at the behest of Lucifer who was the puppet master directing this sad spectacle from behind the scenes.

---

[18] "The power, glory and blessings of the Priesthood could not continue with those who received ordination only as their righteousness continued; for Cain also being authorized to offer sacrifice, but not offering it in righteousness, was cursed. It signifies, then, that the ordinances must be kept in the very way God has appointed; otherwise their Priesthood will prove a cursing instead of a blessing." – Joseph Smith, *Documentary History of the Church*, Vol. 4, 209, October 5, 1840, https://byustudies.byu.edu/content/volume-4-chapter-11; also in Joseph Fielding Smith, ed., *The Teachings of Joseph Smith* (American Fork, Utah: Covenant Communications, Inc., 2002), 172-173.

[19] President Brigham Young, *Journal of Discourses*, Vol. 2, 142-143, December 3, 1854, http://jod.mrm.org/2/136.

Before Cain murdered Abel, however, the Lord intervened and admonished Cain, telling him "Satan desireth to have thee" (Moses 5:23). He warned Cain that if he continued down that path, "it shall be said in time to come — That these abominations were had from Cain; for he rejected the greater counsel which was from God" (Moses 5:25). Sadly, Cain did not heed the Lord's counsel. Instead, his lust to "possess the kingdom" and to rule over the peoples of the earth and to be pampered like a monarch drove him into the outstretched arms of the Adversary:

> "And Cain was wroth, and listened not any more to the voice of the Lord, neither to Abel, his brother, who walked in holiness before the Lord.
>
> "And Adam and his wife mourned before the Lord, because of Cain and his brethren.
>
> "And it came to pass that Cain took one of his brothers' daughters to wife, and they loved Satan more than God.
>
> "And Satan said unto Cain: Swear unto me by thy throat, and if thou tell it thou shalt die; and swear thy brethren by their heads, and by the living God, that they tell it not; for if they tell it, they shall surely die; and this that thy father may not know it; and this day I will deliver thy brother Abel into thine hands.
>
> "And Satan sware unto Cain that he would do according to his commands. And all these things were done in secret.
>
> "And Cain said: Truly I am Mahan, the master of this great secret, that I may murder and get gain. Wherefore Cain was called Master Mahan, and he gloried in his wickedness" (Moses 5:26-31).

This account confirms many of the hints and inferences given about secret combinations in the book of Helaman and elsewhere in *The Book of Mormon*. For instance, we are taught with certainty that *Satan* is the founder of these secret combinations. He is the father of *all* conspiracy. It is he who administered the first blood oaths and wicked covenants to mankind through Cain.

Cain did not invent these oaths and covenants. Lucifer invented them and personally administered them to Cain, telling him what to do and say. Cain simply served as Satan's earthly emissary to initiate his brothers into the same oaths and covenants. Whereas he was formerly a high priest in the true Church, he became, after his initiation into the conspiracy, the first high priest of Satan's counterfeit church. Thus we are told by the Lord that Cain is the mortal father of these "abominations," a word, as noted, that refers to both idol worship and organized conspiracy.

"Conspiracy" is another term used specifically by the Lord. In a revelation to the Prophet Joseph Smith, the Lord revealed that Abel "was slain by the conspiracy of his brother" (D&C 84:16). This conspiracy led Cain to boast and to consider himself a "master." He adopted the title "Master Mahan, and he gloried in his wickedness."

We are informed that, through his wickedness, Cain would "rule over" Satan (Moses 5:23). In what sense would Cain "rule over" the arch-enemy of God? Scholar Hugh Nibley explained the meaning of this curious phrase in these words:

> "Cain rule over Satan? Yes, that is the arrangement—the devil serves his client, gratifies his slightest whim, pampers his appetites, and is at his beck and call throughout his earthly life, putting unlimited power and influence at his disposal through his command of the treasures of the earth, gold and silver. But in exchange the victim must keep his part of the agreement, following Satan's instructions on earth and remaining in his power hereafter. That is the classic bargain, the pact with the Devil, by which a Faust, Don Juan, Macbeth, or Jabez Stone achieve the

pinnacle of earthly success and the depths of eternal damnation."[20]

In truth, Cain does not rule over Satan in any meaningful sense. Rather, he serves as a pawn in the Devil's game. However, because of Cain's oaths, Satan was "at his beck and call" and used his demonic influence and cunning to bring Cain to power and glory in life and to shield him from the unwanted consequences of his actions. Like the genie of Arabic lore[21], Satan appears at the request of his mortal "master" and figuratively grants his wishes and desires — most of which are materialistic and hedonistic.

In the end, Cain's bargain was a fool's bargain, and he got the short end of the stick. He bargained with the Lord of the damned who had nothing but death and hell to offer. Instead of a place in one of God's kingdoms of glory, Cain was conquered by Satan and will receive his eternal reward with his master in the lakes of fire and brimstone prepared for such murderers and apostates. Satan persuaded Cain to commit unpardonable crimes, and he is now a son of perdition. And, ironically, even in mortality Cain did not prosper. He was detected and cursed by the Lord and his name is now synonymous with murder and betrayal. Truly, "the devil will not support his children at the last day, but doth speedily drag them down to hell" (Alma 30:60).

The specifics of the Satanic oaths described above are also interesting. These oaths serve as the prototypical oaths sworn by Satan's henchmen in all generations. We are told that Cain swore by his throat, and his

---

[20] Hugh Nibley, "A Strange Thing in the Land: The Return of the Book of Enoch," Part 8, *Ensign*, December, 1976, accessed March 11, 2018, https://www.lds.org/ensign/1976/12/a-strange-thing-in-the-land-the-return-of-the-book-of-enoch-part-8?lang=eng.

[21] Genies, often referred to as djinn or jinn, are actually demonic entities — the unembodied followers of Lucifer. Though called by a different name, these jinn are evil spirits that tempt and torment mankind. Thus, the modern conception of a genie in a lamp has its basis in reality and is another reminder that Satan's influence spans the globe, cuts across cultures, and infests every religion.

brothers swore by their heads, to never reveal the "great secret." The implication is that an initiate will have his throat cut, or literally lose his head, if he divulges the secrets of the Brotherhood. It is a blood oath whose violation carries the death penalty.

Satan always commands his followers to swear not only by their own heads, but "by the living God." You will recall that the first Gadiantons swore "by their everlasting Maker" to not reveal the secrets of the society (Helaman 1:11). And, in Jaredite times, Satan's initiates swore – in nearly identical fashion to Cain and his co-conspirators – "by the God of heaven, and also by the heavens, and also by the earth, and by their heads, that whoso should vary from the assistance which Akish desired should lose his head; and whoso should divulge whatsoever thing Akish made known unto them, the same should lose his life" (Ether 8:14).

Swearing such an oath is not mere blasphemy, but outright mockery of the true God by the imposter god Lucifer. Satan poses as the Almighty and pretends that he, like God, has authority and power over life and death. He pretends that he, like God, has the power to fulfill the innermost desires of the human heart. In reality, Satan is impotent and possesses no power whatsoever except the power of deception and trickery. The only desires he fulfills are the lusts of the flesh and of the carnal mind. Having no true power of his own, and no original ideas because his soul if full of darkness, Satan endlessly imitates God's methods.

God works through sacred covenants and oaths, the violation of which brings upon us His righteous judgments. In imitation of these methods, Satan offers his followers oaths which serve as a cloak to cover their sins, and which also carry a penalty – a penalty of a brutal death for disobedience. God's covenants are calculated to bind families together, bind individuals to God, inspire the human heart to valiancy in the cause of righteousness, and always point to the redemption of the Savior Jesus Christ. Satan's covenants, by contrast, stimulate fear and inspire no one to good deeds, repentance, or faith in Christ. Through the use of these evil covenants and oaths, Satan binds the gullible to him and, upon threat of death, wields them as weapons in his war against mankind and the Godhead. They are pawns in his game.

After Cain covenanted with Satan, he willfully murdered his brother Abel in cold blood. He "gloried in that which he had done, saying: I am free; surely the flocks of my brother falleth into my hands" (Moses 5:33). It is supremely ironic that Cain believed he had found Freedom in murder. In reality, he had forged an unbreakable chain – a chain which Satan will use to drag him into the abyss at the judgement day.

Trusting Lucifer's hollow promises, Cain assumed he would inherit Abel's glory as well as his property. He believed his crime would go unpunished and that he would escape divine judgement. He believed swearing allegiance to Satan would protect him. By swearing his soul to Lucifer, perhaps Cain believed he would earn mansions in Satan's kingdom – a kingdom that Lucifer no doubt flattered him would eventually triumph over God's.

Members of secret conspiracies in all ages act as if their false god has promised them immunity for their crimes and a seat at his right hand when he will, as they suppose, rule the earth. These men seem to truly believe that Lucifer's side is going to win. As the sad spectacle foreseen in Isaiah 14:4-22 suggests, Lucifer's followers will be shocked to see their master dragged down into the pit in chains at the Judgement Day. When the scales fall from their eyes, they will lament:

> "Art though also become weak as we? art thou become like unto us? Thy pomp is brought down to the grave, and the noise of thy viols: the worm is spread under thee, and the worms cover thee.

> "How art thou fallen from heaven, O Lucifer, son of the morning! how art thou cut down to the ground, which didst weaken the nations!" (Isaiah 14:10-12).

When the curtain falls on Satan's play, the actors he has employed will know they have been deceived. They will realize then that their oaths and covenants earned them a place with their master in hell, not in Heaven.

But until that day, these men will preach Satan's gospel with missionary zeal. They will commit any crime, break any law, tell any lie, start any war, and use any deception to carry out their agenda of conquering total political power by which they can dictate a way of life for the people of the world. The crowning jewel of the global order which the modern conspirators seek to create will be a Luciferian world religion. And it all started with Cain.

Despite his former position in the Lord's Church, Cain hardened his heart against the Lord's ways and failed to fully comprehend His unrivaled omnipotence and supremacy over Satan in all things. Instead, he loved Satan more than God. Yet, the Lord will not be mocked. Shattering Lucifer's promise to shield Cain and conceal his evil deeds, the Lord directly confronted Cain with the death of his brother Abel. Per his training at the hand of the Adversary, Cain lied and denied his involvement. However, the Lord knew his guilt and informed him:

> "The voice of thy brother's blood crieth unto me from the ground.

> "And now thou shalt be cursed from the earth which hath opened her mouth to receive thy brother's blood from thy hand" (Moses 5:35).

Realizing he was caught and his deed was known, Cain at once began deflecting blame away from himself, simultaneously blaming Satan and God. In his petulant tone, Cain said:

> "Satan tempted me because of my brother's flocks. And I was wroth also; for his offering thou didst accept and not mine" (Moses 5:38).

In response to his deflections and excuses, the Lord "set a mark upon Cain" and he was "shut out from the presence of the Lord" (Moses 5:40-41). His murder did not bring him the flocks and property and prestige he coveted; they brought him infamy, a curse, and spiritual darkness. All of Satan's promises, no matter how flattering or temporarily beneficial, lead to ultimate degradation and misery.

Once the Lord had cursed Cain, Cain was ostracized from the community and fled with his family to the land of Nod. Though he was detected, the oath-bound conspiracy he had formed with Satan continued. Cain's great grandson Lamech eventually rose to the position Cain had occupied, that of Master Mahan. We are told that Lamech gathered his wives together and told them he had murdered a man for revealing the conspiracy's secrets to the uninitiated. Of this murder, we are informed:

> "For Lamech having entered into a covenant with Satan, after the manner of Cain, wherein he became Master Mahan, master of that great secret which was administered unto Cain by Satan; and Irad, the son of Enoch, having known their secret, began to reveal it unto the sons of Adam;
>
> "Wherefore Lamech, being angry, slew him, not like unto Cain, his brother Abel, for the sake of getting gain, but he slew him for the oath's sake.
>
> "For, from the days of Cain, there was a secret combination, and their works were in the dark, and they knew every man his brother.
>
> "Wherefore the Lord cursed Lamech, and his house, and all them that had covenanted with Satan; for they kept not the commandments of God, and it displeased God, and he ministered not unto them, and their works were abominations, and began to spread among all the sons of men. . . .
>
> "And thus the works of darkness began to prevail among all the sons of men" (Moses 5:49-52,55).

Here we have the first recorded murder intended to silence a fellow initiate. This murder was committed "for the oath's sake," thus proving the murderous nature and intent of Satan's oaths. It should be remembered that these same oaths given to Cain and Lamech were handed down by Satan to Gadianton (Helaman 6:25). They also exist among today's secret conspiracies, as will be discussed later.

From the time of Cain and his grandson Lamech, this Satanic secret society spread the work of destruction and murder and whoredoms "among all the sons of men." By the time the prophet Enoch was sent to preach, the Lord explained:

> "And for these many generations ever since that day that I created them, have they gone astray, and have denied me, and have sought their own counsels in the dark; and in their own abominations have they devised murder, and have not kept the commandments, which I gave unto their father, Adam.

> "Wherefore, they have foresworn themselves, and, by their oaths, they have brought upon themselves death; and a hell have I prepared for them, if they repent not (Moses 6:28-29).

These verses again suggest that the Lord links "abominations" with the oaths and covenants of the secret societies founded by Satan and Cain. The dark deeds of these conspiracies are frequently at the fore when the Lord warns His people and instructs His prophets. Indeed, the prophet Moroni informed us that secret combinations are the "most abominable and wicked above all, in the sight of God" (Ether 8:18).

Over the centuries, the wickedness stimulated by this secret society became so gross and prevalent that the scriptures record that man's heart "was only evil continually" (Genesis 6:5). "And in those days Satan had great dominion among men, and raged in their hearts; and from thenceforth came wars and bloodshed; and a man's hand was against his own brother, in administering death, because of secret works, seeking for power" (Moses 6:15).

As a last ditch effort to bring back His wayward children, God called Enoch to preach the Gospel to the "sons of men," that is, to the non-members then populating the earth. As part of His call to Enoch, the Lord said:

> "Enoch, my son, prophesy unto this people, and say unto them— Repent. . . .

"For these many generations, ever since the day that I created them, have they gone astray, and have denied me, and have sought their own counsels in the dark; and in their own abominations have they devised murder, and have not kept the commandments, which I gave unto their father, Adam.

"Wherefore, they have foresworn themselves, and, by their oaths, they have brought upon themselves death; and a hell I have prepared for them, if they repent not" (Moses 6:27-29).

This is an interesting passage and reveals some of the chief reasons the Lord was so angry at earth's inhabitants. To my mind, these verses demonstrate the pervasive nature of the secret combinations handed down from Cain and Lamech. Notice that the Lord told Enoch that because of their "abominations" and their "oaths," people had "devised murder," "foresworn themselves," and "brought upon themselves death." To foreswear one's self is to renounce something; in this case, the Gospel and its covenants. As a substitute, they adopted Satan's oaths and abominations. To enter Satan's secret oaths and participate in his covenants is to utterly repudiate God's ways and to rebel against Heaven. This is precisely what the Antediluvians did and, in so doing, "brought upon themselves death."

Because of His mercy and love God decided to cleanse the earth with a flood in order to give His sons and daughters who still had to come into mortality a legitimate chance to grow up in righteousness. If these multitudes had been born to the earth's inhabitants then living – those who had rejected the Gospel and actively participated in Satan's secret combinations – they would have been brought up in iniquity and would have similarly adopted and perpetuated Lucifer's dark covenants.

In sending the Flood upon the earth, the Lord was preserving a righteous posterity through the family of Noah – a posterity with a chance to grow up hearing the words of eternal life free of the deadening influence of secret combinations. Thus, Satan's secret oaths, covenants, and plans were buried, along with his fanatical followers, in the Great Deluge.

When the flood waters receded, Noah established a righteous society following the patriarchal pattern revealed to Adam. However, through transgression, Noah's son Ham was cursed and denied the Priesthood. One of Ham's transgressions was, prior to the Flood, to marry a woman named Egyptus. Egyptus was of the lineage of Cain. It was through Egyptus that the curse of Cain was maintained (Abraham 1:21, 24). Thus, it was through Ham's and Egyptus's cursed lineage that idolatry and a false priesthood would once more enter the world.

Within two generations after the waters receded and Noah's family began to spread, Satan once again forged a beachhead of wickedness on planet earth. Though exact dates are uncertain, two great kingdoms arose almost concurrently: The Babylonian Kingdom of Nimrod and the Egyptian Kingdom under Pharaoh. We will first consider Egypt.

Abraham chapter 1 tells us the origin of Egypt. Egypt was "discovered" by one of Noah's granddaughters, a woman named Egyptus (Abraham 1:23-24). Egyptus was the daughter of Ham, and named after her mother, Egyptus. It is interesting that Egypt was "discovered." Did it exist before the Flood? Were the great pyramids actually constructed *before* the Flood? Could the Flood describe the curious water erosion on the Sphinx? We do not know. But, as described, we do know Egypt's origin *after* the Deluge.

Egyptus's oldest son was named Pharaoh. Pharaoh became the first ruler of the new government of the land thereafter called Egypt. We are told that Pharaoh was "a righteous man" and a wise and just king. Pharaoh was "seeking earnestly to imitate that order established by the fathers in the first generation, in the days of the first patriarchal reign, even in the reign of Adam, and also of Noah, his father, who blessed him with the blessings of the earth, and with the blessings of wisdom, but cursed him as pertaining to the Priesthood" (Abraham 1:26).

In the beginning, the governmental type revealed by the Lord was patriarchal. That is to say, each family constituted a miniature nation, with the father – who was the patriarch – presiding. This divinely-revealed government was a Priesthood government led by the father. Pharaoh "earnestly" wanted to imitate this mode of Priesthood government, but did not have access to the Holy Priesthood because of his Hamic lineage. We are told by the prophet Abraham:

> "Now, Pharaoh being of that lineage by which he could not have the right of Priesthood, notwithstanding the Pharaohs would fain claim it from Noah, through Ham, therefore my father was led away by their idolatry" (Abraham 1:27).

Though he could not hold the Priesthood, Pharaoh and his successors (who adopted the name Pharaoh as their title), imitated the Priesthood order. Egypt's priesthood was, therefore, a false and counterfeit version that led to institutionalized "idolatry." Satan *always* establishes counterfeit churches, priesthoods, covenants, and gospels to lure people away from the true Gospel of the Son of God. He always encourages his followers to intrude where they have no right, and to claim that which is not theirs.

From the earliest days of its existence, Egypt was the cradle of false religion, occultism, and magic. Not having access to the true Priesthood, the rulers of Egypt turned to idol worship and embraced Satan's signs and wonders which had the hollow ring of true Priesthood miracles. No doubt secret societies of the type created through Cain were soon established in idolatrous Egypt. In fact, a number of secret societies have traced their lineage back to secret Egyptian brotherhoods. For instance, one Freemason, Albert Churchward, testified:

> "If Masonry had not its origin in the Sacred Mysteries of the Ancient Egyptians, how could these rites and ceremonies, signs and symbols, have found their way into it? These sacred mysteries were the same amongst the Priests of the Mayas in Central America and Peru in South America.

> "The passwords for the various degrees are the same, or have the same meaning; the signs and symbols are the same; and the

Rituals are identical; which can be proved by any Brother who will take the trouble to learn to read the old hieroglyphic languages. . . .

"From the downfall of the old Egyptian Empire, five thousand years ago, or more, up to the last few hundred years, we have passed through a dark and degenerate age. Then our altars were thrown down, our Brotherhood scattered over the face of the earth, and some of our secrets were lost to many. But there were remnants of the Brotherhood who went forth from Egypt into various parts of the world, carrying the true doctrines and secrets with them, some one part, some another.

". . . the so-called Lodges in England and Scotland were formed by a scattered few, who, to avoid the terrors of the law, and to keep their religious rites and ceremonies pure and unsullied, as they had received them from the parent source – old Egypt – met in secret places and had resort to private meetings. This, therefore, was one original source."[22]

Isn't it curious that what we call Freemasonry – which is an apostate version of true temple worship – was had in ancient Egypt just as the scriptures attest? It was an imitation of the true patriarchal order and the High Priesthood of the Son. Because the Egyptians had no right to that Priesthood, however, it became a curse and led to rampant idolatry, magic, and occultism which has been preserved down through the millennia by a secret Brotherhood and by the personal ministrations of Satan who is the founder of this wickedness.

The historical record is clear that the Egyptian tradition of magic reaches to its very beginnings. E.A. Wallis Budge, one of the early Egyptologists whose work is still very valuable, in fact stated: "The belief in magic . . . is

---

[22] Albert Churchward, *The Arcana of Freemasonry: A History of Masonic Signs and Symbols* (1915; San Francisco: Weiser Books, reprint, 2005), 108-109, 111-112.

older in Egypt than the belief in God."[23] He stated: "In the "white" and "black" magic of the Egyptians most of the magic known in other countries of the world may be found."[24] This magical tradition was so entrenched that Budge noted:

> "As almost every man, woman, and child in Egypt who could afford it wore some such charm or talisman, it is not to be wondered at that the Egyptians were at a very early period regarded as a nation of magicians and sorcerers. Hebrew, and Greek, and Roman writers referred to them as experts in the occult sciences, and as the possessors of powers which could, according to the circumstances, be employed to do either good or harm to man."[25]

There has likely never been a nation as magically-inclined as Egypt or a land where the priesthood of darkness was so thoroughly entrenched as part of the official governing structure of society. And, because of the scriptures, we know the origin of this idolatry.

Elder Bruce R. McConkie gave us this illuminating insight into what magic really is:

> "In imitation of true religion with its miracles, signs, and gifts of the Spirit, Satan has substitute rituals and practices called magic. Attempts by unauthorized and therefore powerless ministers to duplicate the miraculous wonders of true religion result in the degenerate worship of magic. In its nature magic is the art which produces effects by the assistance of supernatural beings or by a

---

[23] E.A. Wallis Budge, *Egyptian Magic: A History of Ancient Egyptian Magical Practices Including Amulets, Names, Spells, Enchantments, Figures, Formulae, Supernatural Ceremonies, and Words of Power* (New York: Bell Publishing Company, 1991), Preface, xiii.

[24] Budge, *Egyptian Magic*, Preface, xvi.

[25] Budge, *Egyptian Magic*, 4.

mastery of secret forces in nature; magicians (those skilled in magic) are necromancers, sorcerers, conjurers, and the like."[26]

Satan's Brotherhood has always included a class of sorcerers, magicians, astrologers, and spiritualists. Today, this segment of society is growing extremely rapidly as tens of millions are engaging in the magical arts and searching out the ancient mysteries first divulged to Cain.

After the Flood, then, occultism came to dominate mankind. Egypt and contemporary nations fell into gross superstitions and sorcery in their unlawful attempt to imitate the Priesthood. From Egypt, these traditions and secrets spread into the rest of the world – Babylon, India, and beyond.[27]

Also through the lineage of Cain came a wicked ruler named Nimrod, a grandson of Ham. Nimrod apparently lived concurrent with Egyptus and Pharaoh. In Genesis 10, we are told that Nimrod founded a kingdom in the land Shinar. One of the principal cities was called Babel, from whence we derive the later name Babylon.

As was happening in Egypt at the same time, Satan was leading Nimrod and his people into an idolatrous imitation of the Priesthood as practiced by Noah (who was alive in his own land outside of Nimrod's rule). The scriptures say precious little about Nimrod and nearly all of what we think we know comes from apocryphal or secular sources, such as the writings of Jewish historian Josephus and the *Book of Jasher*. All the scriptures tell us is that Nimrod established the wicked Kingdom of Babylon (Genesis

---

[26] Bruce R. McConkie, *Mormon Doctrine* (Salt Lake City, Utah: Bookcraft, 1966), 462.

[27] Whether Nimrod's Babylonian Kingdom or the Egyptian Kingdom came first is a question I have not been able to sufficiently answer for myself. The general thought in Christendom is that Babylon came first. However, certain evidence – secular, apocryphal, and scriptural – suggest to my mind that Egypt came first. Whether Babylon or Egypt came first ultimately matters very little. Both of these wicked kingdoms sprang up around the same time. Both instituted apostate forms of religion. Both existed in Noah's day. And Abraham was acquainted with both.

10:10), and that he was a "mighty hunter" (Genesis 10:9), which has been taken to imply a hunter of men as well as beasts.

The *Book of Jasher* describes Nimrod thus:

> "Nimrod did not go in the ways of the Lord, and he was more wicked than all the men that were before him, from the days of the flood until those days.

> "And he made gods of wood and stone, and he bowed down to them, and he rebelled against the Lord, and taught all his subjects and the people of the earth his wicked ways" (Jasher 7:46-47).

From Jasher's tale, we also learn that Nimrod's "conjurors" – his court magicians – witnessed a vision wherein they saw a child who was to become a father of many nations which would eventually overthrow Babylon. This child was Abraham. Nimrod, we are told, attempted to murder Abraham to frustrate the conjurors' prophecy. Another child was substituted and killed instead and "it was the will of Providence" that Abraham survived (Jasher 8).

Whether the apocryphal *Book of Jasher's* account is accurate is not for me to say. However, from what we know of the Tower of Babel and the Kingdom of Babylon, we can surmise that Nimrod was indeed a wicked ruler who left a profound legacy of darkness. Such an evil man is likely to have entered into secret agreements with his master, Lucifer. Thus, it is likely that secret combinations arose in Babylon just as secret brotherhoods grew in Egypt. This assumption is perhaps bolstered by Elder McConkie's description of Babylon.

Elder Bruce R. McConkie explained that "Babylon was the persistent persecutor and enemy of the Lord's people." He said:

> "To the Lord's people anciently, Babylon was known as the center of iniquity, carnality, and worldliness. Everything connected with it was in opposition to all righteousness and had the effect of leading men downward to the destruction of their souls.

"It was natural, therefore, for the apostles and inspired men of the New Testament times to apply the name *Babylon* to the forces organized to spread confusion and darkness in the realm of spiritual things."[28]

If Babylon was the ancient "center of iniquity," then it was surely home to secret combinations, because secret combinations are the "most abominable and wicked above all, in the sight of God" (Ether 8:18).

Of all the deeds done in wicked Babylon, none is more infamous than the failed attempt to build a tower to reach Heaven. Under Nimrod's rule, the peoples of his kingdom united in their efforts to build a gargantuan tower. The purposes of this structure were many. On the one hand, if man could get to Heaven by ascending a tower of his own making, he had no need of God's commandments, laws, ordinances, assistance, or Atonement. And, on the other hand, if God decided to judge the earth and destroy humanity with a flood again, a giant, water-proof tower would be quite handy indeed. There were other uses perhaps more important still to the pagan inhabitants of Shinar.

In a March 1998 *Liahona* segment titled "The Tower of Babel," a question about the infamous Tower was asked. Lee Donaldson, V. Dan Rogers, and David Rolph Seely responded by calling the Tower "a pagan temple" and quoted Hugh Nibley who called Nimrod the creator of a "false priesthood and false kingship in the earth in imitation of God's rule."[29] A Church manual similarly suggests that the Tower of Babel may have served as "a counterfeit temple."[30] Thus, not only was the Tower of Babel a means for

---

[28] McConkie, *Mormon Doctrine*, 69.

[29] Lee Donaldson, V. Dan Rogers, and David Rolph Seely, "The Tower of Babel," *Liahona*, March, 1998, The Church of Jesus Christ of Latter-day Saint, accessed February 12, 2018, https://www.lds.org/liahona/1998/03/i-have-a-question/the-tower-of-babel?lang=eng.

[30] *Old Testament Seminary Teacher Manual*, "Genesis 10-11," Lesson 18, The Church of Jesus Christ of Latter-day Saints, accessed February 12, 2018, https://www.lds.org/manual/old-testament-seminary-teacher-manual/introduction-to-the-book-of-genesis/lesson-18-genesis-10-11?lang=eng.

Nimrod's wayward followers to circumvent God and His Gospel laws, but it served a religious purpose as a counterfeit sanctuary and temple.

Nimrod's leadership was seemingly so successful that his people became united and organized, causing God to lament that "now nothing will be restrained from them, which they have imagined to do" (Genesis 11:6). One of the unifying features of this powerful apostate group was its unity of language. With one language, one religion, and one ruthless leader calling the shots, humanity came close to establishing a one-world order. Instituting a one-world occult system with himself at the head has been Lucifer's dream from the beginning. Such a system, however, is anathema to God's Plan of Salvation and to the progress and happiness of mankind. Therefore, the Lord decided to "confound their language, that they may not understand one another's speech" and later scattered them "upon the face of all the earth" (Genesis 11:7-8).

With one word, the Almighty utterly and in an instant destroyed Satan's schemes and fractured his burgeoning global empire. Nimrod's power was stripped in the blink of an eye. The confounding of man's language forced Satan to regroup and rethink a strategy for once again bringing mankind together under his rule. It has taken the Adversary over 4,000 years to marshal his forces and regain the earthly influence he had in the days of Babel. Yet, now Satan's Brotherhood stands at the head of all nations and they are close to achieving full Satanic dominance.

Chapter 3

Satanic Secret Societies

in the Scriptures, Part 2

As Satan plotted and connived to gain influence, position his forces, and make another a bid for world domination, the Lord preserved unto Himself a righteous nation and led them to the Promised Land of America. This remnant was known as the Jaredites. The Jaredites were led by a man named Mahonri Moriancumer, better known as the "brother of Jared." The Lord told this righteous man that, because of his faith, He would lead him and his family to a land "which is choice above all the lands of the earth" (Ether 1:42). The Lord explained that "there shall be none greater than the nation which I will raise up unto me of thy seed, upon all the face of the earth" (Ether 1:43).

The Jaredites were instructed how to build ships and, being led by the Lord, they sailed from the old world to the land of America. This land – *the very land upon which we live* – was and is the Promised Land. America is the land which is "choice above all the lands of the earth." It was intended, from the beginning, that this special land be a land of Liberty – a land where the inhabitants worshipped the Lord. The prophet Moroni taught *us* – the future "Gentile" readers of his record – this doctrine in an emphatic and straightforward way. He declared:

> "And now, we can behold the decrees of God concerning this land, that it is a land of promise; and whatsoever nation shall possess it shall serve God, or they shall be swept off when the fulness of his wrath shall come upon them. And the fulness of his wrath cometh upon them when they are ripened in iniquity.
>
> "For behold, this is a land which is choice above all other lands; wherefore he that doth possess it shall serve God or shall

be swept off; for it is the everlasting decree of God. And it is not until the fulness of iniquity among the children of the land, that they are swept off.

"And this cometh unto you, O ye Gentiles, that ye may know the decrees of God—that ye may repent, and not continue in your iniquities until the fulness come, that ye may not bring down the fulness of the wrath of God upon you as the inhabitants of the land have hitherto done.

"Behold, this is a choice land, and whatsoever nation shall possess it shall be free from bondage, and from captivity, and from all other nations under heaven, if they will but serve the God of the land, who is Jesus Christ" (Ether 2:9-12).

The Jaredites inherited this choice land – this land of Freedom. They became a righteous and industrious people. They were led by inspired leaders and holy prophets. According to the Lord's promise, they became the greatest nation on the face of the earth. However, also according to the Lord's promise, the Jaredites eventually fell from grace when they ceased to serve the God of this land who is Jesus Christ. This great Jaredite nation was swept off the land when they rejected the prophets and reached a fullness of iniquity. It is the cause of this tragic fall that now becomes our focus.

Generations after the Jaredites landed on the blessed soil of America, a war erupted. A certain man named Jared rebelled against his father, King Omer. The scriptural account tells us that, in similar fashion to the Nephite's arch-conspirator Gadianton, "he did flatter many people, because of his cunning words" (Ether 8:2). Jared successfully took control of the kingdom and made his father "serve in captivity" (Ether 8:3). Omer had additional sons who became angry with their brother Jared, and "they did give battle unto him" and restored Omer to power (Ether 8:5-6).

We are told that Jared "became exceedingly sorrowful because of the loss of the kingdom, for he had set his heart upon the glory of the world"

(Ether 8:7). While in mourning, Jared's daughter – who is described as "exceedingly fair" and "exceedingly expert" – reminded her father of the records brought with the Jaredites from "across the great deep" (Ether 8:8-9). Specifically, she said:

> "Behold, is there not an account concerning them of old, that they by their secret plans did obtain kingdoms and great glory?" (Ether 8:9).

It is intriguing that the Jaredite records contained accounts of ancient secret combinations. Were these the combinations of Cain and the Antediluvians? Or were they records of Nimrod, the secret societies of Egypt, or other post-Flood societies?

In his excellent book *New Age Menace: The Secret War Against the Followers of Christ*, LDS author David Balmforth wrote:

> "The unequaled wickedness in the days of Noah enjoys a close, albeit twisted, parallel in New Age dogma. They reverently speak of a highly-evolved civilization called Atlantis that was utterly destroyed in our earth's prehistory. Believers say that its lost knowledge and mysteries are now being rediscovered and they are reintroducing them into our society.
>
> "These "discoveries" are not welcomed by followers of Jesus Christ. Biblical researcher Dwight L. Kinman states:
>
> ""Occult tradition reveals that the world, prior to the flood, had a unified global government of ten regions called Atlantis. Atlantis is the New Age secret code word for the advanced civilization before the flood. In the day of Noah it was a demonized society that God had to destroy."
>
> "How interesting it is that in this age, where wickedness exceeds that of Noah's age, occult "secrets" from the pre-flood era are making their way back into modern society. Just as the Nephites and Lamanites sought out the ancient secret oaths whenever

wickedness increased, today's growing love affair with New Age organizations is a revival of ancient satanic secrets which flourish among the wicked and the gullible."[31]

How accurate is this "occult tradition" about an advanced occult society that spanned the globe in Antediluvian days? We cannot say with total certainty. However, the scriptural record we have been tracing makes it abundantly clear that secret combinations caused the downfall of society before the Flood, and that pagan conspiracies were revived almost immediately after the Flood waters receded.

Armed with the knowledge of the secret plans Satan had given in former days, Jared's wicked daughter inspired him to form a secret combination of his own. She devised a plan whereby this secret combination could be used to murder King Omer and bring Jared to power. A man named Akish, who was a friend of the king, was called and this "exceedingly fair" woman danced before him and seduced him. When he desired to marry her, Jared gave him his terms: In exchange for his daughter's hand in marriage, Jared required Akish to bring him the head of his father, the king. Sadly, Akish agreed.

The account then describes in some detail how Akish formed his secret combination and accomplished this murderous feat. And note the wicked purposes of Satan's oaths. We read:

> "And it came to pass that Akish gathered in unto the house of Jared all his kinsfolk, and said unto them: Will ye swear unto me that ye will be faithful unto me in the thing which I shall desire of you?
>
> "And it came to pass that they all sware unto him, by the God of heaven, and also by the heavens, and also by the earth, and by their heads, that whoso should vary from the assistance which

---

[31] David N. Balmforth, *New Age Menace: The Secret War Against the Followers of Christ* (Bountiful, Utah: Horizon Publishers, 1996), 13-14.

Akish desired should lose his head; and whoso should divulge whatsoever thing Akish made known unto them, the same should lose his life.

"And it came to pass that thus they did agree with Akish. And Akish did administer unto them the oaths which were given by them of old who also sought power, which had been handed down even from Cain, who was a murderer from the beginning.

"And they were kept up by the power of the devil to administer these oaths unto the people, to keep them in darkness, to help such as sought power to gain power, and to murder, and to plunder, and to lie, and to commit all manner of wickedness and whoredoms.

"And it was the daughter of Jared who put it into his heart to search up these things of old; and Jared put it into the heart of Akish; wherefore, Akish administered it unto his kindred and friends, leading them away by fair promises to do whatsoever thing he desired.

"And it came to pass that they formed a secret combination, even as they of old; which combination is most abominable and wicked above all, in the sight of God" (Ether 8:13-18).

The first thing that should jump out at us is the nature of the oaths sworn by the conspirators. The oaths took the name of God in vain. Initiates swore in the name of their Maker. Violation of this blasphemous oath carried a penalty of violent death. These oaths were administered by the Devil who established similar covenants with Cain. By means of these strict oaths, the conspirators were emboldened to lie openly, murder secretly, indulge the lusts of the flesh, plunder the innocent, and seek power by any means. It is no wonder that God calls such oath-bound secret societies "most abominable and wicked above all."

After enlisting his friends and servants in his conspiracy, Jared was installed on the throne. Fortunately, the Lord warned Omer in a dream and he escaped murder (Ether 9:2-3). Nonetheless, Akish developed a taste for blood and he conspired with this secret society to murder his co-conspirator Jared. The record states: "Akish sought the life of his father-in-law; and he applied unto those whom he had sworn by the oath of the ancients, and they obtained the head of his father-in-law, as he sat upon his throne, giving audience to his people" (Ether 9:5). Once Jared was out of the way, Akish reigned in his place.

This bloodletting opened a Pandora's Box of carnage. The scriptures inform us that "so great had been the spreading of this wicked and secret society that it had corrupted the hearts of all the people" (Ether 9:6). Murder and intrigue became so widespread that Akish imprisoned and starved to death his own son for jealousy (Ether 9:7). By and by, other sons of Akish flattered away the people and initiated a war against Akish. The war resulted in almost the entire destruction of the People. Eventually, Omer was restored to his throne and peace was established once again (Ether 9:10-13).

As sad as it is to recount, this was not the end of the Jaredites' flirtation with secret combinations. At a later period, Heth, the son of Com, the king, "began to embrace the secret plans again of old, to destroy his father" (Ether 9:26). Heth murdered his father and usurped the kingdom. His secret combination corrupted the Jaredite People so thoroughly that the Lord sent "prophets in the land again, crying repentance unto them" (Ether 9:28). When this prophetic voice was ignored, the Lord intervened and cursed the people with famine and poisonous serpents until Heth died and the beleaguered Jaredites humbled themselves sufficiently (Ether 9:28-35).

Satan's conspiracies do not lay dormant for long, however. Eventually, "there began to be robbers in the land; and they adopted the old plans, and administered oaths after the manner of the ancients, and sought again to destroy the kingdom" (Ether 10:33). A righteous king named Com fought against these Satanic robbers, but their grip on the People was too strong. The Lord again sent prophets preaching against this grave wickedness, but the account informs us that "they hearkened not unto the voice of the Lord, because of their wicked combinations" (Ether 11:7). Soon, "there arose a rebellion among the people, because of that secret combination which was built up to get power and gain" (Ether 11:15). Yet again the Lord sent prophets and, like a broken record, "they did reject all the words of the prophets, because of their secret society and wicked abominations" (Ether 11:20-22).

It is highly significant, and no doubt an intentional inclusion in our inspired record, that the *cause* of the People's wickedness, stubbornness, and ignorance, was the Satanic secret society among them. It is no different today. If we look for the true cause of all the confusion, iniquity, perversion, and violence in our society, we need look no further than the modern Satanic secret societies permeating every level of our civilization.

Reading further in Jaredite history, the inspired account attests: "[T]here were many people who were slain by the sword of those secret combinations, fighting . . . that they might obtain the kingdom" (Ether 13:18). Moreover, Gilead, one of the enemy leaders seeking to dethrone King Coriantumr and usurp the kingdom, "received strength to his army, because of secret combinations" (Ether 14:8). After a bitter battle, Gilead's forces took the throne. There is no honor among thieves, however, and Gilead was murdered by his own high priest. Through this secret murder Lib "obtained unto himself the kingdom" (Ether 14:8-10).

In the end, the Jaredite nation destroyed itself in fratricidal war instigated by this Satanic conspiracy seeking for power and gain. Millions of souls – every man, woman, and child – were extinguished in the bestial fighting. Satan no doubt laughed and felt powerful as he watched this once proud race exterminate itself at his instigation.

The Jaredites were the first nation which we are specifically told was destroyed because of secret combinations. As such, this is one of the core messages that should grip even the casual reader. Elder Hans Verlan Andersen made this observation about the book of Ether's message to modern man. Said he:

"Although the book of Ether covers some 2,000 years of history, and concerns itself with what was apparently the greatest nation which was ever on the earth, (Ether 1:43) it is only thirty-two pages long. But within those thirty-two pages (15 chapters), secret combinations and secret societies are mentioned sixteen times. One of the vital messages contained within this severely abbreviated account of this great civilization appears to be: beware of Satan's secret combinations."[32]

Indeed, beware of Satan's secret combinations!

Commenting on the Jaredites' fall, Moroni stated that "their wickedness and abominations had prepared a way for their everlasting destruction" (Ether 14:25). Though the term abominations here alludes to secret combinations, Moroni stated the matter more bluntly when he wrote:

"[Secret combinations] have caused the destruction of this people of whom I am now speaking, and also the destruction of the people of Nephi.

"And whatsoever nation shall uphold such secret combinations, to get power and gain, until they shall spread over the nation, behold, they shall be destroyed; for the Lord will not suffer that the blood of his saints, which shall be shed by them, shall always cry unto him from the ground for vengeance upon them and yet he avenge them not" (Ether 8:21-22).

Writing more than four hundred year earlier, Alma, having read the Jaredite record, confirmed Moroni's later analysis. He stated that the Jaredite record would come forth in the latter days in order that the Lord may "bring forth out of darkness unto light all their secret works and their abominations" (Alma 37:25). He affirmed that the Jaredites had been destroyed because of secret combinations and warned of a curse on the land. Referring to the Jaredites, he told his son Helaman:

---

[32] Andersen, *The Great and Abominable Church of the Devil*, 92-93.

"[Y]e shall teach [the people] to abhor such wickedness and abominations and murders; and ye shall also teach them that these people were destroyed on account of their wickedness and abominations and their murders.

"For behold, they murdered all the prophets of the Lord who came among them . . . and thus the judgements of God did come upon these workers of darkness and secret combinations.

"Yea, and cursed be the land forever and ever unto those workers of darkness and secret combinations, even unto destruction, except they repent before they are fully ripe" (Alma 37:29-31).

Because of secret combinations and the murders and whoredoms which inevitably stemmed from such Satanic oaths and covenants, the Jaredites had slaughtered themselves and killed off their own race. Alma was anxious that such a fate would not befall his own people, the Nephites. Yet, as we have recounted, a short 21 years after Alma issued these warnings to Helaman, the Gadianton sect took root among the Nephites and began its destructive course.

As the generations faded into history, the Nephites were afflicted by the Gadianton Robbers to an ever-increasing degree. So deeply entrenched were the Gadiantons that:

"the Nephites did built them up and support them, beginning at the more wicked part of them, until they had overspread all the land of the Nephites, and had seduced the more part of the righteous until they had come down to believe in their works and partake of their spoils, and to join with them in their secret murders and combinations.

"And thus they did obtain the sole management of the government" (Helaman 6:38-39).

Can you and I relate to this sorrowful passage? Do secret combinations have "the sole management" of our government today? And if so, are we as concerned about our "awful situation" as the Nephite prophets were concerned that their government was taken over by Satan's conspirators?

President Ezra Taft Benson was one modern prophet who lamented about our "awful situation" and endlessly attempted to rouse the Saints to action. In an Independence Day address in 1966, he remarked:

> "[T]oday the Christian constitutionalist mourns for his country. He sees the spiritual and political faith of his fathers betrayed by wolves in sheep's clothing. He sees the forces of evil increasing in strength and momentum under the leadership of Satan, the archenemy of freedom. He sees the wicked honored and the valiant abused. He senses that his own generation faces Gethsemanes and Valley Forges that may yet rival or surpass the trials of the early apostles and the men of '76."[33]

President Benson's words are but an echo of those passionately uttered by the Nephite Freedom Fighters.

The prophet Nephi, grieved for his people's acceptance of the Gadianton secret society, lamented greatly and preached a passionate sermon against secret combinations from his garden tower. Mormon described the occasion thus:

> "Nephi, the son of Helaman, returned to the land of Zarahemla from the land northward.
>
> "For he had been forth among the people who were in the land northward, and did preach the word of God unto them, and did prophesy many things unto them;
>
> "And they did reject all his words. . . .

---

[33] Ezra Taft Benson, in Jerreld L. Newquist, ed., *An Enemy Hath Done This* (Salt Lake City, Utah: Parliament Publishers, 1969), 53.

"And seeing the people in a state of such awful wickedness, and those Gadianton robbers filling the judgement-seats – having usurped the power and authority of the land; laying aside the commandments of God, and not in the least aright before him; doing no justice unto the children of men;

"Condemning the righteous because of their righteousness; letting the guilty and the wicked go unpunished because of their money; and moreover to be held in office at the head of government, to rule and do according to their wills, that they might get gain and glory of the world, and, moreover, that they might the more easily commit adultery, and steal, and kill, and do according to their own wills –

"Now this great iniquity had come unto the Nephites, in the space of not many years; and when Nephi saw it, his heart was swollen with sorrow within his breast; and he did exclaim in the agony of his soul. . ." (Helaman 7:1-6)

As in our day, so in Nephite times the Gadiantons infested society, usurped control over government, and used the levers of power to persecute the righteous and pardon the guilty. The Gadianton Robbers filled the judgement-seats then as they do now.

The prophets and seers in all generations have been greatly agitated by the existence of secret combinations among their peoples. They recognize the truth that secret combinations are the "most abominable and wicked above all, in the sight of God" (Ether 8:18) and that any nation who upholds them "shall be destroyed" (Ether 8:22). Because they infiltrate government and seize its judicial, executive, legislative, and police powers, they wield influence over the whole of society and lead, or even compel, the People to sin. Such was the case among the Nephites.

Among the things Nephi so zealously exclaimed, we find this gem:

"Yea, wo be unto you because of that great abomination which has come among you; and ye have united yourselves unto it, yea, to that secret band which was established by Gadianton!" (Helaman 7:25).

Several Gadianton conspirators were in the audience and heard Nephi rail against their covert criminality and conspiratorial complicity. These men "were judges, who also belonged to the secret band of Gadianton, and they were angry, and they cried out against him" and attempted to incite the crowd to seize the prophet and put him to death (Helaman 8:1). Nephi stood his ground and "spake plainly unto them concerning their secret works of darkness" (Helaman 8:4). During the debate, the Spirit rested upon Nephi and he revealed that the chief judge:

> "is murdered, and he lieth in his blood; and he hath been murdered by his brother, who seeketh to sit in the judgement-seat.
>
> "And behold, they both belong to your secret band, whose author is Gadianton and the evil one who seeketh to destroy the souls of men" (Helaman 8:27-28).

Nephi was honest and bold enough to tell a mob that their chief leaders were, in fact, members of a Satanic secret society. Not only did he say that the People's leaders were Gadiantons, but he told the crowd that many of *them* belonged to the conspiracy. Nephi would doubtless be called a "conspiracy theorist" today, yet he was a prophet and what he said was the truth. It is no less true that today the chief leaders in our government, and many unassuming American citizens, are also members of the modern sect of Red Gadiantons.

Within a handful of years of Nephi's tower sermon, a major war erupted "throughout all the land among all the people of Nephi" (Helaman 11:1). We are told that, in eerie imitation of Jaredite ways, "it was this secret band of robbers who did carry on this work of destruction and wickedness" (Helaman 11:2). To put an end to the work of death caused by Satan's Gadianton conspiracy, Nephi importuned the Lord to send a famine to humble the Nephites. This He did, and the people "swept away the band of Gadianton from amongst them insomuch that they have become extinct, and they have concealed their secret plans in the earth" (Helaman 11:10). With the Gadianton cabal gone, the Nephites revived and became righteous. However, it was not to last.

The scriptures tell us that within five years after sweeping away the Gadianton Robbers, Nephite dissenters went over to the Lamanites and again stirred them up to war. But this war was different than most. It was a more clandestine war utilizing guerilla tactics. It was a tribal war of wanton plunder and destruction.

From the record, we learn that these Nephite and Lamanite dissenters "did commit murder and plunder; and then they would retreat back into the mountains, and into the wilderness and secret places, hiding themselves that they could not be discovered" (Helaman 11:24-25). Because of their growing strength, more dissenters joined them and we read:

> "And thus in time, yea, even in the space of not many years, they became an exceedingly great band of robbers; and they did search out all the secret plans of Gadianton; and thus they became robbers of Gadianton" (Helaman 11:26).

I repeat: Within *five* years, an "exceedingly great" number of Nephites and Lamanites turned from their righteousness and embraced Gadianton's oaths, covenants, and schemes. This mountain-based clan of robbers and guerilla warriors "did make great havoc, yea, even great destruction among the people of Nephi, and also among the people of the Lamanites" (Helaman 11:27). The destruction caused by the Gadianton Robbers was so great that the Nephites and Lamanites sent armies "of strong men into the wilderness and upon the mountains to search out this band of robbers, and to destroy them" (Helaman 11:28). However, these attempts were repulsed and the Gadianton forces grew stronger and "infested the mountains and the wilderness" (Helaman 11:31).

Interestingly, President Brigham Young once told the Saints gathered in Utah that the Rocky Mountains had been one of the abodes of these Gadianton Robbers. He taught:

> "There are scores of evil spirits here—spirits of the old Gadianton robbers, some of whom inhabited these mountains, and used to go into the South and afflict the Nephites. There are millions of those spirits in the mountains, and they are ready to make us covetous, if they can; they are ready to lead astray every man and woman that wishes to be a Latter-day Saint. This may seem strange to some of you, but you will see them. As soon as your spirits are unlocked from these tabernacles, you are in the spirit world, and you will there have to contend against evil spirits as we here have to contend against wicked persons."[34]

These rabid Gadiantons existed in the mountains and wilderness for many years, afflicting the Nephites and Lamanites almost constantly, plundering their goods and kidnapping their women and children (Helaman 11:33). At this stage, *The Book of Mormon* record briefly recounts the preaching of Samuel the Lamanite and the appearance of the great star signifying the birth of the Savior in Bethlehem. By 1 A.D., however, the story comes back to the rising threat of the Gadianton Robbers.

We are told of this secret society that "so strong were their holds and their secret places that the people could not overpower them; therefore they did commit many murders, and did do much slaughter among the people (3 Nephi 1:27). Indeed, we learn that:

> "the Gadianton robbers had become so numerous, and did slay so many of the people, and did lay waste so many cities, and did spread so much death and carnage throughout the land, that it became expedient that all the people, both the Nephites and the Lamanites, should take up arms against them.

---

[34] President Brigham Young, *Journal of Discourses*, Vol. 8, 344, January 20, 1861, http://jod.mrm.org/8/338.

"Therefore, all the Lamanites who had become converted unto the Lord did unite with their brethren, the Nephites, and were compelled, for the safety of their lives and their women and their children, to take up arms against those Gadianton robbers, yea, and also to maintain their rights, and the privileges of their church and of their worship, and their freedom and their liberty" (3 Nephi 2:11-12).

At this critical juncture, the Gadianton ruler, Giddianhi, wrote an epistle to Lachoneus, the righteous and inspired Nephite chief judge. Giddianhi mocked the Nephites and Lamanites for defending their rights and scoffed at the notion that God was preserving them. He demanded that the People "yield up" unto the Gadianton Robbers their cities, lands, and possessions or face destruction (3 Nephi 3:6). He even invited Lachoneus to join the Gadianton Order and share their spoils. He wrote:

"[Y]ield yourselves up unto us, and unite with us and become acquainted with our secret works, and become our brethren that ye may be like unto us – not our slaves, but our brethren and partners of all our substance" (3 Nephi 3:7).

Not only did Giddianhi demand control over all lands and property – a characteristically communist objective codified in Karl Marx's *Communist Manifesto* – but he demanded the Nephites relinquish their "rights of government," demonstrating yet again that the aim of the conspiracy was to control society by controlling government (3 Nephi 3:10). Just as these ancient Gadianton communists took sought power in government by hook or crook, you can find today's Red Gadiantons infesting positions in every branch of government, federal, state, and local.

Worthy of note is the fact that the Gadianton leaders, as well as many of the Jaredite conspirators, often hailed from the upper classes and royal echelons of society and believed they had a right to rule over their fellows. They were elitists who suffered a severe entitlement complex and were enamored with material things. It is highly significant that few of these Gadianton Robbers ever came from the peasantry or lower classes of society. So, too, communism's leaders have come not from the "working classes" they pretend to champion, but from the middle and upper classes. It is the people of money – bankers and other elitists – who use communism as a tool to capture political power and create a monopoly of control over society. The aim was the same in Lachoneus's day.

Furthermore, Giddianhi proudly boasted of his cabal's ancient origins, falsely equating age with goodness and worthiness. His words trumpeted: "I am Giddianhi; and I am the governor of this the secret society of Gadianton; which society and the works thereof I know to be good; and they are of ancient date and they have been handed down unto us" (3 Nephi 3:9).

Finally, Giddianhi swore to avenge the wrongs allegedly perpetrated against members of his order whose right, or so he believed, it was to rule. If the Nephites did not join with the Gadianton Robbers and relinquish their personal rights and personal property, they would be destroyed. And so the die was cast.

The prophetic record states of these Robbers that "there was no way that they could subsist save it were to plunder and rob and murder" (3 Nephi 4:5). In all times, Gadiantons – like modern communists – plunder their victims and live off their spoils. Ideally, secret combinations prefer to take control of the reins of government and "legally" appropriate the People's money through taxation and social welfare programs. However, they were not opposed to outright theft, plunder, and murder when necessary. The end justifies the means.

Elder Hans Verlan Andersen wrote:

> "Satan's great purpose here on earth is to destroy the free agency of man. Communists, like the Gadianton Robbers and secret

combinations before them, undertake to achieve this goal by using government to rob everyone of the fruits of their labor."[35]

Knowing these Devilish tactics, and knowing that these Gadiantons "had wronged themselves by dissenting away unto those wicked and abominable robbers" (3 Nephi 3:11), Lachoneus was "exceedingly astonished" when he read this brash diatribe. In one of my favorite lines in holy writ, Mormon recorded:

> "Now behold, this Lachoneus, the governor, was a just man, and could not be frightened by the demands and the threatenings of a robber . . . but did cause that his people should cry unto the Lord for strength" (3 Nephi 3:12).

No true patriot or disciple of the Almighty is frightened by the demands and threatenings of modern Gadianton Robbers.

Lachoneus prophesied to the People that: "As the Lord liveth, except ye repent of all your iniquities, and cry unto the Lord, ye will in nowise be delivered out of the hands of those Gadianton robbers" (3 Nephi 3:15). Great fear came upon the People and they hearkened to Lachoneus and "did exert themselves in their might to do according to the words of Lachoneus" (3 Nephi 3:16). By the time the Gadianton hordes descended upon the combined Nephite and Lamanite armies, "the Nephites did not fear them; but they did fear their God and did supplicate him for protection . . . yea, in the strength of the Lord they did receive them" (3 Nephi 4:10).

After several years of fighting and siege, the Gadianton Robbers were defeated and their leaders executed. Giddianhi was killed in battle and his successor, Zemnarihah, was:

---

[35] Andersen, *The Great and Abominable Church of the Devil*, 111.

"hanged upon a tree, yea, even upon the top thereof until he was dead. And when they had hanged him until he was dead they did fell the tree to the earth, and did cry with a loud voice, saying:

"May the Lord preserve his people in righteousness and in holiness of heart, that they may cause to be felled to the earth all who shall seek to slay them because of power and secret combinations, even as this man hath been felled to the earth" (3 Nephi 4:28-29).

The Gadianton Robbers who were not killed in the battles were taken prisoner. The Nephites "preached unto them; and as many as would repent of their sins and enter into a covenant that they would murder no more were set at liberty" (3 Nephi 5:4). Those who "did still continue to have those secret murders in their hearts" were put to death and "thus they did put an end to all those wicked, and secret, and abominable combinations" (3 Nephi 5:5-6). In the absence of secret combinations, the Nephites became a righteous people who "did serve God with all diligence day and night" (3 Nephi 5:3). Heartbreakingly, the Nephites could not refrain from the enticing mysteries and covenants of secret societies for long.

Within a short space, "Satan did lead away the hearts of the people to do all manner of iniquity; therefore they had enjoyed peace but a few years" (3 Nephi 6:16). The wickedness of certain segments of Nephite society became so marked that "there were many who testified of the things pertaining to Christ who testified boldly, who were taken and put to death secretly by the judges" and in defiance of the laws of the land (3 Nephi 6:23-24). When their crime was known, the remaining righteous complained to the governor of the land who faithfully arrested the judges. These homicidal judges were tried and sentenced to death. Before the sentenced could be carried out, however, another secret society was formed and the government was overthrown. We read:

"Now it came to pass that those judges had many friends and kindreds; and the remainder, yea, even almost all the lawyers and the high priests, did gather themselves together, and unite with the kindreds of those judges who were to be tried according to the law.

"And they did enter into a covenant one with another, yea, even into that covenant which was given by them of old, which covenant was given and administered by the devil, to combine against all righteousness.

"Therefore they did combine against the people of the Lord, and enter into a covenant to destroy them, and to deliver those who were guilty of murder from the grasp of justice, which was about to be administered according to the law.

"And they did set at defiance the law and the rights of their country; and they did covenant one with another to destroy the governor, and to establish a king over the land, that the land should no more be at liberty but should be subject unto kings" (3 Nephi 6:27-30).

In reading this account of lawyers and judges combining to destroy Liberty, one is reminded of two earlier scriptures and a modern warning from Thomas Jefferson. In the first instance, Alma tells the people of Ammonihah that "the foundation of the destruction of this people is beginning to be laid by the unrighteousness of your lawyers and your judges" (Alma 10:27). The Lord had in fact told Alma that the people of Ammonihah, clearly instigated by their judges and lawyers, "do study at this time that they may destroy the liberty of thy people" (Alma 8:17). And this brings to mind a final statement made by the great Thomas Jefferson in 1821. Said he:

"It has long however been my opinion, and I have never shrunk from it's expression . . . that the germ of dissolution of our federal government is in the constitution of the federal judiciary; an irresponsible body, (for impeachment is scarcely a scare-crow) working like gravity by night and by day, gaining a little to-day & a little tomorrow, and advancing it's noiseless step like a thief, over the field of jurisdiction, until all shall be usurped from the states, & the government of all be consolidated into one. To this I am opposed; because whenever all government, domestic and foreign, in little as in great things, shall be drawn to Washington as the center of all power, it will render powerless the checks provided of one government on another, and will become as venal and oppressive as the government from which we separated. It will be, as in Europe where every man must be either pike or gudgeon hammer or anvil."[36]

In a time when not much attention was paid to the judiciary, which was considered a relatively impotent body, Thomas Jefferson sensed the truth that the judiciary would be the undoing of the American system. When we consider that it is the judiciary that has taken prayer from schools, legalized the killing of babies, and foisted homosexual marriage upon the states, to name only three oppressive measures, we realize that Jefferson had tremendous foresight – and that history repeats itself.

After the formation of this sect of lawyers and judges, the scriptural account continued, explaining that these Satan-worshipping conspirators "did murder the chief judge of the land" in a coup (3 Nephi 7:1). This top-down coup d'état caused a massive division throughout the land. The People "did separate one from another into tribes, every man according to his family and his kindred and friends; and thus they did destroy the government of the land" (3 Nephi 7:2).

The scriptural account emphasized multiple times that this tragedy was brought about because of secret combinations. We read:

"[A]nd all this iniquity had come upon the people because they did yield themselves unto the power of Satan.

---

[36] Thomas Jefferson to C. Hammond, August 18, 1821.

> "And the regulations of the government were destroyed, because of the secret combination of the friends and kindreds of those who murdered the prophets. . . .
>
> ". . . this secret combination . . . had brought so great iniquity upon the people" (3 Nephi 7:5-6, 9).

At the time, it was no secret who had overthrown the government. The People, now separated in their various tribes, knew the culprits. We are told that though they were not righteous, they nevertheless "were united in the hatred of those who had entered into a covenant to destroy the government" (3 Nephi 7:11).

Per their design, the conspirators selected a king to rule over them. His name was Jacob. Jacob led his band into the north countries and built up a kingdom (3 Nephi 7:12). They established a city called Jacobugath. Within four years, this kingdom of robbers was destroyed by the Lord in the destructions that rocked the Americas at the time of His Crucifixion in Jerusalem at the hands of conspiring Pharisees and Jewish leaders.

Mormon recorded that at the time of Christ's death widespread destructions hit the continent, north and south, east and west. However, "there was a more terrible destruction in the land northward" – the very land Jacob and his Satanic Brotherhood inhabited (3 Nephi 8:12). When the wrathful storms subsided, the voice of the resurrected Lord penetrated the darkness. He specifically referenced Jacob's city and listed the chief reason it was destroyed. He declared:

> "And behold, that great city Jacobugath, which was inhabited by the people of king Jacob, have I caused to be burned with fire because of their sins and their wickedness, which was above all the wickedness of the whole earth, because of their secret murders and combinations; for it was they that did destroy the peace of my people and the government of the land; therefore I did cause them to be burned, to destroy them from before my face, that the blood of the prophets and the

saints should not come up unto me any more against them" (3 Nephi 9:9).

Of all the crimes and whoredoms and wicked acts Christ could have mentioned, He singled out that which was most grievous in His eyes – the secret combination that destroyed the government He had previously established. This pronouncement, in conjunction with the dozens of others we have read, should fix in our minds the dire seriousness of secret combinations, and how everlastingly and completely the Lord hates them.

As we know, after the Lord cleansed the land and preached to the spirits in the spirit world, He rose from the tomb in Jerusalem, thus completing the Atonement and shattering the bands of death and hell forever. Soon thereafter, the risen Lord appeared to the Nephites and Lamanites on this continent, established His Church among them, called twelve apostles, and revealed and expounded many precious truths about His ways. For 184 years, the Americas were at peace and the People enjoyed unbounded prosperity and happiness. Then, "a small part of the people . . . revolted from the church" and adopted the name Lamanites (4 Nephi 1:20).

The term Lamanites as used here appears to denote unbelievers and dissenters, rather than those literal descendants of Laman, though we can assume many of Laman's descendants were among their number. This is significant because it shows where the true battle lines were drawn: Those who worshipped Christ occupied one side while all those who rejected Him constituted the opposition. At any rate, from that first dissension by Lamanite unbelievers, society began to change and revert back to its previous ways. They became divided into classes, set their hearts upon material things, and denied the Everlasting Christ.

After 260 years, the scourge of Gadiantonism rose from the grave like a phantom at twilight. We read these somber words: "And it came to pass that the wicked part of the people began again to build up the secret oaths and combinations of Gadianton." (4 Nephi 1:42). After forty years of Gadianton influence:

"both the people of Nephi and the Lamanites had become exceedingly wicked one like unto another.

"And it came to pass that the robbers of Gadianton did spread over all the face of the land" (4 Nephi 1:45-46).

In the days of Mormon, "these Gadianton robbers, who were among the Lamanites, did infest the land" and "there were sorceries, and witchcrafts, and magics; and the power of the evil one was wrought upon all the face of the land" (Mormon 1:18-19). Though he does not specifically say it, Mormon infers that these robbers initiated the great war that began in about 327 A.D. More than once, Mormon draws attention to the fact that "the land was filled with robbers and with Lamanites" (Mormon 2:8). He recorded that "no man could keep that which was his own, for the thieves, and the robbers, and the murderers, and the magic art, and the witchcraft which was in the land" (Mormon 2:10).

The terrible war gradually consumed the Nephite nation. Mormon stated that his "heart did sorrow because of this great calamity of [his] people, because of their wickedness and their abominations." Nevertheless, he led the Nephites in battle "against the Lamanites and the robbers of Gadianton" (Mormon 2:27). Despite their worsening condition, the Nephites refused to repent. After one final battle at the Hill Cumorah in modern day New York state, the Nephite People were swept off the land.

Writing twenty-six years later while in hiding, Mormon's son Moroni recorded that his father had been killed along with all of his family and the whole of the People of Nephi. Said he: "[T]here are none save it be the Lamanites and robbers that do exist upon the face of the land" (Mormon 8:9). These apostates were "at war one with another; and the whole face of this land is one continual round of murder and bloodshed; and no one knoweth the end of the war" (Mormon 8:8). Sadly, the Gadiantons had outlasted the Nephites and were at work tearing down the Lamanites when Moroni wrote this commentary in 401 A.D.

In the years of lonely solitude, Moroni must have pondered the fall of his people thousands of times. Thus, when Moroni put the capstone on *The Book of Mormon* by including the Jaredite record and a few of his own thoughts, he knew precisely what he needed to tell future generations and he crafted his words carefully. With this context fresh in your mind, consider again Moroni's warning to us in the latter days:

> "And it came to pass that they formed a secret combination, even as they of old; which combination is most abominable and wicked above all, in the sight of God. . . .

> "And they have caused the destruction of this people of whom I am now speaking, and also the destruction of the people of Nephi.

> "And whatsoever nation shall uphold such secret combinations, to get power and gain, until they shall spread over the nation, behold, they shall be destroyed; for the Lord will not suffer that the blood of his saints, which shall be shed by them, shall always cry unto him from the ground for vengeance upon them and yet he avenge them not.

> "Wherefore, O ye Gentiles, it is wisdom in God that these things should be shown unto you, that thereby ye may repent of your sins, and suffer not that these murderous combinations shall get above you, which are built up to get power and gain—and the work, yea, even the work of destruction come upon you, yea, even the sword of the justice of the Eternal God shall fall upon you, to your overthrow and destruction if ye shall suffer these things to be.

> "Wherefore, the Lord commandeth you, when ye shall see these things come among you that ye shall awake to a sense of your awful situation, because of this secret combination which shall be among you; or wo be unto it, because of the blood of them who

have been slain; for they cry from the dust for vengeance upon it, and also upon those who built it up.

"For it cometh to pass that whoso buildeth it up seeketh to overthrow the freedom of all lands, nations, and countries; and it bringeth to pass the destruction of all people, for it is built up by the devil, who is the father of all lies; even that same liar who beguiled our first parents, yea, even that same liar who hath caused man to commit murder from the beginning; who hath hardened the hearts of men that they have murdered the prophets, and stoned them, and cast them out from the beginning.

"Wherefore, I, Moroni, am commanded to write these things that evil may be done away, and that the time may come that Satan may have no power upon the hearts of the children of men, but that they may be persuaded to do good continually, that they may come unto the fountain of all righteousness and be saved" (Ether 8:18-26).

Of all the things that Moroni could have warned future generations of Saints about after some twenty-six years of pondering, he emphasized the pernicious influence of secret combinations. It is highly significant that Moroni was not merely speaking from his heart, but, crucially, he was expressing the will of the Lord. Notice the phrase "the Lord commandeth you." That is not a casual expression. It is not a suggestion. It is not merely a bit of sage advice. Rather, *it is a direct command from the Savior Jesus Christ.*

Through His prophet Moroni, the Lord commanded you and me to "awake to a sense of [our] awful situation, because of this secret combination which shall be among [us]." The Lord is not speaking hypothetically; He is warning us of our latter-day reality. Moroni's future is our present. We are living in the days when a great secret combination *is* among us. We are living in the time when the Lord has *commanded* us to wake up to our "awful situation" because of this conspiracy's machinations.

Moroni foretold that a secret combination would exist in our day that would seek to "overthrow the freedom of all lands" – yes, including the United States. This conspiracy would bring to pass "the destruction of all people" if not checked by alert and awake Saints. Moroni explained that the Devil is the author of this latter-day conspiracy that "shall be" among us. He knew that if we allow this secret society to get above us and usurp our power and infest our government, as it did the Jaredite and Nephite governments, and the earlier societies of Egypt, Babylon, and pre-Flood times, "the sword of the justice of the Eternal God shall fall upon [us]" (Ether 8:23). That this evil might be done away with, Moroni was told to command us in the name of God Almighty to awake and arise and resist this Satanic secret combination that *is* among us.

From premortal times, Satan has made war against Christ. Satan's chief tool is deception. Through deception and false promises, he inducts prideful and overzealous individuals into his secret combinations where he administers blasphemous oaths and covenants. These secret combinations seek power and influence in society – most importantly through government – and employ murder to get their way, strike fear into their opposition, and silence internal dissent.

Beginning with Cain, these murderous secret societies have existed in nearly every age. Cain's followers and their collaborators brought such great wickedness upon the earth that God destroyed humanity with a flood. After the Great Flood buried them beneath the waves, secret combinations sprang up again in both the old and new worlds.

From Egypt to Babylon, and from the Jaredites to the Nephites, Satan's conspiracies have destroyed civilizations, toppled empires, subjugated nations, and unleashed a global deluge of blood and idolatry. The Lord's prophets knew that the Lord's people in the last days – that is, you and I – would face off against the same monstrous conspiracies, and they warned us with an emphatic voice. Have we heeded their words?

With the Freedom of all lands hanging precariously in the balance, has the Lord inspired His latter-day prophets and apostles to identify this modern secret combination as Nephi and others did anciently? If so, what have our seers seen and our revelators revealed to the world? What have the Saints been instructed and taught by those authorized representatives of the Lord Jesus Christ? Which ideologies and principles, which movements and creeds, have our Priesthood leaders admonished us to oppose? In short, has the Lord left us to grope in the dark or have His prophets identified the enemy?

Chapter 4

Identifying the Secret Combination Foreseen by Moroni

We begin this chapter the way we ended chapter three, with a question: Have our latter-day prophets identified the secret combination which Moroni prophesied "shall be among [us]" (Ether 8:24)? The answer is an emphatic *yes*. Indeed, the Lord's servants have spoken copiously about this vile secret combination, its tactics, and the threat it poses to mankind and the Gospel. The Lord has *not* left His sheep defenseless against the wolves. The Shepherd is with His flock and will defend them if they listen to His words as delivered through His servants the prophets.

For decades, the Lord's prophets took up the subject of secret combinations and issued candid warnings to the world – and to the Saints in particular. Like Nephi on his garden tower, our prophets have warned us from the General Conference pulpit about these Devilish combinations. They published books and official statements, gave speeches and talks, warned and instructed. These inspired men compared and contrasted the principles and policies of the conspirators with the true principles and policies of the Church, and of the constitutional system of government established by the Lord, so that the Saints would not err.

With great fervor, men like Presidents Ezra Taft Benson and David O. McKay pleaded with the Saints to recognize the enemy and square their shoulders to fight him. They did not mince words or play the political correctness game. With all the honesty, passion, and encouragement of true prophets, our modern seers have led the charge against Satan's secret combinations. In a word, our Heavenly Father has *not* left us without assistance in identifying and combating the secret combination foreseen by Moroni and in understanding exactly what it is, how it operates, who controls it, and what it seeks to achieve.

Latter-day Saints *cannot* plead ignorance on the subject of conspiracy. The members of The Church of Jesus Christ of Latter-day Saints have been given more light and knowledge relating to secret societies and political conspiracies than any members of any other church or group in the world. As disciples of the Lord's Restored Church, we *should* be the most astute and well-informed people on conspiracy to be found anywhere on earth.

Yet, by and large, the average member of this Church demonstrates a stunning lack of understanding and awareness in the realm of conspiracy theory and research, and in the broader realm of politics and government. As this chapter will demonstrate, however, the Saints have been repeatedly and sufficiently warned by the Lord's prophets and therefore have no excuse for their ignorance other than personal apathy, inadequate diligence, and lack of discernment. My aim is not to make anyone feel guilty or dumb, but to encourage the reader to catch the same vision that has inspired our prophets and which causes them to lead the charge against Satan's kingdom.

As cited earlier, the Lord revealed through the prophet Moroni that secret combinations are the "most abominable and wicked above all, in the sight of God" (Ether 8:18). It might be said, then, a secret combination constitutes a Satanic threat to any society – a cancer in the body of a nation. If we think along these lines, the following announcement comes into brighter focus.

During the April 1966 Priesthood session of General Conference, a statement written by then President of the Church, David O. McKay, identified *the greatest threat* facing humanity and the Church. The statement read:

> "The position of this Church on the subject of Communism has never changed. We consider it the greatest satanical threat to

peace, prosperity, and the spread of God's work among men that exists on the face of the earth. . . .

"The entire concept and philosophy of Communism is diametrically opposed to everything for which the Church stands – belief in Deity, belief in the dignity and eternal nature of man, and the application of the gospel to efforts for peace in the world. Communism is militantly atheistic and is committed to the destruction of faith wherever it may be found. . . .

"Communism debases the individual and makes him the enslaved tool of the state, to which he must look for sustenance and religion. Communism destroys man's God-given free agency.

"No member of this Church can be true to his faith, nor can any American be loyal to his trust, while lending aid, encouragement, or sympathy to any of these false philosophies; for if he does, they will prove snares to his feet."[37]

This remarkable declaration and warning has gone ignored by the Church membership as a whole, yet, it has never been rescinded and thus constitutes the *official position* of the Church to this day. The Lord's mouthpiece plainly told the Saints that communism is the "greatest" evil in the world. It is not an ordinary evil, but a "satanical threat" to the Church, to global peace, and to every member of the human family. Without exaggeration, the acceptance of communism is the acceptance of Satanism. It is the embracing of slavery and, thus, the abdication of one's God-given agency. The prophet knew it and warned mankind accordingly.

Furthermore, the prophet made it abundantly clear that no faithful Church member can be a communist or support, encourage, or tolerate any such false philosophy regardless of its label. To do so is rebellion to God and His Gospel. Simply, a person is *not* a real Latter-day Saint if he is

---

[37] President David O. McKay, "Only One Standard of Morality," April 9, 1966, Conference Report, 109-110, http://scriptures.byu.edu/#:t5c7:p51c.

a communist. You must choose between one and the other – you cannot be both simultaneously.

While most Latter-day Saints would not consider themselves "communist," most have regrettably adopted communist principles under other names without even realizing it. They have voted for secret communists wearing Republican and Democratic labels. They have imbibed socialistic ideologies at Brigham Young University as taught by socialist professors who themselves are no doubt deceived. In short, the Devil's philosophy has carefully seduced many of those professing to belong to the Lord's Church.

As promised by President McKay, these "false philosophies" have proved "snares" to the feet of the Saints across the globe. This has become a great hindrance to the progress of the Gospel. If Church members want to come into full conformity with the revealed will of the Lord, this must include embracing the truth that communism – no matter what label it is given and which slogans and names it hides behind – is "the greatest satanical threat to . . . the spread of God's work." Communism *must* be rejected in its entirety by Christ's disciples.

Moroni said that the "most abominable" thing in God's sight was a secret combination and that in the last days one such combination would exist and would menace the world. In fact, we are told that this Devilish conspiracy would seek to "overthrow the freedom of all lands" and would bring to pass "the destruction of all people" (Ether 8:25). It would be a global conspiracy intent on world revolution and world domination. Its founder would be Lucifer and he would persuade his minions to murder and plunder and snuff out Freedom on a global scale. Truly, this latter-day secret combination would be the "most abominable and wicked above all, in the sight of God" (Ether 8:24).

With this description in mind, it becomes highly significant that the Lord's modern mouthpiece declared communism to be the "greatest satanical threat" to mankind. Is it possible that this latter-day conspiracy is simultaneously the "greatest satanical threat" and the "most abominable and wicked above all"? By logical deduction, communism – as the "greatest satanical threat" in the world – *must* be a secret combination, because only secret combinations are "most abominable and wicked above all." Not only must communism be *a* secret combination, but it must rationally be *the* secret combination prophesied to ravage the nations in our day.

Anyone conversant with the history of communism acknowledges that it has caused more destruction and death, and enslaved more people, than any other organization, system, or philosophy in history. The communist conspiracy is the evilest and vilest entity in the world. Rightly have the Lord's prophets labeled it the "greatest satanical threat" in existence. And rightly do we equate this monstrous conspiracy with that foreseen by Moroni.

To confirm this interpretation, I draw a quote from President Ezra Taft Benson, then of the Quorum of the Twelve. He said:

> "Concerning the United States, the Lord revealed to his prophets that its greatest threat would be a vast, worldwide "secret combination" which would not only threaten the United States but also seek to "overthrow the freedom of all lands, nations and countries." (Ether 8:25.). . . .
>
> "The fight against godless communism is a very real part of every man's duty who holds the priesthood. It is the fight against slavery, immorality, atheism, terrorism, cruelty, barbarism, deceit, and the destruction of human life through a kind of tyranny unsurpassed by anything in human history. Here is a struggle against the evil, satanical priestcraft of Lucifer. Truly it can be called, "a continuation of the war in heaven.""[38]

---

[38] President Ezra Taft Benson, "The American Heritage of Freedom – A Plan of God," Conference Report, October, 1961, 69-75, http://scriptures.byu.edu/#:t48d:p401.

Again I say, if the Church has identified communism as the "greatest satanical threat" to mankind, and the scriptures also call the latter-day "secret combination" the greatest threat to mankind, then communism must be *the* secret combination referred to. As noted by President Benson, communism is not merely an earthly conspiracy, but reaches back into the pre-earth life. Communism's true origin is in the pre-existent state when Lucifer proposed to exalt his throne above that of our Heavenly Father, and was consequently cast down for rebellion (Isaiah 14:13; Revelation 12:7-9).

It is a Priesthood duty to "fight against" communism in *all* of its manifestations. In fighting against communism, we are really fighting against "the evil, satanical priestcraft of Lucifer." Communism, then, is priestcraft – *Satanic* priestcraft. Remember what the Lord has instructed His Saints: "Contend against no church, save it be the church of the devil"" (D&C 18:20). If communism is Lucifer's priestcraft in these latter-days, we must fight against it with all our might. To do so, especially for the men of the Priesthood, is a sacred "duty."

Another reason why it is a sacred duty to fight communism is because communism is hate. Hate is anathema to love, which is the crowning characteristic that exemplifies true Christian disciples. "God is love," as the apostle said (1 John 4:8). According to an entry in the Congressional Record of April 12, 1933, Lenin declared: "We must hate – hatred is the basis of communism."[39] Anatoly Lunacharsky, the henchman in charge of education in the USSR, similarly stated:

> "We hate Christians and Christianity. Even the best of them must
> be considered our worst enemies. Christian love is an obstacle to
> the development of the revolution. Down with love of one's

---

[39] Introduced into the Congressional Record April 12, 1933 by Senator Arthur R. Robinson, 1539.

neighbor! What we want is hate. . . . Only then can we conquer the universe."[40]

Christian love is an obstacle to the communist revolution because love is of Christ and communism is of Satan. The two can never mix nor compromise. Disciples of Christ cannot accept one particle of communism because hate and love are opposites and cannot reside in the same heart at the same time.

A professor by the name of Charles C. Wolff once explained:

> "There is no single document in the possession of the serious student of Communism that approaches Sergey Nachayev's *Catechism* in importance for deep insight into the nature of Communism. . . .

> "When you read the *Catechism* you will read (horribly perverted) echoes of the blazing missionary zeal and self-denial of early Christianity. More than any other document, the Catechism is the illustration of the fact that Communism is the perversion of Christianity. . . .

> ". . . there can be no compromise with Communism, no negotiations, no appeasement. . . .

> "People who have wondered at the astounding power of Communism need do so no longer. The secret is out! It begins with the transformation of the spiritually destitute individual into a destructive revolutionary, using a strange process of dehumanization."[41]

---

[40] W. Cleon Skousen, *The Naked Communist* (Salt Lake City, Utah: The Reviewer, 1985), 308.

[41] Des Griffin, *Descent into Slavery?* (Clackamas, OR: Emissary Publications, 1980), 249.

Communism is a perversion of Christianity. Or, rather, it is an inversion of Christianity. Satan's plan is a perversion of the Father's Plan – an inversion of eternal principles. Whereas the Father wanted to give man agency, Lucifer wanted to deny it by destroying accountability (the "I'll save you in your sins" mentality). Whereas the Lord's disciples preach love, Satan's followers preach hate.

The document just mentioned, Nechayev's *The Revolutionary Catechism*, is a short, 26-point paper detailing what it takes to be a true communist revolutionary. Sergey Nechayev was a radical Russian anarchist who walked the walk and ended up dying in prison for his actions. In other words, he knew whereof he spoke. In the opening section of *Catechism*, he wrote:

> "The revolutionary knows that in the very depths of his being, not only in words but also in deeds, he has broken all the bonds which tie him to the social order and the civilized world with all its laws, moralities, and customs, and with all its generally accepted conventions. He is their implacable enemy, and if he continues to live with them it is only in order to destroy them more speedily. . . .

> ". . . He knows only one science: the science of destruction. For this reason, but only for this reason, he will study mechanics, physics, chemistry, and perhaps medicine. But all day and all night he studies the vital science of human beings, their characteristics and circumstances, and all the phenomena of the present social order. The object is perpetually the same: the surest and quickest way of destroying the whole filthy order. . . .

> ". . . He despises and hates the existing social morality in all its manifestations. For him, morality is everything which contributes to the triumph of the revolution. Immoral and criminal is everything that stands in its way. . . .

"The revolutionary is a dedicated man, merciless toward the State and toward the educated classes; and he can expect no mercy from them. Between him and them there exists, declared or concealed, a relentless and irreconcilable war to the death. . . .

"Night and day he must have but one thought, one aim – merciless destruction. Striving cold-bloodedly and indefatigably toward this end, he must be prepared to destroy himself and to destroy with his own hands everything that stands in the path of the revolution."[42]

Each word of the Catechism drips with Nechayev's hatred and brutality. But this hatred is not his own; it belongs to the communist revolution. Communism, being from the Devil, is the embodiment of hatred towards morality, God, justice, sound laws, peace, prosperity, normalcy, sanity, and everything else that is good, wholesome, or heavenly. Communism is a destructive force – the spirit of death, the embodiment of savagery, and the sum of annihilation. As we discuss communism throughout the remainder of this book, keep Nechayev's words in mind. The *Catechism* is the creed of the communist.

In the April 1969 Priesthood session of General Conference, President McKay apparently felt a growing sense of urgency about communist inroads and repeated and elaborated on his earlier remarks wherein he declared communism the "greatest satanical threat." He also echoed many of the words of Moroni in Ether 8. Said he:

"In the United States of America, the Constitution vouchsafes individual freedom, and let us pray also that the Lord will frustrate the plans of the Communists who would deprive us of freedom.

"I desire to refer to some remarks concerning Communism that I made in the general priesthood meeting three years ago. At that

---

[42] Sergey Nechayev, *The Revolutionary Catechism*, 1869, accessed May 8, 2018, https://www.marxists.org/subject/anarchism/nechayev/catechism.htm.

priesthood conference, in addition to encouragement to study the Constitution and be alert to communistic inroads that would undermine it, I said the following: . . . .

""The position of this Church, however, on the subject of Communism has never changed. We consider it the greatest satanical threat to peace, prosperity, and the spread of God's work among men that exists on the face of the earth.""

President McKay went on to refer to the "perils of Communism" and the "dangers of Communism" and then recommended Church members "to become informed on Communism" and "to become better acquainted with forces that are opposed to righteousness." He admonished:

"It is the right and obligation of every citizen, and therefore every member of the Church, to be alert and to be informed about social, educational, communistic, and other political influences that would tend to undermine our free society."

Is it clear yet what the Lord wanted His Saints to know about the threats facing their families? For a prophet to be inspired to mention any topic – be it faith in Christ, the doctrine of repentance, or the communist threat – so many times in one talk should rivet our attention on the message. For the president of the Church – the one man authorized to speak in the name of Almighty God – to stand up in General Conference and declare the "position of this Church" relative to communism twice in three years, it must be important. And for the Lord's mouthpiece to repeat that communism is the "greatest satanical threat" to the Gospel, such knowledge must be of more than normal importance and critical to the progress of the Saints in these last days.

This great prophet of God further explained:

"It must never be forgotten that converts to the Church come from all nations, representing diverse views on controversial issues. Ours must be the responsibility to teach our members from all nations the true doctrines of Christ with such power that they be fortified against all false ideas, regardless of the label under which they may be presented.

"The Melchizedek Priesthood course of study for the coming year will include in the lesson material such subjects as liberty and freedom, religion and the state, the dangers of Communism, and other subjects considered of vital importance in the study of the profound truths of the gospel."[43]

Here we have an acknowledgement by the prophet that the Devil pushes his same old wares under various names depending on his audience. In one country he might call his philosophy socialism while in another country he calls it communism while in yet another he labels it democracy, social democracy, or democratic socialism. Call it what you will, the substance is rotten and leads to slavery.

So emphatic was President McKay and his counselors that the Saints not be deceived by false labels that they commissioned a new Melchizedek Priesthood Handbook for 1970. In its pages, the Saints were warned of communism, taught its principles so that they could be identified under any label, and instructed in the true meaning of Liberty and good government. This drive to unify the Church politically is in accord with statements cited earlier that the Saints must be "one" even in politics.

Some members of the Church believe that our prophets should not mix politics and religion. Yet, every Latter-day Saint familiar with the scriptures knows how often the Lord and His prophets have intermingled religion and politics. Though I discussed this in chapter one, it is so important that I will say another word about it here.

Politics and religion are absolutely inseparable. For instance, how can a faithful Latter-day Saint divorce politics from religion when he remembers the Lord's command in *Doctrine and Covenants* 98:5-7:

---

[43] President McKay, "Let Virtue Garnish Thy Thoughts," Conference Report, April, 1969, 93-97, http://scriptures.byu.edu/#:t69b:p51c.

"And that law of the land which is constitutional, supporting that principle of freedom in maintaining rights and privileges, belongs to all mankind, and is justifiable before me.

"Therefore, I, the Lord, justify you, and your brethren of my church, in befriending that law which is the constitutional law of the land;

"And as pertaining to law of man, whatsoever is more or less than this, cometh of evil."

In this statement, the Lord tells His Saints to embrace the sacred principles of the U.S. Constitution and declares that anything "more or less" than the Constitution "cometh of evil." This is then a moral issue and a religious duty.

Furthermore, Elder Hans Verlan Andersen had a few words to contribute on this subject. He wrote:

"There are those who undertake to keep their "politics" completely separated from their "religion." This is logically impossible for one who accepts the scriptures as the word of God."[44]

Along these lines, we would of necessity have to excise entire chapters in *The Book of Mormon* and other books if we wanted to avoid discussions of politics, secret combinations, and the like. Alma 37, Alma 46, Helaman 6, Ether 8, D&C 98, D&C 123, D&C 134, and Moses 5 are several sections of politically-charged scripture that immediately leap to mind. The Lord evidently wants us to understand the truths these passages contain. He would not have placed so many references to Liberty, politics, government, secret combinations, abominations, and dark works in the scriptures unless they were important to comprehend.

---

[44] Hans Verlan Andersen, *The Great and Abominable Church of the Devil* (1972), 47.

Think of the inspiration that the story of Captain Moroni hoisting the Title of Liberty in defiance of the king-men and the tyrant Amalickiah has given to millions of Saints. Yet, this account would be dropped if we decided to no longer discuss "politics." Who is willing to cut this account out of our Gospel lessons? Certainly, only one entirely unfamiliar with the scriptures and the importance of defending human agency against the forces of darkness would want to brush aside Captain Moroni's story or any of the other myriad accounts dealing with political intrigue, governmental principles, and Liberty.

The simple fact is that Latter-day Saints *cannot* avoid politics. They *cannot* avoid studying secret combinations and understanding their tactics and arguments. Engaging in politics to safeguard our agency and promote righteousness is as much a duty as fulfilling any calling in the Church. Indeed, the War in Heaven was fought over the principle of Liberty and free will. I therefore repeat an admonition given by President Benson to the Saints in 1961:

> "Today the devil as a wolf in a supposedly new suit of sheep's clothing is enticing some men, both in and out of the Church, to parrot his line by advocating planned government guaranteed security programs at the expense of our liberties. Latter-day Saints should be reminded how and why they voted as they did in heaven. If some have decided to change their vote they should repent—throw their support on the side of freedom—and cease promoting this subversion."[45]

As acknowledged by this great apostle, some of us within the Church have been deceived into supporting Satan's plan without knowing it. Yet, we have been warned, and warned, and warned again. We have been taught correctly by inspired prophets. *We have no excuse.* Thankfully, we still have time to acknowledge our error, repent, change our ways, and throw

---

[45] President Ezra Taft Benson, Conference Report, "The American Heritage of Freedom – A Plan of God," October, 1961, 69-75. http://scriptures.byu.edu/#:t48d:p401.

our support behind the Lord's plan of Freedom. But this can only happen if we first correctly identify and understand the secret combination promoting Satan's anti-Freedom agenda today.

Among latter-day prophets, President Ezra Taft Benson raised the loudest and longest voice against the communist conspiracy. Over many decades as an apostle of the Lord, President Benson did battle with Lucifer's minions. Some members of the Church thought (and still think) he was out of touch or that he overstepped his mandate as prophet. Yet, upon his passing into the hereafter, President Gordon B. Hinckley paid him this tribute:

> "Ezra Taft Benson was the fearless and outspoken enemy of communism, a man who with eloquence and conviction preached the cause of human freedom, one who loved and worshipped the Prince of Peace, the Redeemer of mankind. . . .
>
> "He was constantly within the glare of the spotlight of public scrutiny. He was absolutely fearless in speaking out against what he regarded as oppressive programs that shackled the farmer and did injury to him while masquerading as his protector and benefactor. His picture appeared on the covers of the leading national news magazines. Editorialists and commentators denounced him. But without fear or favor, without political or personal consideration, he spoke his mind and won the plaudits of millions across this nation. Even those who disagreed with his policies were forced to respect his logic, his wisdom, and his convictions. They came to know that he knew whereof he spoke. He had once been a dirt-digging, hands-on, sweating farmer. He spoke out of that experience. But he spoke also with the skill and refinement of an educated mind, with the skill of a trained debater, and out of a conviction deep and intense that came of a

love for freedom to live one's own life and direct one's own affairs."[46]

Yes, President Benson "knew whereof he spoke" and was a "fearless and outspoken enemy of communism." It was precisely because he "worshipped the Prince of Peace, the Redeemer of mankind" that he spoke out against the "oppressive programs" of the Adversary of human Freedom. Though President Benson is now doing his work in the world of spirits, the Saints today would do well to heed his words and the fearless teachings he left over the course of many decades in service to the Church. And as the first prophet I can remember as a child, I pay him a special thanks and give him my love for what his words have meant for me.

In the October 1961 General Conference, President Benson, then a member of the Twelve, identified the communist conspiracy as the inheritor of the Gadianton tradition. He explained that modern communism is a mirror image of the alternative plan presented by Lucifer in the pre-mortal realm. This plan, it will be remembered, was rejected by the Father, and by you and me. It caused a War in Heaven which resulted in Lucifer and a one third part of Heavenly Father's children being cast out of His presence for rebellion. This plan, this evil plan, is identified by President Benson as communism:

> "It is time, therefore, that every American, and especially every member of the priesthood, became informed about the aims, tactics, and schemes of socialistic-communism. This becomes particularly important when it is realized that communism is turning out to be the earthly image of the plan which Satan presented in the pre-existence. The whole program of socialistic-communism is essentially a war against God and the plan of

---

[46] President Gordon B. Hinckley, "Farewell to a Prophet," *Ensign*, July, 1994, https://www.lds.org/ensign/1994/07/farewell-to-a-prophet?lang=eng.

salvation—the very plan which we fought to uphold during "the war in heaven" (Rev. 12:7).

"Up to now some members of the Church have stood aloof, feeling that the fight against socialistic-communism is "controversial" and unrelated to the mission of the Church or the work of the Lord. But the President of the Church in our day has made it clear that the fight against atheistic communism is a major challenge to the Church and every member in it. . . .

"The fight against godless communism is a very real part of every man's duty who holds the priesthood. It is the fight against slavery, immorality, atheism, terrorism, cruelty, barbarism, deceit, and the destruction of human life through a kind of tyranny unsurpassed by anything in human history. Here is a struggle against the evil, satanical priestcraft of Lucifer. Truly it can be called, "a continuation of the war in heaven." . . . .

". . . Latter-day Saints should be reminded how and why they voted as they did in heaven. If some have decided to change their vote they should repent—throw their support on the side of freedom—and cease promoting this subversion."

What a stunning revelation! Communism is not only a failed economic or political system, it is not merely a despotic ideology, it is not simply a wrong or different form of government; *communism is, at its core, the very same plan Lucifer presented in the pre-earth life.*

Communism is not a recent invention or a reaction to capitalism; it is Satan's pre-earth plot to "ascend into heaven" and "exalt [his] throne above the stars of God" (Isaiah 14:13). The Prophet Joseph Smith revealed that in vision he and Sydney Rigdon "beheld Satan, that old serpent, even the devil, who rebelled against God, and sought to take the kingdom of our God and his Christ." In order to usurp God's Kingdom, Satan "maketh war with the saints of God, and encompasseth them round about" (D&C 76:28-29).

Satan's overarching goal, then, is not merely to make all men miserable like he is (2 Nephi 2:27), nor even to take away man's agency (Moses 4:3), though he certainly does both. The Adversary's central goal is to usurp God's Kingdom and crown himself king. He wants to be the exalted ruler of Heaven and earth. He wants to sit on the throne. The Lord revealed:

> "Satan rebelled against me, and sought to destroy the agency of man, which I, the Lord God, had given him, and also, that I should give unto him mine own power" (Moses 4:3).

Satan demands to be worshipped. He believes he is superior to all; more intelligent, more enlightened, more benevolent, more powerful. He demands servile obeisance to his whims.

It would be beneficial to briefly discuss how Satan intended on destroying man's agency. Nowhere in the scriptures does it say Satan's proposed pre-earth plan involved force and compulsion. Certainly, compulsion and tyranny have been the results of the implementation of his plan here on earth. However, Lucifer was clever; he would have never proposed forcing anyone to Heaven.

Lucifer knew that people inherently valued their agency, but he also knew that men would misuse their agency and sin. In the Father's Plan, each of us is judged according to our actions. We may choose eternal life or never-ending death. Because of our agency, some of us would inevitably choose death and damnation.

Lucifer therefore sought to manipulate people's emotions and fears by emphasizing that some of us would be lost if the Father's Plan was implemented. He appealed to our emotions and fears and invariably taught that the only loving plan was to save everyone *regardless* of their actions. That "equality" equaled true "justice" in Satan's mind. In order to extend divine "love" equally to all, Satan sought to save all men *in their sins*.

The Adversary's plan, therefore, was to deprive us of the consequences of our actions and save all men no matter what they did. All would receive an "equal" reward – eternal life – irrespective of their failures and sins. While this may sound benevolent and wonderful on the surface, a serious examination of this idea reveals that agency would be nullified under Satan's plan. If we will be saved from the consequences of our actions regardless of how terrible our choices are, then our choices don't matter. All choices are "equal" under this plan – equally irrelevant. Thus, the very core of agency – the ability and right to choose between two opposites – would be crushed.

In the October 1949 Conference, President J. Reuben Clark, Jr., offered this fascinating insight into Satan's scheme:

> "To my mind, as I read the scriptures, the thing boils down rather simply. I do not know whether Satan was offering a new plan or whether he had offered it before, but it sounded as if he thought it was a new plan. Satan offered the Father to take over all the spirits in the great council and save them all. Nobody was going to be lost, and all he asked of the Father was that the Father abdicate. He did not use that word. Maybe it is not used up in heaven, but we know what it means down here. The Father was to turn all of his power over to Satan, was to disappear, get out of the picture. . . .

> "What Satan wanted, quite evidently, was the full possession, ownership, of this creation of spirits that is involved in the peopling of this earth; so he tried to get them by gift, and that being denied, he is following along and trying to get us through the commission of sin. If we sin sufficiently we become his subjects.

> "As I read the scriptures, Satan's plan required one of two things: Either the compulsion of the mind, the spirit, the intelligence of man, or else saving men in sin. I question whether the intelligence of man can be compelled. Certainly men cannot be saved in sin,

because the laws of salvation and exaltation are rounded in righteousness, not in sin."[47]

Since the spirit of man cannot be forced to do anything, Satan's tactic must have been to save us in our sins. You will recall the anti-Christ Korihor. Korihor admitted that Satan had appeared to him and told him what to teach (Alma 30:53). Korihor's primary teaching was that "whatsoever a man did was no crime" (Alma 30:17). If Korihor was on Satan's errand, then this is Satan's teaching.

If we examine anti-Christs, Satanists, New Agers, and other preachers of wickedness throughout history, we find that almost all of them teach: "Do what thou wilt." In other words, "Whatsoever a man did was no crime." According to my study of world religions, it seems the dominant religious philosophy is that all roads lead to Heaven. This was foreseen by Nephi. He wrote:

> "And there shall also be many which shall say: Eat, drink, and be merry; nevertheless, fear God—he will justify in committing a little sin; yea, lie a little, take the advantage of one because of his words, dig a pit for thy neighbor; there is no harm in this; and do all these things, for tomorrow we die; and if it so be that we are guilty, God will beat us with a few stripes, and at last we shall be saved in the kingdom of God" (2 Nephi 28:8).

This "do what thou wilt" dogma is certainly the doctrine of apostate Christendom. But it is also an integral teaching in Hinduism, Judaism, and other religious traditions.

Satan only uses force when he has to as a last resort. Instead, he leads us "by the neck with a flaxen cord, until he bindeth [us] with his strong cords forever" (2 Nephi 26:22). A single flaxen cord is incredibly thin and weak by itself. Yet, when many flaxen cords are bound together, they form a

---

[47] President J. Reuben Clark, Jr., Conference Report, October, 1949, 191-195, http://scriptures.byu.edu/#:t1b5:p527.

strong rope with which to securely bind. Yes, Satan prefers to drag us "carefully down to hell" (2 Nephi 28:21).

Commenting on the phrase "carefully down to hell," President Ezra Taft Benson made this remark that relates to the topic of this book:

> "I like that word "carefully." In other words, don't shake them, you might awake them. But the Book of Mormon warns us that when we should see these murderous conspiracies in our midst that we should awake to our awful situation. Now why should we awake if the Lord is going to take care of us anyway? Now let us suppose that it is too late to save freedom. It is still accounted unto us for righteousness' sake to stand up and fight. Some Book of Mormon prophets knew of the final desolate end of their nations, but they still fought on, and they saved some souls including their own by so doing. For, after all, the purpose of life is to prove ourselves, and the final victory will be for freedom."[48]

Whether through force, as in the case of Russia, or through gradual subversion, careful deception, and ideological warfare as in the United States, Satan is waging war against mankind's agency. His chief weapon is communism. Communism employs both force and deception to bring the human race into servitude. It agents work openly and covertly.

More importantly to Satan, communism is his religion. It is Lucifer's counterfeit religion, and its leading exponents are his high priests. It is his means of exalting himself as god over the earth. Communism is a theocratic despotism that promises utopic and salvation to those who bow and worship the Devil. It is pure Satanism.

Inasmuch as communism is synonymous with Luciferianism, it is every Latter-day Saint's duty to resist it. More specifically, repelling communism is a Priesthood duty – one that has devolved upon the Lord's disciples

---

[48] President Ezra Taft Benson, "Not Commanded in All Things," Conference Report, April, 1965, 121-125, http://scriptures.byu.edu/#:t585:p401.

since pre-mortal times. Though it is "controversial" to buck the tide, our prophets have charged us with fighting Satan's tyranny, a tyranny which is "unsurpassed" in world history and which constitutes the "greatest satanical threat" to the Church.

Truly, no Latter-day Saint can claim he is fully faithful to the Church or to the Lord's prophets if he is not actively resisting the communist conspiracy and its multitude of front movements designed to destroy our culture, sabotage the family, undermine the Constitution, and wreck our Republic. Remember, the Prophet Joseph Smith said that to expose these hidden things of darkness is our "imperative duty."

Additionally, President Benson compared communism not only to Satan's pre-earth plan, but to Gadiantonism. He described the tactics of each group. Consider how thoroughly identical the tactics of the Gadiantons are to modern communist tactics of subversion. As you read, also note the goals of the two conspiracies:

> "When all of the trappings of propaganda and pretense have been pulled aside, the exposed hard-core structure of modern communism is amazingly similar to the ancient Book of Mormon record of secret societies such as the Gadiantons. In the ancient American civilization there was no word which struck greater terror to the hearts of the people than the name of the Gadiantons. It was a secret political party which operated as a murder cult. Its object was to infiltrate legitimate government, plant its officers in high places, and then seize power and live off the spoils appropriated from the people. (It would start out as a small group of "dissenters" and by using secret oaths with the threat of death for defectors (Hel. 11:25-26) it would gradually gain a choke hold on the political and economic life of whole civilizations.)

> "The object of the Gadiantons, like modern communists, was to destroy the existing government and set up a ruthless criminal dictatorship over the whole land."

What are the tactics for seizing power common to both communists and Gadiantons? According to President Benson, both Gadiantons and communists used murder as a potent weapon. In fact, the Gadianton secret society is described as a "murder cult." This description is no less poignant for communism when we consider that more than 100 million lives have been snuffed out by communists in Russia, China, Cambodia, North Korea, Hungary, Cuba, Spain, Angola, and elsewhere. But outright force was only one of the tactics used by these ancient and modern conspirators.

The conspirators also used silent infiltration into sensitive and lofty positions in government to carry forth their agenda. These schemers got themselves and their friends elected to judgeships or appointed to high offices. Once there, they changed laws and instituted self-serving policies. By manipulating government and redistributing wealth through taxes and social programs, the conspirators – now occupying "high places" in government – "live off the spoils appropriated from the people." Thus, communists like Gadiantons use "legal" methods to plunder and subjugate their victims just as readily as they use illegal and coercive methods.

Ultimately, both Gadiantons and communists establish collectivized societies and centralize all power in the hands of their "secret political party." Or, as President Benson stated, they establish "a ruthless criminal dictatorship" over the land. This acquired power is, of course, maintained through secret oaths and covenants made on threat of death, such as those administered to modern Freemasons. This is how Satan operated in the days of Cain, it is the system he delivered to the Gadianton Robbers, it is how he leads the communist kingpins, and it will be his method of operations until the day he is bound.

As his talk progressed, President Benson further identified communism as *the* secret combination foreseen by Moroni, and emphasized that modern prophets had been warning of the communist threat for some time:

"One of the most urgent, heart-stirring appeals made by Moroni as he closed the Book of Mormon was addressed to the gentile nations of the last days. He foresaw the rise of a great worldwide secret combination among the gentiles which " . . . *seeketh to overthrow the freedom of all lands, nations, and countries*" (Ether 8:25, italics added). He warned each gentile nation of the last days to purge itself of this gigantic criminal conspiracy which would seek to rule the world.

"The prophets, in our day, have continually warned us of these internal threats in our midst—that our greatest threat from socialistic-communism lies within our country. Brethren and sisters, we don't need a prophet—we have one—we need a listening ear. . . .

"The prophets have said that these threats are among us. The Prophet Moroni, viewing our day, said, "Wherefore the Lord commandeth you, when ye shall see these things come among you that ye shall awake to a sense of your awful situation" (Ether 8:24).

"Unfortunately our nation has not treated the socialistic-communist conspiracy as "treasonable to our free institutions," as the First Presidency pointed out in a signed 1936 statement. If we continue to uphold communism by not making it treasonable, our land shall be destroyed, for the Lord has said that ". . . whatsoever nation shall uphold such secret combinations, to get power and gain, until they shall spread over the nation, behold they shall be destroyed" (Ether 8:22)."

Do we have a listening ear? Do we have the courage to heed our prophets' words and warnings? Have we truly believed them when they have repeatedly identified communism as the modern Gadianton conspiracy facing mankind? Have we made every effort to make communism "treasonable"? Have we done all we can do to combat communism, or are we ripening for the prophesied destruction which is the lot of every society that upholds secret combinations?

President Benson continued in these words, and yet again identified communism as *the* modern conspiracy facing the world:

> "The Prophet Moroni seemed greatly exercised lest in our day we might not be able to recognize the startling fact that the same secret societies which destroyed the Jaredites and decimated numerous kingdoms of both Nephites and Lamanites would be precisely the same form of criminal conspiracy which would rise up among the gentile nations in this day.
>
> "The stratagems of the leaders of these societies are amazingly familiar to anyone who has studied the tactics of modern communist leaders. . . .
>
> "The world-wide secret conspiracy which has risen up in our day to fulfil these prophecies is easily identified. President McKay has left no room for doubt as to what attitude Latter-day Saints should take toward the modern "secret combinations" of conspiratorial communism."[49]

Yes, the modern conspiracy *is* easily identified – *it is communism*. To be sure, there are other conspiracies at work in the world which are also led by Lucifer. However, the communist conspiracy is the Devil's pet project and remains at this present time the most powerful Satanic sect in existence. Indeed, it is becoming stronger by the day. Though the world believes the myth that communism is "dead," the reality is it has never been more powerful and pervasive than it is now.

Yes, communism is *the* secret combination identified by the prophets. It is *the* secret combination foreseen by Moroni. And this ruthless occult

---

[49] President Ezra Taft Benson, "The American Heritage of Freedom – A Plan of God," Conference Report, October, 1961, 69-75, http://scriptures.byu.edu/#:t48d:p401.

conspiracy will be with us until the Lord cleanses the earth with fire. Hence our duty to be watchmen on the tower and raise our voices to the world (Ezekiel 3:17-19).

Elder Bruce R. McConkie told the Saints assembled for General Conference that modern Gadiantons existed and were seeking to destroy the Freedom of all lands. Said he:

> "We see evil forces everywhere uniting to destroy the family, to ridicule morality and decency, to glorify all that is lewd and base. We see wars and plagues and pestilence. Nations rise and fall. Blood and carnage and death are everywhere. Gadianton robbers fill the judgment seats in many nations. An evil power seeks to overthrow the freedom of all nations and countries. Satan reigns in the hearts of men; it is the great day of his power. . . .

> "The way ahead is dark and dreary and dreadful. There will yet be martyrs; the doors in Carthage shall again enclose the innocent. We have not been promised that the trials and evils of the world will entirely pass us by."[50]

Anciently, the prophet Nephi was shown our day in vision. He saw the "dark and dreary and dreadful" days predicted by Elder McConkie. He also saw Satan's agents seeking to overcome the Saints and overthrow the Freedom of all nations. He saw the martyrs and the persecuted Church of the Lamb.

Nephi described the wickedness and idolatry of our times. He described the formation of a great church which he variously called "the mother of abominations," "the mother of harlots," "the whore of all the earth," and "the great and abominable church of the devil" (1 Nephi 14:9-17). During the experience, Nephi was told by an angel:

---

[50] Elder Bruce R. McConkie, "The Coming Tests and Trials and Glory," General Conference, April, 1980, https://www.lds.org/general-conference/1980/04/the-coming-tests-and-trials-and-glory?lang=eng.

"Behold there are save two churches only; the one is the church of the Lamb of God, and the other is the church of the devil; wherefore, whoso belongeth not to the church of the Lamb of God belongeth to that great church, which is the mother of abominations; and she is the whore of all the earth" (1 Nephi 14:10).

In our day, as in Nephi's, there are only two churches to which a man can belong. On the one hand sits The Church of Jesus Christ of Latter-day Saints, which the Lord has revealed is "the only true and living church upon the face of the whole earth, with which I, the Lord, am well pleased" (D&C 1:30). On the other hand, the Devil's church gathers in the rest of mankind. Among this large congregation are the wicked as well as the good and honorable people of the earth who do not know the truth only because it has been hid from them by Lucifer's craftiness (D&C 123:12). Nevertheless, all who have not repented and been baptized into the Lord's Church are to one degree or another enslaved in Satan's terrible church. There is no middle ground, no neutrality, no third option.

Indeed, Nephi was shown that Satan's church has dominion over the entire earth and all of its nations. He recorded:

"And it came to pass that I looked and beheld the whore of all the earth, and she sat upon many waters; and she had dominion over all the earth, among all nations, kindreds, tongues, and people.

"And it came to pass that I beheld the church of the lamb of God, and its numbers were few, because of the wickedness and abominations of the whore who sat upon many waters" (1 Nephi 14:11-12).

When we look to identify this "church" in our day, we must look for an organization or system which has dominion "over all the earth," including political dominion. Is there a church, in the traditional sense, which has dominion in all lands and also wields the scepter of political power? No. The closest entity is the Roman Catholic Church which at one time did hold political as well as ecclesiastical power in many lands. However, there are many nations where the Catholic Church is not welcome, has few parishioners, or is rapidly decreasing in influence and membership. Russia and China are two poignant examples of major nations where Catholicism has almost no power and few adherents. And at any rate, though it is part of the Devil's system of organized paganism, the Catholic Church alone does not meet all the criteria to be considered *the* great and abominable church of the devil.

Numerous apostles have referred to this prophecy in 1 Nephi 14:10, and to the parallel prophecy recorded by John in Revelation, and have applied the labels "great and abominable church" and "Babylon," to various organizations and denominations. Here are a few examples. Please recognize the general nature of these words. Note that they do not single out merely one church as we consider a church today. And note that they do not refer to the Roman Catholic Church as *the* church of the Devil.

Writing in the April 1854 edition of *The Seer*, Elder Orson Pratt bluntly stated:

> "Both Catholics and Protestants are nothing less than the "whore of Babylon" whom the Lord denounces by the mouth of John the Revelator as having corrupted all the earth by their fornications and wickedness."[51]

Perhaps Elder Pratt took a leaf out of then President Brigham Young's book. President Young taught:

> "The Christian world, so called, are heathens as to their knowledge of the salvation of God."[52]

---

[51] Orson Pratt, *The Seer*, Vol. 2, No. 4, 255, April, 1854, https://archive.org/details/seereditedbyorso01unse.

[52] President Brigham Young, *Journal of Discourses*, Vol. 8, 171, September 16, 1860, http://jod.mrm.org/8/171.

How did the Christian world sink into such a deplorable condition? President Joseph F. Smith taught this about the pagan evolution of Christendom:

> "Notwithstanding, the disciples of Jesus, excepting John the Revelator, suffered ignominious deaths, they sowed the seed of the Gospel among, and conferred the Priesthood upon men, which remained for several generations upon the earth, but the time came when Paganism was engrafted into Christianity, and at last Christianity was converted into Paganism rather than converting the Pagans."[53]

Christianity, through the workings of this abominable church of Satan, became a pagan vessel and a major branch of Babylon. It will be recalled that Nephi foresaw the great and abominable church of the Devil distorting the scriptures and changing the doctrines that came forth from the original apostles called by Christ (1 Nephi 13:20-29). After this major change in doctrine and ordinance occurred, the people were led into darkness by their priests and leaders. To fortify his kingdom from dissent, Satan hunted down and persecuted true believers in Christ wherever they were found. Nephi foresaw that this church "slayeth the saints of God, yea, and tortureth them and bindeth them down, and yoketh them with a yoke of iron, and bringeth them down into captivity" (1 Nephi 13:4-6).

As President George Q. Cannon made clear in the following statement, the objectives and tactics of modern Babylon have not changed. They still hunt down, imprison, and destroy the true Saints of God:

> "One of the chief foundation stones of the great fabric of Government in this land, upon this continent, is religious liberty— liberty for every creed. Persecution of people for religion was unknown at the time this was written, and no man, unless he had been inspired of God, could have contemplated such a possibility

---

[53] President Joseph F. Smith, *Journal of Discourses*, Vol. 22, 44, February 6, 1881, http://jod.mrm.org/22/42.

as that any church would be persecuted for religion's sake. Yet here was a prediction made by Nephi, 2,400 years before it took place, in which he foretold the condition of things in this land, and upon all lands where the church of Christ should exist. There should be combinations and peoples gathered together, by religious influences, against the church of God. Now, what are the facts? Among the first persecutors of this church, when its members were few, were those who were themselves religious teachers. The earliest persecutors of Joseph Smith were religious teachers, and the mobs in Missouri, and the mobs in Illinois, were led by religious teachers. Even the mob that murdered our beloved Prophet and Patriarch, and wounded our revered President—that mob was led by a local Baptist preacher, and our people were driven from Nauvoo, as Brother Wells well knows, by a mob headed by a preacher. And today, those who are inciting mobs against this people; those who go to Congress, and incite persecutions against us; those who fulminate threats and frame petitions; those who meet together in conventions; those who gather together in conferences, are those who belong to this "mother of abominations," this "whore of all the earth," and it is through the influence of that accursed whore, that they gather together and marshal their forces in every land against the Latter-day Saints, the Church of the living God."[54]

President Cannon could see the fingerprints of Babylon all over the persecutions heaped upon the Saints in the United States after the Restoration. Surely no Latter-day Saint would deny that the Prophet Joseph Smith was murdered by men in Satan's employ. However, it is the sad irony that those calling themselves Christians were the ones the Devil used to do his dirty work and expand his abominable church.

---

[54] President George Q. Cannon, *Journal of Discourses*, Vol. 25, 127-128, April 6, 1884, http://jod.mrm.org/25/119.

Elder Bruce R. McConkie, in the second edition of *Mormon Doctrine*, corrected and updated his entry for "Church of the Devil." Whereas he had once explained that the Roman Catholic Church was Satan's church, after receiving counsel from the First Presidency and direct help from then Elder Spencer W. Kimball, Elder McConkie gave this accurate description of the great and abominable church of the Devil:

> "The titles church of the devil and great and abominable church are used to identify all churches or organizations of whatever name or nature – whether political, economic, social, fraternal, civic, or religious – which are designed to take men on a course that leads away from God and his laws and thus from salvation in the kingdom of God."[55]

These above statements should be sufficient to inform the reader that *all* churches and organizations set up or controlled by Satan are part of his great and abominable church. This includes Protestant organizations, the Roman Catholic Church, political fraternities, secret societies, political parties, etc. Whether referring to the persecution of early Christians by the Roman state and, later, by the Roman Church, or to the modern persecution of the restored Church and the murder of the Prophet Joseph Smith at the hand of Protestants and Freemasons, the same "church of the Devil" is responsible.

Bringing our discussion back to communism, Elder Hans Verlan Andersen explained that we should not read the word "church" in Nephi's account to mean a religious church in the traditional sense. Rather, Elder Andersen interpreted the meaning thus:

> "According to this prophecy everyone will eventually take sides and belong either to the Lord's or the devil's church. While a member of Christ's Church will have no difficulty identifying that organization, there is only one organization which will fit the

---

[55] McConkie, *Mormon Doctrine*, 137-138.

description of the other, and that is prostituted government. This is the only "church" to which everyone belongs, and no other organization – religious or otherwise – can possibly meet the test of world-wide membership. . . .

"The only "church" which can exert dominion of that extent, is world-wide government. No apostate religious denomination can ever be expected to wield power of those dimensions. But Nephi also saw that:

""". . . the mother of abominations did gather together multitudes upon the face of all the earth, among all the nations of the Gentiles, to fight against the Lamb of God." (v. 13)

"Only government has the power to assemble armies to fight a war . . . This passage assures us that "nations" belonged to the mother of abominations, and if such be true we can assume that this membership was governmental or political in nature. Such a world-wide government has been formed and is in the process of usurping the power of member nations. . . .

"Heretofore we have concluded that the only organization which fits the description of the Great and Abominable Church of the Devil given by the scriptures, is prostituted government. We have shown that Satan's church and his great secret combinations are one and the same in purpose and method; that according to prophecy, this organization will have dominion over all the earth in these last days; that it will wage war against the Lord's Church and slay his saints and prophets."[56]

If the evil "church" we are seeking to identify is not actually a church, but a political system, which one is it? Perhaps many systems could qualify. For instance, it was the arm of government inspired by demonic priests that crucified the Savior. It was the arm of government, again motivated

---

[56] Andersen, *The Great and Abominable Church of the Devil*, 88, 100.

by evil men of religion, which persecuted and killed the original apostles. It was the acquiescence of Governor Ford that led to the murder of the Prophet Joseph Smith in Carthage Jail at the hands of an organized mob. And so the story has gone for millennia with government being used by men beholden to Satan to crush the Lord's work and enslave mankind.

It is a poignant observation that government is the *only* organization which *all* men and women belong to regardless of their religious creed, race, gender, principles, etc. Government has dominion over *all* people irrespective of their point on the compass. This organ, then, is the chief organ through which Satan reaches all men. It is no wonder the scriptures attest that secret combinations *always* attempted to take command of the reins of government above all else. And today, Satan's secret combination seeks to not only take over individual governments, but *all* governments on an international scale.

If Elder Andersen is correct and "the great and abominable church of the devil" and the secret combination foreseen by Moroni are "one and the same in purpose and method," then what does that mean for identifying this entity? The answer is obvious: If the Devil's church and his secret combinations are the same, then his "church" is communism, because communism has been identified by the Church as a Gadianton-style secret combination which constitutes the "greatest satanical threat" to mankind.

Quoting from Elder Andersen again, we read:

> "[I]f Satan has a church on earth today it cannot be other than corrupted government or "domination by the state." If there is a secret combination among us which is seeking "to overthrow the freedom of all lands, nations, and countries" as Moroni prophesied, then it has to be the great Communist conspiracy and the movement to impose socialism world-wide. The "greatest Satanical threat on the face of the earth" and that "church which

is most abominable above all other churches" must be one and the same organization."[57]

The logic is simple, yet airtight. Communism *must* be the Devil's church, or, at very least, its predominant branch. If the prophets can be trusted, and I testify their words are the words of our Master, then communism is the greatest evil in the world – the same distinction given in the scriptures for Satan's abominable church.

If the Devil's church wields political as well as ecclesiastical authority, it is well to highlight the fact that communism is the absolute worst form of government ever invented. No other organization has been as destructive of God-given rights as has communism. More people have been butchered, enslaved, raped, and plundered by communism than by any other political ideology. The comparisons aren't even close. For instance, the fairly minimal crimes of fascism do not even compare. They aren't in the same ballpark. Communism is in a class all its own. Its atrocities are on an unparalleled scale, boggle the mind, and shock the senses. A minimum of 100 million humans have been massacred by the Bolsheviks, with billions more suffering enslavement.

Unlike most other political ideologies that are confined to an individual country or region, communism is inherently international. Communism seeks to impose itself on the whole of mankind. This is to be expected if, as we have explained, communism is Lucifer's priestcraft. Did not Nephi prophesy that the great and abominable church would have "dominion over all the earth, among all nations, kindreds, tongues, and people" (1 Nephi 14:11).

National socialism – derisively called "Nazism" – *never* sought to dominate the globe and was a regional phenomenon. It was further restricted because of its emphasis on race, German traditions, and a shared Nordic heritage. Zionism, likewise, can only expand so far because of its

---

[57] Andersen, *The Great and Abominable Church of the Devil*, 101.

connection to Judaism. It will never prosper in Arab-dominated regions, for instance. But communism, by contrast, is borderless. Communism has penetrated every region and has made its home among Muslims, Jews, Christians, Buddhists, Asians, whites, Latinos, Indians, blacks, Europeans, Americans, Chinese, Russians, Iranians, Israelis, and so forth. Truly, communism is the only international political system in existence today.[58]

The communist virus is spread through violent revolution. Blood, carnage, and confusion are its fertilizers. Satan's threat to use the armies of the earth to reign with blood and horror has come to pass. It is only fitting that his handcrafted ideology would be transmitted at the barrel of a gun. The spirit of communism is the spirit of the Destroyer.

Hans Kippenberger, the former military leader of the German Communist Party, affirmed:

> "Armed insurrection is the most decisive, severe, and loftiest form of class struggle which the proletariat must resort to, at the right

---

[58] A side note seems necessary. Some readers might immediately protest to my claim that communism is the "only" truly international political system in existence. Capitalism, you may say, dominates the globe more than communism. But a few things must be understood about so-called "capitalism." As practiced today, capitalism bears very little resemblance to the free enterprise system established and practiced by our Founding Fathers. The two systems are incompatible. The "capitalism" we have today is, in truth, a socialized version. It is the same system established by Lenin, for instance, under the title "New Economic Policy." NEP is often touted as "capitalism." It was not. It was socialism, pure and simple. Socialism/communism is all about using the power of government to regulate the "means of production" and harness the economy to line the pockets of the elites. Furthermore, todays' "capitalism" is intimately associated with central banking, and, in the United States, with the Federal Reserve. Please remember that Karl Marx's *Communist Manifesto* calls for the establishment of a national bank. If that sounds like a very capitalist thing to do, you have been the victim of socialist propagandizing. The entire economic system has been inverted. What we call "capitalism" today is in fact socialism. Free enterprise is a thing of the past and is not practiced on planet earth today. Truly, only communism exists on an international scale. You could even say that capitalism *is* communism.

moment in every country to overthrow the rule of the bourgeois and place power in our own hands."[59]

Once communism is coercively established as the ruling authority in any nation, the strong arm of government is used to keep the populace in chains. Freedom is destroyed. The right to worship God is restricted. Slavery is institutionalized. Brainwashing begins on an industrial scale. And armies are raised to assist the global revolution.

Government is used to transport communism internationally. The conspiracy would only be minimally effective if it operated through mafia type organizations. Gadianton-communism can only spread by attaching itself to government. In other words, it can only spread by disguising itself in the trappings of a legitimate social organization. And in our day of global communications, trade, and travel, an international governmental organization like the United Nations becomes a primary organ through which the conspiracy operates.

Furthermore, we recognize the global prevalence of communism when we understand that communism is a way of life. It is a set of attitudes, principles, and policies that blend economics, politics, morals, religion, social behavior, etc. All states acting on communist principles share certain characteristics. Let's examine a few of these.

Every communist state demands religious devotion from its subjects and proclaims power over the minds and hearts of men. The communist philosophy is led by figures, such as Karl Marx, who are venerated as prophets. These false prophets have produced their own de facto set of scriptures and holy books – many of which are mandatory reading at every major university throughout the world. The communist system is a religion, or "church," in nearly every sense of the word, and it occupies prominence worldwide.

---

[59] Richard Tedor, *Hitler's Revolution: Ideology, Social Programs, Foreign Affairs* (Chicago, IL: 2013), 21.

Additionally, the socialist principle of using government to redistribute wealth exists in *all* countries. This theft takes many forms. Most often, it is called "taxation." In his classic text *The Law*, which I recommend every person read and study often, Frederic Bastiat discussed socialism and the way it plunders society through "legal" means. He wrote:

> "Sometimes the law defends plunder and participates in it. Thus the beneficiaries are spared the shame, danger, and scruple which their acts would otherwise involve. Sometimes the law places the whole apparatus of judges, police, prisons, and gendarmes at the service of the plunderers, and treats the victim – when he defends himself – as a criminal. In short, there is *legal plunder*. . . .
>
> "But how is this legal plunder to be identified? Quite simply. See if the law takes from some persons what belongs to them, and gives it to other persons to whom it does not belong. See if the law benefits one citizen at the expense of another by doing what the citizen himself cannot do without committing a crime.
>
> "Then abolish this law without delay, for it is not only an evil itself, but also it is a fertile source for further evils because it invites reprisals. If such a law . . . is not abolished immediately, it will spread, multiply, and develop into a system. . . .
>
> "[I]t is upon the law that socialism itself relies. Socialists desire to practice *legal* plunder, not *illegal* plunder. Socialists, like all other monopolists, desire to make the law their own weapon. And when once the law is on the side of socialism, how can it be used against socialism? For when plunder is abetted by the law, it does not fear your courts, your gendarmes, and your prisons. Rather, it may call upon them for help."[60]

---

[60] Frederic Bastiat, *The Law*, translated by Dean Russell, (1850; New York: The Foundation for Economic Education, Inc., 1996), 16-17, 19.

It is worthwhile to note that this book was published in 1850 – two years after *The Communist Manifesto* openly heralded the communist uprising. It was in direct response to the communist fallacies that Bastiat wrote his classic book.

Another way that communist states legally plunder their subjects is by adopting welfare programs which pick one man's pockets and arbitrarily give the stolen wealth to another. Through the United Nations, this pick-pocketing exists on a global scale as international taxes and foreign aid programs suck the lifeblood and resources out of nations. Frederic Bastiat had a word to say about welfare schemes, too:

> "You say: "There are two persons who have no money," and you turn to the law. But the law is not a breast that fills itself with milk. Nor are the lacteal veins of the law supplied with milk from a source outside the society. Nothing can enter the public treasury for the benefit of one citizen or one class unless other citizens and other classes have been *forced* to send it in . . . The law can be an instrument of equalization only as it takes from some persons and gives to other persons. When the law does this, it is an instrument of plunder."[61]

The prophets have similarly rejected the notion of state-imposed welfare schemes. In the *Church News* of March 14, 1953, President David O. McKay declared:

> "[I]t is not the government's duty to support you.
>
> "I shall raise my voice as long as God gives me sound or ability, against the communistic idea that the government will take care of us all, and that everything belongs to the government. . . .

---

[61] Bastiat, *The Law*, 27.

"It is wrong! No wonder, in trying to perpetuate that idea, that men become anti-Christ, because those teachings strike directly at the doctrines of the Savior.

"No government owes you a living. You get it yourself by your own acts — never by trespassing upon the rights of your neighbor, never by cheating him. You put a blemish upon your character the moment you do."[62]

Despite the fact that government welfare is a "communistic idea" and an "anti-Christ" concept that leaves "a blemish upon your character," every government in the world redistributes wealth in welfare schemes. They call this "charity" and indoctrinate the youth to believe that the purpose of government is to provide a living for its people. But this, as our dear President McKay so pointedly explained, is a "wrong" idea. It is "anti-Christ." Don't be fooled. Don't be duped into believing you are being benevolent, charitable, or kind when you support such Devilish programs.

Finally, as mentioned above, the global financial system, per the official communist plan, dominates the nations through national banks which control the currency, increase inflation, cause recessions and depressions, and redistribute wealth on a whim. When people point to the Federal Reserve and the international bankers as the root of the world's problems, understand that these conspirators are acting according to the stated communist plan. Remember, *communism* is the "greatest satanical threat" to the world.

Yes, Satanic communism holds sway in *every* nation. Most nations are not "officially" communist states, yet they espouse communist principles. Though most nations reject the communist label, they will, however, admit that they are socialist. Some ostensibly anti-communist nations are giddily and proudly socialist states. This is especially true in Europe. Even the United States, as officially anti-communist as she is, has adopted and

---

[62] President David O. McKay, *Church News*, March 14, 29153, in Newquist, ed., *Prophets, Principles and National Survival*, 347.

instituted *all* ten planks of *The Communist Manifesto.* I repeat: Every nation in the world has adopted socialism, churns out socialist legislation, and operates within a socialist paradigm, as a matter of course.

It must be understood that socialism is a wing of the communist conspiracy designed to seduce the nations that are not prepared to openly embrace full communism at the present. Though many "experts" and armchair historians alike protest and claim that socialism is different from communism, this is simply not true. It is thoroughly dishonest to claim that socialism and communism are separate and distinct from one another. It is an outright denial of history and reality to believe such hokum.

The truth is that the socialist movement was created by avowed communists, promotes the same causes with only a slight variation in tactics, achieves the same ends, destroys the same Liberties and personal rights, sees the world through the same collectivist lens, and, finally, rolls out the red carpet which communism marches in on when the time is right. Socialism is communism's wingman. The two are conjoined twins. There is simply no communism without socialism, and socialism inevitably leads to communism.

Furthermore, our prophets have identified socialism as one-and-the-same-thing as communism. These seers have seen and comprehend the truth. They have warned the nations that adopting socialism will inescapably lead us to the horrors of communism. For instance, President Benson wrote an entire book on socialism titled *The Red Carpet: Socialism – the Royal Road to Communism.* In it, he instructed:

> "It is high time we realized the dangerous threat to America of creeping socialism as the ruthless comrade to atheistic communism.
>
> "It is high time that we recognize creeping socialism for what it really is – a Red Carpet providing a royal road to communism. . . .

"This is a most important lesson for all of us to learn, namely, that the communists use the socialists to pave the way for them wherever possible. This is why communists and socialists are often found supporting each other, collaborating together and fighting for the same goals.

"The paramount issue today is freedom against creeping socialism. . . .

". . . the worst thing that can happen to a socialist is to have himself openly identified with the work of the communists who are generally feared and despised. . . .

"We must ever keep in mind that collectivized socialism is part of the communist strategy. Communism is fundamentally socialism. We will never win our fight against communism by making concessions to socialism. Communism and socialism, closely related, must be defeated on principle."[63]

President Benson understood that communists "use the socialists to pave the way for them." The socialist movement was created for this very purpose. It was created by the very same conspirators who would later take the name "communists." The self-proclaimed socialists derive their principles from *The Communist Manifesto* written by arch-communist Karl Marx. Socialism does nothing but "pave the way" for the communist conspiracy. Once softened by socialism, a nation will easily fall into communist hands. The prophets have understood this and have warned us accordingly. Have we heeded their warnings?

In 1966, President Marion G. Romney was asked by the Brethren to give a Conference address contrasting socialism and the United Order. This talk coincided, no doubt intentionally, with President McKay's announcement

---

[63] Ezra Taft Benson, *The Red Carpet: Socialism – the Royal Road to Communism* (Salt Lake City, Utah: Bookcraft, 1962), 65, 69, 75.

already cited on the position of the Church regarding communism. During that landmark talk, President Romney said:

> "[N]otwithstanding my abhorrence of it, I am persuaded that socialism is the wave of the present and of the foreseeable future. It has already taken over or is contending for control in most nations. . . .
>
> "We here in the United States, in converting our government into a social welfare state, have ourselves adopted much of socialism. Specifically, we have to an alarming degree adopted the use of the power of the state in the control and distribution of the fruits of industry. . . .
>
> "We have also gone a long way on the road to public ownership and management of the vital means of production. In both of these areas the free agency of Americans has been greatly abridged. Some argue that we have voluntarily surrendered this power to government. Be this as it may, the fact remains that the loss of freedom with the consent of the enslaved, or even at their request, is nonetheless slavery."[64]

To summarize President Romney's remarks, socialism (i.e. communism with a smiley face) is the "wave of the present" and future and already dominates, or is seeking to control, "most nations." Though we like to boast that our nation is "free," President Romney said socialism (i.e. communism) has largely been adopted in the United States. This system has "greatly abridged" our Liberty and is converting us into slaves – and often with our consent, approval, and applause.

Of course, the communists have admitted that they are presently working to establish socialism. Remember, socialism is merely a precursor to communism and espouses the same goals in a nicer, more public-friendly

---

[64] President Marion G. Romney, "Socialism and the United Order Compared," Conference Report, April, 1966, 95-101, http://scriptures.byu.edu/#:t5c4:p4cb.

way. Several brief points will demonstrate the interrelated nature of communism and socialism.

The unabbreviated name of the USSR was the Union of Soviet Socialist Republics. The word "soviet" means council. These soviets (i.e. councils) promoted socialism as a stepping stone to the ultimate goal of pure communism on a global scale. Furthermore, the actual name of Lenin's Bolshevik sect was the Social Democratic Workers' Party. The 1957 constitution of the Communist Party USA also stated that the "historic mission" of the party was "the establishment of socialism."[65]

Today, nothing has changed. To wit, the preamble to the constitution of Red China states that its goal is "to turn China into a socialist country." The "basic task of the nation is to concentrate its effort on socialist modernization along the road of Chinese-style socialism." This effort is being pushed "under the leadership of the Communist Party of China and the guidance of Marxism-Leninism and Mao Zedong Thought."[66]

Seeing through the deceptive "differences" of communism and socialism, President J. Reuben Clark, Jr. was blunt about their sameness. In the April 1963 General Conference, President Ezra Taft Benson quoted numerous statements by President Clark, such as the following:

> "I have been preaching against Communism for twenty years," said President Clark, over twenty years ago. "I still warn you against it, and I tell you that we are drifting toward it more rapidly than some of us understand, and I tell you that when Communism comes, the ownership of the things which are necessary to feed your families is going to be taken away from us. I tell you freedom of speech will go, freedom of the press will go, and freedom of religion will go. . . .

---

[65] J. Edgar Hoover, *Masters of Deceit* (New York: Pocket Books, Inc., 1958), 126.

[66] "Constitution of the People's Republic of China," The National People's Congress of the People's Republic of China, amended March 14, 2004, accessed February 25, 2018, http://www.npc.gov.cn/englishnpc/Constitution/node_2825.htm.

"The plain and simple issue now facing us in America is freedom or slavery. . .

"Our real enemies," said President Clark, "are communism and its running mate, socialism . . .

"And never forget for one moment that communism and socialism are state slavery . . .

". . . we will not get out of our present difficulties without trouble, serious trouble. Indeed, it may well be that our government and its free institutions will not be preserved except at the price of life and blood . . .

". . . the paths we are following, if we move forward thereon, will inevitably lead us to socialism or communism, and these two are as like as two peas in a pod in their ultimate effect upon our liberties . . .

"We may first observe that communism and socialism—which we shall hereafter group together and dub Statism—cannot live with Christianity, nor with any religion that postulates a Creator such as the Declaration of Independence recognizes. The slaves of Statism must know no power, no authority, no source of blessing, no God, but the State. . . .

"Do not think that all these usurpations, intimidations, and impositions are being done to us through inadvertency or mistake, the whole course is deliberately planned and carried out; its purpose is to destroy the Constitution and our Constitutional government . . .

"We have largely lost the conflict so far waged. But there is time to win the final victory, if we can sense our danger, and fight.""[67]

Socialism and communism are like "two peas in a pod." Both advocate the supremacy of the state, which President Clark called statism and which Elder Andersen identified as the "great and abominable church of the Devil." Statism is the worship of the state as a substitute for the worship of God. Communism is the ultimate statism – its most ruthless and terrifying manifestation. And whether we follow socialism or communism, it matters not – both will reward us equally with chains of slavery.

All those decades ago communism had made such tremendous inroads that President Clark said we had lost the conflict and that perhaps only the shedding of blood would reclaim our lost Liberty. Today the situation is direr and the chains rest heavier upon us. As a People, we have adopted communism without realizing it. Yet, those conspirators who pull the strings from the shadows know full well what they are doing. This is deliberate and according to the plan which Satan has delivered to his receptive followers from the beginning (Helaman 6:30). By slapping the false labels "socialism," "liberalism," "democracy," or "progressivism" on the package, the conspirators have been able to force feed the American People communism until now our constitutional system is a corroded shell of its former self. And now the public is an inch away from electing an avowed socialist to the White House, as the rave popularity of Senator Bernie Sanders attests.

These prophetic statements confirm that communistic government is the "church of the devil" which Nephi saw making war against the Saints in our day, and that this church is synonymous with the secret combination beheld by Moroni. And the Church in modern times has identified *both* of these entities as the Satanic communist conspiracy that exists among all

---

[67] President J. Reuben Clark Jr., in President Ezra Taft Benson, "Righteousness Exalteth a Nation," Conference Report, April, 1963, 109-114, http://scriptures.byu.edu/#:t4fb:p401.

people today and which is fighting for the overthrow of families, faith, and Freedom in every corner of the globe.

Of this great and abominable church, Elder Bruce R. McConkie has written that there exist divisions, or branches. The strongest of these, said he, is communism. Elder McConkie wrote:

> "Basically and chiefly, communism is a form of false religion; it is one of the major divisions of the church of the devil. It denies God and Christ; belittles Christianity; runs counter to the moral and ethical standards of religion and decency; denies men their agency; wrenches from them their inalienable rights; and swallows the individual and his wellbeing up in the formless mass of the state.

> "Communism is also a political movement, one that fosters and promotes world revolution, and has as its aim the subjugation of all free peoples and nations. It necessarily is a dictatorship of the severest and most ruthless type."[68]

When read in context of President McKay's declaration that communism is the "greatest satanical threat," it becomes clear that the communist conspiracy is *the* major division of the Devil's church. Indeed, as Elder Hans Verlan Andersen explained, the Devil's church is "prostituted government." The most international and worldwide version of "prostituted government" is communism. As the most widely accepted political heresy, and as the "greatest satanical threat" to mankind, we can clearly see that communism is Satan's primary vehicle for carrying out his agenda in these last days.

Ex-communist Whittaker Chambers, in his seminal book *Witness*, remarked:

---

[68] Bruce R. McConkie, *Mormon Doctrine*, 151.

"I see in Communism the focus of the concentrated evil of our time."[69]

Communism was the embodiment of evil in our day because it epitomizes man's rejection of God; his rebellion against his Creator. Chambers observed:

"Communism is what happens when, in the name of Mind, men free themselves from God."[70]

In his October 1979 General Conference address titled "A Witness and a Warning," President Benson updated the Saints on the progress of this communist secret combination. He taught that "whenever the God of heaven reveals His gospel to mankind, Satan, the archenemy to Christ, introduces a counterfeit." This prophet then quoted an ancient statement from Isaiah which reads:

"Woe unto them that seek deep to hide their counsel from the Lord, and their works are in the dark, and they say, Who seeth us? and who knoweth us?

"Surely your turning of things upside down shall be esteemed as the potter's clay: for shall the work say of him that made it, He made me not? or shall the thing framed say of him that framed it, He had no understanding?" (Isaiah 29:15-16).

Upon reading this passage, President Benson proceeded to tell us exactly which latter-day group works in the dark, hides its counsel from the Lord, and proclaims the godless creed, "He made me not":

"It is well to ask, what system established secret works of darkness to overthrow nations by violent revolution? Who

---

[69] Whittaker Chambers, *Witness* (Washington, D.C.: Regnery Publishing, 2001), xxxvii.

[70] Chambers, *Witness*, xlv.

blasphemously proclaimed the atheistic doctrine that God made us not? Satan works through human agents. We need only look to some of the ignoble characters in human history who were contemporary to the restoration of the gospel to discover fulfillment of Isaiah's prophecy. I refer to the infamous founders of Communism and others who follow in their tradition.

"Communism introduced into the world a substitute for true religion. It is a counterfeit of the gospel plan. The false prophets of Communism predict a utopian society. This, they proclaim, will only be brought about as capitalism and free enterprise are overthrown, private property abolished, the family as a social unit eliminated, all classes abolished, all governments overthrown, and a communal ownership of property in a classless, stateless society established.

"Since 1917 this godless counterfeit to the gospel has made tremendous progress toward its objective of world domination."[71]

Remember Moroni's prophecy that the latter-day secret combination would seek "to overthrow the freedom of all lands, nations, and countries; and it bringeth to pass the destruction of all people" (Ether 8:25). To my mind, as well as President Benson's, this is a perfect description of communism. The Bolshevik conspirators have destroyed nation after nation, directly and indirectly snuffing out the lives of hundreds of millions of Heavenly Father's children and enslaving billions more. Marx, Lenin, Trotsky, Stalin and other false prophets have overthrown the world's Freedom and corrupted humanity's faith by spreading their communistic ideology.

---

[71] President Ezra Taft Benson, "A Witness and a Warning," General Conference, October, 1979, https://www.lds.org/general-conference/1979/10/a-witness-and-a-warning?lang=eng.

Communism is a counterfeit to the Gospel. It is an inverted gospel with Satan as god and Marx, Lenin, and other gangsters as high priests. In my first book on communism, *A Century of Red*, I made this observation:

> "[T]he Bolsheviks "organized antireligious carnivals on traditional feast days." They opened a museum to officially celebrate atheism, which was purported to house a statue of Baphomet. In Ethiopia, the communist regime taught children to recite a warped version of the Lord's Prayer which began: "Our Party which rulest in the Soviet Union, Hallowed be thy name. . ." In the Chinese prison camps, a Catholic prisoner reported that "meditation, confession, and repentance [were] reinvented as Marxist-Leninist practices." Lin Biao, a leading Chinese communist under Mao, stated that communism was a "spiritual atom bomb." And we have all seen videos of thousands of cheering Russians, Chinese, and North Koreans marching in communist parades, holding aloft giant portraits of their dear prophets, Marx, Lenin, Stalin, Mao, and Kim Il-sung.

> "All of this was done as if to create a parallel religious culture to that of Christianity. Indeed, I interpret the vengeful denunciations and mockery of Christ – which harmonize with those of known Satanists, Theosophists, Freemasons, and occultists – as yet additional evidence of the communist leadership's private Satanic sentiments. They not only hate orthodox religion, but they specifically see Christ as an evil being who stands in opposition to their own god and to the communist religion he has revealed through Marx and other willing servants."[72]

Yes, communism is a counterfeit creed of Satanic origin, complete with religious trappings, holy days, hallowed rituals, sacred writings, and false prophets.

---

[72] Zack Strong, *A Century of Red* (USA: January, 2018), chapter 3,

President Brigham Young made an interesting observation regarding counterfeits to the Gospel. Said he:

> "If true principles are revealed from heaven to men, and if there are angels, and there is a possibility of their communicating to the human family, always look for an opposite power, an evil power, to give manifestations also: look out for the counterfeit.

> "There is evil in the world, and there is also good. Was there ever a counterfeit without a true coin? No. Is there communication from God? Yes. From holy angels? Yes; and we have been proclaiming these facts during nearly thirty years. Are there any communications from evil spirits? Yes; and the Devil is making the people believe very strongly in revelations from the spirit world. This is called spiritualism."[73]

Spiritualism, a sister ideology to spiritism, resurfaced in modern times with the Fox Sisters in 1848. The underlying doctrine of the spiritualist movement is that man can communicate with spirits from the other side. This is a true doctrine. However, spiritualism's methods are counterfeit and false; namely, these otherworldly spirits are summoned in séances, through mediums, during trances, and through other means. These counterfeits are harshly condemned in the scriptures (Leviticus 19:31; Leviticus 20:27; Deuteronomy 18:9-12; Isaiah 8:19; 1 Timothy 4:1). Spiritualism, regardless of how it is practiced, is a counterfeit of the Gospel practice of revelation and angelic ministration.

Elder Bruce R. McConkie has written of spiritualism in these terms:

> "Those religionists who attempt and frequently attain communion (as they suppose) with departed spirits are called spiritualists. Their doctrine and belief that mediums and other mortals can actually hold intercourse with the spirits of the dead is called

---

[73] President Brigham Young, *Journal of Discourses*, Vol. 7, 240, September 1, 1859, http://jod.mrm.org/7/237.

spiritualism. Such communion, if and when it occurs, is manifest by means of physical phenomena, such as so-called spirt-rappings, or during abnormal mental states, such as in trances. These communions are commonly arranged and shown forth through the instrumentality of mediums.

"It is true that some mediums do make contact with spirits during séances. In most instances, however, such spirits as manifest themselves are probably the demons of devils who were cast out of heaven for rebellion. Such departed spirits as become involved in these spiritualistic orgies would obviously be the spirits of wicked and depraved persons who because of their previous wickedness in mortality had wholly subjected themselves to the dominion of Lucifer. Righteous spirits would have nothing but contempt and pity for the attempts of mediums to make contact with them. . . .

"Thus, no matter how sincerely mediums may be deceived into thinking they are following a divinely approved pattern, they are in fact turning to an evil source "for the living to hear from the dead." . . . though some true facts may be found in it, yet its acceptance and use has the effect of leading souls into the clutches of those evil powers which give the data."[74]

Spiritualism, as President Young and Elder McConkie attest, is a counterfeit from an evil source. It is utterly Satanic. It is one of the chief modes through which Satan reveals his will to mortals in every corner of the globe. Through these spiritualist methods, along with personal visitations by demonic beings posing as Masters of Wisdom and angels of light, Satan deceives the nations.

I urge all Latter-day Saints who have become ensnared with divination, astrology, mediumism, and necromancy of all types, to flee from Babylon.

---

[74] Bruce R. McConkie, *Mormon Doctrine*, 759-760.

I personally know several Latter-day Saints, and have a handful of LDS relatives, who are involved in energy healing[75] and various counterfeit forms of occultism, and I know of thousands more who are similarly deceived. Please, resist and reject these counterfeits as you would reject communism.

Curiously, Victoria Woodhull, one of the first radical feminists who led the wicked Women's Liberation movement in the United States, was a fanatical supporter of her contemporary Karl Marx. Woodhull wrote to Marx and urged him to publicly acknowledge what she and others secretly understood; namely, that communism and spiritualism are "one and the same,"[76] and that the Women's Liberation movement embodied both of them.

Indeed, the Women's Liberation movement, as will be touched upon later, is a communist front movement which first gained traction because of the ascendency of modern spiritualism. Feminism was founded by

---

[75] In 2016, the Church's spokesman, Eric Hawkins, released a statement denouncing energy healing as a false practice. In his October 2017 General Conference talk "The Trek Continues!" President M. Russell Ballard repeated this statement and urged the Saints against such practices. Said he:

"In some places, too many of our people are looking beyond the mark and seeking secret knowledge in expensive and questionable practices to provide healing and support.

"An official Church statement, issued one year ago, states: "We urge Church members to be cautious about participating in any group that promises—in exchange for money—miraculous healings or that claims to have special methods for accessing healing power outside of properly ordained priesthood holders.""

As noble as energy healing (also called Christ-centered healing, faith-based healing, Reiki, and therapeutic touch) may seem, it is a Satanic counterfeit. If you need healing, seek out an authorized Priesthood holder for a blessing or find competent medical support. Whatever you do, do not engage in occult practices and then rationalize your behavior as something "harmless" or as a "gift from God." God's house is a house of order and His servants have urged us to avoid all supernatural healing methods "outside of properly ordained priesthood holders." Therein lies safety.

[76] Karlyn Crowley, *Feminism's New Age: Gender, Appropriation, and the Afterlife of Essentialism* (Albany, New York: State University of New York Press, 2011), 16.

Satanic conspirators for the express purpose of destroying the institution of marriage and splitting the patriarchal family unit apart. The feminist movement – dating clear back to the militant Suffragettes – is wrapped up in spiritualism, Wicca, the New Age movement, and the occult. And its leaders have, almost without exception, been either card-carrying members of the Communist Party or furtive adherents of communism.

Communism, like spiritualism, is a counterfeit to the Restored Gospel of Jesus Christ. Its leaders receive revelations and manifestations from Lucifer and his angels just as readily as the Lord's prophets receive inspiration from Heaven. This will be discussed more in a later chapter. Regarding this counterfeit inspiration being given to the world's leaders, President Joseph Fielding Smith observed:

> "The present turmoil and contentions in the world are due to the fact that the leaders of nations are getting their inspiration from Satan, not from the Lord. His Spirit is withdrawn from them, according to his promise, in spiritual things. The Lord would be glad to direct them, but they seek not his counsel. The spirit of the evil one is placing in their minds vain and fantastic notions and leading mankind further away from the truth as they boast in their own strength, while the Almighty sits in the heavens and no doubt laughs at their folly."[77]

Yes, Satan is in charge of this world – at least, as far at the Lord permits him to be. In his temptations of Jesus in the wilderness, Lucifer acknowledged his power to appoint world leaders and control kingdoms. After showing Jesus "all the kingdoms of the world," Satan told Him: "All these things will I give thee, if thou wilt fall down and worship me" (Matthew 4:8-9). As the eternal King of kings, our Savior could not be tempted with such worldly accolades and power.

---

[77] Joseph Fielding Smith, *Answers to Gospel Questions*, Vol. 2 (Salt Lake City, Utah: Deseret Book Company1958), 156.

Conversely, short-sighted mortals *are* tempted by the allure of temporal wealth, power, and glory. From the time Cain murdered Abel to the present, men have been persuaded to murder and steal and compromise their values in order to get gain and power. Those of us who have been through the temple and received our endowment know of Lucifer's threat to use the wealth of the world to buy armies and employ false priests, popes, kings, and presidents to do his bidding and to reign through his mortal surrogates with blood, oppression, and terror. Throughout the ages, Satan has been so successful that the Prophet Joseph Smith was forced to lament:

> "We have learned by sad experience that it is the nature and disposition of almost all men, as soon as they get a little authority, as they suppose, they will immediately begin to exercise unrighteous dominion" (D&C 121:39).

In the same month in 1839, while in unlawful captive in Liberty Jail, Joseph Smith wrote another letter wherein he described the "most damning hand of murder, tyranny, and oppression" and the "iron yoke" that Satan's minion ruled with (D&C 123:7-8). Many of the great leaders, conquerors, and despots of the world – even in our own nation – willingly bow the knee to Lucifer, and he bestows upon them kingdoms, wealth, and the praise of men. We should all keep in mind what Elder Mark E. Petersen taught in 1954:

> "Satan is real; Satan is personal. . . .

> "Satan does give revelation to us, evil revelation, to put us off the track, to lead us astray, and to ease us into sin. . . .

> "Satan is definitely a revelator, devilish and evil as he is."[78]

---

[78] Elder Mark E. Petersen, Address to Teachers of Religion, August 24, 1954, in Gerald N. Lund, *Hearing the Voice of the Lord: Principles and Patterns of Personal Revelation* (Salt Lake City, Utah: Deseret Book, 2007), 235.

Satan is indeed real and he appears to and is known by his zealous followers. The world has been taught that the communist leaders were atheists. This is false. While communism ostensibly rejects all religion and is avowedly "atheist," its chief leaders have in fact been Satanists and occultists. I cover some of the pertinent evidence for this view in my book *A Century of Red*. Later in this work, I will present a drop of that evidence. Here, however, I will simply remind you what the scriptures teach about how and by whom secret combinations are directed and led. They are led personally by Satan. From Cain to Akish to Gadianton, Satan's followers have always known their master personally and intimately.

Recall that Gadianton received the blood oaths and covenants which he administered to his band of robbers and murderers from "that same being who did plot with Cain . . . And he did plot with Cain and his followers from that time forth" (Helaman 6:27). And remember that Cain saw, conversed with, and was instructed by Lucifer face-to-face (Moses 5:18, 29-30). And, finally, recall that Satan "doth carry on his works of darkness and secret murder, and doth hand down their plots, and their oaths, and their covenants and their plans of awful wickedness, from generation to generation according as he can get hold upon the hearts of the children of men" (Helaman 6:30).

In 1979, President Benson reminded us what is at stake in this battle between Freedom and Satanic communism:

> "Today, we are in a battle for the bodies and souls of man. It is a battle between two opposing systems: freedom and slavery, Christ and anti-Christ. The struggle is more momentous than a decade ago, yet today the conventional wisdom says, "You must learn to live with Communism and to give up your ideas about national sovereignty." Tell that to the millions—yes, the scores of millions—who have met death or imprisonment under the tyranny of Communism! *Such would be the death knell of freedom and all we hold dear.* God must ever have a free people to prosper His work and bring about Zion."

Right vs. wrong. Freedom vs. slavery. The Constitution vs. communism. Light vs. darkness. Christ vs. Satan. *This* is our choice. *These* are the alternatives. We either choose Christ and His Gospel plan, or we automatically fall in with Lucifer and, by default, end up promoting one or another version of his communistic conspiracy.

In the same hard-hitting talk, this great leader recounted his personal experiences with communism as he travelled through a Europe besieged by the forces of evil. He then warned us of the dire situation Americans then found themselves in:

> "I have seen the Soviet Union, under its godless leaders, spread its ideology throughout the world. Every stratagem is used—trade, war, revolution, violence, hate, detente, and immorality—to accomplish its purposes. Many nations are now under its oppressive control. Over one billion people—one-fourth of the population of the world—have now lost their freedom and are under Communist domination. We seem to forget that the great objective of Communism is still world domination and control, which means the surrender of our freedom—your freedom—our sovereignty. . . .

> "The truth is, we have to a great extent accommodated ourselves to Communism—and we have permitted ourselves to become encircled by its tentacles. . . .

> "Never before has the land of Zion appeared so vulnerable to so powerful an enemy as the Americas do at present."

Do we believe President Benson's words? Do we believe that our country is surrounded by the tentacles of a Satanic conspiracy? Do we believe this land is "vulnerable" to conquest by an evil and powerful enemy – the most powerful and combined we have ever faced? And, finally, do we believe, as President Benson explained, that this conspiracy, this enemy, this threat, is communism? If we do not believe it, we had better start believing it, because the sad fact is that communism is more powerful and widespread now than it was in 1979.

Finally, President Benson directly compared the communist conspiracy to the secret combination foreseen by Moroni. He said:

> "We must awaken to "a sense of [our] awful situation, because of this secret combination which [is] among [us]" (Ether 8:24). We must not tolerate accommodation with or appeasement toward the false system of Communism. We must demand of our elected officials that we not only resist Communism, but that we will take every measure to prevent its intrusion into this hemisphere. It is vital that we invoke the Monroe Doctrine."[79]

In his talk, President Benson made it crystal clear that communism is *the* secret combination which is among us. He called communism an "anti-Christ" system and reminded us that its dominion sprawls across the earth and that billions of souls are enslaved by its tentacles. He reminded us that communism has given the world "secret works of darkness" and that communism is a false and counterfeit religion headed by false prophets who violently overthrow Freedom wherever they are able to do so. In short, he confirmed the official position of the Church that communism is the "greatest satanical threat" to mankind, and identified it as the same secret combination foreseen by Moroni.

For emphasis of the growing, spreading nature of this communist behemoth, I quote one of President Benson's Conference addresses given while president of the Church. At the October 1988 Conference, President Benson witnessed:

> "I testify that wickedness is rapidly expanding in every segment of our society. (See D&C 1:14–16; D&C 84:49–53.) It is more highly

---

[79] President Ezra Taft Benson, "A Witness and a Warning," General Conference, October, 1979, https://www.lds.org/general-conference/1979/10/a-witness-and-a-warning?lang=eng.

organized, more cleverly disguised, and more powerfully promoted than ever before. Secret combinations lusting for power, gain, and glory are flourishing. A secret combination that seeks to overthrow the freedom of all lands, nations, and countries is increasing its evil influence and control over America and the entire world. (See Ether 8:18–25.) . . . .

"I testify that as the forces of evil increase under Lucifer's leadership and as the forces of good increase under the leadership of Jesus Christ, there will be growing battles between the two until the final confrontation. As the issues become clearer and more obvious, all mankind will eventually be required to align themselves either for the kingdom of God or for the kingdom of the devil. As these conflicts rage, either secretly or openly, the righteous will be tested."[80]

This dear prophet had painstakingly, over many decades, identified communism as *the* secret combination seeking to overthrow our Liberty. Here, in 1988, three years before the alleged and phony "collapse" of communism, President Benson testified that the same cabal was "increasing its evil influence and control over America and the entire world." *Communism was not on its way out; it was ascending and gaining momentum and strength.* Lucifer's forces were in 1988, as they are today, "rapidly expanding" and are causing a cataclysm in which we must choose sides. Yes, Satan is in his end game.

In his marvelous volume *A New Witness for the Articles of Faith*, Elder Bruce R. McConkie spoke of mankind's groping after counterfeit religious systems. He emphasized that communism is a false religion which has mass appeal among the inhabitants of the earth today. He explained:

"Sad as it may be, almost the entire history of mankind is an account of false worship, false gods, and all the ills that attend

---

[80] President Ezra Taft Benson, "I Testify," General Conference, October, 1988, https://www.lds.org/general-conference/1988/10/i-testify?lang=eng.

such a course . . . Communism is in reality a form of religion in which men deny the God of the Bible and worship the gods of compulsion and power and war. . . .

"Since the fall, most of mankind have chosen darkness rather than light because their deeds were evil. The gods of power and wealth and worldliness have always been the favorite deities of fallen man. They are the religion of the natural man, of fallen man, of man in his carnal, sensual, and devilish state. They corrupt the moral sense and open the door to every vice. And nowhere is this more clearly seen than among the idolatrous people who made human sacrifices – religious murders! – a way of worship."[81]

Man loves the "gods of power and wealth and worldliness," and communism offers such idols in abundance. Fanatics like Lenin, Stalin, and Mao Tse-tung have been so enamored with this false god that they have sacrificed over 100 million human beings in its honor. Entire generations have bled out on the altars of communism in Soviet Russia and Red China. As in the days when Satan persuaded the Israelites to sacrifice their children to Moloch, the Master of Sin still requires blood offerings; and his followers dutifully obey.

It is not an emphasis in this book, but it bears noting that Satanic Ritual Abuse (SRA), often accompanied by human sacrifice, is rampant and increasing. Children and adults alike are sacrificed in occult rituals and Satanic ceremonies. Animals are routinely sacrificed by Witches and Satanists on important pagan Sabbats and during significant atmospheric events. For instance, through one of my sisters I know that a group of pagans were seeking a plot of land in Emmett, Idaho on which to sacrifice animals during the August 2017 solar eclipse. One needs only read books such as Jimmy Lee Shreeve's *Human Sacrifice: A Shocking Exposé of Ritual Killings Worldwide* to know this is a serious and rising problem.

---

[81] Bruce R. McConkie, *A New Witness for the Articles of Faith* (Salt Lake City, Utah: Deseret Book, 1985) 54-55.

In a December 13, 1963 address in Logan, Utah, President Benson emphasized that this anti-Christ threat is not unique to Europe or Asia or Latin America, but that communist conquest *can* and *is* happening here in the United States:

> "For a quarter of a century I have seen, at close range, the insidious forward march of creeping socialism and its ruthless companion godless communism. It is a shocking record of bluff, bluster, deception, intrigue, bondage, and mass murder. Never in recorded history has any movement spread itself so far and so fast as has socialistic-communism in the past few years. The facts are not pleasant to review. Communist leaders are jubilant with their success. They are driving freedom back on almost every front. . . .

> "I say to you with all the fervor of my soul: We are sowing the seeds of our own destruction in America and much of the free world today. It is my sober warning to you today that if the trends of the past thirty years – and especially the past three years – continue, we will lose that which is as priceless as life itself – our freedom – our liberty – our right to act as free men. It can happen here. It is happening here.

> "Our greatest need in America today is to be alerted and informed."

This, mind you, was in 1963. In 1979, as recorded earlier, this same prophet told us that the "struggle is more momentous than a decade ago" and that never before had America been in such danger from so powerful an enemy. And again in 1988, as the president of the Church, President Benson testified that Satan's secret combination was expanding and increasing its evil influence as never before. In other words, over the course of recent history, things have gone from bad, to worse, to grim. Moroni said our situation would be "awful," and it truly is because of this Red Gadianton secret society in our midst. With this in mind, let me pose a few questions.

If a prophet told you that you were on the verge of losing your Freedom, would you sit up and take notice? If a prophet told you that modern Gadiantons were "jubilant with their success" in subjugating your nation and the world your children and grandchildren would grow up in, would you care? Yet, a prophet of God *has* warned us that Freedom is being driven back on every front. A prophet *has* told us that the modern equivalent of Gadiantonism is spreading farther and faster than any ideology in world history. And a prophet *has* warned us that this is not simply a European or Asian phenomenon, but that it *is* "happening here."

Furthermore, in the same 1963 speech, President Benson explained, as he so often did, that we are at war with our arch-enemy. He explained that this is no ordinary war and that we cannot afford to compromise:

> "Today we are at war. It is not enough to be against communism. We must shed our complacency and aggressively meet this challenge. . . .

> "There can be no compromise with the communists. They are at war with us – with the entire cause of freedom, and the sooner every American faces this hard fact, the stronger our position will be. It is a real war. The lines are tightly drawn. The war is more insidious, more devious, more devastating, and more satanical than any war in our history. Moral principles, once universally recognized are ignored. International law once respected is thrown to the wind.

> "The socialist-communist philosophy is devastatingly evil – destructive of all that is good, uplifting and beautiful. It strikes at the very foundation of all we hold dear. The communist "has convinced himself that nothing is evil which answers the call of expediency." This is a most damnable doctrine. People who truly accept such a philosophy have neither conscience nor honor.

Force, trickery, lies, broken promises to them are wholly justified."[82]

Whether we want to be engaged in a war or not, we are. This war was foreseen millennia ago. *It is a Satanic war.* In fact, it is "more satanical than any war in our history." It is a war between the forces of good and evil. Our "devastatingly evil" enemy employs every means – no matter how unethical and brutal – to achieve its ends. Moroni warned us that we would be engaged in a titanic struggle for Freedom, and, that, if we failed in our duty, the vicious secret combination which he saw among us would overthrow the Liberty of all lands, including our own. Truly, no one can remain neutral and be counted guiltless.

Not only can we not remain neutral, but we cannot be complacent. Complacency is complicity. If we do not resist evil, we are nearly as guilty as if we are the perpetrators. What we must do is rouse ourselves and remember that communism "strikes at the very foundation of all we hold dear" – our Freedom, our families, our God-given rights, our peace, our culture, and our religion.

President Howard W. Hunter, perhaps admonishingly, questioned:

> "How can men of conscience ignore the teachings of the Master in their daily affairs, in business, or in government? We stand by and wink at many things because we fear to do anything about them. We may be against crime or communism, but what do we do about it? We may be against corruption in government or against juvenile delinquency, but what are we doing about it? We need to push fear into the background and come forward with a definite, positive declaration, and assume responsibility. . . .

---

[82] Ezra Taft Benson, "We Must Become Alerted and Informed," speech, December 13, 1963, in Ezra Taft Benson, *Title of Liberty: A Warning Voice* (Salt Lake City, Utah: Deseret Book Company, 1964), 43, 45-46.

"Can we stand on the sidelines and merely observe? This is a day for action. This is the time for decision, not tomorrow, not next week. This is the time to make our covenant with the Lord. Now is the time for those who have been noncommittal or who have had a halfhearted interest to come out boldly and declare belief in Christ and be willing to demonstrate faith by works."[83]

To prove our faith, we must act. To show our allegiance to the Lord and the men He has called and inspired to warn us of this communist secret combination in our midst, we must step forward and boldly declare that communism is of Satan and that it is alive and menacing. We must back up our verbal declaration with fearless action. In short, we must answer the call of our beloved hymn which thunders:

"Who's on the Lord's side? Who?

"Now is the time to show.

"We ask it fearlessly:

"Who's on the Lord's side? Who?

"We wage no common war,

"Cope with no common foe.

"The enemy's awake;

"Who's on the Lord's side? Who?"[84]

---

[83] President Howard W. Hunter, "Secretly a Disciple?" Conference Report, October 9, 1960, 107-109.

[84] "Who's on the Lord's Side?" LDS Hymn #260, https://www.lds.org/music/library/hymns/whos-on-the-lords-side?lang=eng&_r=1.

Chapter 5

Prophetic Warnings Continued

Thus far we have seen that the enemy is awake and scheming to destroy our Liberty and all that we hold dear. That enemy has been identified by the Church, and the prophets who preside therein, as communism. The communist conspiracy has been declared to be a rehash of the murderous Gadianton conspiracy of Nephite times, which in turn was a repeat of Cain's oaths and covenants made with Lucifer.

As a secret combination, communism is inherently Satanic and intrinsically evil. It is not a mere political or economic philosophy, but a counterfeit religion. Communism qualifies as a branch of the great and abominable church of the Devil foreseen by Nephi. In fact, it is the most powerful and successful branch. In this chapter, we will review additional warnings of this secret combination given to us by General Authorities and wise leaders in the Church.

The communist conspiracy really came into its own during the early years of this final Gospel dispensation. Beginning with the Prophet Joseph Smith, our early prophets – the same as later men like President Benson – recognized the evil in communism and informed the Saints of this reality.

One of the Church's first encounters with communism-socialism occurred in September 1843. On September 13th, an avowed socialist named Mr. Finch arrived in Nauvoo and gave a lecture about the wonders of socialism. Joseph Smith was in attendance. On September 14th, the Prophet attended a second lecture by Mr. Finch on the same subject. He recorded the following about the experience in the *Documentary History of the Church*:

> "I attended a second lecture on Socialism, by Mr. Finch; and after he got through, I made a few remarks, alluding to Sidney Rigdon and Alexander Campbell getting up a community at Kirtland, and

of the big fish there eating up all the little fish. *I said I did not believe the doctrine."*

After the Prophet said he "did not believe the doctrine" of socialism, Mr. Finch castigated the Prophet as a "temporal" prophet and proclaimed himself to be "the spiritual Prophet." Or, in Mr. Finch's own self-righteous words: "I am the voice of one crying in the wilderness. I am the spiritual Prophet—Mr. Smith the temporal."[85]

Taking his cue from the Prophet Joseph Smith, President John Taylor – who spoke about politics more than almost any prophet in this dispensation – also disbelieved the doctrine of communism and let his mind be known to the Saints. In 1881, he stated:

> "I say God bless all men who love the truth, whether here or anywhere else; God bless all men who maintain human rights and freedom; and God confound the opposers of these principles everywhere. These are my principles and feelings. We want nothing like communism, or nihilism, or any of the outrageous infamies that are beginning to vex and perplex the nations. Yet these things will roll on until it will be a vexation to hear the reports thereof, and unless this nation speedily turns round God's hand will be upon them; unless they speedily adhere to the principles of equal rights and freedom, He will be after them. Now, you can set that down if you like, and see whether it will come to pass or not. I say, then God bless every lover of right, whether among this people or anywhere else, and God bless the rulers of this land who rule in righteousness, and God remove those who do not."[86]

---

[85] President Joseph Smith, *Documentary History of the Church*, Vol. 6, 32-33, September 13-14, 1843, https://byustudies.byu.edu/content/volume-6-chapter-2.

[86] President John Taylor, *Journal of Discourses*, Vol. 22, 296, October 9, 1881, http://jod.mrm.org/22/290.

An outrageous infamy is an accurate way of describing communism. And has communism vexed the world? Yes, it has – more than any ideology before it. President John Taylor was indeed a prophet of the living God.

On another occasion, President John Taylor declared the source of this outrageous communist plague:

"I am sorry to see this murderous influence prevailing throughout the world, and perhaps this may be a fitting occasion to refer to some of these matters. The manifestations of turbulence and uneasiness which prevail among the nations of the earth are truly lamentable. Well, have I anything to do with them? Nothing; but I cannot help but know that they exist. These feelings which tend to do away with all right, rule, and government, and correct principles are not from God, or many of them are not. This feeling of communism and nihilism, aimed at the overthrow of rulers and men in position and authority, arises from a spirit of diabolism, which is contrary to every principle of the Gospel of the Son of God. But then do not the Scripture say that these things shall occur? Yes. Do not the scriptures say that men shall grow worse and worse, deceiving and being deceived? Yes. Do not the scriptures tell us that thrones shall be cast down and empires destroyed and the rule and government of the earth be trodden under foot? Yes. But I cannot help but sympathize with those who suffer from their influences; while these afflictions are the result of wickedness and corruption, yet we cannot shut our eyes to the fact that those who engage in these pernicious practices are exceedingly low, brutal, wicked and degraded. I would say "my soul come not thou into their secret; unto their assembly, mine honor, be not thou united.""[87]

---

[87] President John Taylor, *Journal of Discourses*, Vol. 22, 142, July 3, 1881, http://jod.mrm.org/22/139.

Communism is diabolism. Communism is Luciferianism. Communism is occultism. Communism is Satanic. Communism is forever and everlastingly evil because its originator was the Devil himself, the Adversary of our Lord and Master Jesus Christ. The Red Gadiantons who bear the communist standard are "exceedingly low, brutal, wicked and degraded." They are the children of hell and their diabolical dogma ascended from the dark abyss to vex humanity.

Yet another time, President John Taylor referred to the unjust attempts to deprive the Saints of their property and possessions, and left us this interesting observation about communism. Note that communism is referred to as a secret combination:

> "We have peacefully, legally and honorably possessed our lands in these valleys of the mountains, and we have purchased and paid for them; we do not revel in any ill-gotten gain. They are ours. We have complied with all the requisitions of law pertaining thereto, and we expect to possess and inhabit them. We covet no man's silver or gold, or apparel, or wife, or servants, or flocks, or herds, or horses, or carriages, or lands, or possessions. But we expect to maintain our own rights. If we are crowded upon by unprincipled men or inimical legislation, we shall not take the course pursued by the lawless, the dissolute and the unprincipled; we shall not have recourse to the dynamite of the Russian Nihilists, the secret plans and machinations of the communists, the boycotting and threats of the Fenians, the force and disorder of the Jayhawkers, the regulators or the Molly Maguires, nor any other secret or illegal combination; but we still expect to possess and maintain our rights; but to obtain them in a legal, peaceful and constitutional manner. As American citizens, we shall contend for all our liberties, rights and immunities, guaranteed to us by the Constitution; and no matter what action may be taken by mobocratic influence, by excited and unreasonable men, or by inimical legislation, we shall contend inch by inch for our freedom and rights, as well as the freedom and rights of all American

citizens and of all mankind. As a people or community, we can abide our time, but I will say to you Latter-day Saints, that there is nothing of which you have been despoiled by oppressive acts or mobocratic rule, but that you will again possess, or your children after you."[88]

Communism is a secret combination that resorts to "secret plans and machinations" to get its way. It should also be noted that the Nihilists were allied with the communists. The two are often confused, but they constituted two wings of the same bird. Suffice it to say that Nihilists and communists were normally interchangeable and both used terrorism and organized criminal activity to force their socialistic ideology upon the nations of Europe.

In 1878, President George Q. Cannon made an interesting comment about the poisonous impact communism has upon a nation:

"At the present time, in the western States especially, men are greatly concerned about the element known as Communism, which has taken possession of the minds of a numerous class of the people. The working classes are becoming very dissatisfied, and men are trembling for fear of what will come upon the nation. One of the strongest arguments that was made in favor of keeping up the United States army up to its present numbers was, that there would probably be riots in large cities and in populous centers, which would require the presence of the military acting as police to quell. And had it not been for this evil the army would have been cut down. But a good many men were anxious to have it increased, deeming it necessary for the preservation of life and property. When we reflect upon this it shows how changed have become the affairs of our nation, when it is deemed necessary to appeal to military power to maintain good order in the Republic.

---

[88] President John Taylor, *Journal of Discourses*, Vol. 23, 61, April 9, 1882, http://jod.mrm.org/23/47.

There can be no surer sign of the decay of a republic than when human life and property and liberty cannot be sustained by the masses of the people, and the military power, the ranks of which are filled with hired soldiers, has to be appealed to sustain good order in the midst of the people. Let such a state of things continue and there would soon be an end of true republicanism."[89]

Even indirectly, communism's "evil" floods over the nation, adversely impacting law and order and turning the Republic into a police state. Where communism exists, "true republicanism" cannot remain for long. Communism is inimical to republicanism – that is, to the constitutionalism expounded by our Founding Fathers, taught by the prophets, and found in the scriptures.

Elder Erastus Snow, a true champion of Liberty, uttered these inspired words at the April 1881 General Conference. You will notice that he describes a pattern that every student of history knows has played out time and time again across the globe:

"The government which our heavenly Father has exercised, or attempted to exercise over His children on the earth or in the heavens, has not in the least tended to restrain or abridge them in their liberty, but rather to enlarge it, to extend it, to insure, to preserve and maintain it. The Gospel of Christ, and all of the revelations of God to man have sought to mark the line of distinction between liberty and license, between correct principles of government and anarchy or oppression and slavery. Oppression and slavery are the result of sin and wickedness, violations of the principles of the everlasting Gospel either by the rulers or ruled or both, and generally both. True freedom of mind and body and true liberty, even the enjoyment of human rights is

---

[89] President George Q. Cannon, *Journal of Discourses*, 34-35, July 7, 1878, http://jod.mrm.org/20/32.

founded and maintained, and rests upon human integrity and virtue and the observance of those principles of truth on which all true happiness and true freedom is founded. Sin was never righteousness, nor can be; license was never liberty nor can be; misery was never happiness, nor can be; and yet because of the blindness and ignorance of some people, they never appear to be happy only when they are perfectly miserable. And there are some people too who think they are always in slavery and bondage unless they are trying to get themselves into trouble; and they think there is no true liberty only in acting like the devil. The Nihilists of Russia, the Socialists of France and their sympathizers in America, including the "Liberals" of Utah, are panting for liberty; they are restive under the restraint of order and law; they are opposed to government, and like the French Socialists and Communists, they would destroy Jehovah himself and behead the king and burn up Parliament and assassinate every representative of power and government; and when they had reduced the country and themselves to anarchy, they would look upon their condition as the acme of freedom and human liberty. The world today is drifting in this direction, including our own liberal America."[90]

This incredible statement contains many beautiful truths and correct observations about human nature. I urge you to study these principles and to look for them in action as you research history. Specifically, look behind the rhetoric of historical actors to discover their motives. You will find that the communists and others like them use emotionalism to convince people that they are "victims," that they are being oppressed, that law and order are the equivalent of tyranny and suppression, that moral restraints are evil, that libertinism is real Liberty, and, that, to free themselves, they must resort to law-breaking, violence, indulging their every appetite, and "acting like the devil."

---

[90] Elder Erastus Snow, *Journal of Discourses*, Vol. 22, 149-150, April 4, 1881, http://jod.mrm.org/22/149.

Those who hate just laws and moral restraints find a phantom "Freedom" in the anarchic condition that results from following Satan's henchmen. These communist emissaries "would destroy Jehovah himself" if they had the opportunity, because they are led by the Devil who inspired his ancient followers to crucify their King, the Savior Jesus Christ.

I now jump forward in time to show the continuity of thought among General Authorities as relates communism and conspiracy. In his informative work *The Book of Mormon and the Constitution*, Elder Hans Verlan Andersen recapitulated the attitude of the Church toward those members who support communism in any of its form and added an additional witness that the communist cabal is the modern equivalent of the Gadianton Robbers:

> "The Book of Mormon confirms the fact that the secret combinations among the Nephites had the same philosophy and engaged in the same practices as the communists of today. They denied the existence of God, advocated state ownership of all property, and sought control over free governments by murder, intrigue and aggressive warfare. (2 Ne. 3:1-10; Ether 8:25-26; Hela. 2:8; 6:21-24). . . .
>
> ". . . any Church member who lends aid, encouragement, or sympathy to any of the false philosophies of communism is a traitor to both Church and country . . . A person may tentatively judge the extent to which he accepts Communist philosophy by comparing his political beliefs with the Ten Points of the Communist Manifesto."[91]

The scriptures make plain the fact that Gadiantonism is communism, and our prophets have declared communism to be Gadiantonism. Modern prophets and discerning disciples of Christ have testified of this truth repeatedly. We have been told that communism is the world's "greatest

---

[91] Elder Hans Verlan Andersen, *The Book of Mormon and the Constitution* (Orem, Utah: SunRise Publishing, 1995), 16-17.

satanical threat" and that it mirrors Lucifer's pre-earth plan. Considering the multitude of messages on communism our prophets have delivered in print and over the pulpit, it behooves us to go out of our way to become thoroughly informed so that we are not found ignorantly parroting the planks of *The Communist Manifesto.*

One of the major reasons the Lord revealed *The Book of Mormon* record is that it exposes the enemies of the Church, society, and man's free will. President Benson once explained the two paramount ways *The Book of Mormon* fortifies the Saints. He taught:

> "The Book of Mormon brings men to Christ through two basic means. First, it tells in a plain manner of Christ and His gospel. It testifies of His divinity and of the necessity for a Redeemer and the need of our putting trust in Him. . . .

> "Second, the Book of Mormon exposes the enemies of Christ. It confounds false doctrines and lays down contention. (See 2 Ne. 3:12.) It fortifies the humble followers of Christ against the evil designs, strategies, and doctrines of the devil in our day. The type of apostates in the Book of Mormon are similar to the type we have today. God, with his infinite foreknowledge, so molded the Book of Mormon that we might see the error and know how to combat false educational, political, religious, and philosophical concepts of our time."[92]

I am eternally grateful for *The Book of Mormon*! It is an inspired witness of Christ. It is a bold defender of truth. It is an unflinching watchman warning us of Satan's conspiracy to overthrow the Plan of Salvation and drag us down into political and spiritual bondage. It identifies and condemns the very political, economic, social, ideological, and religious

---

[92] President Ezra Taft Benson, "The Book of Mormon is the Word of God," First Presidency Message, *Ensign*, January, 1988, https://www.lds.org/ensign/1988/01/the-book-of-mormon-is-the-word-of-god?lang=eng.

ideas that are so prevalent in our society, and which are even supported by a good many, if not the majority, of the Saints.

Importantly, *The Book of Mormon* testifies of the power of repentance and shows through a myriad of examples how a people steeped in superstition and false principles – yes, even a people who had once supported the Gadianton Robbers – can turn from their evil ways and return to the Lord. When they do so in full sincerity, the merciful Redeemer has promised to forgive and heal them. May we as members of the Lord's Church – who have unprecedented access to the word of God – recognize that we have, in too many instances, accepted and upheld the secret combination that is seeking to destroy us, and turn to the Lord for renewal and protection.

Like the people of Zeniff who, in giving their support to the wicked King Noah, "did . . . labor exceedingly to support iniquity" (Mosiah 11:2-7), but later repented and became stalwart Saints, we, too, can humble ourselves, believe in Jesus Christ, repent, make or renew covenants, and follow the inspired leadership of our modern prophet. This is the only course of safety. If we do not follow this course, the Lord has warned that calamity will befall us.

In the inspired introduction to *The Doctrine and Covenants*, the Lord stated that He revealed afresh His commandments to the world in this dispensation because He knew "the calamity which should come upon the inhabitants of the earth" (D&C 1:17). The Lord, who knows the end from the beginning, inspired His ancient prophets to record very specific messages tailored for our time. Those messages include frequent and emphatic warnings about secret combinations and Satanic deception. Modern prophets have merely confirmed those ancient passages and have identified the modern entity that matches the former descriptions and which carries forward the work of the Adversary.

Nephi, Mormon, Moroni, and others knew exactly which threats we would face, because the Lord revealed them in visions and by the mouth of angels. Moroni, while grieving the destruction of his people at the hands of Gadianton Robbers, foretold that *The Book of Mormon* would come forth "in a day when the blood of saints shall cry unto the Lord, because of secret combinations and the works of darkness" (Mormon 8:27). By 1830 when the Nephite record was translated, the communist conspiracy was alive and well under a different name, and had already committed acts of murder and fomented revolutions throughout Europe. Moroni's prophecy was quite literally fulfilled. And his other warnings are no less valid. Indeed, Moroni specifically addressed you and me as members of the "holy church of God," and stated:

> "I speak unto you as if ye were present, and yet ye are not. But behold, Jesus Christ hath shown you unto me, and I know your doing.
>
> "And I know that ye do walk in the pride of your hearts; and there are none save a few only who do not lift themselves up in the pride of their hearts . . . and your churches, yea, even every one, have become polluted because of the pride of your hearts. . . .
>
> "O ye pollutions, ye hypocrites, ye teachers, who sell yourselves for that which will canker, why have ye polluted the holy church of God? . . . .
>
> "Yea, why do ye build up your secret abominations to get gain, and cause that widows should mourn before the Lord, and also orphans to mourn before the Lord, and also the blood of their fathers and their husbands to cry unto the Lord from the ground, for vengeance upon your heads?" (Mormon 8:35-36,38,40).

Moroni foresaw that in these last days, many members of the Lord's Church would apostatize and join themselves to the "secret abominations" of the Devil, just as Moroni's countrymen had joined themselves to the Gadianton Society of murderers and robbers. Elder Hans Verlan Andersen commented on this passage just quoted and observed:

"Moroni was . . . explicit in predicting false teachings among the Saints. Reflect upon the unmistakable implications of this point-blank indictment of members of the "holy church of God". . . .

"Since there is only one "holy church of God" on earth, and since it is being polluted, the blame therefore appears to rest upon teachers and hypocrites within that church."[93]

Most Latter-day Saints are laboring under the mistaken belief that there can be no latter-day apostasy among members of the Church. True, the organization of the Church and the Priesthood leadership which guides it will never again be taken from the earth. However, numerous scriptural references foretell of a latter-day apostasy among the Saints. And we have been told explicitly by the prophets that the parable of the Ten Virgins refers to the members of the Church. If taken literally, it means half the membership of the Church has gone astray or will go astray.

Anyone who has attended BYU, as I have, knows that straight communism is being indoctrinated into the minds of young Saints. I had one political science professor who even called for a king, justifying himself – despite my very pointed and public protests – with his false interpretations of verses in *The Doctrine and Covenants*. By the time he was done peddling his falsehoods, a number of students were voicing their agreement, demonstrating how easily misled far too many of the Saints are. This and numerous other experiences proved to my mind that BYU is infested with agents of influence working – knowingly or through their own ignorance – for the Adversary.

Additionally, anyone who has paid attention knows that Satanic Ritual Abuse (SRA) and many other forms of wickedness from energy healing (also called "Christ-centered" or "faith-based" healing, or simply Reiki or therapeutic touch) to Tarot readings to astrology to psychic phenomena have crept into the Church and claim tens of thousands of adherents. Is

---

[93] Hans Verlan Andersen, *The Great and Abominable Church of the Devil*, 182.

there an apostasy occurring all around us? Yes, indeed there is. And we must be on guard to protect our families against its ravages.

In 1854, President Jedediah Grant spoke of the apostate condition of the United States, and what she could expect if she did not repent:

> "[T]he result of rejecting the Gospel has been, in every age, a visitation from the chastening hand of the Almighty—which chastisement will be administered in proportion to the magnitude and enormity of their crimes.
>
> "I look for the Lord to use His whip on the refractory son called "Uncle Sam;" I expect to see him chastised among the first of the nations. I think Uncle Sam is one of the Lord's boys that He will take the rod to first, and make him dance nimbly to his own tune of "Oh! Oh!!" for his transgressions, for his high-mindedness and loftiness, for his evil, for rejecting the Gospel, and causing the earth to drink the blood of the Saints—for this, I say, I expect he will be well switched among the first of the sons."[94]

If the United States was so apostate that long ago, what is she like today? Will the Lord have to take His whip and chastise us? Yes, I'm positive He will do just that (D&C 95:1).

One hundred and eleven years after President Grants remarks, in the April 1965 General Conference President Ezra Taft Benson referred to the faltering condition of members of the Church. He cited one of the ways the Lord might correct our wayward behavior:

> "Should the Lord decide at this time to cleanse the Church—and the need for that cleansing seems to be increasing—a famine in this land of one year's duration could wipe out a large percentage

---

[94] President Jedediah M. Grant, *Journal of Discourses*, Vol. 2, 148, April 2, 1854, http://jod.mrm.org/2/145.

of slothful members, including some ward and stake officers. Yet we cannot say we have not been warned."[95]

If President Benson saw the need for a cleansing in 1965, what would he say if he could view our members today? Has our situation improved since 1965? I do not believe it has. Today, more members than ever before are embracing unsound political ideas, adopting occult beliefs and practices, and engaging in every form of socially acceptable wickedness from pornography to gambling to Sabbath day revelry to yoga[96] to energy healing.

---

[95] President Ezra Taft Benson, "Not Commanded in All Things," Conference Report, April, 1965, 121-125, http://scriptures.byu.edu/#:t585:p401.

[96] Unbeknownst to most Yoga practitioners, Yoga is part and parcel of Hinduism. In fact, Yoga is a religious tradition in its own rite. It is a form of prayer, worship, and meditation. One of the objects of Yoga is to tap into and awaken the Kundalini – or Serpent Fire – that allegedly resides in all of us. While many people believe they are "just stretching" when they perform Yoga, the Hindu Yogis and Gurus believe otherwise. I draw a quote from page 174 of Caryl Matrisciana's 1985 book *Gods of the New Age*:

"Most people are surprised to learn that Yoga is a form of Hindu prayer because it is so cleverly packaged as *only* exercise. . . .

"Rabi Maharaj, former guru and author of *Escape in to the Light*, has said, "Many of the people practicing Yoga that I have met say to me that they only practice it because of the physical benefits. Any Hindu will tell you that there is *no* Yoga that is purely physical."

"Prema Nayak, a former Yoga teacher, said:

""One of the first things I learned in my teacher's training class was that I must talk to the students about the philosophy behind Yoga, that this was just as important as the exercises. Relaxation at the end of the Yoga class is really hypnosis, where each part of the body is relaxed. So while they were in this state, I read to them about the Hindu philosophy, or something from one of my guru's books, so they got it whether they wanted it or not!""

Dave Hunt's book *Yoga and the Body of Christ: What Position Should Christians Take* is also highly recommended. On page 18 of that text, Hunt wrote:

Tens of thousands of members have left the Church to join apostate groups and ideologies such as the "Remnant" movement and a rapidly growing sect led by an excommunicated apostate who claims to have new Nephite scripture and a second book of commandments. Yes, the need for a cleansing *is* indeed increasing!

What, it must be asked, is the impetus behind all the wickedness we see about us and even within our own Church membership? Yes, pride, lack of diligence and devotion, ignorance, and other factors play their part. However, the real cause is, as it was in Nephite times (Helaman 6:18), the Devil's secret combination which infests our society like a malignant tumor. Communism has infiltrated the general ranks of the Church and the average member stands deceived in numerous respects. That Latter-day Saints by and large have aligned themselves with this secret combination is never more evident than on election day when the Saints voluntarily cast their votes for members of that conspiracy who deceive them with fake smiles and flattering words. It is this communist ideology, and the wolves in sheep's clothing who propagate it, which prods us to pride and which promotes the "whatsoever a man [does] is no crime" attitude (Alma 30:17).

"If we are honest, the instructors of Hatha Yoga themselves, even in the West, admit that it is *not* purely physical. Richard Hittleman, one of the early pioneers of this so-called "physical" yoga in America, stated that "as yoga students practiced the physical positions, they would eventually be ready to investigate the spiritual component which is 'the entire essence of the subject.'" Such is the consensus of the experts."

Finally, in the preface to their book *The Seven Spiritual Laws of Yoga: A Practical Guide to Healing Body, Mind, and Spirit*, Deepak Chopra and David Simon wrote:

"The word *yoga* is related to the English word *yoke*. Yoga is the union of body, mind, and spirit – the union of your individuality with the divine intelligence that orchestrates the universe. Yoga is a state of being in which the elements and forces that comprise your biological organism are in harmonious interaction with the elements of the cosmos."

I urge my fellow Latter-day Saints to be very careful which "divine intelligence" they yoke themselves to. Avoid Yoga. Nothing good can come from playing with fire – *especially Serpent Fire.*

Elder Hans Verlan Andersen explained communism's appeal to the carnal nature of man:

> "Communism has a greater appeal to the evil in men than any other political philosophy. While enforced priestcraft provides government jobs only for teachers, priests, educators and those who administer the system, under Communism where the state owns all the property and all means for the production and distribution of goods and services, state jobs are created for every activity whatsoever. Also the opportunity to exercise unrighteous dominion is increased to its maximum. And finally those who control government also control all of the things of this world, which lie within their jurisdiction. It is for these reasons that Communism has such an irresistible appeal to the proud, the power-hungry and those who seek to live on the labors of others. It is the perfect system for wickedness of all kinds."[97]

Indolence, pride, selfishness, backbiting, anger, and power-seeking are but a few of the many evil character traits which communism fosters. Unique to communism is the fact that it *institutionalizes* sin and *compels* its subjects to rebel against their Maker and abuse their fellow man. Communism is as much an inherent and eternal enemy to God as the "natural man" spoken of by Nephite prophets. King Benjamin taught: "For the natural man is an enemy to God, and has been from the fall of Adam, and will be, forever and ever" (Mosiah 3:19). Alma likewise taught that carnal people "are without God in the world, and they have gone contrary to the nature of God" (Alma 41:11). What could be a better description of a communist than one who lives "without God in the world"?

President James E. Faust taught that Satan is victimizing the people of this generation because they have indulged the natural man:

---

[97] Andersen, *The Book of Mormon and the Constitution*, 77-78.

> "Satan has had great success with this gullible generation. As a consequence, literally hosts of people have been victimized by him and his angels."[98]

Not only do otherworldly angels on Satan's errand torment those who live contrary to the commandments, but mortal servants of Satan – communists and their associates – victimize their fellow human beings in horrific ways.

Elder Rulon S. Wells spoke of the institutionalized nature of communist wickedness. He first referred to the enforced state religion of the Tsars and of the Russian people's revolt against their rule. However, he then explained:

> "[N]o sooner have they liberated themselves from this condition of thralldom till the Soviet seeks to plunge them into the still more deadly slavery of atheism. These Soviet masters are still greater oppressors and tyrants than any who have preceded them, for they have even undertaken to prevent them from serving God in any form whatever, and when men cease to serve God, at that moment they begin to serve the devil, which means slavery. Such rulers have no conception of human rights."

Because communism imposes atheism on the peoples it subjugates, by default it leads them into servitude to Satan. Said more bluntly, communism ushers people into Satan-worship by robbing them of the ability to worship God freely. In a country like the United States where people *voluntarily* embrace this depraved system of diabolism, I cannot help but believe Almighty God is even more displeased. And for Latter-day Saints to adopt a Luciferian ideology antithetical to the Restored Gospel is tantamount to apostasy and blasphemy.

Elder Wells made several additional worthwhile statements that directly apply to our topic. Said he:

---

[98] Faust, *Finding Light in a Dark World*, 76.

"The Gospel is a plan of liberating mankind from bondage . . . the truth from heaven has a mission to perform, namely, to liberate us and make us free. . . .

"What is freedom? What is liberty? Does it mean license to do evil? No, indeed it does not. To be free means to liberate ourselves from the bondage of sin. We, in this country, boast of our human liberty and we have great reason to be proud of the liberty that we enjoy under our Constitution; but after all is said and done it is only a measure of civil liberty, but the greatest measure to be found among all the governments of the world. We sometimes boast of being in the land of the free, the home of the brave. Nevertheless, we are not free until we have overcome evil – until we liberate ourselves from the bondage of sin.

"The Gospel of the Lord Jesus Christ is destined to make us free. . . .

"What a blessed boon is liberty. The free agency of man! The right to live upon the earth with a knowledge of good and evil. Blessed are we if we choose the good and reject the evil, provided, of course, we do so of our own volition, in the exercise of our free agency. Many there were even in the very beginning who opposed this plan. We are told in holy writ that one-third of the hosts of heaven followed Lucifer in his rebellion against God and were cast out of heaven. That war begun in heaven, is continued here on earth. To follow the enemies of God means to follow them into slavery, but to serve God means freedom, and we are under necessity of choosing whom we will serve – God or the adversary of our souls, the archenemy of God. Many there have been in all ages who have endeavored to enslave mankind – to dominate the minds and conscience of men. All such are enemies to God. They have instituted despotic governments and have ruled with an iron hand. They have established state religions and punished non-conformists as heretics and even burned them at the stake. All enemies of God are they who seek to destroy the free agency of man or to deprive them of their inherent – their inalienable rights of life and liberty, the right to worship God according to the dictates of their own consciences. The establishment of a state religion is an abomination in the sight of God."[99]

Communism has done precisely what Elder Wells said is an abomination; namely, it has set itself up as a state religion. Communism is only atheism in the sense that it prohibits people from worshipping other gods or attending other churches – particularly those inclined to worship Christ. Yet, communism is inherently religious. It is a jealous and fearful master that requires its subjects to worship her and her alone. It is idolatry by another name, and we know that "the devil of all devils deligtheth" in idolatry (2 Nephi 9:37). By worshipping this incarnate and state-mandated Satanism, people subject themselves – or are subjected – to the will of the Devil.

Christ's Gospel, on the other hand, is the epitome of Freedom. Freedom is the one word that sums up the entire Gospel plan. It is Freedom from sin, from death, and from the Devil. Because of the Lord's Atonement, "hell must deliver up its captive spirits, and the grave must deliver up its captive bodies" (2 Nephi 9:12). Because of our Redeemer's sacrifice, we are not "shut out from the presence of our God . . . to remain with the father of lies, in misery, like unto himself" (2 Nephi 9:9). Because of Jesus, that humble Man of Nazareth, the way is prepared "for our escape from the grasp of this awful monster; yea, that monster, death and hell" (2 Nephi 9:10).

Unfortunately, Satan and his agents are actively and successfully promoting communistic ideologies, under various names, throughout the earth. Through deception, the Adversary has convinced men to carry on the same conspiracy he established with Cain. The scriptures tell us that

---

[99] Elder Rulon S. Wells, Conference Report, October, 1930, in Ralph C. Hancock, ed., *Just and Holy Principles: Latter-day Saint Readings on America and the Constitution* (Boston, MA: Simon and Schuster Custom Publishing, 1998), 75-77.

Satan "transformeth himself nigh unto an angel of light, and stirreth up the children of men unto secret combinations of murder and all manner of secret works of darkness" (2 Nephi 9:9). Just as Freedom is the epitome of the Gospel of Christ, communism, with its inherent idolatry and slavery of mind, body, and soul, is the epitome of Satan's counterfeit gospel.

Can these two philosophies coexist? Is there a peaceful solution to be found? Can we live side by side with communists? President Marion G. Romney declared that there can be absolutely *no* compromise between the people of God and the anti-Christ philosophy of communism. Said he:

> "Liberty loving people can no more expect to secure cooperation from communism in the establishment of peace than Christ could secure such cooperation from Satan. Communism being what it is, will never voluntarily yield in its evil purposes. Every time it negotiates, it advances its own cause or it does not deal."[100]

Communism, being a godless conspiracy that seeks to undermine our agency, is incompatible with Christ's Gospel of Liberty. Thus, true Christians cannot dabble in communism with impunity. They cannot embrace its tenets without being spiritually seared in the process. "Can one go upon hot coals, and his feet not be burned?" (Proverbs 6:28). To imbibe communism is to ingest the deadliest spiritual poison in existence; a poison manufactured in hell and sold by the mortal and otherworldly anti-Christs who stalk the earth. Also, make a mental note that communism "will never voluntarily yield in its evil purposes," for this notion is the fundamental basis of my comments in chapter eight.

Joseph Fielding McConkie similarly remarked on the incompatibility of Devilish philosophies with servants of Christ. He observed:

> "We cannot march with both the Israelites and the Philistines. Light and darkness will never meet. Christ and Satan will never shake hands. As to Christ and His gospel, there can be no middle

---

[100] President Marion G. Romney, BYU devotional, March 1, 1955.

ground, no neutrality. You stand with the prophets or against them."[101]

Truly, there is *no* middle ground on the question of communism. We either stand with the prophets who have declared communism to be the "greatest satanical threat" to mankind, or we reject their witness and throw our support to Lucifer by default. While some of us squabble as to whether it is the Jesuits, the Zionists, the Bilderbergers, or some other group that has wrecked the globe, our prophets have had no such quandary; they have consistently singled out communism as *the* greatest threat to the world.

In a December 10, 1963 BYU address, President Ezra Taft Benson explained the matter in blunt terms:

> "We must not become confused over side issues. Our enemy is not the Catholic, not the Protestant, not the Negro, not the white man, not the Jew, not the Gentile, not employers, not employees, not the wealthy, not the poor, not the worker, and not the employer. Our mortal enemies are the Satanic Communists and those who prepare the path for them."[102]

Can it be stated any plainer? The "Satanic Communists" are the #1 threat to mankind. Without question, communism is the secret combination which threatens us. The Red Gadiantons are at the pinnacle of the conspiracy pyramid.

It is high time we humbled ourselves and gained this same witness through the Holy Spirit. Having acquired this testimony for myself through

---

[101] Joseph Fielding McConkie, "The First Vision and Religious Tolerance," in *A Witness for the Restoration: Essays in Honor of Robert J. Matthews*, ed. Kent P. Jackson and Andrew C. Skinner (Provo, UT: Religious Studies Center, Brigham Young University, 2007), 177–99.

[102] President Ezra Taft Benson, "A Race Against Time," BYU address, December 10, 1963, https://www.latterdayconservative.com/ezra-taft-benson/a-race-against-time/.

the ministering of the Holy Ghost, I add my fervent witness to those of the prophets that communism is *not* dead, that its tentacles have our society by the throat, that the doctrine of communism is of Lucifer, and that no greater threat exists. The communists are public enemy number one. It is high time we treated them as traitors to our free institutions and as enemies of the Republic.

In his phenomenal book on the socialist/communist conspiracy titled *The Red Carpet*, President Benson explained that communism, as a de facto religion, fills a spiritual void created by the false religious creeds of the apostate world. He said that communists zealously evangelize their beliefs and draw people in with their bold claims and their total devotion to their cause. He also chastised our nation for not standing up for its infinitely better system of principles. Instead of defending our own system, he lamented, we have gone along with the communist plan in the name of "tolerance":

> "The communists bring to the nations they infiltrate a message and a philosophy that affects human life in its entirety. Communism seeks to provide what in too many instances a lukewarm Christianity has not provided – a total interpretation of life. Communists are willing to be revolutionary; to take a stand for this and against that. They challenge what they do not believe in – customs – practices – ideas – traditions. They believe heatedly in their philosophy.

> "But our civilization and our people here in America are seemingly afraid to be revolutionary. We are too "broadminded" to challenge what we do not believe in. We are afraid of being thought intolerant – uncouth – ungentlemanly. We have become lukewarm in our beliefs. And for that we perhaps merit the bitter condemnation state in the Book of Revelation 3:16: "So then because thou art lukewarm, and neither cold nor hot, I will spue thee out of my mouth."

"That is a sad commentary on a civilization which has given to mankind the greatest achievements and progress ever known. But it is even a sadder commentary on those of us who call ourselves Christians, who thus betray the ideals given to us by the Son of God Himself. I ask, are we going to permit atheistic communist masters, fellow travelers and dupes to deceive us any longer?

"There is a deception going on in our country this very moment which is just as dangerous to the United States as the false pretentions of Fidel Castro were to Cuba. It is amazing to me that some of our citizens seem to take special delight in ridiculing the warnings of government investigators and the cry and alarm which comes from Iron Curtain refugees when they see how the United States is being led carefully down the trail of disaster." [103]

Have we been deceived and lured as a fly into the communist web? Have we been "led carefully down the trail of disaster" with false promises, utopian ideas, and a counterfeit worldview? Have the communists exploited our so-called "tolerance" and "open-mindedness" to further their agenda of enslaving us? Have we, without realizing it, replaced our true religious principles with communist doctrines wearing the veneer of "equality," "peace," "cooperation," "sharing," and "brotherhood"?

The United States was founded by the hand of God. He reserved this land for a righteous People. That People was led here and was prompted to declare Independence from British tyranny. Under divine inspiration, Thomas Jefferson penned The Declaration of Independence and the Founding Fathers drafted the U.S. Constitution. Our forefathers were good, independent people of high moral character, and devout Christians. They loved the Lord and they loved their Liberty. With a just framework of law and order to work within, our forefathers forged this great nation.

---

[103] Benson, *The Red Carpet*, 53-54.

Any objective student of history acknowledges that the United States rose faster and farther than any nation ever has. We are the most powerful, influential, technologically-advanced, and wealthiest country in history. It was precisely because of our Christian political and religious philosophies that we became great. Yet, over time we have abandoned our tried and true principles for a worldview that has destroyed Freedom, caused wars, precipitated oppression, and driven people to ruin wherever it has been implemented.

President J. Reuben Clark, Jr. recognized that, like the Nephites, our years of prosperity and peace have made us weak and blinded us to the incremental burrowing of Satan's termites. In 1935, during the rule of FDR's severely communist-infiltrated administration, he stated:

> "We are deaf today to the approach of tyranny because we have lived so long under the protection of the Constitution that we take for granted the blessings of liberty. But the Framers of the Constitution, having had bitter experience with tyranny, wrote it with the purpose to preserve the right of local self government – which had been the fundamental principle on which the war of the Revolution was fought. They were not dreamers, but practical men of wide experience, and they wrote into that document the fruition of human experience in self-government. Prospering under the privileges insured by the Constitution this country has advanced as no other in a like period in all history. We need more people today with strong convictions in support of the Constitution and with courage to stand back of their convictions. We need men with courage to refuse support to every effort aimed at undermining the Constitution. Any change in our social order which is really desirable can be effected under the Constitution or by orderly Constitutional amendment rather than

by efforts to evade its provisions. We must continue to protect ourselves against the approach of tyranny in any guise."[104]

Because of the blessings poured out upon them through adherence to the principles set forth in the Constitution, and through righteous living, the American People became safe, powerful, prosperous, and great. Yet, because of the power, prosperity, and ease we have enjoyed for so long, we have forgotten what Liberty requires to preserve. We have seemingly forgotten that tyrants exist in this world and that they are willing to fill mass graves with the bodies of their ignorant supporters here in the United States just as readily as they did in Soviet Russia and Red China.

We have increasingly allowed the "experts" to manage our national, and even local, affairs. We have renounced our sovereignty bestowed upon us by Heaven. We have abdicated our responsibility to self-govern and to be actively engaged in the political process, trusting it instead to charlatans calling themselves "Republicans" and "Democrats." We have taken for granted the Constitution and do not understand what it says, or why what it says is important or relevant to us.

Communists have filled the void left by our abdication of the duties of self-government. The communists work harder and longer than other groups to promote their worldview and to bring about changes to our political system. They flatter others and promise them their hearts' desire for the sake of power. They work and sweat, cheat and steal, lie and mislead, maim and destroy, whenever necessary.

The U.S. House Committee on UnAmerican Activities gave this description of why the communists are so successful:

"They work. Others won't. They come early and stay late. Others don't. They know how to run a meeting. Others don't. They demand the floor. Others won't. They do not hesitate to use physical violence or ANY form

---

[104] J. Reuben Clark., Jr., July 12, 1935, in J. Reuben Clark., Jr., *Stand Fast by Our Constitution* (Salt Lake City, Utah: Deseret Book Company, 1973), 4.

of persecution. They stay organized and prepared in advance of each meeting. The thing to remember is that Communists are trained agents under rigid discipline, but they can always be defeated by facts."[105]

These subversive agents have worked hard and have been all too successful. The seeds they planted decades ago have matured into gigantic redwood sequoias which now cast long shadows over the breadth of our nation. Generation after generation has adopted more and more of the communist plan and philosophy. It has become, in numerous important respects, the dominant ideology in the United States.

In a 2010 survey, only 28 of 988 people polled had read the U.S. Constitution in its entirety. Only 55% of those polled believed the Constitution actually worked to limit power.[106] I do not believe there is a greater interest in, and knowledge of, the Constitution today than eight years ago. Indeed, several recent polls are disturbing and show the rising popularity of communism.

In a November 2017 poll, 23% of those polled considered Joseph Stalin – the communist dictator and mass murderer – a "hero." And though 71% of those polled could not give an accurate definition of the philosophy, 26% nevertheless had a favorable view of socialism.[107] If those numbers were not disturbing enough, 44% of those who responded to a 2017 poll said they would prefer to live in a socialist country rather than a capitalist

---

[105] U.S. House of Representatives Committee on UnAmerican Activities, *100 Things You Should Know About Communism* (1949), 18-19.

[106] Sharon C. Fitzgerald, "Survey: U.S. admires, but hasn't read, Constitution," *The Daily Progress*, September 17, 2010, accessed February 24, 2018, http://www.dailyprogress.com/news/survey-u-s-admires-but-hasn-t-read-constitution/article_a4d58bd4-3e2d-50e3-859b-fcede87ec145.html.

[107] Rob Shimshock, "Education Fail: Almost One-Quarter of Millennials Consider Notorious Communist Butchers 'Heroes'," *Freedom Media Group LLC*, November 2, 2017, accessed February 24, 2018, https://thepolitistick.com/education-fail-almost-one-quarter-millennials-consider-notorious-communist-butchers-heroes/.

one.[108] From my personal experience dealing with thousands of people as an administrator on various social media platforms, and my five years observing the rising generation in college classrooms, I believe the numbers cited above are actually low. The number of people who have embraced socialism – albeit under different labels – is much higher than 23, 26, or even 44 percent. Truly, our culture has a serious infection that must be treated at once.

Elder Joseph F. Merrill of the Quorum of the Twelve Apostles made a remark in an April 1949 General Conference address about the "Satan inspired" power that was increasing across the globe. Read his words carefully. He observed:

> "[T]he agencies operating under this wicked influence are steadily growing more numerous and more powerful, making the future of America more dark and precarious. Unless this rapidly developing tendency changes for the better, the time is probably not far away when the America of the fathers, the America where free enterprise with all its associated blessings of personal freedom and liberty for its citizens, will have been relegated to the pages of history. And is it not strange, very strange, from the standpoint of reason and logic, that the means and the conditions by which and under which America has grown to be the greatest, the most powerful, and the most prosperous nation on earth have become odious to vast numbers of our people, who therefore are scheming, planning, working, hoping, even praying, for changes that would put an end to America as "the land of the free and the home of the brave"? Among all the unrighteous organized agencies now working in the world to further the cause of Satan, perhaps the largest and most wicked are those given to the cause of communism. Communism is organized wickedness and crime of

---

[108] Ben Steverman, "Get Rid of Capitalism? Millennials Are Ready to Talk About It," *Bloomberg L.P.*, accessed February 24, 2018, https://www.bloomberg.com/news/articles/2017-11-06/get-rid-of-capitalism-millennials-are-ready-to-talk-about-it.

the blackest type. Harsh terms, certainly! Its objectives are confiscation of property, robbery of those who have, slavery of its productive workers, and death to its opponents. Its beneficiaries are ne'er-do-wells, those who own nothing, but want everything, especially power and its emoluments.

"What is the explanation of all this? I think that it lies in the fact that Satan has more influence and power in the world today than ever before. And Satan's purpose is to overcome righteousness, to entice God's children into ways of sin, misery, and suffering, to handicap those who would do good, and to darken the minds of those who would like to know what is best in the great confusion of conflicting ideas. And so struggles and conflicts multiply with the result that men's hearts are failing them. Selfishness is growing. Demands are increasing for more and more for less and less—more pay, less work—for more privileges, but fewer responsibilities. Merit as a condition for reward is disappearing and Satan is riding high."[109]

Yes, in these last days "Satan is riding high" and relishing his unprecedented power. He is riding the wave generated by his communists and their sympathizers – and those who sit idly by and do nothing to stop it. This wave, like a surging tsunami, destroys everything in its path – marriages, families, culture, good institutions, economic stability, rule of law, public order, common decency, common sense, and faith in Christ.

Communism is, without a doubt, "organized wickedness." In every aspect, it is criminal and monstrous. If we are to judge an ideology based upon its fruits, as our Lord taught us to do (Matthew 7:20), then the unprecedented spectrum of murder, rapine, theft, blasphemy, persecution, priestcraft, degradation, and misery perpetrated by

---

[109] Elder Joseph F. Merrill, "Some Fundamentals of Gospel Teachings," Conference Report, April, 1949, 24-29, http://scriptures.byu.edu/#:t17d:p523.

communists worldwide places it in a category all its own. It is surely the "greatest satanical threat" to humanity.

As the polls cited above demonstrate, that day when our forefathers' achievements and principles would be "relegated to the pages of history" is upon us. These prophetic words of an apostle of God have come true. We are now entering upon the great day of Satan's power, a day in which men's hearts fail them for fear (Luke 21:26) and when the whole of mankind is beginning to bow the knee and worship before Satan's unholy altar (Revelation 13:4, 8; Revelation 17:2).

President Benson once remarked:

> "Communism is not a political party, nor a military organization, nor an ideological crusade, nor a rebirth of Russian imperialist ambition, though it comprises and uses all of these. Communism, in its unmistakable reality, is wholly a conspiracy, a gigantic conspiracy to enslave mankind; an increasingly successful conspiracy, controlled by determined, cunning and utterly ruthless gangsters, willing to use any means to achieve its end."[110]

This "gigantic conspiracy" has gnawed on our society for so long that we have largely succumbed. We are now led with a flaxen cord by Satan. As sad as it is, the prophets of old knew it would happen and painted a graphic picture of our day. Nephi, for instance, wrote of our day:

> "And there are also secret combinations, even as in times of old, according to the combinations of the devil, for he is the founder of all these things; yea, the founder of murder, and works of darkness; yea, and he leadeth them by the neck with a flaxen cord, until he bindeth them with his strong cords forever" (2 Nephi 26:22).

---

[110] Ezra Taft Benson, "We Must Become Alerted and Informed," speech, December 13, 1963, in Newquist, ed., *Prophets, Principles and National Survival*, 273.

Prophets in the old world saw our plight as well and students of the Bible have had a front row seat to the end of the world for two millennia. In the Book of Revelation, John tells us of a Beast he saw "rise up out of the sea" (Revelation 13:1). We are told that "all the world wondered after the beast" and that "they worshipped the dragon which gave power unto the beast" (Revelation 13:3-4). John then prophesied something quite disturbing and ominous:

> "And all that dwell upon the earth shall worship him, whose names are not written in the book of life of the Lamb slain from the foundation of the world" (Revelation 13:8).

Save those true followers of Christ, the entire world – the whole of humanity – will worship Satan, who is the Dragon, and will give obeisance to this Beast empowered and directed by him. The world will be deceived by "miracles" and "wonders" and will be compelled to "make an image to the beast" (Revelation 13:13-14). Those who refuse to "worship the image of the beast [will] be killed" (Revelation13:15). And, finally, the peoples of the earth will be required "to receive a mark in their right hand, or in their foreheads," without which it is impossible to "buy or sell" in the beast's political system (Revelation 13:16-17).

We are living in the day when this prophesy is to be acted out on the world's stage. The curtain has closed on many of the acts already, and the others are imminent. Ours is a day of wickedness. It is a time when the dominant religion is one form or another of thinly-veiled Satan-worship. It is a time when the "mark of the beast" is to be issued.

This "mark of the beast" has been a point of contention for centuries. Just what is the mark of the Beast? Is it a literal mark, like a tattoo, or perhaps an implantable RFID chip as many suppose?[111] Unfortunately, the prophets have not given an official interpretation. However, one Church study manual gives us several enlightening insights into John's Beast and the mark which the world's inhabitants will take upon themselves.

The manual notes a Joseph Smith translation to verse 1 of Revelation chapter 13. It emphasizes that the Beast is "in the likeness of the kingdoms of the earth." That is to say, in the words of the Prophet Joseph Smith, the beast represents "those kingdoms which had degenerated and become corrupt, savage and beast-like in their dispositions, even the degenerate kingdoms of the wicked world." Additionally, several characteristics of these kingdoms are noted, such as their anti-Christ natures and their predatory behavior. The writers note: "It could be said that any kingdom or government that exhibits these characteristics manifests the spirit of the beast."

As for the mark that the people will have to "receive . . . in their right hand, or in their foreheads," the writers suggest the following:

> "This may symbolize that the wicked show by their actions (hands) and beliefs (heads) that they do the will of the beast and accept his ideology."[112]

While we do not know the precise meaning and identification of this terrible Beast and his infamous mark, it is clear that the earth's

---

[111] As a note of interest, certain corrupt individuals have indeed advocated chipping the population to better manage them, reduce crime, etc. After the recent school shooting in Parkland, Florida, a bill was introduced by Republicans in Congress calling for mentally disabled people to be chipped. On a more practical level, RFID technology has proliferated society. The entire population of Red China now has state-issued documents that utilize RFID technology, so it is a very real and present danger. Inasmuch nothing definitive has been revealed by our prophets, this is an option to consider. Yet, I defer to the wisdom of those who wrote the Church manual cited on this page, and to their interpretation of John's words as symbolic of behavior and ideology rather than a literal mark.

[112] *New Testament Student Manual*, "Revelation 12-16," The Church of Jesus Christ of Latter-day Saints, 2014, https://www.lds.org/manual/new-testament-student-manual/revelation/chapter-55-revelation-12-16?lang=eng.

inhabitants are following – whether knowingly or not – Satan and his false prophets who preach his doctrines. Mankind is in Satan's camp and does his bidding. And no nation has been more savage and beastlike than Russia and China, the homelands of communism.

Also, recall that anciently Nephi was shown the exact same vision which John saw. Though he was not allowed to reveal most of what he witnessed, Nephi explained that those who do not belong to the Lord's Church belong to the "great and abominable church of the devil" (1 Nephi 14:10). And we have previously acknowledged that this great and abominable church is the same organization as the secret combination foreseen by Moroni, which our prophets have identified as communism.

Following a similar line of thought, LDS author Farley Anderson gave us his opinions about the Beast in his *The Book of Revelation Today*. He wrote:

"Let us compare the beast with communism. . . .

"The beast is like unto a leopard (Revelation 13:2). Leopards are creatures of the night, of shadows and darkness. The most often seen evidence of their existence are the carcasses left behind. This analogy fits with communism. Nations and kingdoms are enslaved while one hundred million people have been murdered this past century by the communists. This beast has the feet of a bear (Revelation 13:2) and thus leaves bear tracks. Politically speaking, the bear tracks of today lead back to the Russian bear, the first communist country of our era. The beast has the mouth of a lion. This may be a little more difficult to understand, but consider Karl Marx, the false prophet and mouth for communism. Marx is a false prophet because his manifesto promises utopia, yet delivers Hell on Earth. Karl Marx was born in Germany, but did most of his writing from England, which uses the banner of the lion. He was born of Jewish ancestry, which also uses the banner of the lion. . . .

"In Revelation 13:3 we see an unmistakable feature of the beast that should be recognized by all today. The beast is wounded in the head unto death, but is not really killed. This important warning (that communism's death is not a reality) is repeated five times in the Book of Revelation (Revelation 13:3, 13:12, 13:14, 17:8, 17:11). We next see the beast is a military superpower (Revelation 13:4). From Revelation 13:8 we learn that almost all the earth shall worship the beast. The word *worship* is strong, but consider how doctrines of communism are taught and learned, and how, directly and indirectly, the world financially supports communism . . . Last, but not least, we see in Revelation 17:3 that the beast is scarlet colored. Identifying the beast as satanic communism may be as simple as asking who the reds are. Lucifer used red as his banner in the pre-mortal world. The Marxist followers of our day are likewise known as Red communists or socialists."[113]

Whether or not Brother Anderson's interpretations are completely accurate is not for me to say. However, I strongly agree with the overall premise based on the fact that communism has been simultaneously identified by our prophets as the "greatest satanical threat" to the world, the great and abominable church of the Devil from Nephi's vision (the very same witnessed by John), and the latter-day secret combination foreseen by Moroni.

Additionally, Nephi and John both describe this latter-day organization as the "mother of harlots" (Revelation 17:5; 1 Nephi 14:16-17). Both of these ancient prophets describe this Devilish system as having control over the whole earth, and in fact use the same phrase that she "sat on many waters" (Revelation 13:4, 8; Revelation 17:1-2, 18; 1 Nephi 14:11). In the light of these facts, it seems highly improbable, if not outright impossible,

---

[113] Farley Anderson, *The Book of Revelation Today: The Last of the Last Days: Who, What, Where, When, Why and How* (Paradise, Utah: Replenishing Press, 2011) 21-22.

that communism – the wickedest entity in the world which serves as the Devil's church and which controls the politics of the world – would not be the same scarlet Beast witnessed by John.

President Joseph Fielding Smith explained that Satan is *personally* governing the nations of the world. His dominion encircles the globe like an iron net. The Dragon is actively engaged in promoting the Beast and giving him power. President Smith observed:

> "*Satan has control now.* No matter where you look, he is in control, even in our own land. *He is guiding the governments as far as the Lord will permit him.* That is why there is so much strife, turmoil, confusion all over the earth. One master mind is governing the nations. It is not the President of the United States; it is not Hitler; it is not Mussolini; it is not the king or government of England or any other land; it is Satan himself."[114]

From this quote, and the mountain of other evidence presented so far, we can unequivocally state that it is *Satan* who controls the men who appear to pull the strings in our society. The string pullers are mere puppets themselves, pawns in Satan's crusade against the Eternal Father whose crown, power, and glory he both hates and covets. Always remember that organized evil *does* really exist and that conspiracy is not some wild notion, but a scripturally-substantiated reality. It is the reality we live each day and from which we cannot escape. Latter-day Saints are bound by their religion to acknowledge this conspiracy and do their utmost to thwart its intrigues.

President Ezra Taft Benson famously told the Saints in his fantastic 1972 April Conference talk that conspiracy is a *fact*. He affirmed:

> "There is no conspiracy theory in the Book of Mormon — it is a conspiracy fact."

---

[114] Bruce R. McConkie, ed., *Doctrines of Salvation*, Vol. 3 (Salt Lake City, Utah: Bookcraft, 1956), 315.

Perhaps it would be more powerful to cite this statement in its proper context. President Benson adroitly taught:

> "[T]he greatest handbook for freedom in this fight against evil is the Book of Mormon. . . .
>
> "Joseph Smith said that the Book of Mormon was the "keystone of our religion" and the "most correct" book on earth. (*DHC,* vol. 6, p. 56.) This most correct book on earth states that the downfall of two great American civilizations came as a result of secret conspiracies whose desire was to overthrow the freedom of the people. "And they have caused the destruction of this people of whom I am now speaking," says Moroni, "and also the destruction of the people of Nephi." (Ether 8:21.)
>
> "Now undoubtedly Moroni could have pointed out many factors that led to the destruction of the people, but notice how he singled out the secret combinations, just as the Church today could point out many threats to peace, prosperity, and the spread of God's work, but it has singled out the greatest threat as the godless conspiracy. There is no conspiracy theory in the Book of Mormon —it is a conspiracy fact. . . .
>
> "This scripture should alert us to what is ahead unless we repent, because there is no question but that as people of the free world, we are increasingly upholding many of the evils of the adversary today. By court edict godless conspirators can run for government office, teach in our schools, hold office in labor unions, work in our defense plants, serve in our merchant marines, etc. As a nation, we are helping to underwrite many evil revolutionaries in our country."[115]

---

[115] President Ezra Taft Benson, "Civic Standards for the Faithful Saints," General Conference, 1972, https://www.lds.org/general-conference/1972/04/civic-standards-for-the-faithful-saints?lang=eng.

President Benson's analysis and interpretation of *Book of Mormon* warnings is important. Not only did Moroni point out that his people, and the Jaredites, were destroyed because of the secret Satanic conspiracy among them, but Mormon, Alma, and other prophets did, too. Prophets both ancient and modern are in full agreement as to the source and cause of the disturbances which plagued their respective societies. The cradle of corruption among the Nephites was the communistic secret conspiracy among them, and it is the same in modern times.

In our day, in our land, President Benson saw the same secret society at work subverting our Liberty. This cabal not only uses organized crime, street gangs, and labor unions to do portions of its work, but, more importantly, it embeds its agents in all levels of federal, state, and local government. These conspirators work as advisors to presidents, bureaucrats in the many government agencies, diplomats, heads of the Federal Reserve, federal investigators, FBI, CIA, and NSA agents, law enforcement officers, and, yes, as congressmen, judges, and even presidents. They have left no stone unturned and no sector untargeted; their agents infest every nook and cranny of our society.

In more recent times, J.R. Nyquist has poignantly observed:

> "Soviet strategy is not conspiracy theory. It is conspiracy history. It has already happened and continues to happen. We are seeing it unfold before our eyes."[116]

Despite the factual, historical reality of communist conspiracy, the Lord has given us *The Book of Mormon* which is the "greatest handbook for freedom in this fight against" Satan's secret combinations. Armed with this divine defense manual, the Latter-day Saints are fully prepared to step forward and be the ultimate bulwark against conspiracy, and the supreme voice in favor of Liberty and the Constitution. The fact that the

---

[116] Cliff Kincaid and J.R. Nyquist, *Red Jihad: Moscow's Final Solution for America and Israel* (Owings, MD: America's Survival, Inc., 2016), 89-90.

membership of the Church has *not* done so is a damning condemnation of our criminal lack of devotion to the Restored Gospel of Christ.

We must repent, become vocal and active in the fight against tyranny, and lead our country by example. We should be the Lord's shock troops in this eternal war for agency, goodness, and light. If we do not lead the way, who else will? If we, who have the scriptures foretelling of secret conspiracies, say nothing, who will? If we, who enjoy the counsel of living prophets, fail to act upon their warnings, who will?

In a 1962 speech in Chicago, President Ezra Taft Benson spoke of the "forces" laboring to undermine our society from within. He observed:

> "I hear that some people, and more particularly the Communists and the Social Democrats, don't want us to examine this internal threat, but I believe we should. I think we should study Communism and study Socialism so that we can recognize the influence of each. We can leave the spies to the FBI, but learning how our enemies are trying to subvert us is everybody's job. I also recognize that it is not popular in some circles to be called an anti-communist but I consider Communism a God-less political and economic disease. I do not believe an American citizen can be patriotic and loyal to his own country, and its God-inspired Constitution of freedom, without being anti-Communist.
>
> ". . . We should expose to the light of public inquiry those forces which would destroy our country and our way of life. We should pay no attention to the recommendations of men who call the Constitution an 18th Century Agrarian document – who apologize for capitalism and free enterprise. We should refuse to follow their siren song of concentrating, increasingly, the powers of government in the Chief Executive, of delegating American sovereign authority to non-American institutions in the United Nations, and pretending that it will bring peace to the world by

turning our armed forces over to a U.N. world-wide police force."[117]

Those dark communist forces overrun our society. They use many labels to confuse people, such as Social Democrat (which is the label adopted by communist Senator Bernie Sanders), but they all work toward the same objectives. They call themselves "Republicans" and "Democrats." They are your local sheriffs and judges. They are your congressional representatives. They are the president and his cabinet. They are Supreme Court justices and national lawyers. They are FOX News and CNN reporters. They are "conservative" and "liberal" talk show hosts. They are authors and actors. They are doctors and CDC researchers. They are your children's public school teachers. They are in your ward and quorums. They are there, as President Smith said, "no matter where you look."

These subversives are not patriots, *they are traitors*. Like the king-men of Captain Moroni's day, they are "desirous that the law should be altered in a manner to overthrow the free government and to establish a king over the land" (Alma 51:5). They are enemies to our "God-inspired Constitution of freedom." They are a fifth column working from the inside to sell us into the hands of the enemy. They are carriers of the communist disease – the Red Plague that has infected the world.

President Benson rhetorically asked whether these turncoats are merely incompetent or whether they know what they are doing. He remarked:

> "In view of the life-and-death nature of this struggle, it is incredible that our leaders in Washington for over thirty years consistently have followed a policy of hopeful coexistence, of fearful containment, and now even of building bridges of trade and friendship to our enemies. Are they deaf and unable to hear the communists daily reaffirm their declaration of war against us? Are they blind and unable to see how the communists are

---

[117] Ezra Taft Benson, "Our Freedom is Threatened," speech in Chicago, September 22, 1962.

maneuvering into strategic positions, both at home and abroad, from which to strike the fatal blow? Are they ignorant and unable to learn the lessons of history?

"Unfortunately, they are none of these. The problem could be easily corrected if it were merely a question of competency. Our leaders and opinion-molders are well aware of everything I have just outlined, but they are steering us along a course of non-resistance to communism just the same."[118]

President Benson said that these fifth columnists serve an essential function in the Soviet strategy. He described this strategy thus:

"They have taken over one-third of the world without a single Soviet invasion. Their formula has been takeover from within by inspiring civil wars, revolution and through acts of treason. Countries fall into the Red slave empire, not at the hands of invading Russians, but at the hands of native communists who secretly work for the overthrow of their own government. This has been their successful pattern of operation for over fifty years, and they certainly are not going to abandon it now.

"Nikita Khrushchev explained it this way:

""It is not an army, but peace that is required to propagate communist ideas, disseminate them, and establish them in the minds of men. . . .

""Marxism-Leninism is our main weapon.""[119]

These "native communists" in the United States are spreading the ideological work of destruction. Though Moscow has prepared for war and trained many of its operatives in military tactics, Marxism-Leninism is

---

[118] Benson, Newquist, ed., *An Enemy Hath Done This*, 166.

[119] Benson, Newquist, ed., *An Enemy Hath Done This*, 170-171.

their "main weapon." *The Book of Mormon* famously declares that the preaching of the word of God had a "more powerful effect upon the minds of the people than the sword" (Alma 31:5). It should not be surprising, then, to learn that the communists also believe their teachings are the most powerful armament in their arsenal.

In accordance with their communist dogma, the "native communists" have assaulted their opposition with an unrestrained, unrelenting smear campaign; a veritable war of words. We must expose this fifth column to the light and *never* apologize for our principles, no matter how "intolerant," "bigoted," "racist," "nationalist," "chauvinistic," or "anti-Semitic" our enemies claim we are. Remember, this is a "life-and-death" struggle and risk-taking is a requirement. No price is too high for Freedom.

President Ezra Taft Benson spoke frequently of the smear tactics used by the communists and their allies. He taught:

> "The smear seems to be the most widely used and effective tool of the Conspiracy to discredit and weaken any effective anti-communist effort. The smear of any individual or organization by the Communists, their dupes and fellow-travelers is certain evidence of effectiveness. If any of you are affiliated with patriotic organizations reportedly opposed to the Communist Conspiracy, which are not extensively smeared, you can rest assured your opposition is largely ineffective. You had best look for a more fruitful affiliation."[120]

Another time, he noted:

> "It is the current anti anti-communism drive and the branding as "super-patriots", "fanatics" and "right-wing extremists", those

---

[120] Ezra Taft Benson, December 13, 1963, in Newquist, ed., *Prophets, Principles and National Survival*, 251.

who defend the freedom, traditions and principles on which this great nation was founded. . . .

"No more should we condone name calling and castigating those who would defend American freedoms. This is what the communists want."[121]

The communists' favorite "smear" is to call its opponents "Nazis" and "anti-Semites." Because of the mass brainwashing that has occurred regarding the true history of World War II and the "atrocities" that may or may not have been committed by Germany, people recoil and have a kneejerk reaction any time the epithet "Nazi" or "anti-Semite" is used to label someone. Once the public has been sufficiently convinced that you are a "Nazi," the conspiracy has largely neutralized you in the fight. Yet, it is our duty to fight through such absurd smears and labels and to proclaim the truth boldly regardless of consequence.

Satan will use any tactic to derail opposition to his plan. In 1942, in the midst of the terrible conflagration of war brought upon the world – not by Hitler, as the propagandists claim, but by members of the Satanic communist conspiracy and their Western allies – the First Presidency warned the Church in these fervent words:

"Infidelity, atheism, unchastity, intemperance, civil corruption, greed, avarice, ambition – personal, political, national – are more powerful today than at any other time in the lives of us now living. They are pulling and thrusting us almost at will into new fields of action, new lines of thought. They are shaking the faith, undermining the morals, polluting the lives of the people. They have thrown many so far off balance in all of their activities, economic, social, political, and religious, that they stand in real danger of falling. Satan is making war against all the wisdom that has come to men through their ages of experience. He is seeking

---

[121] Benson, *The Red Carpet*, 197.

to overturn and destroy the very foundations upon which society, government, and religion rest. He aims to have men adopt theories and practices which he induced their forefathers, over the ages, to adopt and try, only to be discarded by them when found unsound, impractical, and ruinous. He plans to destroy liberty and freedom – economic, political, and religious, and to set up in place thereof the greatest, most widespread, and most complete tyranny that has ever oppressed men. He is working under such perfect disguise that many do not recognize either him or his methods. There is no crime he would not commit, no debauchery he would not set up, no plague he would not send, no heart he would not break, no life he would not take, no soul he would not destroy. He comes as a thief in the night; he is a wolf in sheep's clothing. Without their knowing it, the people are being urged down paths that lead only to destruction. Satan never before had so firm a grip on this generation as he has now."[122]

Satan's grip on mankind was strong and widespread in 1942, and it is even more threatening now.

Contrary to popular belief, Stalin – not Hitler – started World War II. In 1963, President Ezra Taft Benson, in fact, stated: "World War II . . . was largely brought on through the world-wide diplomatic conniving of Stalin's agents."[123] And so it was. In his book *The Chief Culprit: Stalin's Grand Design to Start World War II*, Soviet defector, Viktor Suvorov, wrote:

"The Soviet Union entered World War II as an aggressor. Poland, Finland, Estonia, Lithuania, Latvia, Romania – all the western neighbors of the Soviet Union – fell victim to the Red Army. During talks in Berlin, Stalin's envoy Molotov demanded strongholds in Yugoslavia, in the Adriatic Sea, in Greece, in the Bosporus and Dardanelles, in the Persian Gulf; he demanded that

---

[122] First Presidency message, Conference Report, October, 1942, 13.

[123] Newquist, ed., *Prophets, Principles and National Survival*, 265.

countries south of the Baku-Batumi line, in the direction of the Persian Gulf, be given over to Soviet control, including eastern Turkey, northern Iran, and Iraq. He also declared the Soviet Union's interest in southern Bukovina. Molotov constantly asked Hitler and Ribbentrop whether Germany had reconsidered its position on the fate of Finland, seeing that the Soviet Union was not going to let that country be independent. Finally, Stalin's major demand at the Berlin talks in November 1940 was for Germany to acquiesce to a Soviet military presence in Bulgaria. Molotov added, in a conversation with Hitler, that "the USSR was ready to support Bulgaria in its desire for an outlet to the Aegean Sea, and considered said desire to be just." Stalin never specified which countries his puppet Bulgaria would have to invade to reach this outlet – Greece, Turkey, or both."[124]

I discuss more of the evidence for Stalin's culpability in beginning, intensifying, and facilitating World War II in my book *A Century of Red*. Suffice it to say that the communists, strategically stationed around the world as they were in their role as subversives, brought on World War II. No honest person can deny that. The facts and evidence are too overwhelming. Germany and Hitler have merely been the scapegoats held up by the communist-controlled press and court historians who wish to deflect attention away from their own guilt.

Viktor Suvorov added this note about Soviet expansion and desires for expansion:

> "The Soviet Union finished World War II as an aggressor as well. It was the only country that expanded its borders as a result of World War II. Stalin annexed Estonia, Latvia, Lithuania, northern Bukovina, western Ukraine, and western Byelorussia, as well as parts of eastern Prussia with Koenigsberg, Trans-Carpathian

---

[124] Viktor Suvorov, *The Chief Culprit: Stalin's Grand Design to Start World War II* (Annapolis, Maryland: Naval Institute Press, 2008), 278.

Ukraine, the Kuril Islands, South Sakhalin, and Bessarabia. Under the banner of the "great patriotic war," Stalin punished entire peoples and nations. On Stalin's orders, all the Chechens, Ingushes, Crimean Tatars, Volga Germans, and other peoples were transported to empty frozen fields or waterless, lifeless steppes, and abandoned there to die. . . .

"The Red Army came to Central Europe with the supposedly noble goal of liberating it from the Nazis, but it left only after establishing puppet governments in most of those countries. Poland, Czechoslovakia, East Germany, Hungary, Romania, Yugoslavia, part of Austria, and Albania were forced under Stalin's control, as well as China, North Korea, and Vietnam in Asia. On July 22, 1945, the Soviet delegation suggested that the Soviet Union, the United States, and Great Britain separately or jointly oversee the former Italian colonies in Africa and the Mediterranean. On July 23, Stalin demanded the right to create Soviet military naval bases in the Black Sea region, in the straits of Bosporus and Dardanelles. He also wanted parts of Turkey – the Kars and Ardagan regions – to belong to the Soviet Union. Stalin tried to take control of West Berlin by strangling it through blockade. Soviet agents appeared in France, Italy, and Greece . . . Stalin declared northern Iran to be a part of Azerbaijan, and right until the end of his life never gave up trying to take control of this province. Stalin set up the People's Democratic Republic of Southern Azerbaijan, and the Kurdish People's Democratic Republic, respectively in northern and western Iran."[125]

Yes, the Soviet Union was the unquestioned beneficiary of the spoils of World War II. Among those wicked accomplishments just mentioned, we note several others. Using the cover of a war which their agents started, the communists: Bankrupted Britain and separated her from her colonies; destroyed Germany, the leading anti-communist nation in Europe;

---

[125] Suvorov, *The Chief Culprit*, 278-279.

occupied half of Europe; converted the American People into a warlike and interventionist nation by embroiling us in the war (and later in wars in Korea and Vietnam); heavily infiltrated the U.S. government under ally and sympathizer FDR; established the United Nations, the first head of which was the Soviet spy Alger Hiss; stole the materials and data needed to construct an atom bomb; set up the North Korean regime; set the stage for conquest of China (which was intentionally allowed by complicit American fellow travelers like General George C. Marshall in 1949); and used the phony threat of "the Nazis" to justify aggression and military buildup.

Whittaker Chambers, one of the most famous ex-communists to break with the conspiracy, also saw communism as the only beneficiary of the world wars. He stated:

> "The chief fruit of the First World War was the Russian Revolution and the rise of Communism as a national power. The chief fruit of the Second World War was our arrival at the next to the last step of the crisis with the rise of Communism as a world power. History is likely to say that these were the only decisive results of the world wars.
>
> "The last war simplified the balance of political forces in the world by reducing them to two. For the first time, it made the power of the Communist sector of mankind (embodied in the Soviet Union) roughly equal to the power of the free sector of mankind (embodied in the United States). It made the collision of these powers all but inevitable. For the world wars did not end the crisis. They raised its tensions to a new pitch. They raised the crisis to a new stage. All the politics of our time, including the politics of war, will be the politics of this crisis."[126]

---

[126] Chambers, *Witness*, xxxvii.

Communism is the only true beneficiary of the world wars. Satan has manipulated the affairs of the world so as to place his ideology at the head. Lucifer's communist crown was bought with blood; the blood of tens of millions of innocent human beings.

Working under "perfect disguise," Satan's agents used the Second World War to establish a framework for global government. This tyrannical government, as foreseen by John and other ancient prophets, is in the final stages of construction, and we will yet see its banners fly over the earth. It will be "the greatest, most widespread, and most complete tyranny that has ever oppressed men," as the First Presidency warned.

I repeat: *The communists started World War II as a means of advancing communism.* The resources and troops provided by the Allies were used by the Bolsheviks in their war against humanity. They used the conflict to their advantage and expanded across the globe, enslaving a myriad of nations in the process. They used the war as a launchpad for further aggression against mankind — aggression which has never ceased. All of this served the secret agenda because, to the conspirators, order can only come out of chaos.

Communists are masters of chaos. They deliberately stoke the fires of contention and seek to bring about total bedlam. This mayhem is seen as the nursing mother of progress.

Creating chaos by exacerbating differences between peoples and groups is part and parcel of communist ideology. They see it as their destiny — the hand of fate working through the conflict they create to bring about a brighter future for the race. In other words, they seek to bring about order out of chaos. However, inherent in that notion is the necessity of bringing about that chaos and giving fate a friendly push.

In 1957, Chinese tyrant Mao Tse-tung explained:

> "Marxist philosophy holds that the law of the unity of opposites is the fundamental law of the universe. This law operates universally, whether in the natural world, in human society, or in

man's thinking. Between the opposites in a contradiction there is at once unity and struggle, and it is this that impels things to move and change. Contradictions exist everywhere . . . In any given phenomenon or thing, the unity of opposites is conditional, temporary and transitory, and hence relative, whereas the struggle of opposites is absolute."[127]

This is a very occult notion. It is the ancient concept of Yin and Yang which says there is a dark side and a light side to everything and, that, when merged together, these opposites form a whole. This pagan idea dictates that even God is made up of two parts – both good *and* evil, both light *and* darkness. In order to be complete, God must partake of both aspects. If we follow this to its conclusion, it means we must also merge both aspects – good and evil – in our own lives to create a oneness of soul. In other words, the concept of utopia, wholeness, or order is the offspring of the conflict sparked by contradictions.

We learn from the scriptures that there is indeed an "opposition in all things" (2 Nephi 2:11), but we are firmly told to reject the evil and cleave only to the good. Everything good comes from God and everything evil comes from Lucifer (Moroni 7:11-14). There can be no merger of the two; no Yin and Yang. The conflict we face is to choose to do only "good continually" (Mosiah 5:2). Only by promoting goodness, righteousness, morality, light, and truth can true peace, order, and happiness be brought about.

Marxists, however, twist this notion of opposition in all things. In essence, the communists have chosen the wrong "opposite" and are using the inherent friction between good and evil to bring about an evil agenda. They exploit the inherent contradictions in all things and use them as wedges to pry apart and tear down the pre-existing social order that they believe is the root of evil. They see their work as benevolent; as

---

[127] Mao Tse-tung, *Quotations from Chairmon Mao Tse-Tung* (BN Publishing, 2007), 78.

promoting the greater good. After all, you have to crack a few eggs to make an omelet.

Similar to Latter-day Saints, communists believe they should act rather than be acted upon (2 Nephi 2:13-14). However, they act on the side of Satan to bring about chaos, disorder, misery, suffering, and struggle rather than to being "anxiously engaged in a good cause, and [doing] many things of their own free will, and [bringing] to pass much righteousness" (D&C 58:27). Indeed, they will bring about a devastating nuclear war if they feel that's what it takes to create the sufficient chaos out of which true and universal order can be established over the globe.

This process is the old Hegelian dialectic at play. In this dialectic, two opposites create friction and conflict, or "struggle." Out of this struggle emerges a synthesis of the two contradictory parts – a superior product. It is often written as thesis–anti-thesis–synthesis. In other words, a third way – a compromise – is created by the struggle between two opposites.

Thus, in communist philosophy, there must *always* be struggle. It is inherent. There is no communism without struggle. This struggle between opposites is perpetual. What this means for us is that as long as communists walk the earth, we will be in a war for our survival whether we want to be or not.

An anonymous intelligence operative interviewed by Cliff Kincaid described how fundamental dialectical theory is to communism. He said:

> "One of the things that is so fundamental to understanding Marxism Leninism is "struggle." Lenin said there's not a Marxist who doesn't probably believe this – that without struggle there is no development. Why do we see chaos appearing in different places? Because, it is through struggle that development takes place, not through negotiations but through struggle. We have to disrupt things in order to move it . . . So wherever there is oppression there is resistance. When these organizations come up and talk about being oppressed, the idea is to promote resistance

to it because, that resistance is disruptive and it means that somebody can do something about the disruption. Somebody is going to have to take action to quell it, to pacify it, so it's a way of moving things forward, struggle promotes development and there's no question about it. . . .

"Dialectics is a scientific method and they call it science. It's the algebra of revolution which is pretty scientific."[128]

Just as bacteria cannot grow in a pristine environment, but breed and spread best in filth, communism cannot ascend in the absence of chaotic conditions. According to a deliberate, scientific plan, the communists create chaos, throw fuel on the fire until it the madness reaches a frenzied pitch, then ride in as the saviors promising, as Lenin promised the Russian peasants, "Peace! Land! Bread!"[129] But the communists will always deliver just what Lenin delivered to Russia – slavery, moral degradation, and an unsurpassed orgy of death.

Pope Pius XII gave a succinct overview of this dialectical notion and what it means to both communists and the rest of the human race:

"Insisting on the dialectical aspect of their materialism, the Communists claim that the conflict which carries the world towards its final synthesis can be accelerated by man. Hence they endeavor to sharpen the antagonisms which arise between the various classes of society. Thus the class struggle with its consequent violent hate and destruction takes on the aspects of a crusade for the progress of humanity. On the other hand, all other

---

[128] Cliff Kincaid, *The Sword of Revolution and the Communist Apocalypse* (Owings, MD: America's Survival, Inc., 2015), 73-74.

[129] Linda Delaine and Evgenia Sokolskaya, "Peace, Land, Bread," *Russian Life*, April 23, 2014, accessed, May 8, 2018, https://russianlife.com/stories/online-archive/peace-land-bread/.

forces whatever, as long as they resist such systematic violence, must be annihilated as hostile to the human race."[130]

It is in chaos that the Red Gadiantons can push forward their agenda and establish themselves in positions of power. War is perhaps the greatest agent of chaos. Society can be restructured much faster in wartime conditions than during peacetime. Thus, those who serve the conspiracy always agitate for war. Whether it is the unconstitutional "War on Terror" or a proposed strike against North Korea, these subversives are prepared to sacrifice your sons on the altar of global government and self-aggrandizement.

We cannot afford to allow our "representatives" in government to squander American wealth and blood in pointless, unconstitutional, immoral wars abroad, nor in the service of the communist-controlled United Nations, which President J. Reuben Clark, Jr. once described as a "scheming, brawling, word-mauling" organization. He also stated: "I believe American manhood is too valuable to be sacrificed on foreign soil for foreign issues and causes."[131] I wholeheartedly agree.

Whether for Israel, Britain, or South Korea, American blood is too precious to spill on foreign soil. Refusing to allow our men to be used as a "world-wide police force" – a modern Praetorian Guard for the conspiracy – is a good place to begin if we truly desire to stop the profusion of blood and put an end to the conspiracy's machinations.

President Ezra Taft Benson warned that the conspirators were attempting to do one of two things: 1) Either transfer American military might to the communist-controlled United Nations; or 2) so severely disarm and weaken the U.S. military that it could not stand up to communist power. He explained:

---

[130] Kincaid, *The Sword of Revolution and the Communist Apocalypse*, 31.

[131] President J. Reuben Clark, Jr., address, November 14, 1947, in J. Reuben Clark, Jr., *Stand Fast by Our Constitution*, 72, 76.

"The only real worry to the planners in Washington and Moscow is that the American people will not appreciate the "wisdom" of their long-range strategy and will insist on real anti-communist action for a change. And so, occasionally, the planners go through the motions of opposing communism to placate the voters at home, but make it clear to the enemy that they really do not intend to do anything rash – like winning. In the meantime, it is a race against the clock. While they are still in power, they are attempting to build a world organization and to transfer our military might to that organization just as rapidly as possible so that, even if the anti-communist public should finally wake up to their plans, it will be too late to do anything about it."[132]

Many people refer to the "globalist" conspiracy without understanding that the "globalists" serve the communist conspiracy. This is plain to see when we realize that nearly every move the Western "globalists" make is calculated to weaken the United States while strengthening the international communist position. For instance, it only benefits Moscow and Beijing when the United States weakens her military or when she transfers her sovereignty and resources to the communist-controlled United Nations.

The American, British, and French "globalists" (the three most powerful subsections) are, in truth, anti-Americans who promote a world government under communism/socialism. The Hillary Clintons and Barack Obamas are little more than mid-level dupes serving this conspiracy. When the Anti-Christ ushers in his global government, you can be absolutely certain it will operate on communist principles such as the centralization of all political power, the use of military force to enforce its dictates, the abolition of private property, and the redistribution of wealth. And the means to bring this communist world order about is war and conflict.

---

[132] Benson, Newquist, ed., *An Enemy Hath Done This*, 167-168.

Mao Tse-tung, the greatest mass murderer in world history, affirmed the unsurpassed importance of revolutionary war and force to the communists:

> "According to the Marxist theory of the state, the army is the chief component of state power. Whoever wants to seize and retain state power must have a strong army. Some people ridicule us as advocates of the "omnipotence of war". Yes, we are advocates of the omnipotence of revolutionary war; that is good, not bad; it is Marxist. The guns of the Russian Communist Party created socialism. We shall create a democratic republic Experience in the class struggle in the era of imperialism teaches us that it is only by the power of the gun that the working class and the labouring masses can defeat the armed bourgeoisie and landlords; in this sense we may say that only with guns can the whole world be transformed."[133]

Satanic communists in all ages are the masters of death. Cain brought murder into the world. His fellow Luciferian initiates carried forward the practice. Nimrod was a mighty hunter of men. The Jaredite secret societies spread the work of death so thoroughly among that once great race that it exterminated itself. The Nephite Gadiantons assassinated and murdered wantonly and eventually led the Lamanites to annihilate the Nephites. And in our own day the cycle of war continues under their guidance.

War hardens our hearts and ultimately destroys our faith in God and His laws. In 1976, President Spencer W. Kimball chastised the American People for supporting militarism rather than following the Savior's teachings. He said:

> "We are a warlike people, easily distracted from our assignment of preparing for the coming of the Lord. When enemies rise up,

---

[133] Mao Tse-tung, *Quotations from Chairman Mao Tse-Tung*, 28.

we commit vast resources to the fabrication of gods of stone and steel—ships, planes, missiles, fortifications—and depend on them for protection and deliverance. When threatened, we become antienemy instead of pro-kingdom of God; we train a man in the art of war and call him a patriot, thus, in the manner of Satan's counterfeit of true patriotism, perverting the Savior's teaching:

""Love your enemies, bless them that curse you, do good to them that hate you, and pray for them which despitefully use you, and persecute you;

""That ye may be the children of your Father which is in heaven." (Matt. 5:44–45.)

"We forget that if we are righteous the Lord will either not suffer our enemies to come upon us—and this is the special promise to the inhabitants of the land of the Americas (see 2 Ne. 1:7)—or he will fight our battles for us (Ex. 14:14; D&C 98:37, to name only two references of many)."[134]

The Lord has promised His Saints to protect them and fight their battles. This promise is conditional, however, and depends upon our faithfulness to His words. We receive His words from His prophets. How can we expect the Lord to make good on His promise if we do not uphold our end of the bargain and heed the warnings about secret combinations, communism, and political intrigue delivered to us so forcefully by the Savior's servants? If we do not live righteously and heed the words of the prophets, we will be brought into literal, physical captivity by Satan's minions (1 Nephi 14:7).

President Marion G. Romney gave a warning relative to this subject of divine protection. He said:

---

[134] President Spencer W. Kimball, "The False Gods We Worship," *Ensign*, June, 1776, https://www.lds.org/ensign/1976/06/the-false-gods-we-worship?lang=eng.

"In distinguishing communism from the United Order, President David O. McKay said that communism is Satan's counterfeit for the gospel plan, and that it is an avowed enemy of the God of the land. Communism is the greatest anti-Christ power in the world today and therefore the greatest menace not only to our peace but to our preservation as a free people. By the extent to which we tolerate it, accommodate ourselves to it, permit ourselves to be encircled by its tentacles and drawn to it, to that extent we forfeit the protection of the God of this land."[135]

To the extent that America has adopted communism, to that extent she has forfeited the Savior's generous promises to defend her and fight her battles. The reason for this is simple: *Communism is anti-Christ.* Everything that is anti-Christ is of Satan, and people cannot embrace that which comes from Satan and still receive the Lord's blessings.

Anciently, Mormon taught this doctrine:

"[W]herefore, a man being a servant of the devil cannot follow Christ; and if he follow Christ he cannot be a servant of the devil.

"Wherefore, all things which are good cometh of God; and that which is evil cometh of the devil; for the devil is an enemy unto God, and fighteth against him continually, and inviteth and enticeth to sin, and to do that which is evil continually. . . .

". . . whatsoever thing persuadeth men to do evil, and believe not in Christ, and deny him, and serve not God, then ye may know with a perfect knowledge it is of the devil" (Moroni 7:11-12, 16).

Our prophets have declared communism to be "the greatest anti-Christ power in the world today" and, therefore, we "may know with a perfect knowledge it is of the devil." If we embrace communism, we take into our

---

[135] President Marion G. Romney, "America's Promise," *Ensign*, September, 1979, https://www.lds.org/ensign/1979/09/americas-promise?lang=eng.

soul a deadly poison which, if not quickly treated with the antidote of repentance and faith in Christ, leads to certain spiritual death now and in the eternities. We simply cannot afford to adopt one particle of the communist plan. Communism is pure Satanism.

Because the people of this nation have rejected Christ's message, they have been lured into the arms of the Adversary. The communistic philosophy which now governs the lives of tens of millions of Americans is incompatible with true Americanism and authentic constitutionalism. It is incompatible with the twin pillars of Liberty – morality and religion. We are reaching a boiling point of friction between Liberty, religion, and morality on the one hand and communistic tyranny coupled with occult theocracy on the other. Yet, our prophets have made clear on which side we must stand. President Benson wrote:

> "I say to Americans and to people everywhere; no true Christian, no true believer in Christ, can be a communist. These dangerous philosophies of communism are anti-Christ and are wholly incompatible with our God-given freedom and the true gospel of Jesus Christ.
>
> "It is not alone hunger and poverty and oppression that afflict so many in this sweeping program of man's inhumanity to man. In country after country faith in God has been ruthlessly destroyed.
>
> "We have long known that the abolition of all religion is the ultimate goal of communism. Lenin has said: "Atheism is a natural and inseparable portion of Marxism, of the theory and practice of scientific socialism. Our propaganda necessarily includes propaganda for atheism.""[136]

If any Latter-day Saint has deluded himself into believing that he can be both a disciple of Christ *and* a proponent of communist principles (no

---

[136] Benson, *The Red Carpet*, 35.

matter their outward label; no matter how they are presented), he is grossly mistaken. *A true Christian cannot support communism in any form with impunity.* Communism is anti-Christ! It is destructive of faith in God and of all true religion wherever it is implemented.

President David O. McKay confirmed that two opposing forces are engaged in a fight to the death. He said:

> "Today two mighty forces are battling for the supremacy of the world. The destiny of mankind is in the balance. It is a question of God and liberty, or atheism and slavery. The success of Communism means the destruction of Religion."[137]

Light dispels darkness, and darkness conquers whenever light retreats. Only one can occupy a given space at the same time. We either preserve our Liberty and our rights of free worship, or we automatically embrace Satan's despotism.

In a 1947 *Improvement Era* piece, President McKay again highlighted the alternatives encompassed in this war:

> "Today America is reputedly the only nation in the world "capable of sustaining western civilization."

> "Opposed to her is Russia, which has renounced faith in God and in his overruling power in the universe.

> "The threatened impending clash between these two nations is more than a test of political supremacy, more than a fight between capitalism and communism – it is the ever-contending

---

[137] President David O. McKay, *Church News*, July 18, 1953, cited in Jerreld Newquist, ed., *Prophets, Principles and National Survival*, 215.

conflict between *faith* in God and in the gospel of Jesus Christ, and *disbelief* in the philosophy of Christian ideals."[138]

As it was in the days of our pre-mortal existence, our choice is between Jesus Christ's Gospel on one hand and Lucifer's scheme on the other. The United States is the Lord's base of operations and the headquarters of the Lord's Church. Russia is Satan's base of operations and the headquarters of the Devil's great and abominable church. We have a very clear choice, and it is dismaying to see so many Americans openly embracing Vladimir Putin and the Russian regime while denigrating their own nation. Despite our many grave flaws, this is still the Promised Land – the Zion of our God. Will you fight against Zion or with her?

In April 1948, President McKay stood at the podium during General Conference and again presented the Saints with the same choice. He declared:

> "The choice today is between dictatorship with the atheistic teachings of communism, and the doctrine of the restored gospel of Jesus Christ, obedience to which alone can make us free."[139]

This struggle between the polar opposites of communism and Christianity is so momentous that President McKay warned of a third world war unless communism was quickly vanquished. He said:

> "The Church of Jesus Christ of Latter-day Saints looks with deep concern upon the attitude of communism toward the Christian religion.
>
> "A third World War is inevitable unless communism is soon subdued. Communism yields to nothing but force.

---

[138] President David O. McKay, *Improvement Era*, Vol. 50, 562-563, 1947, in *Gospel Ideals: Selections from the Discourses of David O. McKay (Salt Lake City, Utah: The Improvement Era, 1953)*, 275.

[139] President David O. McKay, Conference Report, 117-118, in *Gospel Ideals*, 273.

> "Communism looks upon the individual as a mere cog in the wheel of the state. That is a false doctrine. The state exists for the welfare of the individual."[140]

In the sixty-eight years since that statement was made, have we defeated communism? Not hardly. One look at American culture confirms that communism has nearly completely conquered us. In the process of this gradual communist conquest, the Constitution's guarantees of protection have been shredded. The nation has been set on a course of endless war. The fruit of our labor is being confiscated and redistributed at alarming rates under the guise of "taxation" and "welfare." Fewer Americans than ever before believe in God. And so on and so forth. Is the third world war that President McKay warned us about "inevitable"? I believe it is. And it will take the intervention of God Himself to rescue us from the trap set by the communists.

To the Saints gathered for Conference in April 1951, President McKay again warned of Satan's deceptions. He warned that American were being tricked into supporting a ruling clique of gangsters. He taught:

> "More destructive to the spreading of Christian principles in the minds, particularly of the youth, than battleships, submarines, or even bombs, is the sowing of false ideals by the enemy. . . .

> "Misrepresentation, false propaganda, innuendoes soon sprout into poisonous weeds, and before long the people find themselves victims of a pollution that has robbed them of their individual liberty and enslaved them to a group of political gangsters."[141]

The context of President McKay's remarks makes it clear that Soviet Russia was the sower of these dangerous seeds in the minds of men.

---

[140] President David O. McKay, *Salt Lake Telegram*, April 26, 1951.

[141] President David O. McKay, Conference Report, April, 1951, 96, in *Gospel Ideals*, 284.

More destructive than any number of nuclear warheads Russia or China could hurl at the United States is the malicious propaganda spread through the communist-controlled press, communist-dominated textbooks, communist-staffed public schools and universities, etc. Communist agents of influence – operating under a multitude of names and through numerous organizations that are ostensibly non-communist – have deceived our nation and warped our minds with vulgar falsehoods.

Through deception, Satan has taken away from us light and truth (D&C 93:39) and we are left groping in the dark. With our hearts in a darkened state, even the Saints can falter and turn to the pagan ways of old. Communism is the incubator of modern-day paganism, the instigator of wickedness and apostasy. Remember President Romney's words: Communism is "the greatest anti-Christ power in the world today."

As we have seen, President J. Reuben Clark, Jr. raised one of the most articulate and strident voices against the communist menace. Having served in the government in many capacities, such as in the state department, as ambassador to Mexico, and as an advisor to several U.S. presidents, President Clark had an incredible working knowledge of politics and international intrigue. Thus, when we read President Clark's politically incorrect declarations, we would do well to take note.

This great servant of the Lord frequently used the podium at General Conference to educate and inform the Saints in these thorny matters. In the October 1959 General Conference, President Clark warned the Saints of the greatest threat facing them. Foreshadowing President McKay's dire warnings, President Clark stated:

> "[W]e have the man [Soviet dictator Nikita Khrushchev] described by President McKay and commented upon so well, who in effect is the directing head of this whole great body of paganism in their ideology and in their non-belief in God. I think this is the first time in all history when God's people have been faced with an organized paganism more or less guided and directed by one who denies God and says he is unconvertible from his atheism.

"We get the impression that he has in mind that his Marxian ideology, and his atheism, shall gain control somehow and make of all of us the followers of his doctrines. He preaches peace, I may say, and then he preaches the abandonment of certain weapons of war, then he preaches that we go back to traditional warfare, where numbers count, he preaches that we shall destroy our military installations, and if he gets rid of these, I see no end to what he may try to do.

"Now, let us have no illusions about this, brethren and sisters. The plan is really one of exterminating God and Christianity. Into our hands has been placed through divine ordinations the Holy Priesthood after the Order of the Son of God. In our hands is the responsibility of carrying forward.

"We do not have now a united front to this united paganism. We are still torn and divided among many sects. But the problem we face, if the plans of the Marxian paganism are carried out, is our extermination."

Read that again. And again. Let it sink in. Internalize the truths this great disciple of Christ is teaching. Study his words until you grasp the danger that faces you and your family.

In this landmark statement, President Clark equated communism with paganism. Communism can be thought of as "organized paganism." It is the church of the Devil, the synagogue of Satan. This vicious brand of modern paganism is united under the communist banner. The Communist Party is *the* secret society pushing this "Marxian paganism" upon the world. And what is their stated goal? Their goal is the extermination of Christians and the obliteration of faith in Christ wherever it is found. As will be discussed later, these Red Pagans have already slaughtered some 40-60 million Christians in the Soviet Union alone. We are next if we allow these Satanists to continue subverting our society.

President Clark was not finished with his solemn warnings, however. He explained the persecution that awaited the Saints, identified the force leading this persecution, and expounded the remedy that could see us through these awful trials:

> "There are good people in Russia. There are faithful people in Russia. Elder Benson has recently met a few of them. But they live under this Marxian theory, and one of the elements of that is the destruction of free agency which was given to the sons of God before the world was created. Through it there was the rebellion in heaven. Through free agency we climb to the heights that lead us into exaltation. The Marxian theology repudiates God.
>
> "I have a feeling, brothers and sisters, that any man or woman who voluntarily subjects himself to this pagan ideology, who voluntarily lives within its jurisdiction, who voluntarily under this theory gives up his free agency, has lost his testimony and is on the road to apostasy.
>
> "I cannot bring too strongly that here in the last days, paganism is under one head, and that head is guided by Satan himself. Please, brethren and sisters of the Church, keep the home fires of testimony and knowledge of the gospel and of God and of Jesus Christ, keep the home fires burning in your homes, in your priesthood quorums, and all the rest, for I am sure, one way or another, we shall have to face dire persecution."[142]

The communist paganism threatening the Saints is "under one head," and that head is led directly and personally by Satan. Satan is the being guiding the communist conspiracy. The Satanic communists are his servants and do his bidding. At his behest, they destroy the lives of anyone opposing Lucifer's burgeoning world order. And they have targeted true believers in Christ for liquidation.

---

[142] President J. Reuben Clark, Jr., "The Task Ahead," Conference Report, October, 1959, 45-46, http://scriptures.byu.edu/#:t402:p527.

President Clark was clear that anyone who supports this pagan system and lives its principles has no testimony of Christ and "is on the road to apostasy." Because of those who repudiate their testimony and acquiesce to the forward march of this pagan conspiracy, the true Saints of God will suffer "dire persecution." Because of traitors and tyrants, America may totally lose her Liberty for a short season. To survive this persecution, one must nurture his testimony of the Savior and, most importantly, nurture it within the walls of his own home. Those lacking a true testimony will be consumed by this communist leviathan.

In other statements, President Clark taught that this wicked conspiracy is foreign and alien to American institutions. He said in 1943:

> "This influence is in leadership largely alien, – in birth, or in tradition, or in training and experience, or possessing alien concepts and alien philosophies. With them are some American-born rebel conspirators. These all form a vast army, some 3,000 of whom, handpicked, are said to swarm in Government offices, many in key positions, all ready, able, and willing to take over if their opportunity shall come, or be made."[143]

And make it they have. The communist agents of subversion have used our society's momentum against us. They have fomented chaos, strikes, protests, and public violence. They have salted old wounds in order to stir up fresh hatred. They have marched for "Civil Rights," called for a false form of "tolerance," and have indulged Americans in their own perverse desires and lusts. In this distracted condition, their specially trained and "handpicked" agents – this "vast army" of traitors, foreign agents, and Satanic special forces – have transferred greater power to the government which they thoroughly dominate. Through the arm of government, these Red Pagans have plundered and degraded these once great United States.

---

[143] President J. Reuben Clark, Jr., October 7, 1943, in Newquist, ed., *Prophets, Principles and National Survival*, 221-222.

To the Soviets, the United States was always the "Main Enemy." "Main Enemy" was the euphemism used to describe our American Republic. The Bolsheviks knew the United States would be the grand prize in their scheme of global conquest. They also knew we would be the toughest nut to crack – the last domino to fall. So, they developed a long-range strategy that they knew would take decades to achieve. They prepared for the long haul. They knew that generations of subversion would be required before the United States would crumble. But they also knew that unless the American People united against this "organized paganism," they would become demoralized, divided, and decadent under the withering barrage of Satan's cultural assault.

Just as President Clark termed communism "paganism," President McKay labeled the philosophy "barbarism." In an October 1952 article for the *Deseret News*, President McKay warned the Saints of the "awful situation" Moroni foresaw and foretold (Ether 8:24) that we would be in:

> "During the first half of the twentieth century we have traveled far into the soul-destroying land of socialism and made strange alliances through which we have become involved in almost continuous hot and cold wars over the whole of the earth. In this retreat from freedom the voices of protesting citizens have been drowned by the raucous shouts of intolerance and abuse from those who led the retreat and their millions of gullible youth, who are marching merrily to their doom, carrying banners on which are emblazoned such intriguing and misapplied labels as social justice, equality, reform, patriotism, social welfare.

> "Intoxicated with pride in our achievement, enmeshed in the interesting problems still unsolved, we have left unguarded the gate through which are pouring the destructive hordes and forces of a new invasion of barbarism."[144]

---

[144] President David O. McKay, *Deseret News*, October 18, 1952, 2, 4, in *Gospel Ideals: Selections from the Discourses of David O. McKay* (Salt Lake City, Utah: The Improvement Era, 1953), 273.

Please note that the Lord's prophet said the United States was in full "retreat from freedom" in 1952. Have conditions improved or regressed since then? Clearly, our situation is far direr than that which our grandparents tackled and disaster looms on every side. Today we are so "intoxicated with pride" that we have allowed the "destructive hordes" of the communist conspiracy to spread their paganized barbarism. Like the barbarians who sacked Rome and helped usher in the Dark Ages, the communists are extinguishing the light of Christ, the light of experience, and the light of reason, and are ushering in a new Dark Ages her in America.

Under the guise of "equality," "social justice," and other such communist notions, the nation has injected itself with deadly poison. Even in its death throes, our society pats itself on the back for its supposed "tolerance" and "egalitarianism." The soul-destroying socialism peddled by the communist conspiracy is the cause of this rampant degradation. If we do not immediately stop the bleeding, communist pagans will overthrow our society and impose a new reign of medieval barbarism of a distinctly Satanic nature.

In 1936, the people of the Church and of the United States were warned by the First Presidency of the fate they would reap if communism was not made treasonable and eradicated. On July 3, 1936, the First Presidency under President Heber J. Grant published a message in the *Improvement Era*. It read in part:

> "With great regret we learn from credible sources, governmental and others, that a few Church members are joining directly or indirectly, the Communists and are taking part in their activities. . . .

> ". . . Communism is not a political party nor a political plan under the Constitution; it is a system of government that is the opposite of our Constitutional government, and it would be necessary to destroy our government before Communism could be set up in the United States.

"Since Communism, established, would destroy our American Constitutional government, to support Communism is treasonable to our free institutions, and no patriotic American citizen may become either a Communist or supporter of Communism.

"To our Church members we say: Communism is not the United Order, and bears only the most superficial resemblance thereto; Communism is based upon intolerance and force, the United Order upon love and freedom of conscience and action; Communism involves forceful despoliation and confiscation, the United Order voluntary consecration and sacrifice.

"Furthermore, it is charged by universal report, which is not successfully contradicted or disproved, that Communism undertakes to control, if not indeed to proscribe the religious life of the people living within its jurisdiction, and that it even reaches its hand into the sanctity of the family circle itself, disrupting the normal relationship of parent and child, all in a manner unknown and unsanctioned under the Constitutional guarantees under which we in America live. Such interference would be contrary to the fundamental precepts of the Gospel and to the teachings and order of the Church. Communism being thus hostile to loyal American citizenship and incompatible with true Church membership, of necessity no loyal American citizen and no faithful Church member can be a Communist.

"We call upon all Church members completely to eschew Communism. The safety of our divinely inspired Constitutional government and the welfare of our Church imperatively demand that Communism shall have no place in America."[145]

---

[145] First Presidency Message, *Improvement Era*, July 3, 1936, http://www.josephsmithfoundation.org/reference/first-presidency-message-on-communism-1936/.

This 1936 statement was a very public salvo in the Church's long war against communism. Communism is so vile and evil that the Church has declared that *no Latter-day Saint can be a faithful member of the Lord's Church and be a communist.* Furthermore, no American is loyal to his country who supports communism. Additionally, no Saint is faithful to the Lord's revelation concerning the sacredness of the U.S. Constitution who supports communistic principles which necessarily destroy the Constitution. The Lord's servants have declared communism to be "treasonable" and have commanded all Latter-day Saints "completely to eschew" communism. They did not mince words – they wanted everyone to know the Lord's view on the matter.

The First Presidency warned that the safety of our Heaven-inspired Constitution and the welfare of the Church depend upon eradicating communism from the United States. In so doing, they added their testimony to the chorus of prophets, ancient and modern, who warned of secret combinations. Their declaration was the standard which successive presidents of the Church referenced and quoted in their condemnations of communism.

Yet, even earlier than 1936, Church leaders were warning the Saints from the pulpit. In 1952, President J. Reuben Clark, Jr. reminded the Saints of his warnings thirty years previous:

> "Thirty years ago, from this pulpit, in a public meeting, I voiced a warning against what we then knew as Bolshevism and Socialism, and what we now know as Communism. I thought I saw it coming, and it came . . . thank God for this country and for our citizenship. And there is nothing that we should not do to preserve this country, and its liberties, and its free institutions.

There is absolutely nothing we shouldn't do to preserve our Freedom. Communism is the antithesis of Freedom. President Clark described communism as:

"A system destructive of the great principle which lies behind our great plan, that utterly wipes it out and makes it as if it did not exist, the great principle of free agency."

He then gave an ominous warning of what would happen if the rapid advance of communism was not checked:

"Brethren, I do not suppose that any of you have had communistic leanings. I suppose that all of you love your country, love the Constitution, love the free institutions under which we live, love our freedoms. But if there be any, may I ask you, prayerfully and humbly, think this thing over, because if it comes here it will probably come in its full vigor and there will be a lot of vacant places among those who guide and direct, not only this government, but also this Church of ours."[146]

If I read this statement correctly, President Clark is warning that if communism ever comes in its full might to the United States, many leaders both in society and in the Church would be slaughtered.

In Nephite times, the prophets raised a continuous warning voice against the Gadianton Robbers. You will also recall that in seasons when the Nephites and Lamanites were righteous, they used every means to hunt down and destroy the Gadianton Robbers from among them. It was the righteous prophets and leaders who initiated these purges. Several examples of their inspired anti-conspiracy actions will suffice to demonstrate how seriously the threat of secret combinations has always been taken by the Lord's true sheep.

When the existence of the Gadianton sect was discovered, Helaman sent soldiers to hunt down and execute its members (Helaman 2:10). Later, the converted Lamanites "did use every means in their power to destroy them off the face of the earth" (Helaman 6:20). During his landmark tower

---

[146] President J. Reuben Clark, Jr., Conference Report, April, 1952, 80-82, http://scriptures.byu.edu/#:t248:p527.

sermon, Nephi publicly labelled the Gadiantons murderers and traitors (Helaman 7:25-28) and exposed the Nephite chief judge and his brother as Gadianton Robbers (Helaman 8:26-28). Around 12 B.C., the Nephites and Lamanites "sent an army of strong men into the wilderness and upon the mountains to search out this band of robbers, and to destroy them" (Helaman 11:28). And when the Nephites and Lamanites were besieged by an army of Gadiantons, the chief judge Lachoneus snubbed the Gadiantons' threats and commissioned Gidgiddoni to defend against their attack, which he successfully did, killing the Gadianton leader Giddianhi and hanging his successor Zemnarihah from a tree (3 Nephi 3:12; 4:14; 4:28-29). Similarly, Captain Moroni used force of arms to eradicate the traitorous and subversive king-men who were actively undermining Nephite Liberty (Alma 46 and 51).

In our day, our prophets have stood firmly against the Red Gadiantons who infest our land. They have exposed them as traitors and have refuted their lies. They have called for action – both grassroots and official – against the communist conspiracy. They have recommended that we root out the Communist Party and its subversive agents. Their witness against the evil secret combination of communism has been as firm and unrelenting as was the witness born by the ancient Nephite Freedom Fighters and prophets. Yet, by and large, members of the Church have not heeded their warnings or are oblivious of their existence. And the American People have similarly ignored them.

Not only have the Saints ignored these warnings particular, but they have ignored similar warnings in Church publications for at least a century and a half. As early as 1879, communism had been identified as the secret combination of prophecy. Its evil works were detailed and the Saints were warned.

An April 21, 1879 article in *The Latter-Day Saints' Millennial Star* written by President William Budge – at the time serving as a mission president in England – offers a startling look at the state of the earth because of the existence of the communist secret combination which was at that time coming into its own. President Budge began his piece by emphasizing that war is a sign of the times and that the nations of the world are being thrown into turmoil by secret combinations. He wrote:

> "The universal kingdom of God cannot be co-existent with the kingdoms of this world. War is set forth as a demolisher of obstacles in the way of the introduction of a peaceful reign. This warlike spirit will not be confined to nationalities. It will assume forms that will be much more pregnant with terror to the peacefully disposed than that, causing not only the downfall of weaker nations by victory being perched upon the banners of their opponents, but will make a crumbling mass of the institutions of the proudest and most powerful governments under the sun. We refer to secret combinations and societies that are silently and surely undermining the foundations of the governments of the earth. To warn the people in the nations of those destructive and murderous associations, is a portion of the message of the servants of God in this dispensation."

President Budge then quoted an 1831 revelation found in D&C 42:63-64 in which the Lord tells His people to "flee to the west, and this in consequence of that which is coming on the earth, and of secret combinations." He then identified the chief qualities of these secret combinations. Please note that nearly every infamous act he referred to was committed by the Satanic communists and their allies:

> "At the time this revelation was given, secret combinations of a murderous and communistic description were comparatively unknown in civilized nations, but since then they have increased most alarmingly on both hemispheres. The character of those combinations is well known by their outcroppings, as observable in the sanguinary, murderous history of the French commune; the destructive course of a similar element in the United States, scarce two years since, during the great railroad strikes; the Nihilistic assassinations of government officials in Russia; the

socialistic attempts at murder in Germany, and the various late attempts against monarchy, in the efforts to take the lives of several of the crowned heads of Europe. These show the objects to be the possession of gain and power, the necessity of shedding blood to obtain them being considered no obstacle. This internal strife in the bodies politic is even more threatening to national existence than conflicts ensuing from kingdom rising against kingdom. A gentleman of prominence who recently gave the subject of these secret combinations some investigatory attention, was alarmed at the discovery that, to use his own phrase, they "fairly honeycombed the nations of Europe."

From the communist-inspired French commune to the bloody, revolutionary spirit of Russia, President Budge understood that communists and socialists were the most dangerous of all secret societies. He also rightly stated that these subversive cells "honeycombed" Europe. And from Europe this Red Plague eventually migrated to America.

President Budge then turned his attention to the means of redress against secret combinations. He pointed out that the governments of Europe, lacking the truths of the Restored Gospel, were going about eliminating the problem in the wrong way. He predicted, correctly as history shows, the expansion of these secret societies and foretold the fate that awaited nations that tolerated or failed to eliminate this socialistic conspiracy. He explained:

> "The governments in which the socialistic element assumes the more dangerous aspect – Germany and Russia, seek to crush it out of existence by repressory measures, but the effect of these efforts will be the rapid increase of the institutions they are desirous of killing. A nation is an individualism. When the body of a man is attacked with a violent eruptive disease, the only safety lies in adopting means to throw the poisonous matter upon the surface of the skin. If, on the other hand, it be kept in the system, it will spread through every artery, attack and corrupt the vitals,

and mortification, dissolution and death are the inevitable results. So it is with the violent socialistic element in the nations; the poison may be smothered and kept from the surface by repressive legislation, but it is still in the body politic, vitiating its channels, knawing [sic] at the national vitals, and the doom of that government is merely a question of time. And what a doom, to be torn in fragmentary shreds by murderous mobs, united only in their aim to break down every restrictive barrier that restrains them in the gratification of their lawless desires.

"Did the nations but know of the impending ruin that is at their doors, surely they would tremble, with fearful looking forward, for even now the sword of justice hangs over them by a slender thread, liable soon to snap and let the shining blade descend upon their devoted heads.

"The fate of the nations of the world is plainly depicted in that most clear and precious record, the Book of Mormon. The existence of the numerous secret orders and societies of the present day are a standing proof of the divine authenticity of that book. They fulfill some of its most emphatic prophecies."

Truly, Moroni and other inspired men of the past saw this same group of modern Gadianton Robbers and foretold of the destruction they would bring upon mankind. They gave us "emphatic prophecies" to warn us and forewarn us of the threats to our way of life. It must have wrenched Moroni's soul to see the same group of Satan-worshipping conspirators menacing the world in our day that destroyed his own people, his friends, and his family. No doubt this painful acknowledgement inspired Moroni's "emphatic" warnings.

Ultimately, these warnings about secret combinations constitute a unique evidence for the "divine authenticity" of *The Book of Mormon*. No other book of scripture in the world discusses conspiracy in any depth. No other holy book explicitly warns of Satanic conspiracies seeking to overthrow Liberty. No other scripture details the oaths, covenants, objectives, and

216

tactics of these secret societies. Have you ever paused to drop to your knees and thank your Father in Heaven for giving you such an important and unique warning about the threats to your Freedom, faith, and family?

As a brief aside, President George Q. Cannon likewise said that the rise of secret combinations is a sign of the fulfillment of prophecy. He taught:

> "Among the many signs of the times concerning which the prophets have spoken, there are none scarcely that are of a more threatening character than the combinations of various kinds which are being formed in the land. These combinations are ominous of evil. If they go on increasing as they have done for some years past, the consequences to our nation will be of a most serious, not to say dreadful, character.

> "In Europe, a condition of feeling has arisen, among socialists, nihilists, anarchists, and people of this type, that is exceedingly threatening to the governments under which people of this description live. They are agitating, and plotting, and spreading dissatisfaction among all classes."

President Cannon noted that "thousands of these dissatisfied people" had "flocked to the United States" and had "become agitators of a dangerous character." He warned that, if not stopped, these Satanic combinations would "overthrow" the U.S. government.[147]

Proceeding with President Budge's comments, this great man next quoted from Moroni's warnings of a great secret combination in Ether 8. He said:

> "With what pointed plainness did Moroni predict the present condition of some of the Gentile nations. Although his inspired predictions were penned nearly fourteen hundred years ago, his

---

[147] President George Q. Cannon, *The Juvenile Instructor*, Vol. 25, 536, in Newquist, ed., *Prophets, Principles and National Survival*, 219-220.

statements are as clear an exposition of existing difficulties as if written at the present hour."

President Budge witnessed the unfolding of these ancient "inspired predictions" and bore his testimony of their accuracy, just as Presidents Benson, Clark, McKay, and others have in more recent times.

Further, President Budge related additional evidence of a communist secret combination at work in Europe and the world. He accurately recounted the rampant assassinations and nihilistic spirit of the conspirators. He explained that these revolutionary tactics would lead, as Moroni prophesied, to the "overthrow of every nation" harboring such subversive elements. Finally, he urged the elect to flee Europe and other besieged lands and make join the Saints in Zion. Said he:

> "One of the latest of the many murderous deeds of these secret agencies was perpetrated at St Petersburg, Russia, on the 14th of April, in the form of an attempted assassination of the Emperor Alexander. A leading paper, commenting upon this outrage, says: "The hallucination of Nihilists and Socialists in supposing that by homicidal crime they can accelerate human progress must be accounted – gross and insane as it is – one of the most serious political dangers of the times." This is true, and it is beyond the power of human agency to avert the danger. It portends the utter overthrow of every nation in which this socialistic element has gained a foothold. The prophecies foretelling the arising of this combination are receiving an unqualified and literal fulfillment, and we look with equal confidence for the effects of its existence – the utter overthrow and destruction of every country where it appears.

> "Hear it, O ye nations, and know that your doom is nigh at hand, for already the chill hand of dissolution is laid upon your institutions. Soon will your pride be laid low in the dust. Not only will there be wars, "nation against nation and kingdom against kingdom," but the peoples of the earth will be torn and rent

asunder by internal disturbances, for, as declared in the Book of Mormon, "The Lord will send a great division among the people." It will come to pass that the people of Zion will be the only people who will not be at war one with another. Zion will be the refuge to which the peace-loving in all countries will turn their eyes and direct their steps, for the time will come when "every man who will not take up his sword against his neighbor must needs flee to Zion for safety.""[148]

In 1879, President Budge could read the handwriting on the wall. He knew then that the "doom" of the nations was "nigh at hand." A century and a half later, the enemy is entrenched and occupies the positions of power throughout the world and humanity is hanging on by its fingertips.

Our choice, as explained by President David O. McKay and other great apostles of Christ, is between Freedom and slavery, right and wrong, light and darkness, truth and error, Christ and Satan. Satan operates through many channels and uses numerous disguises, but his most successful disguise yet has been the Red mask of communism. With this cunning disguise in place, the Devil has openly carried on his work of destruction – the final danse macabre in earth's sordid history.

Through the instrumentality of the high priests of communism – Weishaupt, Marx, Lenin, Trotsky, Stalin, et al – Lucifer has established a global system of tyranny infinitely more powerful and dangerous than any before it. Communism is none other than "Mystery Babylon." It has proven to be the very same scarlet Beast recorded in John's Revelation and the same great and abominable Church of Nephi's vision. Moroni foresaw this same secret combination and knew that the colossal conflict against Freedom and God's authority in the last days was driven by a modern band of Gadianton Robbers.

---

[148] President William Budge, "Secret Combinations," *The Latter-Day Saints' Millennial Star*, Vol. 41, 248-250, April 21, 1879, https://contentdm.lib.byu.edu/digital/collection/MStar/id/38679/rec/9.

Latter-day seers have likewise identified a secret combination as the greatest threat to society. Communism has been repeatedly singled out as *the* secret combination of our day – the "greatest satanical threat" to mankind. Our prophets have expressed the Lord's will that His Saints fight communism and "eschew" it as "the greatest anti-Christ power in the world today." It is the "organized paganism" that threatens our extermination unless we defeat its intrigues.

I repeat: The Lord's prophets have identified the communist conspiracy as *the* secret combination foreseen by Moroni and as *the* "greatest satanical threat" to mankind. For some 150 years, latter-day prophets have denounced communism and its socialist spawn. At what point will we, as Latter-day Saints and the elect of God, believe our inspired leaders and heed their emphatic warnings? At what point will we step forward and, armed with the power and authority of the Holy Priesthood, eradicate communism from our midst? Do we believe our prophets or don't we? Will we follow them or won't we? Everything hinges upon the fundamental question of whether God has really called prophets who declare His will for our day.

Ultimately, there is only one question we must ask ourselves: Do we believe our prophets and are we willing to follow their counsel? I, for one, believe them and sustain them will all my heart and soul. Through the Holy Ghost I know their message is accurate and true. In my imperfect way, I have made every effort to warn my fellow Saints of the "awful situation" we are in because of this secret combination, and the horrifying future that awaits us if we remain apathetic.

I end this chapter with one additional quote which sums up the attitude of the latter-day prophets toward the communist abomination. This comes from a piece written by President David O. McKay for the Church Section of the *Deseret News* on July 9, 1952. On that occasion, President McKay exclaimed:

"Communism is anti-Christ! That alone condemns it as idiotic."[149]

---

[149]President David O. McKay, *Deseret News*, July 9, 1952, 2, in *Gospel Ideals*, 10.

Chapter 6

Modern Origins of the

Communist Conspiracy

Now that we have demonstrated that a Satanic secret combination *is* among us, and that our prophets have identified this combination as the communist conspiracy, it is time to discuss the origins of communism. Communism, as an ideology, has existed since pre-earth times when Lucifer presented a communistic plan to Heavenly Father's children – a plan which was categorically rejected. Communism has existed under various names and has been espoused through the centuries by such historical figures as Plato whose proposed system of "philosopher kings" bears a striking resemblance to communism with its planned economy and centralized authority. However, more important to our discussion is communism's modern origins.

Inasmuch as our latter-day prophets have declared communism to be a Gadianton-style secret society, it should not surprise us that communism has its origins in the infamous Order of Illuminati. While our prophets have not used the term "Illuminati" to refer to the communist threat, they may as well have, for the communist movement can be traced directly back to the Order of Illuminati founded by Adam Weishaupt in 1776. As I hope to demonstrate, the terms Illuminism and communism are as interchangeable as communism and Gadiantonism.

A quick note before we begin. This chapter will give you the cliff notes and salient points of communism's recent rise. For a more in depth study of this history, I refer the reader to my book *A Century of Red*.

This conspiracy began in 1776 when the Order of Illuminati was founded in Bavaria by Adam Weishaupt. Research suggests that Weishaupt was most likely an ethnic Jew. However, his family ostensibly converted to

Catholicism. After his father's death, Weishaupt was raised by a devout Roman Catholic family. He was trained in Catholic dogma and eventually joined the Society of Jesus, better known as the Jesuit Order. In 1773, the Jesuit Order — a fierce secret combination in its own right — was temporarily disbanded by Pope Clement XIV following an international backlash against Jesuit intrigue.

In his book *Apostasy from the Divine Church*, LDS author James L. Barker gave this brief description of the Jesuits and of the reaction to their machinations:

> "The principle object of the Jesuits was the maintenance of papal authority and the overthrow of Protestantism.
>
> "They established missions in practically every country. Their complete obedience to the slightest command of their leader made of them a compact and powerful army.
>
> "They interfered in political affairs and incurred the hostility of every nation in Europe. France, Germany, Switzerland, Spain, Great Britain and other nations expelled the society from their territories.
>
> "The Jesuit movement was suppressed in many Catholic countries. Perhaps they thought there was danger to a country when a group of men, sworn to absolute obedience, blindly obeyed a foreign commander."[150]

The fact that Weishaupt was trained by the Jesuits is significant. The stamp of Jesuit discipline, underhandedness, and fanaticism left its mark on Weishaupt and can be seen in ample supply in later communist dogma and actions. Additionally, it is worth noting that the Jesuits not only established missions throughout the world, but they secretly established

---

[150] James L. Barker, *Apostasy from the Divine Church* (Salt Lake City, Utah: Bookcraft, 1984), 529.

totalitarian slave labor camps in Latin America which helped fund their intrigues elsewhere. These camps were known as "reductions."[151] It is altogether plausible that the idea of concentration camps rubbed off on Weishaupt and was handed down by his successors until Lenin and the Bolsheviks established the most ruthless system of slave labor camps in world history inside the Soviet Union.

After the Jesuit Order was disbanded, Weishaupt became a professor of Catholic canon law at Ingolstadt University in Bavaria. While there, he studied – and apparently embraced – occultism. The term occult refers to hidden or secret knowledge – the type handed down by Lucifer through secret combinations from the days of Cain. By his own admission, Weishaupt "interrogated the Cabala."[152] The Kabbalah (also spelled Cabala and Qabalah) is a body of Jewish occult mysticism dating back to ancient times. The word "cabal," a term denoting a secret faction or league, is derived from the word Kabbalah. It is no surprise, then, that Kabbalistic doctrines undergird most modern secret societies and therefore have a tremendous influence in the world.

While the corpus of Kabbalistic texts contains some scattered gems of truth, Kabbalism is, fundamentally, occultism. While the average Kabbalist may not understand the dark nature of Kabbalism, elite Kabbalists understand that their god is Lucifer. They worship him and fight against Christ. Indeed, the ranks of Kabbalism have produced numerous Jewish anti-Christs, such as Sabbatai Zevi who proclaimed himself the Messiah in 1666, and Jacob Frank who followed in Zevi's footsteps.

These bitter fruits of Kabbalism are not surprising considering the fact that Kabbalism denies the existence of our Father in Heaven and His Son Jesus Christ, and rejects the need for a Savior. In Kabbalistic thought, God

---

[151] Bill Hughes, *The Enemy Unmasked* (Eustis, Florida: Truth Triumphant, 2006), 12-13.

[152] John Robison, *Proofs of a Conspiracy*, (1798; Belmont, MA: Western Islands, reprint, 1967), 80.

is not a corporeal Being, but, rather, is an essence or force that emanates throughout the universe, is both male and female, and embraces both good *and* evil. It has in fact been the perverse teaching of several prominent Kabbalists that one must commit sin so as to comprehend the full spectrum of godliness. This smacks of Korihor's teachings as recorded in the thirtieth chapter of Alma.

As sad as it is to recount, modern Judaism is largely a product of Kabbalistic and Talmudic beliefs, as opposed to the true teachings of their forefathers found in the Old Testament. Anciently, the Jewish rabbis, Pharisees, and Sadducees adopted Kabbalism and imported this false dogma from Babylon when the Israelites returned from captivity. This is why the Talmud is more properly referred to as the Babylonian Talmud. The Talmud today is the most important book from which rabbis learn their craft. Additionally, many apostate and pagan traditions were carried out of Egypt during the Exodus.

So entrenched was this occult ideology in ancient Israel that LDS researcher Ken Bowers has suggested – in his superb book *Hiding in Plain Sight* – that Kabbalism "may be the oldest secret society in existence," and that it was likely adherents of the Kabbalah who conspired to murder Jesus Christ while He dwelt in the flesh.[153] To be sure, the Lord referred to His murderers as "hypocrites," "fools," "blind guides," "serpents," and a "generation of vipers" whose teachings would make a man who believed them a "child of hell" (Matthew 23:14-37). The Apostle John likewise referred to these types of apostates, both Jew and Gentile, as constituting the "synagogue of Satan" (Revelation 2:9; 3:9). Both Old and New Testaments are filled with denunciations of the pagan, occult elements among the Jewish people.

On May 1, 1776 – an ancient pagan, Wiccan, and Satanist holiday, not coincidentally celebrated by the communists as their holy day – Adam

---

[153] Ken Bowers, *Hiding in Plain Sight: Unmasking the Secret Combinations of the Last Days* (Springville, Utah: Bonneville Books, 2010), 193.

Weishaupt founded the Order of Illuminati. Weishaupt's clique declared war against the entire world and sought to dethrone God. Weishaupt's special enemy was religion – and Christianity in particular. As did his later successors Marx, Lenin, and Stalin, he swore to destroy all organized religion and "liberate" mankind from false superstitions. His Illuminati agents thus became the vanguard in Satan's war against Christ.

Latter-day Saint author J.R. Ledkins wrote of the Illuminati in a booklet on secret combinations. He observed:

> "The Illuminati is literally the secret combination warned of throughout the pages of the Book of Mormon. . . .
>
> ". . . The latter day manifestation of the secret combination, the whore of all the earth, the beast, the church of the devil, or whatever name is used, is in fact the Illuminati."[154]

If the description of the Illuminati fits that of the "church of the devil," and we know that communism is the church of the Devil, then Illuminism and communism must be one and the same. Later in the booklet, Ledkins explained the aims of this Satanic cabal:

> "The objective of the Illuminati is to establish a one world government with Lucifer as its prince. Members of the Illuminati have literally sworn an oath to dethrone the Christ and to replace Christianity with pure Satanism. . . .
>
> "The leaders of the Illuminati . . . are a small but very powerful group of international bankers. They have induced others into their order to include educationalists, economists, etc. These men have accepted the Luciferian doctrine of Adam Weishaupt."[155]

---

[154] J.R. Ledkins, *Wherefore the Lord Commandeth You* (1993), 15.

[155] Ledkins, *Wherefore the Lord Commandeth You*, 41.

Lucifer's pre-earth goal was to exalt himself above the Father and steal His crown. He wanted to be worshipped. After his rebellion, Satan retained the same selfish desires. It is still his object to be worshipped and to have dominion over all things.

In his delirious tantrum before Moses, the Adversary "cried with a loud voice, and ranted upon the earth, and commanded, saying: I am the Only Begotten, worship me" (Moses 1:19). It is no surprise, then, that the object of Satan's secret combinations – apart from seizing worldly power – is to install Lucifer as god over the earth. Through his chosen illumined communists, his Red Gadiantons, Satan works to deify himself and popularize his dark deeds.

Author Henry Makow, in his hit book *Illuminati: The Cult that Hijacked the World*, has also written of the Illuminati's mission:

> "The essence of political struggle is actually spiritual, a cosmic battle between God (Good) and Satan (Evil) for the soul of man.
>
> "The struggle is between an international financial elite dedicated to Satan led by the Illuminati, and the remnants of humanity that still uphold God's Plan.
>
> ". . . This occult elite creates and controls both sides of every conflict in order to obscure and at the same time advance its long-term agenda.
>
> "The elite plan is to remake the planet as its private neo feudal preserve. This involved the reduction of the world's population through plague, catastrophe or war; mind control/breeding of the survivors as serfs; and the elevation of Lucifer as god. . . .
>
> "The "Illuminati" sounds fantastic but it is NOT a chimera. Hidden within Freemasonry, it is the Church of Satan. Its membership was known; its premises were raided. Plans and correspondence were seized and published. At formal inquiries, defectors testified to the grave danger. It was suppressed but went underground. It has

since grown so powerful that it has literally defined the modern age (under the guise of "progress," "reform" and "revolution") and now threatens the future of humanity. . . .

"The term "Illuminati" means "enlightened ones" and refers to Lucifer, the "light bringer." . . . .

""Do as thou wilt" (i.e. "tolerance") was the Freemason-Illuminati motto. The Illuminati will define reality, not God or nature. Illuminism or "humanism" is a secular religion and a transition to Satanism. The decline of public decency makes this increasingly apparent. Look for the world to increasingly resemble the game "Grand Theft Auto" or a Hollywood horror or disaster movie.

"Whether it's a plant, a dog or a child, given a little nourishment and love, each will flourish according to an innate design. The Illuminati wishes to unplug us from this inherent design by promoting dysfunction in such guises as "sexual liberation" and "equality.""[156]

Using shining slogans like "equality," "rights," "tolerance," and "liberation," the conspirators have instigated massive cultural rot and political "reform." This subversion falls under the umbrella term "cultural revolution." It is a total transformation of American values, morals, norms, attitude, and behavior; in other words, culture. The Luciferian doctrine of Illuminism – the communist counterculture that reared its ugly head during the 1960s – is being incrementally substituted for the former reign of Christian Americanism that brought our society so much prosperity, peace, hope, and Freedom.

Elsewhere in his book, Makow explained that this very Illuminati created communism:

---

[156] Henry Makow, *Illuminati: The Cult that Hijacked the World* (Winnipeg, Canada: Silas Green, 2011), 81-82.

"The Illuminati bankers created Communism to harness the working class to their program of a comprehensive world dictatorship (now known as "globalization.") The Illuminati and Communists are Masonic secret societies that celebrate the same anniversary, May 1, 1776 and share the same Satanic symbols. . . .

"Communism is a Satanic movement devoted to human degradation and enslavement, not public ownership and social justice. . . .

"Communism and the New World Order is basically monopoly capitalism taken to its logical outcome. Government is the ultimate monopoly. The Illuminati bankers despise capitalism because it involves competition and market forces. It allows other people the opportunity to prosper and be independent. Monopoly or state capitalism allows the bankers to own everything and everyone. Of course, this is disguised as "public ownership" but they control the government, its wealth and its security apparatus. . . .

"Communism is nothing but a sugar-coated goon squad for the Illuminati bankers."[157]

Through communism, the riches, governments, and manpower of the earth have been mobilized by the secret combinations with the aim of establishing an occult world order led directly by Lucifer. The Illuminati/communists are Satan's shock troops in bringing about his global dictatorship.

We have previously established that communism is a Satanic ideology and that the prophets have identified the communist conspiracy as *the* secret combination of Moroni's prophecy. We have now given an overview of the Illuminati. By further reviewing the nature, goals, tactics, and history of the Illuminati, we can discern that it is one and the same conspiracy as

---

[157] Makow, *Illuminati*, 141-143.

the communist conspiracy; the forerunner to the global leviathan making war against God and His Church.

Illuminati founder Adam Weishaupt harnessed his agents to not only destroy faith wherever it was found, but to destroy the very fabric of society. Specifically, Weishaupt sought to breakdown the traditional family unit by promoting what he termed the "emancipation" of women, of which more will be said later. He vowed to overthrow the governments of the earth and to install his Order in their place. He envisioned a centralized world government controlled by Illuminists. This global government would abolish private property, redistribute wealth, and promote communist-style social justice. The Illuminati's methods for achieving these objectives were blackmail, deceit, murder, organized criminal activity, and violent revolution.

I trust that the reader notices the stunning similarities between the Illuminati's goals and tactics and what we have learned thus far about the ancient Gadiantons and modern communists. It is *not* a coincidence that the comparisons are so precise.

Furthermore, it not a coincidence that at the very time Weishaupt and his co-conspirators founded the Illuminati and set into motion their plan for world revolution, the American Founding Fathers were convened in Philadelphia and Thomas Jefferson was preparing to write the Declaration of Independence. Satan knew the Lord's design to establish the United States as a free nation under a constitutional government and, thus, he created a counterfeit system of governance across the ocean in apostate Europe at the exact same time.

Weishaupt patterned the Illuminati off of two major groups: The Jesuits and the Freemasons. From the Jesuits, Weishaupt appropriated a strict hierarchical structure, rigidly enforced discipline and obedience, and a penchant for craftiness and intrigue. This structure was wrapped in Masonic language and adopted numerous Masonic rituals, code words, oaths, handshakes, signs, titles, and values. These oaths and rituals – as did the covenants administered by Cain, Gadianton, Akish, and others –

kept Illuminati adepts in line. And an internal network of spies closely monitored all participants within the Order.

Before proceeding, a brief aside may be beneficial. One group of conspiracy researchers believes the Jesuits rule the world and that the Catholic Church is that Mystery Babylon spoken of by John. They believe the Illuminati is a Jesuit front. However, this view is not supported by the evidence, nor by the declarations of our prophets already cited. Though Weishaupt had formerly been a Jesuit and learned their ways, he developed a seething hatred for the Jesuits and Catholicism. Weishaupt went so far as to ban Jesuits from his Order and told his co-conspirators to avoid Jesuits "like the plague."[158]

Weishaupt later boasted that his Illuminists had ousted "all" Jesuit professors from Ingolstadt University.[159] And another time he wrote with reference to Jesuits:

> "What these men have done for altars and empires, why should I not do against altars and empires? By the attraction of mysteries, of legends, of adepts, why should I not destroy in the dark what they erect in the light of day?"[160]

Weishaupt began making good on his threat against the Catholic Church during the French Revolution – a revolution inspired by the Jacobin Clubs which were created as Illuminati fronts. Operating through fronts is a deceptive sleight of hand the communists have employed with stunning success. During the melee in France, Illuminati agents abolished church marriage, outlawed tithing, nationalized the Catholic Church's property, and forced priests to swear an oath of allegiance to the new secular state

---

[158] Nesta H. Webster, *World Revolution: The Plot Against Civilisation* (1921; Palmdale, CA: Omni Publishing, 1994, reprint), 26.

[159] Nesta H. Webster, *Secret Societies and Subversive Movements* (London: 1924; Buffalo, New York: Eworld Inc., reprint), 219.

[160] A. Ralph Epperson, *The New World Order* (Tucson, Arizona: Publius Press, 1990), 110.

constitution.[161] Simply, the Illuminati's words *and* actions demonstrate genuine antipathy towards the Jesuits and the Catholic Church. And their later communist progeny showed at least an equal level of hatred for Catholicism and have worked hard to infiltrate and subvert the Catholic Church from within.

One of the most prominent writers who has exposed the Jesuits is the Catholic Father Malachi Martin. His best work on the subject is *The Jesuits: The Society of Jesus and the Betrayal of the Roman Catholic Church*. It is intriguing that the first chapter of Martin's book is devoted to exposing the communist takeover of the Jesuit Order. For instance, Martin wrote:

> "[T]he brute fact is that many Jesuits wish to see a radical change in the democratic capitalism of the West, in favor of a socialism that seems inevitably to come up smelling just like totalitarian Communism. . . .

> "Though the movement has been global since its inception, it was above all in Latin America that the strange alliance between Jesuits and Marxists gathered its first practical momentum. It was there that this new Jesuit mission, entailing as it does nothing less than the transformation of the sociopolitical face of the West . . . scores of Jesuits began to work with the passion and zeal that has always been so typical of them, for the success of the Sandinocommunists in Nicaragua; and, when the Sandinistas took power, those same Jesuits entered crucial posts in the central government, and attracted others to join at various regional levels. In other Central American countries, meanwhile, Jesuits not only participated in guerrilla training of Marxist cadres, but some became guerrilla fighters themselves. . . .

---

[161] James B. Collins, *The Ancien Régime and the French Revolution* (Canada: Thomson Learning, Inc., 2002), 109-112.

"The fact of life for Jesuits now is that our bipolar world spins inexorably around Soviet Marxist-Leninism and Western-style capitalism. The only contest that seems to matter for the Society of Jesus in this last quarter of the twentieth century is the one between those two spheres of influence. And the fact is that though the Society itself is not officially Marxist, individual Jesuits who were and are self-proclaimed Marxists . . . are not for that reason expelled from the Society or censured or silenced. Rather, the greatest pains are taken to protect them from attack. So blatant has this element become that not long ago, when Pope John Paul II met an Indian Jesuit who, as he found, was not a Marxist, he exclaimed in surprise, "So you're not all Marxists!""[162]

This observation just goes to show how thoroughly successful Weishaupt and his communist successors have been in infiltrating and distorting the Catholic Church they so hated. When you read of modern Jesuit intrigues, and there are many, know that the Jesuit Order has been taken captive by the communists who have infiltrated. From Father Martin to Bella Dodd to Manning Johnson, researchers and ex-communists alike have detailed this massive communist infiltration of the Catholic Church. The entire Catholic Church is now at the mercy of a hierarchy full of communist priests and cardinals, including Pope Francis who is not only a Jesuit, but an all-but-avowed communist who openly preaches communist-inspired Liberation Theology. But all of this is tangential.

In 1782, an immensely important event happened in the history of the Illuminati conspiracy. In that year, a large conference of Freemasons was convened in Wilhelmsbad, Germany at the behest of Illuminati agents within Freemasonry's ranks. This has become known as the Wilhelmsbad Congress. It was at this Congress that Weishaupt's Illuminati enlisted certain sects of Freemasons to their cause. As oath-bound secret societies, Masonic lodges would be the perfect incubators for worldwide

---

[162] Father Malachi Martin, *The Jesuits: The Society of Jesus and the Betrayal of the Roman Catholic Church* (New York: Simon and Schuster, 1987), 16-17, 21.

subversive activity. In the words of researcher George Dillon, Weishaupt's plan was "to reach all humanity by means of Masonry." Furthermore:

> "He wanted a kind of General Council of the Masonry extended at the time throughout the earth to be called together; and he hoped that, by adroitly manipulating the representatives whom he knew would be sent to it by the lodges of every nationality of Masons, his own Illuminism might be adopted as a kind of high, arch, or hidden, Masonry, throughout its entire extent."[163]

The Congress convened in secret and the delegates were sworn to secrecy, so very little information has come out of the meetings themselves. However, the Illuminati plan evidently worked and various Masonic groups were brought under Illuminati leadership. One attendee, the Comte de Virieu, was thoroughly disturbed by what he heard and gave us this intriguing warning:

> "The conspiracy which is being woven is so well thought out that It will be, so to speak, impossible for the Monarchy and the Church to escape from it."[164]

Virieu was so shaken by this Freemasonic/Illuminati "conspiracy" – of which he had firsthand knowledge – that he subsequently abandoned Freemasonry and became a devout Catholic.

Masonry has always been looked upon as a disguise with which to hide the true identity of the conspirators. Weishaupt wrote:

> "[W]e shall have a masonic lodge of our own . . . we shall regard this as our nursery garden . . . to some of these Masons we shall not at once reveal that we have something more than the Masons

---

[163] George F. Dillon, *Grand Orient Freemasonry As the Secret Power Behind Communism* (London: Britons Publishing Company, 1965), 59.

[164] Webster, *World Revolution: The Plot Against Civilisation*, 19; and Dillon, *Grand Orient Freemasonry As the Secret Power Behind Communism*, 60.

have . . . at every opportunity we shall cover ourselves with this . . . All those who are not suited to the work shall remain in the masonic Lodge and advance in that without knowing anything of the further system."[165]

In agreement with his predecessor, the communist revolutionary and Satanist Mikhail Bakunin said simply that Freemasonry will "serve as a mask" for the cabal.[166] Behind the Masonic mask sat a seething den of darkness and death that threatened to consume the world.

In his book *My Life*, Leon Trotsky – second in command during the Bolshevik coup in Russia – acknowledged his deep interest in and study of Freemasonry and described its revolutionary spirit. He wrote:

> "In the eighteenth century, freemasonry became expressive of a militant policy of enlightenment, as in the case of the Illuminati, who were the forerunners of revolution; on its left, it culminated in the Carbonari."[167]

Even Trotsky recognized that the Order of Illuminati was the forerunner of modern revolution – the spark that lit the blaze. Through his study of Freemasonry, Trotsky became acquainted with Marxism. His intensive study of Freemasonry was his introduction to the concepts and ideas of revolution. Freemasonry was for Trotsky what Weishaupt had intended – a "nursery garden" where revolutionaries could be grown, groomed, and selected for advancement.

Trotsky thereafter joined the "enlightened" revolutionary tradition and never looked back. He rose to nearly the highest ranks of the conspiracy. Certain evidence suggests that apart from his communist activities,

---

[165] Webster, *Secret Societies and Subversive Movements*, 209-210.

[166] Webster, *Secret Societies and Subversive Movements*, 268.

[167] Leon Trotsky, *My Life* (1930), 92. https://www.marxists.org/archive/trotsky/1930/mylife/1930-lif.pdf.

Trotsky also joined one or more Freemasonic lodge, including the fanatical and powerful Jewish Masonic order known as B'nai B'rith.[168]

At this same Wilhelmsbad Congress mentioned above, another significant merger took place. Not only did the Illuminati successfully enlist a number of Freemasons to their cause, but they also merged with the lords of high finance – the international bankers. Many of these bankers were Jewish. The more revolutionary minded Jews developed their own Masonic orders whose desires meshed nicely with Weishaupt's. It appears that the Rothschilds – the wealthiest and most powerful dynastic family in the world – joined forces with Weishaupt at this conference, though other researchers suggest Weishaupt had been bankrolled from the beginning by the Rothschilds. At any rate, what came out of the Wilhelmsbad Congress was an amalgam of evil – a fusion of Masons, Illuminists, and Jewish conspirators.

With the Illuminati contributing the plan and organization, the Rothschilds and Jewish sects providing the funds and foot soldiers, and the Masons contributing lodges and oath-bound secret meetings wherein to recruit members and hide in plain sight, this Satanic cabal spread rapidly. Its agents were soon in the United States as well as all the major nations of Europe. So entrenched was this secret society that when the Bavarian government discovered its existence in 1784 and attempted to crush them over the following two years, the conspirators were little affected and simply went underground or migrated to other countries and carried on their work.

The Illuminati spread far and wide, reaching the United States fairly early. Though mainstream "historians" allege that the Order went extinct by 1786, the reality is otherwise.

---

[168] Juri Lina, *Under the Sign of the Scorpion* (2002), chapter 5, https://ia800300.us.archive.org/35/items/UnderTheSignOfTheScorpion/sign_scorpi on.pdf.

On Independence Day 1798, the president of Yale University,[169] Timothy Dwight, gave a powerful and enlightening speech in which he warned of the Illuminati's influence in America and the world. He highlighted their damnable doctrines, demonstrated Illuminism's spread around the globe, and warned that the Illuminati sought the destruction of Christianity, the misery of mankind, and the overthrow of America. I quote from this patriot at length:

> "This order is professedly a higher order of Masons, originated by [Weishaupt], and grafted on ancient Masonic institutions. The secresy, solemnity, mysticism, and correspondence of Masonry, were in this new order preserved and enhanced; while the ardour of innovation, the impatience of civil and moral restraints, and the aims against government, morals, and religion, were elevated, expanded, and rendered more systematical, malignant, and daring.

> "In the societies of Illuminati doctrines were taught, which strike at the root of all human happiness and virtue; and every such doctrine was either expressly or implicitly involved in their system.

> "The being of God was denied and ridiculed.

> "Government was asserted to be a curse, and authority a mere usurpation.

> "Civil society was declared to be the only apostasy of man.

---

[169] Interestingly enough, Yale University was the birthplace of the Order of Skull and Bones (and offshoot societies such as Wolf's Head), often simply called "the Order." Skull and Bones is most likely an Illuminati branch that was transplanted from Germany by its founders in 1832. The Order boasts an elite membership, including such figures as President George H.W. Bush, President George W. Bush, President William Howard Taft, Senator John F. Kerry, Secretary of State W. Averell Harriman, William F. Buckley, Jr., current Secretary of the Treasury Steven Mnuchin, and hundreds more. For information on this sinister secret society, read Antony C. Sutton's book *America's Secret Establishment: The Order of Skull and Bones*.

"The possession of property was pronounced to be robbery.

"Chastity and natural affection were declared to be nothing more than groundless prejudices.

"Adultery, assassination, poisoning, and other crimes of the like infernal nature, were taught as lawful, and even as virtuous actions.

"To crown such a system of falshood and horror all means were declared to be lawful, provided the end was good.

"In this last doctrine men are not only loosed from every bond, and from every duty; but from every inducement to perform any thing which is good, and, abstain from any thing which is evil; and are set upon each other, like a company of hellhounds to worry, rend, and destroy. Of the goodness of the end every man is to judge for himself; and most men, and all men who resemble the Illuminati, will pronounce every end to be good, which will gratify their inclinations. The great and good ends proposed by the Illuminati, as the ultimate objects of their union, are the overthrow of religion, government, and human society civil and domestic. These they pronounce to be so good, that murder, butchery, and war, however extended and dreadful, are declared by them to be completely justifiable, if necessary for these great purposes. . . .

"Multitudes of the Germans, notwithstanding the gravity, steadiness, and sobriety of their national character, have become either partial or entire converts to these wretched doctrines; numerous societies have been established among them; the public faith and morals have been unhinged; and the political and religious affairs of that empire have assumed an aspect, which forebodes its total ruin. In France, also, Illuminatism has been eagerly and extensively adopted; and those men, who have had, successively, the chief direction of the public affairs of that country, have been members of this society. Societies have also been erected in Switzerland and Italy, and have contributed probably to the success of the French, and to the overthrow of religion and government, in those countries. . . .

"Nor have England and Scotland escaped the contagion. Several societies have been erected in both of those countries. Nay in the private papers, seized in the custody of the leading members in Germany, several such societies are recorded as having been erected in America, before the year 1786.

"It is a remarkable fact, that a large proportion of the sentiments, here stated, have been publicly avowed and applauded in the French legislature. The being and providence of God have been repeatedly denied and ridiculed. Christ has been mocked with the grossest insult. Death, by a solemn legislative decree has been declared to be an eternal sleep. Marriage has been degraded to a farce, and the community, by the law of divorce, invited to universal prostitution. In the school of public instruction atheism is professedly taught; and at an audience before the legislature, Nov. 30, 1793, the head scholar declared, that he and his schoolfellows detested a God; a declaration received by the members with unbounded applause, and rewarded with the fraternal kiss of the president, and with the honors of the sitting. . . .

"Where religion prevails, their system cannot succeed. Where religion prevails, Illuminatism cannot make disciples, a French directory cannot govern, a nation cannot be made slaves, nor villains, nor atheists, nor beasts. To destroy us, therefore, in this dreadful sense, our enemies must first destroy our Sabbath, and seduce us from the house of God. . . .

". . . Shall we, my brethren, become partakers of these sins? Shall we introduce them into our government, our schools, our families? Shall our sons become the disciples of Voltaire, and the dragoons of Marat; or our daughters the concubines of the Illuminati?

"Some of my audience may perhaps say, "We do not believe such crimes to have existed." The people of Jerusalem did not believe, that they were in danger, until the Chaldeans surrounded their walls. The people of Laish were secure, when the children of Dan lay in ambush around their city. There are in every place, and in every age, persons "who are settled upon their lees," who take pride in disbelief, and "who say in their heart, the Lord will not do good, neither will he do evil." Some persons disbelieve through ignorance; some choose not to be informed; and some determine not to be convinced. The two last classes cannot be persuaded. The first may, perhaps, be at least alarmed, when they are told, that the evidence of all this, and much more, is complete, that it has been produced to the public, and may with a little pains-taking be known by themselves."[170]

Yes, every person may comprehend the truth of these things for himself "with a little pains-taking." Truth frankly and happily reveals itself to a person who is sincere and who is willing to act upon the knowledge. "Ask, and it shall be given you; seek, and ye shall find; knock, and it shall be opened unto you" (Matthew 7:7).

The truth is that the Order of Illuminati did *not* die, but spread across oceans and continents. Within two decades of its creation, it had fomented the French Revolution, took control of Germany, and entrenched itself in Italy, Switzerland, England, the United States, and elsewhere. Timothy Dwight understood this clear back in 1798.

Dwight knew that the Illuminati was an anti-Christ conspiracy. He understood that their doctrines "strike at the root of all human happiness

---

[170] Timothy Dwight, "The Duty of Americans, at the Present Crisis," address, July 4, 1798, http://consource.org/document/the-duty-of-americans-at-the-present-crisis-by-timothy-dwight-1798-7-4/.

and virtue." He recognized their handiwork in the French Revolution. He saw that if their machinations were not opposed manfully, America's sons would partake in the conspiracy's sins and her daughters would become its concubines. Strong imagery, to be sure; but necessary in order to convey the magnitude of this occult conspiracy against mankind.

In 1798, no less a man than George Washington, the Father of America, also acknowledged the Illuminati's existence and their attempts to subvert the United States. In a letter, George Washington told G.W. Snyder:

> "It was not my intention to doubt that, the Doctrines of the Iluminati, and principles of Jacobinism had not spread in the United States. On the contrary, no one is more fully satisfied of this fact than I am.

> "The idea I meant to convey, was, that I did not believe that the *Lodges* of Free Masons in *this* Country had, as *Societies,* endeavoured to propagate the diabolical tenets of the first, or the pernicious principles of the latter (if they are susceptible of seperation). That Individuals of them may have done it, and that the *founder,* or *instrument* employed to found, the Democratic Societies in the United States, may have had these objects—and actually had a seperation of the *People* from their *Government* in view, is too evident to be questioned."[171]

If the Illuminati's machinations here in America were "too evident to be questioned" in 1798, why do we still question them in 2018? George Washington was a sober man; he was no "conspiracy theorist." Yet, he was fully aware of the Illuminati's "diabolical" plan to overthrow the U.S. government. He was even aware that certain Freemasons and others posing as "democrats" were involved in the intrigues. If General

---

[171] George Washington to G.W. Snyder, October 24, 1798.

Washington was so convinced of these facts, shouldn't we also be persuaded to believe rather than doubt their veracity?

Though the Illuminati spread everywhere, France became the conspiracy's major hub. It was there that Illumined Freemasons, as they have been dubbed by researchers, created the Jacobin Clubs and fomented the French Revolution. The red flag of revolution was hoisted in France as the conspirators overthrew the government and erected their own radical, communistic government in its place. Unlike the American Revolution, this was not a grassroots uprising. Rather, it was a completely contrived coup by a group of largely foreign gangsters bound together by secret oaths. No sooner did the Jacobins take control than blood flowed in the streets of Paris and the war against Christ began afresh.

The French Revolution was little more than a test run for the Bolshevik putsch in 1917. Its orgy of violence, its assault on Christianity, and its theft of property can be viewed as Bolshevism 101. Numerous writers have acknowledged the links between this first Illuminati revolution in France and the later uprising in Russia. I cite just two.

In the 1930s, German writer Karl Ganzer observed:

> "If liberalism can be described as the socially established form of the French Revolutionary trend, then Marxism is a radicalized variety, strongly rooted in the brutality of that revolution. Its basic premise, class warfare, is an intellectual transformation of the French reign of terror into a sociological concept."[172]

A more prominent figure, Winston Churchill, also noted the parallels between the Illuminati, the shadowy groups who launched the French Revolution, and those who carried out the 1917 coup in St. Petersburg. In 1920, before he sold his soul to the Zionist wing of the same conspiracy, he wrote this frank observation in a newspaper article titled "Zionism versus Bolshevism":

---

[172] Tedor, *Hitler's Revolution*, 23.

"From the days of Spartacus-Weishaupt to those of Karl Marx, and down to Trotsky (Russia), Bela Kun (Hungary), Rosa Luxembourg (Germany), and Emma Goldman (United States), this world-wide conspiracy for the overthrow of civilization and for the reconstitution of society on the basis of arrested development, of envious malevolence, and impossible equality, has been steadily growing. It played, as a modern writer, Mrs. [Nesta] Webster, has so ably shown, a definitely recognizable part in the tragedy of the French Revolution. It has been the mainspring of every subversive movement during the Nineteenth Century; and now at last this band of extraordinary personalities from the underworld of the great cities of Europe and America have gripped the Russian people by the hair of their heads and have become practically the undisputed masters of that enormous empire."[173]

In this powerful paragraph, Churchill links Adam Weishaupt with the French Revolution and with later communist kingpins such as Karl Marx and Leon Trotsky. He identified the French Revolution, the upheavals across Europe in the 1800s, the Bolshevik coup in Russia, and other international subversive undertakings as the handiwork of the same clique of underworld conspirators. If Winston Churchill so plainly saw these connections in 1920, how is it that the average person cannot grasp this truth nearly 100 years later in the internet age of the 21st Century?

For Latter-day Saints, the French Revolution should sound strikingly familiar. Jaredite secret combinations behaved in remarkably similar ways as they led coup after coup, overthrowing king after king, and leaving a trail of blood and debauchery in their wake. Gadianton seizure of power during certain periods of Nephite history also resembled this modern "revolution" in France and subsequent aggression by the communists in other lands.

---

[173] Winston Churchill, "Zionism versus Bolshevism: A Struggle for the Soul of the Jewish People," *Illustrated Sunday Herald*, February 8, 1920, 5, accessed May 15, 2018, http://www.fpp.co.uk/bookchapters/WSC/WSCwrote1920.html.

In each case, modern and ancient, the struggle was sparked by a Satanic secret society intent on installing itself as the ruling authority. In each case, laws were altered and the government subverted. In every instance, blood was shed. And, in each of these tragic events, Christians were targeted for persecution.

The uncanny resemblances do not end there, however. Just as the Gadianton Robbers suffered an initial setback and went underground during Helaman's rule, the Illuminati conspiracy faltered in France after initial successes and the society went underground. It will be recalled that, while underground, the Gadianton Order infiltrated both the Nephites and the Lamanites and carried on their criminal activity in silence.

Similarly, while underground, the Illuminati shed its skins and reemerged under new names as a series of unions, leagues, and organizations all across Europe. These organizations worked hard to win converts to their cause, to entrench themselves in positions of power, and to marshal their forces for a future attempt at seizing power in Europe.

Weishaupt had previously instructed his followers to never use the society's real name, but to always use a fake name to deflect unwanted attention and deceive the unsuspecting public. Illuminists were instructed to infiltrate preexisting organizations and use them as a cover. Weishaupt coached his co-conspirators thus:

> "The great strength of our Order lies in its concealment; let it never appear in any place in its own name, but always covered by another name, and another occupation. None is fitter than the three lower degrees of Free Masonry; the public is accustomed to it, expects little from it, and therefore takes little notice of it. Next to this, the form of a learned or literary society is best suited to our purpose, and had Free Masonry not existed, this cover would have been employed; and it may be much more than a cover, it may be a powerful engine in our hands. By establishing reading societies, and subscription libraries, and taking these under our

> direction, and supplying them through our labours, we may turn the public mind which way we will."[174]

In accordance with Weishaupt's diabolically clever strategy, the conspirators emerged under new names after the French Revolution. In Germany, the German Union was born, followed later by the Tugendbund, or League of Virtue. In Italy, Giuseppe Mazzini – a leader of the powerful Masonic Carbonari faction – created the mafia and carried forward the Illuminati's agenda of destroying the Catholic Church. In France, the League of Outlaws was created. By 1836, this League split into two. The more radical and violent faction renamed themselves the League of the Just and removed to England.

As they grew in strength, the League of the Just prepared to take Europe by storm as its Illuminati predecessor attempted in France in 1789. In 1847, the League recruited an exiled Jewish German revolutionary and Satanist using the alias Karl Marx. Marx was given the task of writing a constitution for the League. This document was to announce to the world the League's principles and objectives. About the time of publication, the League rebranded itself the Communist League. Therefore, Marx's finished product was given the title *The Communist Manifesto* when it was published in February 1848 by the Communist League.

Friedrich Engels, coauthor with Marx of the *Manifesto*, admitted in the preface to the 1888 English edition of the document that the communist movement was "unavoidably a secret society." As we have seen, that secret society was the League of the Just, and that the League derived from the League of Outlaws which in turn stemmed back to the revolutionary front groups founded by the underground network of Illuminati conspirators and their Masonic and Jewish allies.

Elder Hans Verlan Andersen made this remark about the intriguing origin of the communist movement:

---

[174] John Robison, *Proofs of a Conspiracy* (1798; Boston, MA: The Americanist Classics, 1967), 112.

"The preface to the Manifesto admits that the Communist League commenced as a "secret society" which is only to be expected in view of the fact that this has always been Satan's method of operation . . . Satan's combinations of the past had one unvarying aim which took precedence over all others – seizure of the control of government. The Manifesto announces that purpose in these words:

""The Immediate aim of the Communists is . . . conquest of political power.""[175]

As the earlier chapters of this book make clear, Satan inevitably works through secret societies. The Lord's prophets have at all times condemned secret societies. The latter-day Church has consistently warned its members to avoid joining secret societies and fraternities. As worthy as the intentions of some of them may be, they are liable to be hijacked, infiltrated, or misdirected over time. And, what's more, they steal away the talents, efforts, and time of people who could otherwise devote such service to the Church and to the building up of God's Kingdom.

On October 6, 1865, Presidents John Taylor and George Q. Cannon of the First Presidency cautioned the Saints about secret societies in these words:

"A great number of secret societies are being formed with which we cannot affiliate. Such organizations are generally inimical to law, to good order, and in many instances subversive of the rights of man. We cannot amalgamate with them. They are very distinctly spoken against in the Book of Mormon, as among the calamities which should afflict the people."[176]

---

[175] Andersen, *The Great and Abominable Church of the Devil*, 109.

[176] First Presidency epistle, October 6, 186, in James R. Clark, *Messages of the First Presidency*, Volume 3 (Salt Lake City, Utah: Bookcraft, Inc., 1966), 29-30.

While each organization should be taken on its individual merits, the general rule of thumb is to *avoid secret societies*. Indeed, one of our temple recommend questions asks the individual whether he supports or affiliates with any group whose teachings are not in harmony with Church doctrine. If we belong to secret societies, odds are we cannot honestly answer that question in the negative.

Moroni taught that "the Lord worketh not in secret combinations" (Ether 8:19). Any secret society should be immediately suspect in our eyes; yes, even Freemasonry, despite the fact that some early Church leaders belonged to Masonic lodges.[177] At any rate, one thing is absolutely certain – the communist secret combination is of Satan and has been a calamity that has afflicted the peoples of the earth.

In his book *Secret Combinations Today*, Robert E. Hales described Satan's latter-day secret society and summarized the consequences *The Communist Manifesto* has had for mankind:

> "To blind, deceive and captivate those in other parts of the world, Satan employed the on-going work of the secret combinations. Through instruments responsive to his teachings, Satan

---

[177] I frequently encounter Latter-day Saints who find nothing wrong with Freemasonry – even considering it a wonderful and benign fraternity – simply because the Prophet Joseph Smith and other early Church leaders were Masons. It is not the topic of this book, so I will not embark on a lengthy discussion of why this rationalization is flawed, historically-nearsighted, and dangerous. Instead, I will simply say that the Prophet Joseph Smith considered Masonry an apostate version of the ancient temple ceremony. In his eyes, introducing Masonry in Nauvoo was a way to ease his fellow Latter-day Saints into the coming temple endowment – an endowment which had already been largely revealed to the Prophet *before* he ever stepped foot inside a Masonic lodge. If the rituals and dogma of Masonry are apostate and incomplete versions of our temple endowment, as they clearly are, then why would we who have the fullness waste our time with them? Nothing can be gained from associating with Freemasonry. While the average Mason is no doubt a good person, Masonry has been, and is being, used by its leaders to further an evil, anti-Christian, ecumenical, occult agenda that is politically anathema to everything true Latter-day Saints hold dear. Avoid association with Freemasonry at all costs. In the "Recommended Reading" section in the back of this book, you will find a number of titles dealing with Freemasonry that will give you a clearer picture regarding its apostate beliefs and practices.

influenced the creation of an organization with teachings and philosophies in direct opposition to the teachings of Christ. He structured this organization for the purpose of binding the souls of men. This organization spawned a new political order and found its most successful exposure through a document titled *The Communist Manifesto. . . .*

". . . *The Communist Manifesto* has had great effect upon the children of Adam, and literally billions have been and are currently held captive by those who have adopted, professed and espoused its tenets. Despite the recent crumbling of the iron curtain, hundreds of millions of people are still captivated by its tentacles."[178]

Yes, the principles of Marx's *Manifesto* were the principles of the Illuminati offshoot the League of the Just, which renamed itself the Communist League. The continuity of thought and deed amongst Satan's combinations from the days of Cain to the present is nothing short of remarkable. Fortunately for us, this continuity allows us to identify the Devil's handiwork and fortify ourselves against his schemes.

Upon publication of *The Communist Manifesto*, Europe erupted, like clockwork, in revolutions. Luckily, these revolutions fizzled out. The ground was not ripe enough for a communist takeover and in 1852 the Communist League was formally dissolved. However, per Illuminati tradition, other organizations sprung up in its place and carried forth the same agenda as outlined by Weishaupt and *The Communist Manifesto*. Like the fabled Hydra, when one head is chopped off, two more grow back in its place.

Throughout the nineteenth century, the communist movement spread its tentacles and underwent numerous makeovers. At one point, it went by the name International Working Men's Association. The infamous

---

[178] Robert E. Hales, *Secret Combinations Today: A Voice of Warning* (Bountiful, Utah: Horizon Publishers, 1996), 140.

Internationals emerged next. Both the Communist and Socialist Internationals were founded by diehard communists – some by Karl Marx himself – and were used to promote the same agenda with different tactics best suited to the target country.

In May 1871, communists briefly overthrew the government in Paris, an event known as the Paris Commune or French Commune. The word communist actually stems from the French word *commun*, meaning common or general.[179] Referring to this insurrection and the form of government it briefly introduced, Joseph Stalin said: "The Paris Commune was the embryo of this form; Soviet power is its development and culmination."[180]

Eventually, the Social Democratic Workers' Party was founded in 1898. This party was more of a secret society than a traditional political party. Its leaders and operatives worked to subvert the nations of Europe and bring communist regimes to power. They engaged in criminal activity and organized crime. They met behind closed doors and developed plans and strategies for carrying out revolutions. Almost from the start, a man named Vladimir Ilyich Ulyanov came to power over the most violent faction within the Party.

Ulyanov is better known to history by his criminal alias "Lenin." Lenin was an elitist from a wealthy family. It is generally believed that Lenin was set on his downward course when his older brother Alexander was executed – justly, I might add – for his part in an assassination plot against Russian Tsar Alexander III in 1887. Lenin, always the activist, swore revenge upon the Tsar and spent the rest of his life plotting to seize power in Russia and punish the royal family. Lenin literally never held a job, but spent his life as a professional revolutionary and criminal mastermind. More than

---

[179] "Communism," *Online Etymology Dictionary*, accessed May 6, 2018, https://www.etymonline.com/word/communism.

[180] Joseph Stalin, *The Foundations of Leninism* (1924), chapter 4, https://www.marxists.org/reference/archive/stalin/works/1924/foundations-leninism/ch04.htm.

almost any other individual, Lenin has shaped the ideology and tactics of the communist conspiracy. Not surprisingly, certain evidence suggests that Lenin participated in occult and Satanic rituals while in exile in Italy.[181]

In 1903, the Social Democratic Workers' Party split in two. Lenin headed a faction he named the Bolsheviks. The term Bolshevik comes from the word Russian word *bolshinstvo*, or "majority," and was selected to denote that Lenin's clique held a majority among communists. In truth, the second group, later named Mensheviks (after the Russian word "minority"), actually held a majority. Both blocs were communist and sought political power by hook or by crook. The only difference of opinion was which type of revolutionary activity would be most effective. While both sides believed in violent revolution when necessary, Lenin's Bolsheviks were fanatical and infinitely more violent. They declared violent revolution to be a *prerequisite* for communist conquest.

At this time, Russia was ablaze with terrorist activity. It was gripped by a subversive, revolutionary spirit. The large Jewish population within the empire produced the most radical and involved terrorists and gangsters. Both the communist and Zionist movements gained traction with them.

Assassinations, bank robberies, and kidnappings became routine as the Russian Imperial Government failed to handle the problem. The revolutionaries only became more radicalized as the government attempted to fight fire with fire. The anarchy became so common that Lenin's Bolshevik faction was routinely financed by bank robberies. They euphemistically called these robberies "expropriations." Indeed, Joseph

---

[181] Lyndon H. LaRouche, Jr., "The Truth About Temporal Eternity," part 2, The Schiller Institute, March 14, 1994, accessed October 30, 2017, https://www.schillerinstitute.org/fid_91-96/943-2_temp_eternity.html; and The New Federalist, "Is Satanism in Your Schoolyard?" *Rense*, January 17, 2005, accessed October 31, 2017, http://www.rense.com/general61/satanism2.htm; and Joseph D. Douglass, Jr., *Red Cocaine: The Drugging of America and the West* (second edition, 1999), introduction, X.

Stalin got his start in the communist movement by "expropriating" funds for Lenin through bank robberies, piracy, and other criminal activities.

In 1905, the Russo-Japanese War gave the communist terrorists an opportunity. Most Bolshevik leaders were out of the country at the time and only returned in the late stages of the short-lived revolution. It was actually the Mensheviks, led by men like the Jewish communist Lev Davidovich Bronstein – better known by his codename Leon Trotsky – who directed the coup attempt. These revolutionaries were funded by their banker allies in the West.

Fortunately, the Russian Imperial Government took control of the situation and thwarted the coup and communism was not imposed upon Russia at that time. Unfortunately, the conspirators who were captured were not executed, but were merely exiled abroad or to Siberia where they plotted and waited for a new opportunity to strike. These same men would return to Russia with a vengeance in 1917 and initiate the greatest deluge of blood the world has ever seen.

In February 1917, in the midst of World War I, the Russian People rose up against the Tsar's tottering authority and a provisional government was established. The leader of this government was a Jewish socialist named Alexander Kerensky. Kerensky immediately instituted two policies which were to have devastating consequences for Russia and the whole of mankind. First, Kerensky lifted all restrictions on Jews, allowing large numbers of radicalized individuals to flood into business, government, and other sectors of society. And second, the Russian government pardoned all those formerly exiled by the Tsar for subversive activity, including the Bolsheviks and Mensheviks. These two acts opened the floodgates and allowed the communist tsunami to sweep over Russia.

Lenin and his cohorts were elated to know that they had been pardoned and could return to the nation they had vowed to conquer by violent revolution. Trotsky, at the time enjoying a Wall Street-subsidized life in New York City, embarked on a ship destined for Russia with some 300 primarily Jewish revolutionaries. These insurgents were detained in

Canada, but, with wrangling by the U.S. government, and documents furnished by socialist President Woodrow Wilson, Trotsky's band returned to Russia as scheduled.

At the same time, Lenin and a handful of future Soviet leaders were making a deal with the German government allowing them safe passage to Russia with the tacit understanding that Lenin would foment a revolution which would knock Russia out of the war and free up German troops and supplies for the struggle against Britain and France in the West. Stalin returned from his exile in Siberia to meet Lenin and Trotsky in St. Petersburg. And so it went, with at least 90,000 – and as many as 250,000, by some accounts – revenge-seeking communists flooding into Russia between February and October 1917.

On October 25, 1917, the Bolshevik conspirators – aided by seditious units of the Russian military – overthrew the provisional Russian government and seized power. This event is erroneously referred to in the history books as the "Russian Revolution." In truth, few native Russians contributed to the planning and leadership of the insurrection. This was no popular uprising – it was a violent coup d'état led by a foreign element of anti-Christ communists. This group of predominately Jewish, non-Russian gangsters was funded by foreign bankers and elitists in Britain, France, Germany, and the United States. Essentially, the "Russian Revolution" was a foreign invasion by an international criminal conspiracy funded by international bankers, merchants, and would-be tyrants.

In his 1920 article previously cited, Winston Churchill revealed exactly who dominated the leading posts within this conspiracy. He said:

> "There is no need to exaggerate the part played in the creation of Bolshevism and in the actual bringing about of the Russian Revolution, by these international and for the most part atheistical Jews, it is certainly a very great one; it probably outweighs all others. With the notable exception of Lenin, the majority of the leading figures are Jews. Moreover, the principal inspiration and driving power comes from the Jewish leaders.

Thus Tchitcherin, a pure Russian, is eclipsed by his nominal subordinate Litvinoff, and the influence of Russians like Bukharin or Lunacharski cannot be compared with the power of Trotsky, or of Zinovieff, the Dictator of the Red Citadel (Petrograd) or of Krassin or Radek -- all Jews. In the Soviet institutions the predominance of Jews is even more astonishing. And the prominent, if not indeed the principal, part in the system of terrorism applied by the Extraordinary Commissions for Combating Counter-Revolution has been taken by Jews, and in some notable cases by Jewesses. The same evil prominence was obtained by Jews in the brief period of terror during which Bela Kun ruled in Hungary. The same phenomenon has been presented in Germany (especially in Bavaria), so far as this madness has been allowed to prey upon the temporary prostration of the German people. Although in all these countries there are many non-Jews every whit as bad as the worst of the Jewish revolutionaries, the part played by the latter in proportion to their numbers in the population is astonishing."

The number of Jews involved in communism and occupying the chief positions within the conspiratorial apparatus truly is "astonishing." What is even more astonishing is how few people are aware of this fact. It should be noted that the communist conspiracy is *not* Jewish; rather, it is Satanic. However, as noted, the percentage of Jews involved is wildly disproportionate to their overall numbers.

Every communist revolution that I am aware of was led, or strongly influenced, by Jews. The communist uprisings in Spain, Russia, Mexico, Hungary, and China, for instance, were either led directly by Jews or saw Jews serving as chief advisors to native revolutionaries. Again, this is not to suggest that Judaism is to blame or that the Jewish people are the root cause of communism. *Satan* is the supreme author of communism. Yet, we cannot deny the facts. We cannot deny the massive Jewish involvement in communism. To do so would be intellectually dishonest.

In my first book, *A Century of Red*, I discussed the Jewish connection to communism in much greater detail. Among other things, I attempted to answer the question of why Jews found a home, as it were, in the communist camp. I will not say much in this book on the topic, but I will quote my own synopsis found in *A Century of Red*:

> "[I]t is my belief that, owing to the Jewish people's highly secular culture and lack of true religion – which results from their rejection of Christ who *is* the Messiah – many Jews have a severe identity crisis. Humans are children of God. We have an innate longing in our souls for the divine. This desire for spirituality cannot be erased, suppressed, or beat out of a person. When a person grows up in a spiritually-anesthetized, materialistic environment – which is a perfect example of the international Jewish community – he longs for something higher. He needs a purpose. The spiritual void *must* be filled. Unfortunately, for most of Russia's Jews, communism filled the void and became their religion."[182]

The Jewish race has produced the best and the worst of humanity – the prophets and plotters. The Savior of the world came through the Abrahamic lineage as well as not only His condemners and murderers, but Adam Weishaupt, Karl Marx, and most of the communist hierarchy. Even Lenin, according to recent research, was part Jewish and spoke Yiddish in his home.[183]

While we point out the fact that Jews have been over-represented within the highest echelons of global conspiracy, let's be careful to avoid the error of blaming "the Jews" for the evil in the world. Let's recognize that these are *not* Old Testament-believing Jews, but, rather, are either

---

[182] Zack Strong, *A Century of Red*, chapter 16.

[183] David Duke, *The Secret Behind Communism : The Ethnic Origins of the Russian Revolution and the Greatest Holocaust in the History of Mankind* (Mandeville, LA: Free Speech Press, 2013), 67-68; and Dmitri Volkogonov, *Lenin: Life and Legacy* (London: HarperCollinsPublishers, 1995), 5.

atheists or outright Satanists, as in the case of Marx and Lenin. Let's not conflate Old Testament religion revealed through the prophets with modern Sabbatean/Kabbalistic Judaism which is, of a truth, anti-Christ. Sabbatean dogma was devised in the bowels of hell, and the Kabbalah is littered with occult teachings. Thus, let us always be as honest as we can without falling into the trap of undue bias, overreaction, or unfair generalization.

While cautioning the reader to not give into hatred for the Jews or Israel, let me also warn against confusing the modern state of Israel with the spiritual Israel spoken of in scripture. They are two different entities. Far too many Christians turn a blind eye to the treachery of the Israeli regime – including the theft of American military secrets through espionage and the sale of those secrets to the Soviets and Red Chinese, and the bombing of the U.S.S. Liberty in 1967, to name only two Israeli attacks on America. These American Zionists turn a blind eye to these crimes because they erroneously believe the state of Israel is the Israel of prophecy. In my estimation, such a sycophantic and blind love for the state of Israel, regardless of its wrongdoings, is a sure sign of scriptural ignorance.

In a talk of such importance that President Spencer W. Kimball had it reprinted for the entire Church in 1977, Elder Bruce R. McConkie explained the differences between spiritual Zion and physical Zion. In part, he taught:

> "As is well known, ancient Israel was scattered among all the nations of the earth because they forsook the Lord and worshipped false gods. As is also well known, the gathering of Israel consists of receiving the truth, gaining again a true knowledge of the Redeemer, and coming back into the true fold of the Good Shepherd. . . .
>
> "Our tenth Article of Faith says, "We believe in the literal gathering of Israel." This gathering occurs when the lost sheep of Israel come into the Church. It occurs when their sins are washed

away in the waters of baptism, so that once again they have power to become pure in heart; and Zion is the pure in heart."[184]

Conspicuously absent in Elder McConkie's talk is any mention of a physical gathering to the Holy Land. Though that is in fact part of the divine plan, it is a much lesser part. The primary gathering of "Israel" foretold in scripture is the spiritual gathering we see taking place across the globe through missionary work. A person becomes a part of Israel when he embraces the Gospel and joins The Church of Jesus Christ of Latter-day Saints. Though one's lineage is highly significant and is largely a result of one's valiancy in the pre-earth life, ultimately, a person is *not* justified merely because he is of Jewish/Israeli ethnicity. Rather, the important thing is whether the individual comes to the Savior Jesus Christ, repents of his sins, and joins the Restored Church.

Jacob gave an incredible sermon on this topic. The record is contained in 2 Nephi, chapters 6-10. Jacob informs his audience that the Jews were scattered because "they have hardened their hearts and stiffened their necks against the Holy One of Israel" (2 Nephi 6:10). At that day, still future, "when [the Jews] shall come to the knowledge of their Redeemer, they shall be gathered together again to the lands of their inheritance" (2 Nephi 6:11). In the future, "they shall be restored to the true church and fold of God" and will thereafter "be gathered home to the lands of their inheritance, and shall be established in all their lands of promise" (2 Nephi 9:2).

Despite their current state of near total spiritual blindness, the Jews have a glorious future ahead. However, the path to redemption is rocky; the road steep; the price high. Until the day that they believe in Jesus Christ, their true Messiah, they will be "scattered, and smitten, and hated" (2 Nephi 6:11). They will be tried in the furnace of affliction and all the wicked destroyed from among them *before* they receive the word of the

---

[184] Elder Bruce R. McConkie, "Come: Let Israel Build Zion," February 25, 1977, https://www.lds.org/general-conference/1977/04/come-let-israel-build-zion?lang=eng.

Lord. The prophet Brigham Young in fact said that through the furnace of affliction is the only way the Jews will convert to the Gospel. He taught:

> "Jerusalem is not to be redeemed by the soft still voice of the preacher of the Gospel of peace. Why? Because they were once the blessed of the Lord, the chosen of the Lord, the promised seed. They were the people from among whom should spring the Messiah; and salvation could be found only through that tribe. The Messiah came through them, and they killed him; and they will be the last of all the seed of Abraham to have the privilege of receiving the New and Everlasting Covenant. You may hand out to them gold, you may feed and clothe them, but it is impossible to convert the Jews, until the Lord God Almighty does it."[185]

Many events will occur before this time of restoration and revival among the Jews. At a future day, the forces of Magog (whom I interpret as Russia and her allies) will besiege Israel and two of the Lord's servants will testify there and will preserve that nation with the Lord's power despite Magog's overwhelming strength and numbers. The Lord will perform this great miracle in accordance with the promises He made anciently to Abraham and the patriarchs and *not* because of any righteousness on the part of the Jews.

Indeed, the nation of Israel is highly secular and immoral. Israelis openly support immorality like homosexuality and have a very loose system of values stemming from the anti-Christian perversions of modern Judaism. 58% of Israelis, according to a recent survey, support gay marriage.[186] Homosexual culture – particularly the popularity of gay porn – has spread

---

[185] President Brigham Young, *Journal of Discourses*, Vol. 2, 142, December 3, 1854, http://jod.mrm.org/2/136.

[186] Staff, "Most Israelis favor same-sex marriage, but half of MKs mum on issue," *The Times of Israel*, June 5, 2018, accessed June 5, 2018, https://www.timesofisrael.com/most-israelis-favor-same-sex-marriage-but-half-of-mks-mum-on-issue/.

like wildfire throughout Israel.[187] And at least 42% of Israelis openly classify themselves as "secular."[188]

Not only is Israel's culture rotten to the core, but the modern regime in Tel Aviv was founded in blood and is led by men as corrupt, warmongering, and evil as the leaders in Washington, D.C., Moscow, Beijing, London, Pyongyang, or Tehran. Though officialdom promotes a sanitized version of Israel's founding, the truth is much uglier. Certain Jewish researchers, such as Ilan Pappe and Miko Peled, have attempted to counter the whitewashed narrative by presenting the true story in an academic, factual way. Unfortunately, their research is either ignored or ironically called "anti-Semitic."

In his book *The Ethnic Cleansing of Palestine*, Ilan Pappe detailed how entire Palestinian villages were either massacred or expelled in coordinated Israeli military attacks coinciding with the founding of the state of Israel in March 1948 and beyond. Thousands of Palestinians were murdered and hundreds of thousands were dispossessed of their homes. In one assault on the town of Lydd, for instance, 426 Palestinians were killed and 50,000 people were rounded up and expelled from their homes.[189] These sorts of atrocities happened frequently during the founding of the Israeli state, yet the world press has covered them up. Particularly in the United States, there is a deliberate agenda to gain support among Christians by painting the state of Israel as a holy nation where God's "chosen" people live – and where they are innocent victims

---

[187] Shakked Auerbach, "Israeli Porn Is Booming, and the Industry Insists It's About More Than Just Sex," *Haaretz Daily Newspaper Ltd.*, June 4, 2017, accessed June 2, 2018, https://www.haaretz.com/life/MAGAZINE-israeli-porn-is-booming-and-the-industry-insists-it-s-about-more-than-just-sex-1.5472336.

[188] Moti Bassok, "Poll: Fewer Than Half of Israelis See Themselves as Secular," *Haaretz Daily Newspaper Ltd.*, September 13, 2010, accessed June 2, 2018, https://www.haaretz.com/jewish/1.5112262.

[189] Ilan Pappe, *The Ethnic Cleansing of Palestine* (London: Oneworld Publications, 2014), 167.

of hostile neighbors. Unfortunately, these propaganda efforts have been largely successful.

Other factors also lead one to the conclusion that the state of Israel is a depraved place. In a 2009 memo, the U.S. embassy in Israel called the nation the "promised land for organized crime."[190] Jews have always been involved with, and are the leaders of, organized crime. In the United States, for instance, Jews led the infamous Murder Inc. society that operated during the heyday of mob activity. Jews ran the black-market smuggling of alcohol during Prohibition. And so on and so forth. This criminal activity has followed the Jewish people to Israel.

A recent article in *The Times of Israel* titled "Is Israel becoming a mafia state?" referred to:

> "the massive growth of organized crime in Israel over the past ten years, as well as the fact that Israel has become one of the world's leading exporters of investment scams, stealing an estimated $5 billion to $10 billion per year from victims worldwide.

> "Despite the fact that Israeli police recently announced that these investment scams are largely run by organized crime, which has grown to "monstrous proportions" as a consequence of little to no law enforcement for years, the Israeli government, parliament and authorities have to date proved unwilling or unable to shut them down, in part because these fraudulent industries have a powerful lobby in the Knesset."[191]

---

[190] Barak David, "WikiLeaks: U.S. Worried Israel Becoming 'The Promised Land' for Organized Crime," *Haaretz Daily Newspaper Ltd.*, December 3, 2010, accessed June 1, 2018, https://www.haaretz.com/wikileaks-u-s-worried-israel-becoming-the-promised-land-for-organized-crime-1.328480.

[191] Simona Weinglass, "Is Israel becoming a mafia state?" *The Times of Israel*, September 11, 2017, accessed June 1, 2018, https://www.timesofisrael.com/is-israel-becoming-a-mafia-state/.

The Knesset is essentially Israel's Congress. From sources I've read in the past, the Knesset is inexorably linked with international and domestic organized crime. The Likud Party is particularly infested. And Benjamin Netanyahu, one of the most ruthless leaders in the world today, is currently under fire for massive corruption.[192]

Israel is not only a paradise for organized crime, but for human trafficking as well. A massive sex slave industry is centered in Israel. Women (and even boys) from all points of the compass are brought there to be used or sold. Beautiful Eastern European women are the delicacies of the Israeli slave market. *Thousands* of Eastern European women are taken there after being kidnapped abroad or are lured there under false pretenses of work and then forced into prostitution. While certain nominal steps have been taken to reduce the problem, it still persists and thousands of victims remain enslaved in Israel.[193]

Sadly, in almost all measurable ways, the Israeli nation is wicked beyond belief and is host to parasitical Satanic organizations that take advantage of its wealth and power. The Israel of today is similar to the Israel of yesteryear – the Israel that sacrificed her children to Moloch, cast out the prophets, and crucified the Son of God.

---

[192] Josh Breiner, "Head of Netanyahu's Coalition Suspected of Receiving More Than a Million in Bribes From Mob Figure," *Haaretz Daily Newspaper Ltd.*, December 4, 2017, accessed June 4, 2018, https://www.haaretz.com/israel-news/.premium-bitan-suspected-of-receiving-millions-in-bribes-from-underworld-figure-1.5627645; and "Netanyahu Criminal Investigations" archive, *The Times of Israel*, accessed June 4, 2018, https://www.timesofisrael.com/topic/netanyahu-criminal-investigation/.

[193] Dick Eastman, "Astonishing Israeli Profits From White Sex Slavery: Young Women Kidnapped from Ukraine And Russia," *Rense*, December 24, 2009, accessed June 2, 2018, http://rense.com/general88/aston.htm; Lazar Berman, "Thousands of slaves in Israel, global study finds," *The Times of Israel*, October 20, 2013, accessed June 2, 2018, https://www.timesofisrael.com/thousands-of-slaves-in-israel-global-study-finds/; and Eric Silver, "Destination Israel for sex 'slaves'," *Independent*, March 1, 1998, accessed June 2, 2018, https://www.independent.co.uk/news/destination-israel-for-sex-slaves-1147678.html.

Israel has many sore trials to pass through before she shall be truly free and her people righteous. Those who will be left after the vortex of war and judgment hits them will be the humble and upright. Those who are left will be those who are prepared to receive the Lord at His appearance in Palestine. And just when all hope is lost and Magog finally is allowed to conquer Jerusalem temporarily, the Jews' Messiah, the resurrected Lord Jesus Christ, will appear on the Mount of Olives to smite the enemy and save His covenant people who are waiting for Him and who have by now been refined and are prepared to receive Him and join His Restored Church.

But all of this is somewhat tangential. The key thing to remember is that it is *not* the Jews as a race, but the Satanic communists who are the enemies of mankind. Many Jews have tragically betrayed their heritage and have joined themselves to this great and abominable church, just as many Gentiles have. All who do so, though they may enjoy temporary power and earthly glory, will eventually be destroyed unless they repent. "Thus shall be the destruction of all nations, kindreds, tongues, and people, that shall fight against the twelve apostles of the Lamb" (1 Nephi 11:36).

We return to the tragic tale of the communist ascent to supremacy. Shortly after seizing power and declaring themselves the only legitimate authority in Russia, the Bolshevik conspirators adopted the name Communist Party. In time, the Party christened Russia the Union of Soviet Socialist Republics (USSR). The Communist Party existed as an extralegal body that was forever and always above the law and accountable to no one.

The Communist Party was and is organized gangsterism. The communists were ruled by the laws of this conspiratorial organization much the same way that the members of Gadianton's sect were ruled "not according to the laws of their country, but according to the laws of their wickedness" which were given by Lenin and his co-conspirators (Helaman 6:24). In short, the Soviet Union was ruled by a ruthless secret society which adopted the trappings of a legitimate government.

It took years of savage fighting, engineered famines, and sheer brutality to bring the Russian subjects to heel. Millions of peasants who opposed the regime were shot, tortured, or sent to slave labor camps in Siberia. Rapine and debauchery ran rampant. Barbaric torture was commonplace. We read this description of the vicious conduct of communist agents in the Russian city of Yaroslavl:

> "The Cheka are looting and arresting everyone indiscriminately. Safe in the knowledge that they cannot be punished, they have transformed the Cheka headquarters into a huge brothel where they take all the bourgeois women. Drunkenness is rife. Cocaine is being used quite widely among the supervisors."[194]

In my book *A Century of Red*, I describe the savagery of the communists at length. In a section titled "Medieval Barbarism," I gave this graphic depiction in order to cement in the reader's mind the utterly demonic nature of communism:

> "As horrendous as these engineered famines were, starvation was not the worst death inflicted upon communism's victims. Many others – especially in the open-air prison known as the Soviet Union – were tortured, flayed, impaled, and even crucified.[195] Victims were often put on display and humiliated before being murdered or sent to a labor camp. Show trials were common in both China and the USSR. Every inhuman method of murder was utilized to repress and terrorize the peoples within the communist sphere.

---

[194] Stephane Courtois, Nicolas Werth, Jean-Louis Panne, Andrzej Paczkowski, Karel Bartosek, and Jean-Louis Margolin, *The Black Book of Communism: Crimes, Terror, Repression* (Cambridge: Harvard University Press, 1999), 105.

[195] Orlando Figes, *A People's Tragedy: The Russian Revolution 1891-1924* (New York: Viking Penguin, 1997), 647, 775.

"Mimicking and intensifying the methods of the Medieval Inquisition, the communists boiled or steamed people to death, drowned victims in icy rivers, and buried them alive in coffins with dead bodies. They used tools to tear open skulls and extract brains. People were branded like animals. Skin was ripped from the bodies in an excruciating manner. Eyes were gouged out. Limbs and body parts were amputated. Heads were decapitated or slowly crushed with steam hammers.[196] Victims were forced to eat their own excrement.[197]

"In several recorded instances, men's stomach was split open and their intestines were pulled out and nailed to a tree. In this condition, communists beat them with their rifle butts or whips to force them in circles around the tree, unwinding their intestines and inflicting a painful death.[198]

"Priests and nuns were special targets of the anti-Christ Bolsheviks. It was not enough, however, to kill the physical body – the communists wanted to degrade and defile the human spirit. In one account, a pentagram – the symbol universally adopted by modern Satanists – was burned into the foreheads of the sufferers. Priests were often rounded up and killed in brutal ways after being forced to verbally blaspheme, conduct mock baptisms in buckets of feces, or otherwise deny Christ.[199] Nuns were routinely raped.[200] These same vicious gang rapes would later be

[196] Benton L. Bradberry, *The Myth of German Villainy* (Bloomington, IN: AuthorHouse, 2012), 100-103.

[197] Richard Wurmbrand, *Marx & Satan* (Bartlesville, OK: Living Sacrifice Book Company, 1986), 19.

[198] Harun Yahya, *Communism in Ambush: How the Scourge of the 20th Century is Preparing for Fresh Savagery* (Istanbul: Global Publishing, 2003), 35; Bradberry, *The Myth of German Villainy*, 103.

[199] Wurmbrand, *Marx & Satan*, 74-75.

[200] Wurmbrand, *Marx & Satan*, 75.

carried out on an unprecedented scale against innocent Germans in the closing days and aftermath of World War II.

"When German soldiers liberated Lviv, Ukraine in 1941, they found a priest crucified on a cross in a local jail. His stomach had been slashed open and an unborn baby – ripped from its mother's womb – was inserted inside.[201] It was not uncommon for Bolshevik fanatics to bind pregnant women to trees or posts and cut their babies out of their stomachs.[202] Beginning in 1917, this orgy of madness and viciousness went on decade after painful decade.

"In short, every vile thing the human mind can imagine was enacted by these sadists against the enslaved populations under their rule. Their cruelty was the fruit of blind hatred. This hatred was inspired by infidels like Marx and Lenin who so loved bloodshed and violence and who bowed the knee before the throne of Abaddon."

Such was the unequaled terror and barbarity of the Bolshevik regime.

After a full generation of enduring such horrific, Satanic abuse, the Russians were beat down and subjected to the will of the Bolsheviks. The iron yoke rested upon their necks and their communist taskmasters employed them in building a base of operations from whence they could wage war against the globe. Author Des Griffin observed:

"It took the communists twenty one years of unrelenting terror to completely subjugate the Russian people, to break their will and to bring them to a state of near mindless conformity. Students of history recognize that what happened in Russia was the

---

[201] Wurmbrand, *Marx & Satan*, 62.

[202] Bradberry, *The Myth of German Villainy*, 101.

fulfillment of the first stage of the Illuminati's master plan for the total domination of the world."[203]

With the resources and population of Russia at her disposal, the communist conspiracy was poised to launch a global war against the forces of Freedom. This war has been ongoing for over a century. Shooting wars have been instigating by the communists, including World War II, and a future war is currently being prepared for by Russia and China and their allies. However, the most devastating work of the enemy has come in the field of subversion.

Using fronts of a hundreds types and hiding behind idealistic slogans like "equality" and "peace," the communists have gradually corrupted our culture, undermined our homes, and hardened our hearts. They have taken us to the brink of ruin because we have trusted and followed them. We have not been wise enough to comprehend that those who lead us are wolves in sheep's clothing. They are the blind leading the blind – though we who voluntarily follow these charlatans to the execution chamber are perhaps more blind.

The First Presidency under President Brigham Young once declared that "our national institutions will never fail, unless it be through the wickedness of the people, and the designs of evil men in brief authority."[204] Though their authority has been brief in comparison to earth's total span, communists and their dupes have dominated the United States for over a century. Their power grows stronger as we plunge into the abyss of immorality, vice, and ignorance and make a wreck of the institutions erected by our inspired forefathers.

We now turn our attention to several specific front movements created by the communist conspiracy to destabilize our society and make us easy

---

[203] Griffin, *Descent into Slavery?* 113.

[204] First Presidency, "Seventh General Epistle," in James R. Clark, ed., *Messages of the First Presidency*, Vol. 2 (Salt Lake City, Utah: Bookcraft, Inc., 1965), 98.

prey for the communist leviathan. You will discover that the communist hand has been secretly guiding all of the major social "trends" that have transformed us from a Christian Republic with rule of law and order into an amoral free-for-all and budding collectivist state.

Chapter 7

Communist Fronts

During the Cold War, kids could sometimes be heard singing: "Here a commie, there a commie, everywhere a commie, commie" to the tune of "Old MacDonald." As amusing as that jingle might be, the truth is that communists *were* and *are* everywhere. It is no exaggeration to say that every significant aspect American life that has been influenced or manipulated by communist agents and their unwitting dupes. This is not "McCarthy fearmongering," but cold, hard reality.

Senator Joseph McCarthy, so unjustly vilified by the conspiracy-controlled press, was right. He has been vindicated over the years as more research has been made available. Books like M. Stanton Evans' *Blacklisted by History: The Untold Story of Senator Joe McCarthy* sufficiently set the record straight. The fact is that communist infiltration of American institutions was far greater than even Senator McCarthy imagined.

If one searches for definitive proof of the communist conspiracy in the published papers and documents released by the communists, there's not much to find. Yes, you will find Marx threatening to abolish all property or Lenin advocating revolutionary terror. However, you will find few if any admissions by the communist leaders that communism is a Satanic conspiracy and that their goal is to enslave all of mankind. But when you realize how communists operate, you cannot help but be struck by the fact that everything the communists do is aimed at subjugating mankind and destroying all opposition to their power.

Communists are like chameleons. They blend into their surroundings. In our day, they are usually white-collar criminals rather than street thugs or underworld mob bosses (though communism embraces all of these). To better deceive mankind, the communists – beginning in the days of the

Illuminist Adam Weishaupt – adopted the tactic of concealing their subversion behind front movements. They are the master infiltrators.

Everything the Red Gadiantons do is masked with cheery slogans, fake overtures, and misleading narratives. They will forever operate behind a sophisticated façade because they know their plan of death and misery would never be accepted if they honestly admitted that those were their goals. In short, they take after the founder of their movement, Lucifer, the Father of Lies. It is the Devil who promises the world, but delivers only hell, regret, and pain.

In 1949, the U.S. House Committee on UnAmerican Activities published a book titled *100 Things You Should Know About Communism*. In its question-and-answer format, the book asked, "What is a Communist front?" and responded:

> "An organization created or captured by the Communists – to do the Party's work in special fields. The front organization is Communism's greatest weapon in this country today and takes it places it could never go otherwise – among people who would never willingly act as Party agents. It is usually found hiding among groups devoted to idealistic activities."[205]

Fronts are the communists' "greatest weapon" to destroy America. And they involve people – millions of them – who would never openly work for the enemy. Yet, through trickery, these "idealistic" and naïve Americans are led to labor for the Soviet cause.

J. Edgar Hoover, former head of the FBI and one of the staunchest anti-communist crusaders who ever lived, explained more about what a communist front is and how it operates:

---

[205] U.S. House of Representatives Committee on UnAmerican Activities, *100 Things You Should Know About Communism* (1949), 17.

"A front is an organization which the communists openly or secretly control. The communists realize that they are not welcome in American society. Party influence, therefore, is transmitted, time after time, by a belt of concealed members, sympathizers, and dupes. Fronts become transmission belts between the Party and the noncommunist world. . . .

"Some may be newly created, or, as often happens, they may be old-line organizations captured by infiltration. . . .

"The Party has operated hundreds of major fronts in practically every field of Party agitation: "peace," civil rights, protection of the foreign-born, support of the Smith Act "victims," abolition of H-bomb tests, exploitation of nationality and minority groups. Some are based on specific appeal, to teachers, writers, lawyers, labor, women, youth. . . .

". . . The danger of a Party front rests not on its physical appearance or size but on its ability to deceive."[206]

As always when we are dealing with Lucifer and his henchmen, deception is the name of the game. A front is nothing more nor less than organized deception. By playing upon people's fear or flattering their desires, prejudices, or self-interest, communists come to power over them and mobilize them in myriad causes – more particularly causes with warm and fuzzy sounding slogans like "liberation," "Go green," or "free love." Unbeknownst to most of the "dupes" in these fronts, they are being used strategically by a ruthless cadre of Satanic gangsters to break down our society and bind us in thick chains.

In fact, communist doctrine dictates that much of its work be done by non-communists who have been deceived into following the Party line. J. Edgar Hoover noted:

---

[206] J. Edgar Hoover, *Masters of Deceit: The Story of Communism in America and How to Fight It* (New York: Pocket Books, Inc., 1964), 213-214.

"Above the surface a gigantic propaganda and agitation campaign is in progress, a campaign that depends for success upon the support of noncommunists. Basic communist strategy dictates that noncommunist hands, knowingly or unknowingly, under communist guidance, must further the influence of the communist world."[207]

Read that again and let it sink in. The communists specialize in using non-communists to carry out their agenda.

In fulfillment of this plot to use non-communists to do the dirty work, the Red Chinese have a concept known as wu wei, "which means to get other nations to do your work for you."[208] Not to be outdone, European communists have organized affairs in such a way that their oblivious and idealistic allies work for them without knowing it. Bulgarian communist Georgi Dimitrov explained:

"As Soviet power grows, there will be greater aversion to Communist Parties everywhere. So we must practice the techniques of withdrawal. Never appear in the foreground; Let our friends do the work. We must always remember that one sympathizer is generally worth more than a dozen militant Communists. A university professor, who, without being a party member, lends himself to the interests of the Soviet Union, is worth more than 500 poor devils who don't know any better than to get themselves beaten up by the police. Every man has his value, his merit. The writer without being a party member defends the Soviet Union, the union leader who is outside our

---

[207] Hoover, *Masters of Deceit*, 185.

[208] Michael Pilsbury, *The Hundred-Year Marathon: China's Secret Strategy to Replace America as the Global Superpower* (New York: Henry Holt and Company, 2015), 42.

ranks but defends Soviet international policy is worth more than one thousand party members."[209]

Remember, the most valuable work done for the communist cause has been, and is being, carried out non-communists. The groundwork is instead being done by communism's dupes and sympathizers. The genius of the conspiracy is that its agents are trend-starters and manipulators. That is, they start a movement and then let its own momentum carry it to destructive ends. Or, if a movement has already been started, they infiltrate it, subtly derail it, and divert its energy toward their own causes. Just because an organization or group or ideology doesn't openly embrace communism does not mean it isn't directly following the communist game plan.

Most of the sympathizers and dupes are unaware that they are supporting communism. Most would truthfully — at least as far as they comprehend — deny furthering communist objectives or having any formal affiliation with communist organizations. Yet, because of mass brainwashing, sophisticated and high-tech indoctrination, and scientifically calculated propagandizing, most of communism's "friends" do the footwork that allows the more clandestine conspirators to manipulate situations, events, and popular trends in their favor.

President Benson stated in unmistakable terms the incontrovertibly insidious disposition of the communist cancer that has infected America. Pay attention to the deceptive tactics used by this Luciferian gang as documented in this quotation:

> "The American branch of the Communist party is comparable to a commando detachment of enemy troops working on our own soil to create the conditions necessary for the eventual communist conquest of our nation. The only difference is that, unlike our enemies of the past, the communists plan to conquer from the

---

[209] Nevin Gussack, *Red Dawn In Retrospect: Soviet-Chinese Intentions for Conquest of the United States* (USA), 14.

> inside using such weapons as riots, civil war, political manipulations, brainwashing, blackmail, false leadership, and treason. Whether we like it or not, the international communist organization has declared total war against the United States, and we are fighting for survival."[210]

Yes, we are in an all-out war of attrition – a war for our very survival! This war is being instigated by the communists and those unknowingly working for them. This cadre forms a fifth column in our midst – a veritable commando unit of spiritual, societal, ideological, economic, political saboteurs. Unless we have the discernment of mind and spirit to see through the red fog of manipulation and deception that has descended over these United States, we *will* fall. We are currently dying a death of a thousand cuts.

The Red Gadiantons are brilliant in the execution of their sinister plot. Their success has been unparalleled and their ideology has come to dominate the world. But this astounding accomplishment would *not* have been possible without fronts and without millions of enthusiastic dupes who have allowed themselves to be manipulated by cold-hearted men operating from the shadows.

Edward Bernays, considered the father of modern propaganda, referred to this elite network of manipulators as an "invisible government." He explained:

> "There are invisible rulers who control the destinies of millions. It is not generally realized to what extent the words and actions of our most influential public men are dictated by shrewd persons operating behind the scenes.

> "Now, what is still more important, the extent to which our thoughts and habits are modified by authorities.

---

[210] Benson, Newquist, ed., *An Enemy Hath Done This*, 263-264.

"In some departments of our daily life, in which we imagine ourselves free agents, we are ruled by dictators exercising great power. . . .

"The invisible government tends to be concentrated in the hands of the few because of the expense of manipulating the social machinery which controls the opinions and habits of the masses."[211]

Bernays also wrote:

"We are governed, our minds molded, our tastes formed, our ideas suggested, largely by men we have never heard of. . . .

"Our invisible governors are, in many cases, unaware of the identity of their fellow members of the inner cabinet. . . .

"Small groups of persons can, and do, make the rest of us think what they please about a given subject."[212]

Through modern technology and mass media, a small group of self-appointed aristocrats and "experts" manipulate our minds and lead us by the nose. These manipulators are largely "invisible" and are not household names. Yet, they exist the same as the Gadianton Robbers existed in the shadows during Nephite times and exercise tremendous influence over the course of our daily lives.

Millions of people go to work each day to defend and further the communist position without having the slightest inkling that they do so. With the indispensable help of ignorant idealists and average folks who just want to live their lives in peace and therefore don't object to anything that goes on in Washington or even in their local city council, the

---

[211] Edward Bernays, *Propaganda* (Brooklyn, New York: Ig Publishing, 2005), 61, 63.

[212] Bernays, *Propaganda*, 37, 57.

communist conspiracy has spread until now its web covers the entire earth.

Nearly half of my book *A Century of Red* is devoted to exposing and detailing communist fronts. I refer you to that work for additional information about communist cultural subversion. What follows is an abbreviated, albeit explosive, exposé of several major communist fronts at work in the United States.

Red Feminism

At the heart of our Heavenly Father's Plan of Happiness is the home. The home is the central building block of society. My Dad once taught me an analogy relative to the home and its importance to society. He compared homes to cells in a body. The body represents society. When enough cells die, a body dies. Similarly, when enough homes crumble, society perishes. The inevitable result of broken homes is a broken nation. By contrast, strong homes make for a strong society.

President Benson famously stated:

> "[N]o nation ever rises above its homes. This Church will never rise above its homes. We are no better as a people than are our firesides, our homes. The school, the church, and even the nation, I feel confident, stand helpless before weakened and degraded homes. The good home is the rock foundation, the cornerstone of civilization. It must be preserved. It must be strengthened.
>
> "There has never been and there never will be a satisfactory substitute for the home established by the God of heaven. If this nation is to endure, then the home must be safeguarded, strengthened, and restored to its rightful importance."[213]

---

[213] President Ezra Taft Benson, "Strengthening the American Home," Conference Report, October, 1953, 120-123, http://scriptures.byu.edu/#:t2a8:p401.

Truer words were never spoken. The home is the bulwark of society; the purveyor of culture; the incubation chamber for the rising generation's morals, ethics, and politics. The home is the center of God's Plan of Happiness, the focus of the Gospel, the very reason the Church exists.

Founding Father Elias Boudinot likewise observed:

> "Good government generally begins in the family and if the moral character of a people once degenerate, their political character must soon follow."[214]

It is the home which teaches the values that mold the people who shape society in the coming generations. Freedom is won or lost at the dinner table. Morality waxes or wanes by the fireside. Culture is refined or tarnished by mothers and fathers who put their families first. It is the home, therefore, that must be our focus if we wish to change the political and cultural standards of the future.

The communists, receiving their inspiration and orders from Satan, understand the vital importance of the home. They realize that in order to subjugate a society, they must first weaken its institutions — most importantly the home. Consequently, from the days of Adam Weishaupt, the conspiracy has targeted families and marriages, and both men and women individually.

It cannot be argued that men have always been the defenders of society and of the home. Men have been specially equipped for this task and it is a divine duty they must shoulder. In order to destroy a civilization — including its homes — men must first be neutralized. A man's Achilles' heel, however, is women. This being obvious, Weishaupt instructed his Illuminati that manipulating and controlling women must be their #1 goal in their war on the family. He explained:

---

[214] Elias Boudinot, Oration, July 4, 1793, in David Barton, ed., *Celebrate Liberty! Famous Patriotic Speeches and Sermons* (Aledo, Texas: WallBuilder Press, 2004), 137.

"There is no way of influencing men so powerfully as by means of the women. These should therefore be our chief study; we should insinuate ourselves into their good opinion, give them hints of emancipation from the tyranny of public opinion, and of standing up for themselves; it will be an immense relief to their enslaved minds to be freed from any one bond of restraint, and it will fire them the more, and cause them to work for us with zeal, without knowing that they do so; for they will only be indulging their own desire of personal admiration."[215]

Women are emotion-driven and it is therefore no surprise that so many of them have fallen for the siren song of "equality" and "emancipation." By claiming to "emancipate" women from the so-called oppression of what feminists hatefully call "the patriarchy," the enemy has successfully mobilized women into a hammer with which it bludgeons society and corrupts its traditional institutions.

In following this wicked agenda – an agenda made to seem noble through misleading phrases like "equal rights," "pro-choice," and "we can do it" – feminist women work for the communist conspiracy "without knowing that they do so." Feminists really are the vanguard of the communist conspiracy. They are the standard-bearers; the diseased carriers of the Red Plague that corrupts society one marriage, one family, one home at a time.

Of all the front movements that have served the communist cause, none has done so as effectively as feminism. Feminism, from its earliest beginnings in the Suffragette movement, was a front designed to bring about the destruction of the patriarchal family. The ironically named Women's Liberation movement – as almost all movements that utilize the term "liberation" – was founded by the communists. Nearly every major feminist icon has been a card-carrying member of the Communist Party or

---

[215] John Robison, *Proofs of a Conspiracy*, (1798; Belmont, MA: Western Islands, reprint, 1967), 111.

an open adherent of Marxist doctrine. And a great many feminist leaders have been occultists, Wiccans, or spiritualists.

Author Ted Flynn gave us this frank description of feminism:

> "Over the years, feminism has been so closely aligned with Marxism that feminist writers have described the two doctrinal systems as being one and the same. Where socialist and communist organizers attempt to impose economic standards, radical feminists want to control matters that touch us in a deeper way, extending their influence beyond simply the free enterprise system. . . .
>
> "Radical feminism is the most destructive and fanatical movement to come down to us from the sixties. This is a revolutionary, not a reformist movement, and it is meeting with considerable success. Totalitarian in spirit, it is deeply antagonistic to traditional Western culture and proposes the complete restructuring of morality and human nature. Radical feminism is today the counterpart of sixties radicalism. "Feminism rode into our cultural life on the coattails of the New Left, but by now it certainly deserves its own place in the halls of intellectual barbarism.""[216]

Totalitarian barbarism is a great way of describing feminism. Feminism is indeed as inimical to Western culture as barbarianism was to Roman law anciently. Simply, Christian culture and feminism cannot coexist. Christ's Gospel of true Liberty and communist-inspired Women's Liberation are incompatible.

Speaking of 1960s feminism, Kylie Malchus and Danelle Malchus, two wonderful Latter-day Saint women and personal friends, wrote this in their excellent book *End Feminism; Save the World*:

---

[216] Ted Flynn, *Hope of the Wicked: The Master Plan to Rule the World* (Herndon, Virginia: MaxKol Communications, Inc., 2000), 318, 324-325.

"Equality was never the goal. The true agenda of the 1960s feminist was nothing more than to blend the genders and legalize abortions. Abortions were the biggest significant legal change for which the Second-Wave Feminist fought. In other words, feminism was birthed simply for the desire to end births. Taking into account the true history of feminism, it's not a correct notion to say that it was built upon the desire for equality. Legal equality already existed. When you get right down to it, what feminism was actually built on was the blood of innocent children."[217]

Few things make feminists happier than the knowledge that they can legally kill their offspring. They consider themselves "emancipated" and "liberated" when society finally bows to their bullying and gives them the "right" to snuff out their children. This giddy outpouring was recently seen after Ireland voted in a national referendum to repeal a decades-old ban on abortion.[218]

Let's not mince words: Abortion is infanticide. It is perhaps the greatest act of selfishness anyone has yet devised. Every nation that permits abortion is only aborting its own future. A just God cannot abide the wanton murder of His most innocent children forever.

J.R. Nyquist sarcastically described the sick feminist mentality of self-destruction:

"I think that pregnancy itself has become synonymous with disease, as all pregnancies are increasingly a course of irritation. Anything is preferable to parenthood. People are realizing this more and more. The secret dirty thought of today is: "Liberate me

---

[217] Danelle Malchus and Kylie Malchus, *End Feminism; Save the World* (Salt Lake City, Utah: Pyxis Publishing, 2016), 26. Go support this mother-daughter team by buying their books and purchasing Kylie's beautiful art. Kylie's Amazon profile is at this link: https://www.amazon.com/Kylie-Malchus/e/B00L6A7QE6/ref=sr_tc_2_0?qid=1521432158&sr=1-2-ent.

[218] Zack Strong, "Death of the Irish," *The American Citadel*, May 26, 2018, https://theamericancitadel.com/2018/05/27/death-of-the-irish/.

from my children." – a viewpoint that posits sterility as good luck. Only when they become old and frightened do people adhering to this viewpoint rush off to find pathways back to fertility. But sometimes it is too late. And then there's the wreckage of so many past "relationships" behind one, a series of regrettable pedestrian accidents mucking up the soul. And a woman with direct experience of this cynical new world cannot be sure that her husband won't cashier her for a newer model when midlife crisis takes hold of him. On the other hand, women ought to be independent – right? – and learn to live like bachelors. Everyone knows that the traditional role of housewife is to be sneered at. The age-old safeguards, the age-old chivalries, are but masculine condescensions and should be rejected out of hand as patronizing and arrogant. Such trappings diminish the feminine personality. Therefore, an alternative to the old ways has been proposed. It name is "women's liberation.""[219]

Feminists are fond of saying: "My body; my choice." This selfish creed dominates their worldview. They want to be able to sleep around without consequences and play with fire without getting burned. Yet, they fail to understand the contractual nature of sex. They only ask: "What does it benefit me?" The gift of sex begets the miracle of life. It is a beautiful gift to be enjoyed within the covenant bond of marriage. Yet, promiscuous people only see the hedonistic implications and place pleasure on a pedestal and despise responsibility.

The truth is that once a woman helps create a new life, she is no longer dealing with her body only; she is dealing with the body and life of another human being. It is a body with a heartbeat and a pulse; a body that can yawn and kick and feel pain; a body that needs nutrition to survive. In language even a feminist can understand: *Not your body; not your choice.*

---

[219] J.R. Nyquist, *Origins of the Fourth World War* (Chula Vista, CA: Black Forest Press, 1999), 172.

What's more, sex is a joint venture and a man has equal say in the situation, though this right is routinely denied the father by biased courts. But as usual the feminist is "independent," makes her own decisions, and only sees herself. She would rather kill her unborn child than accept the responsibility of motherhood. And it is the ideology of feminism that facilitates this criminality.

Under the corrosive influence of "Women's Liberation," modern women have rejected the God-ordained gender roles calculated to make all members of society healthy, happy, and safe. Instead, they act on their selfish impulses and seek to live a "bachelor's" life devoid of real responsibility. They don't want to be "burdened" with children or marriage. And they certainly don't want to "honor and obey" their husbands. After all, they are "strong, independent women" who can "do it all" and "have it all."

Feminism is a frightening symptom of the communist cancer at work in our midst. Feminism is *not* fascist, as we so often hear, but is *communist* and promotes a uniquely communist agenda.[220] Feminism promotes slavery and moral degradation while claiming to help, empower, and liberate women. Feminism is code for selfishness. As just discussed, this selfishness often leads women to kill their offspring rather than be "burdened" by pregnancy or motherhood. Feminism is truly a bloody, demonic ideology spawned in hell.

Nothing the Women's Liberation movement has ever achieved has been positive or beneficial. *Absolutely nothing!* No "rights" have been gained that women did not already possess. No health advantages were gained – women are unhealthier and more stressed, more depressed, and lonelier than ever before. No inner fulfillment has been gained, but, rather, a caustic bitterness has overtaken the female gender. Feminism did not gain for women greater respect, but, rather, has earned them the

---

[220] Zack Strong, "Feminism is Not Fascist – It is Communist," *The American Citadel*, June 2, 2018, https://theamericancitadel.com/2018/06/02/feminism-is-not-fascist-it-is-communist/.

contempt and disdain of men who once treated them like princesses. When women stopped being proper ladies, men stopped being honorable gentleman.

Soviet feminist Inessa Armand was very forthright about feminism's indissoluble links to communism. She said:

> "If women's liberation is unthinkable without communism, then communism is unthinkable without women's liberation."[221]

This is the cold, hard reality. We must internalize this crucial truth: *Feminism is communism and communism is feminism.*

Sergey Nechayev, the heartless Russian anarchist quoted earlier, classified men and women in various categories. There were five categories for men and three for women. They were distinguished according to their usefulness to the communist world revolution. Nechayev said:

> "[Women] can be divided into three main groups. First, those frivolous, thoughtless, and vapid women, whom we shall use as we use the third and fourth category of men."

For greater clarity, I quote how the third and fourth categories of men are defined by Nechayev:

> "The fourth category comprises ambitious office-holders and liberals of various shades of opinion. The revolutionary must pretend to collaborate with them, blindly following them, while at the same time, prying out their secrets until they are completely in his power. They must be so compromised that there is no way out for them, and then they can be used to create disorder in the State.

Quoted in Sharon Smith, "Women's Liberation: The Marxist Tradition," *International Socialist Review*, Issue #93, summer, 2014, accessed on March 14, 2018, https://isreview.org/issue/93/womens-liberation-marxist-tradition.

"The fifth category consists of those doctrinaires, conspirators, and revolutionists who cut a great figure on paper or in their cliques. They must be constantly driven on to make compromising declarations: as a result, the majority of them will be destroyed, while a minority will become genuine revolutionaries."

The women who occupied Nechayev's first category are the "ambitious" types – those who fancy themselves "liberals." These should be spied on for blackmail purposes. If they have no skeletons in their closet, they are to be led into compromising situations and then blackmailed. "They must be so compromised" that they can never, if they were to learn the truth, speak out in opposition to the communist plan. Women like Hillary Clinton fall into this category of ambitious women who are compromised and blackmailed into submission to the greater conspiracy.

Of the second and third categories of women to be used by the communists, Nechayev wrote:

"Second, women who are ardent, capable, and devoted, but whom do not belong to us because they have not yet achieved a passionless and austere revolutionary understanding; these must be used like the men of the fifth category. Finally, there are the women who are completely on our side – i.e., those who are wholly dedicated and who have accepted our program in its entirety. We should regard these women as the most valuable or our treasures; without their help, we would never succeed."[222]

Always and forever the communists "use" their followers as pawns in their game. Women are no different than men in this regard. Those women who both consciously and unknowingly embrace or promote feminism are communist dupes. *They* are the true slaves. They are slaves to a small clique of men who rule from the shadows and use them as fodder.

---

[222] Sergey Nechayev, *The Revolutionary Catechism*, 1869, accessed May 8, 2018, https://www.marxists.org/subject/anarchism/nechayev/catechism.htm.

By contrast, traditional wives find Freedom in faithfully following the Lord's pattern and submitting to their husbands in the covenant of marriage. These traditional women have what the feminists inwardly want – happiness, security, purpose, Liberty, and love. In submitting to Moscow's dictates, feminists prove themselves both slaves and tools of destruction to abolish that which they claim to be fighting for – the emancipation and advancement of women. Ultimately, "without their help, [the communists] would never succeed."

The feminists *have* joined the communists, however, and their plot *is* succeeding in consuming our once proud culture. Ted Flynn has observed:

> "Culture is everything and culture can be changed so that all male-female differences, other than in their reproductive organs, will disappear. The totalitarian implications of this are obvious. Culture is a stubborn opponent. To defeat it requires the coercion of humans. The Soviet Union attempted to create the New Soviet Man with gulags, psychiatric hospitals, and firing squads for seventy years and succeeded only in producing a more corrupt culture. The feminists are having a similarly corrupting effect on our culture with only the weapon of moral intimidation. The contention that underneath their cultural conditioning men and women are identical is absurd to anyone not blinded by ideological fantasy. . . .
>
> "Young women today are lured into women's studies, and what they obtain there is a total immersion in a false world view coupled to a fourth-rate education. While other students are studying history, mathematics, science, languages, and similarly useful disciplines, those in women's studies programs are working on acquiring belligerent attitudes and misinformation. Instead of preparing students for the world, the programs impose severe handicaps upon them."[223]

---

[223] Flynn, *Hope of the Wicked*, 325.

Feminism radicalizes women, thus upending and destroying the tried and true cultural structure that produced the happiest, freest, most productive society in history. A New Soviet Woman has been created right here in America. Their ideological fantasies and ingrained delusions – learned from the controlled media and through brainwashing in public institutions – have led these women to fight for communism without knowing they do so. Then again, some have fought through the Stockholm Syndrome and know full well that they are furthering the revolution. These malicious women help the communists oppress and manipulate their fellow women.

Conspiracy researcher Henry Makow has been one of the most vocal critics of feminist militancy. Makow authored the book *Cruel Hoax: Feminism and the New World Order* which I cannot recommend too highly. In the book, the fact that feminism is a communist/Illuminati front is made extremely plain. The incestuous relationship between feminism and communism is so obvious that Makow commented:

> "It is hard to escape the conclusion that feminism is Communism by another name."[224]

In an article on his website, Makow made another blunt but relevant observation in relation to the communist holiday International Women's Day and what it says about our society:

> "This satanic cult subjects us to the same social engineering as the USSR. We have de facto Communism and don't even know it. . . .

> "International Women's Day (March 8) is a longtime Communist propaganda tool. What does it say when an official Soviet holiday is enshrined in our mainstream culture? Clearly, Communism isn't dead; it has just morphed into other forms like Feminism. . . .

---

[224] Henry Makow, *Cruel Hoax: Feminism and the New World Order* (United States: Silas Green, 2010), 37.

"Through its feminist surrogate, Communists have stripped women of a secure and honored social identity as wives and mothers, and made them workers and sexual commodities, hostages of the economy and the ravages of age. . . .

"International Women's Day is hate against women and society perpetrated by the traitorous banker colonial establishment, which includes most "feminist" politicians, educators and the mass media. Women who participate are dupes and "useful idiots."

"It is a vestige of Communist "popular front" movements first organized in the 1930's to ensnare naive idealistic people using feel-good platitudes like "equality," "peace" and "human rights." These rubes didn't know that the movements were funded and run by Moscow. The purpose was to alienate the intelligentsia from their own society and make them amenable to the Communist agenda, ultimately "world government." This seems to have largely succeeded."[225]

Feminism is a disease. It is a spiritual sickness. It is a disorder of Biblical proportions. It is a confusion of the God-ordained pattern of patriarchal families established with Adam and Eve and sustained by prophets throughout time. It is a perversion and betrayal of the female gender and the very concept of femininity. It is arrested development of the most severe sort.

President Boyd K. Packer once pondered aloud about the dangerous logic – or lack therefore – of feminism. In the October 1964 General Conference, he remarked:

---

[225] Henry Makow, ""Women's Day" is Old Soviet Propaganda Ploy," *henrymakow.com*, March 7, 2018, accessed March 8, 2018, https://www.henrymakow.com/why_we_celebrate_communist_fes.html.

> "There is a trend in the world today—and unfortunately in the Church—for women to want to be emancipated. And we wonder at times—emancipated from what? From domesticity? From motherhood? From happiness? And to what are you in slavery? Your children? . . . .
>
> "Mothers, do not abandon your responsibilities!"[226]

Indeed, where is the so-called sexism against women we hear so much about in the media? Where is the alleged anti-female discrimination in the workplace? Where is the "unfairness" that women suffer on college campuses – campuses where women outnumber men and where feminists fill most professorships? The fact is, "oppression" of women and "discrimination" against females is a *complete myth* in this country. Yes, there have been individual cases of abuse. This is indisputable. But it is likewise indisputable that such abuse was never prevalent; no, not in 1964, not in 1864, not in 1764. American women have traditionally been the most privileged and blessed class of people ever to have lived on this planet.

In the past, women were held up as examples of virtue, piety, and goodness and held enormous power over the course of society by virtue of their exalted role as mothers. Good mothers were honored and revered. A good woman was the finest jewel in a man's crown.

Mothers were the most cherished of all Americans. As a group, their legacy resounds to the present and countless generations will remember the good deeds their mothers and grandmothers performed in the home. In the next life, the eternities will praise the work of women in the home.

Mothers were so influential because of their dedicated, selfless work in the home that President Brigham Young remarked:

---

[226] President Boyd K. Packer, Conference Report, October, 1964, 85.

"The mothers are the moving instruments in the hands of Providence to guide the destinies of nations. Mothers are the machinery that give zest to the whole man, and guide the destinies and lives of men upon the earth."[227]

Yes, women had true power when they embraced their divine calling as mothers and focused their unique talents and sensibilities on the home. It is when women leave the home that they leave behind their influence and venture onto unequal ground. In the home, however, mothers are queens with a unique, blessed, and holy calling.

Today, however, feminists look upon their parents and grandparents remorsefully as if they were in bondage or as if motherhood is a demeaning and repressive role. In fact, most diehard feminists reject reality and think women are still in chains! They are following Adam Weishaupt's game plan of tricking women into pursing the phantom of "emancipation" at the expense of the stability of the home.

Instead of embracing the things that earned women so much respect and honor in past generations, feminists think they know better. They have been so thoroughly bombarded with anti-family, anti-marriage, anti-mother, anti-male propaganda that they are legitimately fearful of becoming mothers and believe that motherhood and homemaking are conspiracies designed by men to keep them as second-class citizens (though women have *never* been second-class citizens in America).

As a consequence of their delusions, feminists reject the tried and true course of marriage, homemaking, and motherhood and instead embrace everything lewd, obnoxious, and unwomanly. Feminists adopt the worst qualities of men and somehow think that makes them "equal." They complain about, compete with, and demonize men, yet wonder why they don't receive the same attention and respect as before.

---

[227] President Brigham Young, in Laura M. Hawkes, ed., *Quotes from Prophets on Mothers and Families* (Salt Lake City, Utah: Hawkes Publishing, Inc.), 13.

Rather than cultivate feminine characteristics and dress and behave like ladies, feminists hold raucous rallies, march topless in the streets, demand their "right" to murder their unborn offspring, swear like sailors, live selfishly with no thought of marriage or family, put off womanly responsibilities to indulge their own misguided goals of education and career, and simply do not behave, dress, or speak like ladies. And they certainly reject the scripturally-supported doctrines of submission and patriarchal marriage. Instead, they claim they are "strong, independent women" and lack all humility, submissiveness, and femininity.

Feminism has smashed the good and positive doctrine of submission, replacing it with selfishness and so-called "independence." It is my opinion that selfishness is the #1 cause of divorce. With over 80% of divorces in the United States being initiated by women, and the vast majority of these being so-called no-fault divorces, I believe there is a tremendous need for women to be informed of their God-given duties and the blessings that can come from fully, cheerfully embracing them.

Latter-day Saint educator and mother of seven, Charlotte S. Maxfield, in an article for the informative book *The Joy of Being a Woman*, wrote of submission and gave this beautiful advice and encouragement to wives:

> "The solution I suggest to you for overcoming your problems in marriage and bringing peace to your family is exactly what Paul commanded: *Submit* to your husband in everything! [Ephesians 5:22-24]

> "It's crazy, you say? It can be done, and I've seen it accomplished many times. The changes and blessings it brings are so great that I can hardly express the difference. I have seen several hundred women accomplish it in their lives and as they relate the results of their change in behavior and the reaction within their whole family, their happiness brings tears of joy to your eyes.

> "Can you dare to do it? Have you the courage and faith? What have we really got to lose that is of eternal importance? . . . .

"Don't allow yourself to have hurt feelings. It is a sign that you are not truly dedicated yet, and are indulging yourself in childish self pity and it is a form of rebellion against him. If you have displeased him, just honestly tell him that you are sorry and that you'll correct it. When you really mean it, he'll know by your actions and respect and worship you for it. . . .

"Your single and most compelling desire is to obey and please him 100% As you do this you'll never have to worry about yourself again: your needs, wants, or welfare.

"The women who have succeeded in this attitude have found that their husband has become even more confident and manly, more fully accepting of his authority and the responsibility for the welfare of everyone's needs. Soon, before she even realizes that she has a need, he has provided for it. . . .

"I know that there are some women who might read these things and the idea of complete submission sends chills of agonizing fear into their hearts, but I have heard fear referred to as lack of faith. In order to succeed in this challenge you must believe that your husband is good. It is frightening to place yourself at the mercy of someone else, but you will find that it will become the most glorious dedication of your existence. The two of you shall reach such realms of exalted joy in your lives together that you will finally begin to know what "home – a heaven on earth" really means. . . ."

Profound words from a humble woman with years of experience walking the walk. Sister Maxfield next addressed herself to those women who are apprehensive about following the ancient scriptural counsel to submit to their husbands. She wrote:

"Let me talk to the woman who might tend to feel that she wouldn't dare to obey everything her husband tells her, because he isn't perfect and therefore doesn't have the right. This kind of woman is usually manipulative. Though she's deathly afraid to admit it to herself, others can see it. She may be the kind of woman who has been unconsciously looking down on her husband in self-righteousness, and treating him like a child who is not permitted to grow into complete manhood. Such a woman will often laugh at such an approach to her future happiness and try to find some logical reason why she couldn't possibly do it. This justifies her failure to commit herself. It is easier to condemn something as foolish, impractical, faulty, and ridiculous than it is to say, "I haven't the humility or faith to do it," or "I'm scared." Remember, "Thy desire shall be to thy husband, and he shall rule over thee." (Gen. 3:16) Some women would like to erase that from the scriptures, but I don't think that our Father in Heaven could have made it more clear.

"The only reason a woman will look for an excuse to rationalize or justify her behavior is because she is defending her inside self who is frightened of the truth and afraid of having to humbly dare to change.

"You must have faith. It is difficult to believe that any man who is entrusted with the welfare and safety of a loving woman who has completely sacrificed all her selfish desires and wishes and pledged her undying obedience unto him would ask such a submissive and delicate possession to commit sin. If he did, I feel that the sin would be upon his head, if she were obeying God's law. And I cannot believe that any of our husbands are that corrupted.

"You must have faith in him and in yourself, and in God – that He will bless your sincere efforts. I believe that He will answer you beyond your most vivid imaginings. Ask, knock – for His greatest desire is to have heavenly marriages. Remember that you and the Lord are an "invincible team."

"After all, isn't that what the Lord is asking of you? He has commanded us to place nothing before Him in importance. . . .

"Well, are you willing to set aside your pride? Are you willing to obey God's law? Can you willingly obey the head of your home as a similitude of your love for your Savior as Eve did? You know what your husband can become, but only if you will cease to resist and fight him. Your pride may be the only thing which is stifling his spiritual growth into what he can become.

"Is there any price too great to pay for this promise? If we are to become worthy of this tremendous reward, we must practice and grow now. We must take those few frightening babysteps with faith and courage and humbly pray to the Lord to guide us. I have faith that He will.

"Great blessings are in store for you if you can now give life to the words and beliefs you have merely been giving lip service to all these years."[228]

What an inspiring testimony! Yes, great blessings are in store for women who courageously follow the revealed scriptural pattern for marriage. The patriarchal pattern was not a social construct. It certainly was not invented by men to oppress women. It was revealed to Adam by God the Father and was faithfully performed by Adam and Eve.

Now, an additional word about submission. Submissive does not mean subservient or inferior. Far from it! Submission is a sign of strength and humility. It requires an extraordinary amount of faith. Being submissive is God's way.

---

[228] Charlotte S. Maxfield, "A Husband – To Have and To Hold," in Duane S. Crowther and Jean D. Crowther, ed., *The Joy of Being a Woman: Guidance for Meaningful Living By Outstanding LDS Women* (USA: Horizon Publishers, 1973), 198-202.

And husbands do not have a right to take advantage of a woman's submission. On the contrary, husbands must preside in righteousness. No woman is obligated to follow her husband to hell. Yet, as the Lord established it in the beginning, the husband is the head of the home; it is his right and duty to preside. It is a heavy burden to bear, yet God has appointed that men bear it.

Elder A. Theodore Tuttle of the Quorum of the Twelve once explained:

> "In reality, each family is a dominion within itself. Father heads that government . . . In the beginning it was the only government on the earth and was passed down from Adam to his descendants . . . Heaven, to us, will be simply an extension of an ideal home. As the presiding priesthood officer, the father fills an irreplaceable role."[229]

To preside over the family is a duty filled with grave responsibility. Fathers have a God-given duty to teach, preach, discipline, protect, provide, comfort, inspire, and lead. And I believe with Sister Maxfield that the sins of the family will be heaped upon the father's head if he is derelict in his profound leadership duties.

A woman's submission, then, is an added protection for her both in mortality and in the hereafter. This gift of submission allows a woman to focus her considerable talents on motherhood, childrearing, and homemaking. Women, you have the wonderful responsibility to keep house and be mothers. Considering what we discussed earlier about the central importance of the home in God's Plan, in the economy of the Church, and in the sound function of society, what more could a woman ask for? What could be better than serving in the home where you have an unparalleled opportunity to shape society? As full-time mothers, you

---

[229] Elder A. Theodore Tuttle, "The Role of Fathers," General Conference, October, 1973, https://www.lds.org/general-conference/1973/10/the-role-of-fathers?lang=eng.

are still full partners with your husbands in the marriage covenant; you simply have a different role to play.

Elder N. Eldon Tanner once taught this beautiful doctrine about a woman's lofty position in our Father's Plan:

> "What woman could want any greater glory or tribute than that which comes from an appreciative and loving husband? The applause and homage of the world fades into insignificance when compared with the approbation of God and expressions of love and appreciation which come from the hearts and lips of those who are nearest and dearest to her.

> "From the beginning God has made it clear that woman is very special, and he has also very clearly defined her position, her duties, and her destiny in the divine plan. Paul said that man is the image and glory of God, and that woman is the glory of the man; also that the man is not without the woman, neither the woman without the man in the Lord. (See I Cor. 11:7,11.) You will note that significantly God is mentioned in connection with this great partnership, and we must never forget that one of woman's greatest privileges, blessings, and opportunities is to be a co-partner with God in bringing his spirit children into the world. . . .

> ". . . [Woman] is a co-partner with God in bringing his spirit children into the world. What a glorious concept! No greater honor could be given."

Elder Tanner also warned of the Adversary's assault on womanhood. He did not use the term "feminism," but he might as well have. Said he:

> "It is of great concern to all who understand this glorious concept that Satan and his cohorts are using scientific arguments and nefarious propaganda to lure women away from their primary responsibilities as wives, mothers, and homemakers. We hear so much about emancipation, independence, sexual liberation, birth control, abortion, and other insidious propaganda belittling the

role of motherhood, all of which is Satan's way of destroying woman, the home, and the family – the basic unity of society. . . .

"To mothers, daughters, and women everywhere, let me stress the fact that because of your great potential and influence for good in the lives of all of us, Satan is determined to destroy you. You cannot compromise with him. You must have courage, the strength, the desire, and the determination to live as the Lord would have you live – good clean lives."[230]

There is no greater position in the Heavenly pantheon than the role of mother. Satan knows this, and he has done everything he can to distract you, instill in you a sense of selfishness and "independence" and a desire to abandon your post in the home. But embracing the domestic life, submitting to a righteous husband, and stepping gladly into your role as wife, mother, and homemaker, is what the Lord expects.

Women, do not feel that in embracing homemaking and motherhood you are being held back from opportunities or that you are being shunted aside and left behind by the world. You are not being shortchanged – *you have the most important role of all!* Motherhood is the grandest, highest, most impactful calling in eternity. Generations will praise your memory if you faithfully fulfill this calling and the riches of celestial eternities will be yours. So, I say, have the courage to set aside pride and humbly follow God's pattern. If you do so, all will be well, you will be happy, and you will please your Father in Heaven.

Yet, feminism – so prevalent today, even among the Saints – is a rejection of this revealed patriarchal pattern. It is a rejection of the duties of wifehood, homemaking, and motherhood. It is a rejection of the divine doctrine of submission. It is a rejection of the domestic life. It is a rejection of the Father's Plan. Women who reject this Plan inevitably

---

[230] Elder N. Eldon Tanner, "No Greater Honor: The Woman's Role," General Conference, October, 1973, https://www.lds.org/general-conference/1973/10/no-greater-honor-the-womans-role?lang=eng.

reject the blessings that are attached to it and which are predicated upon humble obedience (D&C 130:21).

Ladies, something you will not often hear is that men *need* you in the home. Your husbands *need* you to stay at home. It is where your children need you. It is where society needs you, too. There never was a more pressing time for women to return to the home and embrace their divinely-appointed role as now.

I know far too many LDS women who have rejected their divine role in favor of "getting an education" or pursuing a career or, in some cases, just plain pleasure-seeking. This must cease. Not only are you forfeiting eternal blessings and setting yourself up for everlasting failure, but you are undermining your home, which undermines society. Everyone suffers when women choose career, work, hobbies, or fun over homemaking, being wives, and rearing children.

Feminism has made modern women so unappealing, and so unproductive and unskilled in the things that actually matter, that men have begun swearing off marriage and relationships altogether. To many men, what is the point? Women can't cook, they don't want children, they're too busy studying to have a relationship, they'd rather be in an office cubicle than at home, they don't dress and behave like ladies, and they are the polar opposite of submissive and feminine. And in the 50/50 chance of divorce, men stand to lose everything in a totally biased and rigged judicial system. So, what's in it for them?

Of course, this is a selfish attitude; yet it is founded on reality. It is a logical reaction to feminism and the havoc it has caused. There is also another item to factor in – sex. Though men don't want any sort of relationship with these caustic feminists, they still want sex. So, these types of degenerate "men" have created the Men Going Their Own Way (MGTOW) movement which denounces marriage and any responsibility, yet allows for sexual liaisons.

I caution you that the rapidly rising MGTOW movement is nothing but feminism for men and is just as dangerous as the Women's Liberation movement. It is certainly as immoral as feminism and stands in violation of the seventh commandment. But we must also understand that it all comes back to Women's Liberation. MGTOW is just another perverse byproduct of Red Feminism.

In their book *The Flipside of Feminism*, authors Suzanne Venker and Phyllis Schalfly commented on the tragic role reversals our society had endured, and what women have lost in the process:

> "Women of yesteryear had enormous power, just of a different variety. Today when we talk about power, we're referring to money and status. That makes sense, for this kind of power reflects modern values. In the past, when marriage and family took center stage, women were exalted on the home front. Husbands deferred to wives on virtually all household matters, including child rearing. Women were revered for their unique sensibilities.

> "When women usurp men's role in society, as they do now, it messes up the order of things. Most men don't want to compete with women; they want to take care of them. It makes men feel important and boosts their self-esteem. What's more, statistics prove women want men to have the dominant role in the relationship. Recognizing this doesn't give men carte blanche to treat women as subordinate – and most men don't do this, or want to do this. That's a feminist scare tactic to convince women otherwise."[231]

In communist fashion, feminists lie about everything. They lie about history and about reality. They use scare tactics and peer pressure to coerce women into acting against their best interests. Feminism fosters a

---

[231] Suzanne Venker and Phyllis Schlafly, *The Flipside of Feminism: What Conservative Women Know – and Men Can't say*, 89-90.

materialistic mentality that has no time for family or motherhood. It is a "me, me, me" ideology – a selfish sham of an existence.

When women are shocked they haven't found fulfillment from a desk job or a life of partying, feminists manipulate their emotions by blaming men and society, traditions and religion, laws and expectations. In the end, however, one fact remains: American women were once respected and cherished for embracing their inspired roles of wives and mothers. Women will *never* receive that same level of appreciation and respect when they pursue careers and compete with men as they would if they embraced their femininity and stayed at home to create the best family possible.

Women must be taught that feminists do *not* have their best interest at heart and that feminism will *not* empower them in any sense that really counts. The first step must be to convince women that feminism is a communist front movement – a diabolical conspiracy designed to lead them away from true happiness and fulfilment as mothers and wives. We must inform them that feminism then and now was never about equal rights, equal opportunities, or equality in any sense. The only equality feminism can give is equal misery.

The next step is to point out that feminism has repeatedly failed to deliver on its promises and that women are the worse for giving any heed to such pipedreams. Are women better off today than in the past? Hardly! Divorce is off the charts. More women than ever are addicted to harmful substances. More women than ever are seeing therapists. More women than ever are hooked on anti-depressants and suffer from anxiety attacks. More women than ever before are unhappy. Yes, today's women have more stuff – more material things – but what does that matter?

Also, it's sad that some feminists love to say "evolution" has chosen women to lead. Women are smarter than men, they claim. Women have greater capacities, they allege. "The future is female," they cheer. They are proud that women are dominating the workplace, the college campus, public schools, etc. To me, however, this is a further indictment on feminism and a black mark on women.

Think of it; in the time since women have risen to leadership positions and have infiltrated the workplace, particularly the education profession, society has dropped to pitifully low levels of greatness, intelligence, education, courage, morality, Freedom, imagination, and common sense. Is this the feminist legacy? Yes, it is. Women should not be proud of the fact that they hold so much conspicuous influence in our self-destructing society.

It is curious to me that Isaiah lists women being in leadership positions as one of the signs of a decaying society (Isaiah 3:12). It is in defiance of the established pattern for women to lead in society. From the beginning, men were called to be the head of the home and to fill society's leadership roles (Genesis 3:16). Yes, women should lead by example in the home as mothers, and no one has a greater impact on society than mothers, but a woman's place is not to hold formal positions of leadership. The home is the woman's sphere. The home is where she was designed to shine.

President Brigham Young once stated:

> "You cannot read in the Bible that women take the lead, that the responsibility is upon the women, for it is not so.

> "One thing is very true and we believe it, and that is that a woman is the glory of the man; but she was not made to be worshipped by him. As the scriptures say, "Man is not without the woman, neither is the woman without the man in the Lord." Woman has her influence, and she should use that in training her children in the way they should go; if she fails to do this she assumes fearful responsibilities."[232]

---

[232] President Brigham Young, in Laura M. Hawkes, ed., *Quotes from Prophets on Mothers and Families* (Salt Lake City, Utah: Hawkes Publishing, Inc.), 12.

Men are the head of the home and women are the heart. Neither can function without the other, but each has a separate role to perform. Women were designed by the Almighty to work in the home – the most important sphere of activity, education, and growth in mortality. What a blessing for them! What a wonderful calling to be mothers in Zion – co-creators with God.

Suzanne Venker and Phyllis Schlafly have written of the ploy used by communist agents to lure women out of the home and away from their God-given responsibilities as mothers and down the path to loneliness, bitterness, and distress:

> "One of the ways 1970s feminists lured women out of the home was to demand that they focus their education on subjects that would advance their careers, rather than focus on subjects related to homemaking or teaching. Elite feminists push all women to plan their lives around careers. The result is that young women give little thought to marriage and motherhood and instead spend upwards of a decade becoming highly qualified for the workplace. Women believe this is the better life plan, since their mothers' lives, they are told, were empty and meaningless. Women in previous decades may have had jobs, but they didn't have careers. Like tempting children with candy, feminists assured women that there was a better life to be had. "Whether girls heard the call of independence from their family or the outside culture, they listened," wrote Dr. Jean Twenge in *Generation Me*."[233]

These voices that have called to women and filled their heads with fairytales about being "strong" and "independent," and about "having it all" while neglecting the most important mission they have in mortality,

---

[233] Suzanne Venker and Phyllis Schlafly, *The Flipside of Feminism: What Conservative Women Know - and Men Can't Say*, 51-52.

are duplicitous and have an agenda. Don't be hoodwinked by their siren song.

President Ezra Taft Benson referred to these same devious voices and urged women not to heed them and not to buy into their flattery. In 1981, he delivered a profound Conference address entitled "The Honored Place of Woman." I believe it is the greatest talk ever given on this subject by a General Authority. In it, President Benson declared:

> "Before the world was created, in heavenly councils the pattern and role of women were prescribed. You were elected by God to be wives and mothers in Zion. Exaltation in the celestial kingdom is predicated on faithfulness to that calling.
>
> "Since the beginning, a woman's first and most important role has been ushering into mortality spirit sons and daughters of our Father in Heaven.
>
> "Since the beginning, her role has been to teach her children eternal gospel principles. She is to provide for her children a haven of security and love—regardless of how modest her circumstances might be.
>
> "In the beginning, Adam was instructed to earn the bread by the sweat of his brow—not Eve. Contrary to conventional wisdom, a mother's place is in the home!
>
> "I recognize there are voices in our midst which would attempt to convince you that these truths are not applicable to our present-day conditions. If you listen and heed, you will be lured away from your principal obligations.
>
> "Beguiling voices in the world cry out for "alternative life-styles" for women. They maintain that some women are better suited for careers than for marriage and motherhood.

"These individuals spread their discontent by the propaganda that there are more exciting and self-fulfilling roles for women than homemaking. Some even have been bold to suggest that the Church move away from the "Mormon woman stereotype" of homemaking and rearing children. They also say it is wise to limit your family so you can have more time for personal goals and self-fulfillment."[234]

Can a prophet speak any more directly? In one fell swoop, President Benson refuted the core feminist dogmas with the uncompromising word of God. From the pulpit, this great leader urged women to reject not only the organized feminist movement, but the feminist way of thinking, its attitude, and its incorrect principles. He spoke firmly and frankly. Do you have the courage to heed his words or will you choose instead to follow the worldly voices blaring nonstop from the great and spacious building?

I have been verbally threatened and accosted many times in the past by Latter-day Saint women who have been intellectually swindled by feminism. In fact, I have received no more violent, vile, and vicious hate mail than that which has come from LDS feminists who took offense to the fact that I believed in and quoted the prophets relative to a woman's role.

On several occasions, I have had LDS women tell me they hope I get divorced or that my wife leaves me because I dared to quote the above Conference talk by President Benson. From their warped point of view, I must be "oppressing" my wife if I believe these principles. I have also had numerous LDS women complain to me that the Biblical mentality is archaic and outmoded. Others have outright told me that President Benson was wrong in this talk or that he was a misogynist. LDS women have told me that *I* am what is wrong with the world and that I am just scared because the "patriarchy" is dying. One LDS woman even retorted

---

[234] President Ezra Taft Benson, "The Honored Place of Woman," General Conference, October, 1981, https://www.lds.org/general-conference/1981/10/the-honored-place-of-woman?lang=eng.

to an online post I made about feminism: "I didn't think people still thought like this in the 21st Century!"

These women are the epitome of how feminism corrupts the sweet feminine spirit with the dreadful influence of anti-Christ. They have been duped and deceived. They have been led by the nose to reject the traditional Christian viewpoint and the revealed word of God. Instead of looking inward and questioning what they have been told by the media and their feminist university professors, they lash out, threaten, swear, and accost when confronted with truth by someone like myself who unapologetically sustains our latter-day seers. "[T]he guilty taketh the truth to be hard, for it cutteth them to the very center" (1 Nephi 16:2).

If you, as a Latter-day Saint, have been persuaded to follow any of these feminist principles – even if you do not consider yourself a "feminist" – I urge you and plead with you to abandon such false ideas and bring your life into harmony with the teachings of the Gospel and our latter-day prophets. For the sake of your home, your marriage, your happiness, and the progress of our society, please, reject the feminist ideology. It is a poison to the soul.

The simple reality is that women were not designated to have careers outside the home; their greatest career is inside the home as a wife and mother. They were designed to submit to their husbands in righteousness and to sustain him as the head of the home. Humble homemaking and mothering children are the Gospel ideals for women. It is for these purposes that the Lord equipped them so richly with talents and inclinations that can be used in the setting of a home filled with children.

Yet, "beguiling voices" in our society "spread their discontent" and "propaganda" in the attempt to lure women away from their "principal obligations" as daughters of God and mothers in Zion. And please remember that as a woman your exaltation in the Celestial Kingdom "is predicated on faithfulness" to your calling as a mother in the home.

Embrace your noble calling and reject Satan's feminism. Your exaltation is quite literally at stake.

Satan wants nothing more than for women – especially LDS women – to abandon their post in this critical hour of earth's history. The success of his mission to destroy humanity requires women to acquiesce and abandon, or at least misprioritize, their domestic responsibilities. If women do not abandon the home, Lucifer cannot prevail. Strong homes are anathema to Satanic conquest. But homes where women embrace feminism or put careers, schooling, and other pursuits ahead of childrearing and homemaking are homes ripe for destruction. Sisters, you cannot afford to abandon your home or let any other thing divide your attention. Society is counting on you!

At the risk of sounding like a broken record, I want to repeat the salient point of this section; namely, that *feminism is communism by another name*. Feminism is a communist front movement led by card-carrying members of the Communist Party and their fellow travelers. The Women's Liberation movement was first embraced and pushed by Soviet Russia.

The earlier Suffragette movement had gained its traction because of the spread of occult spiritualism sparked by the Fox Sisters. It was Adam Weishaupt who set the Women's Liberation movement in motion. His Illuminati agents, and their communist successors, have used every resource available to manipulate women and use them as a battering ram against their husbands and homes, and against the very institution of marriage and family.

When the Bolshevik conspirators overthrew the Russian government and established its Party as the ruling force, they immediately began to make good on *The Communist Manifesto's* threat to "abolish the family." The first step was to dismantle traditional, patriarchal, Church-sanctioned marriage.

It is highly significant that the first nation to legalize no-fault divorce was Soviet Russia. The communists have led the worldwide assault on marriage. In the USSR, divorce became so easy that one party could send the other a letter through the mail informing them that their marriage was terminated. Church marriages were abolished and state-approved and regulated marriages filled their place. Many couples opted to have so-called "red weddings" – a ritualistic substitute for former Church marriages. Being divorced from its Christian context and fully under the control of the Satanic Soviet state, the institution of marriage thus became fairly meaningless.

In a wonderful article titled "The Communist Roots of No-Fault Divorce," writer Joe Carter explained:

> "Lenin became the dictator of first Marxist state in the world and "set in motion political and social changes that would lead to the formation of the Soviet Union." One of the most profound changes was an attempt to abolish marriage using divorce as the hammer and sickle that would destroy and sweep away the institution. . . .
>
> "A primary goal of the Bolsheviks was, as Elizabeth Brainerd explains, to "break down the traditional 'bourgeois' structure of the family in order to equalize the status of men and women." They did this by implementing a number of changes to the Family Code: allowing civil marriages (whereas before only religious marriage was allowed), granting equal rights to illegitimate and legitimate children, making abortion legal (and free if done in a hospital), and instituting no-fault divorce. . . .
>
> "No-fault divorce and related policies nearly destroyed the Russian family. Will it do the same to the American family?"[235]

---

[235] Joe Carter, "The Communist Roots of No-Fault Divorce," *The Gospel Coalition*, September 18, 2015, accessed February 16, 2018, https://www.thegospelcoalition.org/article/the-communist-roots-of-no-fault-divorce/.

In the long list of tactics used to upturn the traditional family, the assault on the unborn's right to life came next. As with no-fault divorce, the first modern state to legalize abortion was communist-controlled Russia. Abortion became rampant – a deadly plague. Entire generations of Russians were snuffed out before they could see the light of day. Russia boasted the highest abortion rates in history.

In the atmosphere of communist morality, and with legal restraints on divorce and abortion removed, Russian subjects became wildly promiscuous. Promiscuity leads to "unwanted" pregnancies. "Unwanted" pregnancies lead to rampant abortion. The problem became so evident that Stalin – the second greatest mass-murderer in all of history after Red China's Mao Tse-tung – restricted abortion. There is no doubt in my mind that Stalin did not end the practice out of compassion for the unborn, but, rather, because he was planning a future world war and needed men to fill his armies.

Another change to the fundamental structure of the family was that the Soviet state forced women out of the home and into the workplace. Though feminists count this as a "victory" and see it as a sign of "liberation," such a move is contrary to God's will as expounded in the scriptures and by modern prophets. It was *not* a victory – it was a tragic setback that not only damaged women but severely weakened families. A family with a good mother in the home is usually a strong family. A family where a mother is absent from the home and has little time for her children is a weak family whose children are exponentially more likely to have rough lives, to commit more crime, and to grow up to forge weak families themselves. Instead of being homemakers, Russian women became factory workers with little time for their families; factory workers who depended upon the government for their meager existence.

In much the same way, the world wars forced American women out of the exalted sphere of the home and into the competitive, dog-eat-dog workplace. The absence of men – who were abroad fighting in contrived and unjust wars for this very clique of gangsters we have been discussing

– necessitated women working. Rosie the Riveter told women "we can do it" and encouraged this dramatic shift from home life to work outside of the home. The United States has never recovered from this shift; our homes have been exponentially weaker as a result.

The world wars thus forced a radical restructuring of American society by eliminating, to a very large degree, a woman's powerful influence in the home. It is absolutely no surprise that exactly one generation after American women were forced from the home during World War II that the rebellious, drug-fueled, promiscuous, communist-inspired 1960s ravished our nation. If American women had remained at home to train their children and lead by example, the 1960s simply would not have happened. The 1960s were *not* a push back to the alleged rigidity and prudishness of the 1950s, but, rather, were a result of the dismantling of the American home and the efforts of communist agents and feminist dupes to subvert our culture.

For a greater discourse on what I have deemed Red Feminism, I encourage you to read my book *A Century of Red*. But I hope you are impressed with the fact that communism – by promoting "Women's Liberation" in all its horrible hues – has destroyed the American family just as they destroyed the Russian family during Soviet rule. Unless we recognize that the communist contagion has infected our familial and marriage institutions, the abolition of the family – the dream of communist agents and the dark master who leads them – is assured. Women, the choice is yours. Everything hinges upon your willingness to submit to the Father's Plan for the happiness of mankind and to fulfill your role as a wife and mother in the home.

Homosexuality and Transgenderism

A subdivision of the broader feminist movement is the militant homosexual and transgender agenda. There has been a very concerted and deliberate push to make homosexuality and transgenderism appear "normal" and "natural." The drive to legalize, encourage, and expand these twin movements is nothing but the ongoing effort to destroy the traditional family unit, assault the notion of gender, redefine marriage as originally defined by God, and weaken America through immorality and sexual degeneracy. Said differently, the homosexual/transgender movement is part of the communist conspiracy's attempt to decimate and reshape society.

It is disheartening that the issue of homosexuality is so divisive and contentious among Latter-day Saints. It is one of the great wedges preventing unity and provoking argument. The honest individual will admit that the Gospel's teachings on gender, marriage, and sexuality are some of the plainest and simplest. This should be one issue we as a Church can unite on. Yet, through his cunning, Satan has hoodwinked a large segment of Church members into believing his lies regarding gender, marriage, and sexuality.

Specifically, Satan has persuaded thousands of Church members that homosexuality is "normal." He has convinced many that people are born gay or that God created them that way. He has lured others to his side using false ideas such as "Who are we to judge?" "If they love each other, what is wrong with it?" "They have a right to marry, too," "Homosexuality isn't a choice," and "God loves everyone just how they are." Lucifer smiles when the Saints parrot his lies.

The truth is that no one is born gay and God does not create anyone gay. Homosexuality is a sin. It is a sexual sin, which means that only denying the Holy Ghost and murder are worse crimes. Both the Old and New Testaments, as well as myriad statements by latter-day apostles, make this point abundantly clear. Leviticus 18:22, for instance, plainly states:

> "Thou shalt not lie with mankind, as with womankind: it is abomination."

Yes, homosexuality is an abomination. It is an aberration of nature. It is a perversion.

If homosexuality, then, is evil, we must admit that God does *not* create His children gay, nor does He give them homosexual inclinations. If He did, He would be a liar. He would be a cruel, arbitrary Being who damns some and saves others on a whim. I could never believe in such a Being; and reason forbids such misguided faith.

The first chapter of James teaches us a valuable principle:

> "Let no man say when he is tempted, I am tempted of God: for God cannot be tempted with evil, neither tempteth he any man:
>
> "But every man is tempted, when he is drawn away of his own lust, and enticed" (James 1:13-14).

These verses tell us that God does not tempt us. He never entices us to do something that is wrong, sinful, or evil. Instead, man is drawn away by his own lusts. He is enticed to sin – and not by God. By whom, then, is man enticed to evil? Mormon gives us the answer:

> "Wherefore, all things which are good cometh of God; and that which is evil cometh of the devil; for the devil is an enemy unto God, and fighteth against him continually, and inviteth and enticeth to sin, and to do that which is evil continually.
>
> "But behold, that which is of God inviteth and enticeth to do good continually; wherefore, every thing which inviteth and enticeth to do good, and to love God, and to serve him, is inspired of God" (Moroni 7:12-13).

Satan is the being who entices mankind to commit sin and do evil. God tempts no one, but instead "inviteth and enticeth to do good continually." Everything good comes from God and everything evil comes from Satan. Homosexuality, being evil, cannot come from God. It can only come from the Adversary.

If we acknowledge these truths, we must also acknowledge the falsity of the notion that people are "born that way" or that homosexuality is "normal." Only Satan would tell you perversion is normal. Only the Devil would seek to convince you that Heavenly Father created His children in a state of sinfulness and perversion. To believe that is to deny the Atonement and the mercy of our Redeemer. It is to believe that man is inherently evil. Yet, the scriptures refute the notion and, instead, speak of the innocence of children, the inherent spark of divinity within each of us, and the capacity for growth and godhood present in our spiritual make up.

In the beginning, men and women were created in the image of Heavenly Father and Heavenly Mother (Genesis 1:27; Moses 2:26-27). Heavenly Father is not an amorphous entity possessing both male and female attributes as is depicted in Eastern religions and occult traditions. Rather, He is a Man – an exalted and holy Man. One of His titles is Man of Holiness (Moses 6:57). Our Holy Father is wedded to His wife, our Heavenly Mother. Together, through their union, our spirits were brought forth and we lived as sons and daughters, men and women, males and females, in the pre-earth realm before coming to earth.

The knowledge of our origin as children of Heavenly Parents, and the fact that we had a pre-mortal existence as distinct individuals, should cement in our mind the eternal importance of gender. Indeed, the Family Proclamation states: "Gender is an essential characteristic of individual premortal, mortal, and eternal identity and purpose."[236]

When Adam and Eve were placed on this earth, they – and, by extension, we – were instructed to cleave to one another in the marriage covenant (Genesis 2:24). From day one, marriage was between a male and a female, a man and his wife. Men and women in the marriage covenant were commanded: "Be fruitful, and multiply, and replenish the earth" (Genesis 1:28). The command to procreate – the first commandment –

---

[236] The Church of Jesus Christ of Latter-day Saints, "The Family: A Proclamation to the World," September 23, 1995, https://www.lds.org/topics/family-proclamation?lang=eng&old=true.

nullifies homosexuality as legitimate because of same-sex couples' inability to fulfill the commandments.

If these examples from the scriptures are not sufficient, we have the words of modern prophets to guide us relative to the issues of homosexuality and gender. For instance, President Boyd K. Packer taught the Saints:

> "Some suppose that they were preset and cannot overcome what they feel are inborn temptations toward the impure and unnatural. Not so! Remember, God is our Heavenly Father."[237]

Simple. Straightforward. To the point. We simply do *not* have "inborn temptations" that are "unnatural" – such as same-sex attraction.

While it is absolutely true that we bring into mortality many of the predilections and tendencies, talents and proclivities, desires and wants that we developed in pre-mortality, I doubt same-sex attraction was one of them. However, even if that was the case, one could still not blame God for "creating you that way." And, additionally, God bestowed free will and agency upon each of us and we are "free according to the flesh . . . to choose liberty and eternal life" (2 Nephi 2:27). To have an inclination or tendency, or to be tempted, is not a sin. It is when we exercise our agency to act on those temptations that we cross the line and enter the Devil's territory.

I will quote one more prophet before moving to the meat of our topic. President Spencer W. Kimball wrote and spoke more on the topic of homosexuality than perhaps any other prophet. He was blunt. He raised the warning voice. He laid to rest the numerous myths that are so popular even among Latter-day Saints. I urge anyone who is confused or troubled on the subject to consult President Kimball's myriad writings and talks.

---

[237] President Boyd K. Packer, "Cleansing the Inner Vessel," General Conference, October, 2010, https://www.lds.org/general-conference/2010/10/cleansing-the-inner-vessel?lang=eng.

In a hard-hitting 1980 statement, President Kimball used his prophetic mantle to teach the Saints these timely truths:

"The unholy transgression of homosexuality is either rapidly growing or tolerance is giving it wider publicity. If one has such desires and tendencies, he overcomes them the same as if he had the urge toward petting or fornication or adultery. The Lord condemns and forbids this practice with a vigor equal to his condemnation of adultery and other such sex acts. And the Church will excommunicate as readily any unrepentant addict.

"Again, contrary to the belief and statement of many people, this sin, like fornication, is overcomable and forgivable, but again, only upon a deep and abiding repentance, which means total abandonment and complete transformation of thought and act. The fact that some governments and some churches and numerous corrupted individuals have tried to reduce such behavior from criminal offense to personal privilege does not change the nature nor the seriousness of the practice. Good men, wise men, God-fearing men everywhere still denounce the practice as being unworthy of sons and daughters of God; and Christ's church denounces it and condemns it so long as men and women have bodies which Can be defiled. . . .

"This heinous homosexual sin is of the ages. Many cities and civilizations have gone out of existence because of it. It was present in Israel's wandering days, tolerated by the Greeks, and found in the baths of corrupt Rome.

"This is a most unpleasant subject to dwell upon, but I am pressed to speak of it boldly so that no youth in the Church will ever have any question in his mind as to the illicit and diabolical nature of this perverse program. Again, Lucifer deceives and prompts logic and rationalization which will destroy men and women and make them servants of Satan forever. . . .

""God made me that way," some say, as they rationalize and excuse themselves for their perversions. "I can't help it," they add. This is blasphemy. Is man not made in the image of God, and does he think God to be "that way"? Man is responsible for his own sins. It is possible that he may rationalize and excuse himself until the groove is so deep he cannot get out without great difficulty, but this he can do. Temptations come to all people. The difference between the reprobate and the worthy person is generally that one yielded and the other resisted. It is true that one's background may make the decision and accomplishment easier or more difficult, but if one is mentally alert, he can still control his future. That is the gospel message—personal responsibility."[238]

What is there to add but "Amen"? I pray that as a Church body we will unite and rally around the teachings given to us by our prophets. They should be our gold standard by which we judge everything.

As we will see below, homosexuality is not merely a social trend, but part of a larger conspiracy to wreck our society by degrading our culture and gutting the institution of marriage. Though we ought to always go back to revealed religious sources to discover the truth on any given subject, science confirms Gospel truth on this issue. Let's examine a few points.

Basic human anatomy and biology refute and reject the idea that homosexuality is "normal" and "natural." Men and women are created to fit together anatomically. This divine design allows for procreation and a full expression of love between wedded couples. While in the act of love, men and women are intended to be as nearly "one flesh" as is possible (Genesis 2:24). This unity is anatomically, physically impossible for same-sex couples.

---

[238] President Spencer W. Kimball, "President Kimball Speaks Out on Morality," *Ensign*, November, 1980, https://www.lds.org/ensign/1980/11/president-kimball-speaks-out-on-morality?lang=eng.

Even those who believe in the heretical, anti-Christ theory of Darwinian evolution must logically conclude that homosexuality is a preposterous idea. After all, the species must procreate; this is the purpose of so-called "evolution." Yet, those afflicted by homosexuality *cannot* procreate. According to Darwinism, homosexuals would have been weeded out eons ago. Thus, even science affirms that homosexual relationships are against nature and the eternal laws of procreation and perpetuation of the species.

I will not say much about transgenderism other than that is a truly bizarre phenomenon that constitutes little more than mental illness. For a man to believe he is a woman and employ plastic surgery to indulge this fantasy is the very definition of a mental disorder. Perhaps more accurately, transgenderism is a serious spiritual disorder and a symptom of total confusion of soul. Homosexuality can be described in similar terms, for it, too, is a symptom of spiritual confusion, lust, and self-delusion. No one is born transgender just as no one is born gay. Both lifestyles are a result of choice.

A former psychiatrist at John Hopkins, Dr. Paul R. McHugh, incurred the wrath of the media last year when he called transgenderism a "mental disorder." Dr. McHugh cited studies which prove that upwards to 80% of children who once professed transgender feelings "spontaneously" lost those feelings over time. Those who persist in the lifestyle and have sex-change operations have a suicide rate 20 xs higher than the average. This is not a result of bullying or social stigma, but a result of living a life not in harmony with God's laws.

In his comments, Dr. McHugh made this important statement:

> "At the heart of the problem is confusion over the nature of the transgendered. "Sex change" is biologically impossible. People who undergo sex-reassignment surgery do not change from men to women or vice versa. Rather, they become feminized men or masculinized women. Claiming that this is [a] civil-rights matter

and encouraging surgical intervention is in reality to collaborate with and promote a mental disorder."[239]

Precisely! Transgenderism is a mental/spiritual illness and those who facilitate such fantasies and delusions are harming, not helping, those who suffer them. The same is true of homosexuality. If the activists truly loved these people, they would get them the proper help they needed rather than using them as fodder to promote an anti-family, anti-Christian agenda.

It should not be surprising to learn that the soul-destroying homosexual and transgender movements were founded by communist agents and promoted by communist organizations. Under terms such as "gay rights" and "gay liberation," communists pushed this confusion in order to further weaken American cultural institutions and to decrease our level of national morality.

In his 1958 book *The Naked Communist*, W. Cleon Skousen compiled a list of "current communist goals." The information was synthesized from investigations into communist subversion and the orders communist agents had received from Moscow. One of the objectives was to: "Present homo-sexuality, degeneracy and promiscuity as "normal, natural, health.""[240]

Skousen recorded that "many well-meaning citizens have become involved in pushing forward the Communist program without realizing it. They became converted to Communist *objectives* because they accepted superficial Communist *slogans*. Soon they were thinking precisely the way

---

[239] Scott Osborn, "Liberals Furious! Johns Hopkins Chief Psychiatrist: Transgender Is A 'Mental Disorder'," *Joe For America*, October 30, 2017, accessed May 8, 2018, https://joeforamerica.com/2017/09/ohns-hopkins-transgender-mental-disorder/.

[240] Skousen, *The Naked Communist*, 261.

the Communists wanted them to think."[241] Unfortunately, this is exactly what has happened regarding homosexuality and the LGBT movement.

The founder of the destructive homosexual movement was an active communist named Henry "Harry" Hay. Hay was afflicted with homosexuality and was a card-carrying member of the Communist Party USA. Hay's life mission was to normalize homosexuality in the public mind and to promote so-called "gay rights" on an international scale. To achieve this goal, Hay founded several groups, including the Mattachine Society, the Radical Faeries, and the North American Man Boy Love Association (NAMBLA).

Through the tireless efforts of these vile organizations, homosexuality made its way into the public discourse and received wide support with literally tens of thousands of individuals joining these societies nationwide, and more internationally. In a short period of time, homosexuality went from a largely undiscussed perversion shunned by society to an accepted "alternative lifestyle."

Other insidious groups joined forces to foist homosexuality on the American People and to change our laws to support and enforce "gay rights." It is worth noting that there is no such thing as "gay rights" – there are only human rights that apply to everyone equally. If something cannot apply to everyone equally, it is not a right. Thus, no exclusive group – not gays, not women, not blacks, not Jews – has its own set of "rights." To imply that they do makes of them a politically protected class. When you see political pundits, politicians, and media personalities referring to the "rights" of this or that group and saying they must be promoted, know that they are using an old political talking point and likely have an ulterior agenda that is not in your best interest.

One anti-American group that has heavily promoted the LGBT agenda is the American Civil Liberties Union (ACLU). The ACLU was founded by

---

[241] Skousen, *The Naked Communist*, 262.

Fabian Socialists and other radicals promoting the communist agenda. The ACLU continues to spew their propaganda about how LGBT people are "discriminated" against and how they are not "full participants" in society. They try hard to make it appear as if there is institutionalized bigotry against gays, though no such bigotry exists. Indeed, our culture has almost fully embraced homosexuality as a "normal" part of life. Yet, the radicals at the ACLU and in likeminded organizations are not satisfied. They consider anyone who opposes their agenda an "extremist" who must be defeated. On their website, the ACLU explains:

> "Despite these advances into the American mainstream, however, LGBT people continue to face real discrimination in all areas of life. . . .
>
> "In 1986, after more than two decades of support for lesbian and gay struggles, the American Civil Liberties Union established a national Lesbian and Gay Rights Project. Working in close collaboration with the ACLU's affiliates nationwide, the Project coordinates the most extensive gay rights legal program in the nation. Increasing opposition from a well-organized, well-funded coalition of radical extremists and fundamentalists promises many battles and challenges ahead."[242]

Where is the "increasing opposition" they speak of? The Supreme Court has flaunted American tradition and moral law by making gay marriage legal nationwide. Courts frequently rule against those who refuse to make cakes for homosexual weddings. Those afflicted by homosexuality are found in government, in positions of leadership, in Hollywood. They are promoted in the media every single day. They are held up as icons. For instance, Bruce Jenner – a man who pretends he is a woman named

---

[242] "The Rights of Lesbian, Gay, Bisexual and Transgendered People," American Civil Liberties Union, accessed March 17, 2018, https://www.aclu.org/other/rights-lesbian-gay-bisexual-and-transgendered-people.

Caitlyn – has been featured on the front page of national magazines and has been widely called a "hero."[243]

Unfortunately, there is *no* real societal opposition to the LGBT juggernaut. Yet, those few of us who stand up and speak out against it are labeled "radical extremists and fundamentalists" and are depicted as "intolerant," "bigoted," or "Nazis." Yours truly even had his Facebook page titled "Feminism is a Disease" temporarily "unpublished" by Facebook based on a calling transgenderism a mental disorder. In fact, the purpose of the post was to highlight the same article just cited where Dr. Paul McHugh of John Hopkins also referred to transgenderism as a mental illness.[244] Stating the obvious is apparently "hate speech" according to Facebook. Yes, the cultural tide has decisively turned in favor of the communists with their amorality.

The Communist Party USA has also openly supported the LGBT community. Of many statements that could be cited, I quote from an article featured on the CPUSA website written by C.J. Atkins. It states:

> "Communists have been at the forefront of this movement from the very beginning. It was Harry Hay, a former Communist Party member and union organizer in New York's department stores, who founded the first gay organization in the United States – the Mattachine Society.

---

[243] Rebecca Ruiz, "Why Caitlyn Jenner represents a new type of American hero," *Mashable*, June 2, 2015, accessed May 13, 2018, https://mashable.com/2015/06/02/caitlyn-jenner-hero/#a.YE0FGcsZqm.

[244] Scott Osborn, "Liberals Furious! John Hopkins Chief Psychiatrist: Transgender Is A 'Mental Disorder'," *Joe For America*, October 30, 2017, accessed April 21, 2018, https://joeforamerica.com/2017/09/ohns-hopkins-transgender-mental-disorder/.

> "Today, we are proud to celebrate this heritage and stand together with the LGBTQ community in its struggle for equality."[245]

Yes, communists have been at the forefront in foisting homosexuality and like perversions upon the American People. They and their allies have been the vanguard in changing constitutional law to accommodate "hate speech" regulation, "gay rights," and other such agenda-driven assaults on traditional law and order. As is so often the case, communists create the spark that ignites the blaze that burns through our institutions and leaves us weak and on the verge of collapse.

Homosexuality and transgenderism constitute a convoluted brew of irrationality and immorality. It requires serious mental gymnastics to wrap your head around how anyone can think they are "normal" and "natural." On the one hand, the LGBT movement says its members were "born that way," and on the other they defend their "right to choose" to be a different gender and orient their sexuality whichever way they please. Which is it? It is a choice or are they "born that way"? Simply put, these people are spiritually confused. They do not understand what the *Family Proclamation* so boldly proclaims; namely, that:

> "ALL HUMAN BEINGS—male and female—are created in the image of God. Each is a beloved spirit son or daughter of heavenly parents, and, as such, each has a divine nature and destiny. Gender is an essential characteristic of individual premortal, mortal, and eternal identity and purpose."[246]

---

[245] "What is the Communist Party's Stance on LGBTQ Equality?" Communist Party USA, April 30, 2016, accessed March 17, 2018, http://www.cpusa.org/faq/what-is-the-communist-partys-stance-on-lgbtq-equality/.

[246] "The Family: A Proclamation to the World," The Church of Jesus Christ of Latter-day Saints, September 23, 1995, accessed March 18, 2018, https://www.lds.org/topics/family-proclamation?lang=eng&old=true.

We are each of divine and royal lineage. Our Father is the very God who upholds the universe. Our eternal identity is wrapped up in our gender and designation as a son or daughter of the Eternal Father. Males have certain qualities, traits, expectations, and roles, and females have their own. Each is unique and complementary. Adam without Eve is a lone man in the Garden of Eden. Eve without Adam is left to wander in the wilderness of sin without fulfillment, happiness, and progression. To tamper with one's gender or to convert the purpose of sex into an instrument of lust is a serious sin – one that has brought past societies to total destruction.

Additionally, science does *not* support the claims of "normalcy" of the LGBT community. LGBT members suffer *far more* from disease, depression, domestic violence, and other such criminality and disorders than do normal heterosexuals. This is not, as the ACLU and others claim, a result of "discrimination" by society. Rather, it is a direct result of living contrary to God's laws, the laws of nature, and the principles of basic biology. Inasmuch as homosexual or transgendered marriages provide only a corrupt atmosphere devoid of true love and contrary to the true order of marriage, it is child abuse to allow homosexuals or transgenders to adopt and raise children.

If we want to preserve our society from utter destruction, we must defeat this particular prong of the communist assault on families, gender, and marriage. We must recognize that communism sparked this devastating blaze. We must understand that the homosexual agenda is part and parcel of the greater Satanic agenda aimed at destroying and subjugating our society. There is no room for compromise on issues of morality; we either stand with God or against Him.

Environmentalism – Green Communism

I have termed the radical environmental movement Green Communism. The push to convince mankind that they are destroying the earth through "global warming" and "climate change" is led by communists and their pagan allies in the New Age movement. Through the communist-controlled United Nations, the conspirators have pushed the lie that man is destroying the globe. The modern environmental movement kicked off on the first "Earth Day," or April 22, 1970 – the 100th anniversary of Lenin's birth. Whether environmentalism's founding day being the same day as Lenin's birthday is a mere coincidence, I'll let you decide.

The United Nations has developed a plan for global "sustainable development" called Agenda 21, or, the Agenda for the Twenty-First Century. It has since been updated and is now referred to as Agenda 2030, but the core elements of Agenda 21 are firmly in place. Of this agenda, Rosa Koire has written:

> "Familiarize yourself with Communitarianism. It's the political philosophy behind all of this. It states that the individual's rights are a threat to the global community. Everyone is an individual, so we are all a threat to the global community. Our rights to property ownership, to personal mobility and life choices, to feed and clothe ourselves, are a danger to the global community. So we must be rationed. We must be controlled. We must be watched. We must be regulated, restricted, and balanced. Our individual rights must be balanced against those unnamed rights granted to the world community by the United Nations, as codified by Agenda 21/Sustainable Development."[247]

Communitarianism is simply a fancy way of saying communism. It is a collectivist ideology that demeans and dismisses the individual while glorifying the collective (and, by consequence, the state). Individual rights mean nothing; community interests take precedence. The state, which represents the collective, then becomes the supreme arbiter of all things, restricting and regulating whatever it must to "protect" the collective and "defend" its interests.

---

[247] Rosa Koire, *Behind the Green Mask: U.N. Agenda 21* (Santa Rosa, CA: The Post Sustainability Institute Press, 2011), 31.

If we believe the claptrap that community interest takes precedence over individual rights, the only thing left is to be convinced that individuals are endangering the collective through their actions and embracing communism is a step away. For instance, if global warming is destroying the globe, and SUVs cause pollution, then, according to collectivist logic, the state has a right and duty to regulate or ban SUVs to prevent the problem and, thus, save humanity. Literally nothing is sacred in a system that exalts the collective over the individual and exists to please the whims of the majority. There is no Freedom in such a system, because such a system is democracy, or, more appropriately, mobocracy.

Our controlled media outlets daily inform us that *we* are destroying the earth, that mankind is a threat to itself and the planet, that man is harming the ecosystem and animal life, that we are destroying the rainforests, that factory pollution is obliterating the ozone and exposing us to danger, that humanity will go extinct within a manner of years because of our irresponsibility, and so on. To date, zero credible evidence has emerged to support these absurd allegations, yet the lies never end. We are subjected to a constant stream of indoctrination and are called "conspiracy theorists" when we object.

Under the guise of "saving the planet," the United Nations has been mobilized to pressure the nations of the world into raising taxes and expanding regulations on everything from factories to vehicles. Through this immoral taxation, the wealth of Western and developed nations is redistributed to poorer, third-world nations (a good many of which are controlled directly by Moscow or Beijing). It is a gigantic Ponzi scheme that serves no purpose other than to destroy the sovereignty and wealth of nations in the ostensibly non-communist world. Interestingly, Red China is the world's #1 polluter, yet the U.N. never targets them or demands that they pay taxes to "save the planet."

Furthermore, what are tax dollars supposed to do to protect the ozone layer or preserve the trees in the Brazilian rainforests? Have you ever stopped to ask yourself *how* a tax can ever help? Because the media propagandizes you with dramatic reports of a dying planet, your emotions kick in and override your rational thought processes. There is zero possible way that increasing taxes – such as the carbon tax – could ever save the planet from the ravages of the non-existent "global warming." Because the globe is in nearly two straight decades of global cooling, the term global warming has been increasingly referred to as "climate change" – as if humanity is responsible for earth's ever-changing climate.

Perhaps all one needs to do to know that the communists are behind the rabid environmentalist movement is to understand that the United Nations is leading the charge against sanity by promoting Agenda 21 with the intent of centralizing world authority and wealth in the hands of an international body which then will redistribute it into their own pockets or to nations in the communist world. When one realizes that the United Nations is itself a veritable communist front, it all falls into place.

A few facts about the United Nations are worth noting. First, the leaders of the U.N. have coupled with earth-worshipping pagan cults. Together, they promote an earth-worship spirituality straight out of Medieval history. In the name of the great goddess, otherwise known as Mother Earth or Gaia, these delusional occultists feel the need to restrict human kind's Liberty in order to save their goddess from extinction. Ted Flynn has written of this merger of paganism and United Nations policy in these terms:

> "In Greek mythology, Gaia, or Ge, was the goddess of the earth . . . gaia ideology supports the Green Movement claim that modern man is responsible for maintaining Nature's fragile balance.

> "The gaia hypothesis of saving "mother earth" is the basis for the Endangered Species Act, the United Nation's Biodiversity Treaty, and the President's Commission on Sustainable Development. . . .

> "Agenda 21 is the far-reaching UN blueprint for global eco-socialism. Endorsed by over hundred heads of state, this

voluminous plan threatens to destroy American property rights, while proposing specific changes in activities of all people. . . .

"Today, what is commonly termed New Age is in reality an amalgam of many ancient concepts. Babylonian paganism and selected mythologies are combined with elements of Hinduism and Buddhism and a mixed assortment of philosophies and psychobabble. Western pseudo-scientific language is then added to form the modern day New Age philosophy. Environmentalists have found that repackaging religious ideas from the distant past can be quite useful in winning new converts.

"The beginning of the more widespread infiltration of New Age into the environmental movement took place on Earth Day in 1990, when the concept of recognizing the earth as a living being, worthy of worship, was introduced to the world at large. Many environmental publications view biblical teachings as the cause of significant ecological problems . . . In the opinion of these environmental zealots, the spread of Christian beliefs led to the detrimental development of technology that would harm the earth. . . .

"Not surprisingly, environmentalists are adopting New Age religious views. Using the term loosely, scientists have become mystics in the pursuit of environmental purity. People of faith are increasingly being portrayed as enemies of the earth. Many propagators of international law are consistently ant-Christian, anti-family, and anti-freedom. A "new" religion with occult overtones is subtly being introduced, and, in some cases, reintroduced on a global scale. When more and more signs point to a growing relationship among paganism, nature worship, and the preservation of natural resources, an unsettling feeling descends upon those who cherish religious freedoms.

"Private property ownership is viewed by environmentalists as another threat to the earth. The strategies of environmentalists to eliminate private property rights are slowly surfacing each year."[248]

The elimination of private property; the assault on Christianity; the resurrection of ancient paganism; the implementation of "eco-socialism" – all of this smacks of the Satanic communism we have discussed hitherto.

As seen by Flynn's accurate analysis, the U.N. is virulently anti-Christian and cavorts with avowed pagans. Recall that President J. Reuben Clark, Jr. described communism as "organized paganism" and said that all modern paganism, ultimately, is "under one head," and "that head is guided by Satan himself.   This earthly head is the leader of the communist conspiracy and his dark Brotherhood. They direct the course of the United Nations and other significant entities and government. To wit, the United Nations uses occult organizations, such as the New Age Lucifer Publishing Company (renamed Lucis Trust), to distribute educational material. And inside the U.N. building in New York there is even a "meditation room" furnished with occult symbols and a black, Masonic altar.[249]

Benjamin Creme – the late New Age guru and servant of the coming Lord Maitreya – has stated:

> "The energy of the Avatar of Synthesis actually plays through the United Nations Assembly and is slowly but surely bringing the nations together. It is one of the major groupings through which that energy flows."[250]

If that statement seems confusing, let me take a moment to explain. As briefly discussed earlier, Maitreya is the name of a spiritual figure – a highly advanced and enlightened man – expected to come (or return) to

---

[248] Flynn, *Hope of the Wicked*, 328-330, 348.

[249] Des Griffin, *Fourth Reich of the Rich*, 159-160.

[250] Benjamin Creme, *The Reappearance of the Christ and the Masters of Wisdom* (North Hollywood, CA: Tara Center, 1980), 170.

the earth and usher in a golden age for humanity. Maitreya goes by the names Imam Mahdi, Krishna, Avatar, the Fifth Buddha, the Messiah, and the Christ. In other words, members of every major faith on the planet are expecting the appearance, or reappearance, of this illustrious figure.

It appears obvious to me that Maitreya is simply another way to say "Anti-Christ" – the very same prophesied of in Revelation. It is revealing that numerous world leaders have privately claimed to have met this entity, whom they normally refer to as either "the Christ" or "Lord Maitreya." Among the list of prominent world leaders who have seen and conversed with Maitreya are Soviet dictator Mikhail Gorbachev, the communist revolutionary Nelson Mandela, and Saddam Hussein. Others in the West, Middle East, and elsewhere have purportedly seen Maitreya and follow his lead.

Not only does Maitreya personally appear to influential world leaders, but his associates, known as the Ascended Masters of Wisdom, do as well. Together, this group of disembodied beings constitutes what is called the Hierarchy. This Hierarchy's goal is to bring mankind together as one in a new political and religious order. Through global "sharing" of wealth and power, the world will allegedly achieve peace.

In truth, these figures are Satan and his hosts who were cast down after the War in Heaven. Their everlasting goal is to subjugate the whole of humanity under their dominion. To achieve this, they appear as mentors, spirit guides, guardian angels, advanced men, and Masters of Wisdom. They do not appear gnashing their teeth and breathing fire, but, rather, they teach doctrines that are "pleasing to the carnal mind" (Alma 30:53). These "seducing spirits" preach "doctrines of devils" (1 Timothy 4:1) and hand down a counterfeit gospel to receptive individuals the same way Cain and his successors received them from the mouth of Lucifer.

It seems apparent from the descriptions of Maitreya's various appearances that he loves to appear as an angel of light. When I read descriptions of Maitreya written by his followers, an image of Satan appearing to Korihor "in the form of an angel" and teaching him false doctrines immediately leaps to my mind (Alma 30:53). Yes, Satan is active and is giving false manifestations and revelations just as frequently, if not more so, than our Lord does to His Saints.

When Maitreya appears to mankind, he will coalesce the governments of the world together. The world leaders – many of whom will have previously been acquainted with Maitreya – will step forward and offer their nation's sovereignty to him and to the world government he will head. According to Benjamin Creme, all nations will give up their property and wealth to the United Nations to be redistributed by them based on need.[251] Furthermore, Creme has explained:

> "At the head of several of the governments of the world and in the great world agencies, like United Nations agencies, and so on, there will be either a Master of at least a third degree Initiate. So the great international agencies will be under the direct control of a high member of the Hierarchy. The Christ will be, not distant from humanity, but the leader . . . The Masters will gradually be coming in with Their high Initiates and will oversee the administrative and technical detailed work. The Christ Himself will have a great deal to do – with the release of energies . . . and in stimulating and inspiring the formation of the New World Religion."[252]

According to Creme, Satan and his fellow cursed souls will have "direct control" of the mechanisms of global government in a coming day. They will work openly as they bring humanity together under their command. They will inspire "the formation of the New World Religion." This religion will be Luciferianism – a type and a shadow we can see in communism.

In another book, Creme wrote:

---

[251] Creme, *The Reappearance of the Christ and the Masters of Wisdom*, 171.

[252] Creme, *The Reappearance of the Christ and the Masters of Wisdom*, 169.

"Maitreya says that no nation can work on one wheel. If you see a nation as a cart, it must have two wheels; otherwise it will not go. If one wheel alone is capitalism, it will not move. If one wheel alone is socialism, it will not move. The only thing that will make the cart, that is your political/economic structure, work properly is to have the best of socialism and the best of capitalism. The Masters advise 70 per cent socialism to 30 per cent capitalism as the best proportion."[253]

This notion is in direct contradiction to what the prophets of God have taught about socialism and communism, and what the Lord has revealed about the U.S. Constitution which He established. The prophets have said that communism is the "greatest satanical threat" to mankind – an ideology spawned by the Devil. What Creme is really describing in these quotations is a one-world communist order led personally by Lucifer through his mortal Anti-Christ surrogate.

One such surrogate was Karl Marx. President Ezra Taft Benson included Marx in his list of modern anti-Christs. In a powerful October 1970 Conference address, President Benson taught the Saints:

"As a watchman on the tower, I feel to warn you that one of the chief means of misleading our youth and destroying the family unit is our educational institutions. President Joseph F. Smith referred to false educational ideas as one of the three threatening dangers among our Church members. There is more than one reason why the Church is advising our youth to attend colleges close to their homes where institutes of religion are available. It gives the parents the opportunity to stay close to their children; and if they have become alert and informed as President McKay admonished us last year, these parents can help expose some of the deceptions of men like Sigmund Freud, Charles Darwin, John

---

[253] Benjamin Creme, *The World Teacher for All Humanity* (London: Share International Foundation, 2007) 74.

Dewey, Karl Marx, John Keynes, and others. Today there are much worse things that can happen to a child than not getting a full college education. In fact, some of the worst things have happened to our children while attending colleges led by administrators who wink at subversion and amorality."[254]

Freud, Darwin, Marx, and the rest belonged to the same cabal of subversive thinkers and plotters. Through their writings and work, these men aided Satan's plan and helped establish for him a global network of minions ready and willing to do his bidding.

To Benjamin Creme, Marx was not merely an adherent of the Hierarchy, he was one of its members who appeared in bodily form to give the world a better political system. Said Creme:

"Marx was indeed a member of the Hierarchy, of a certain degree. . . .

"He came into the world to release a certain teaching about new economic possibilities, new relationships, a new theory of social change, and he built it into a very structured dialectic. . . .

"Marxism is feared today, in some countries, because it means change – that's what it's about; he is the apostle of change. . . .

"Marxism is not only a narrow economic theory, it is to do with the basic laws of mankind's nature and inter-relationship. Man is One. That, essentially, is what Marx is saying. Man is One, Humanity is One. Eventually, all social systems will tend towards a system which encourages that brotherhood or Oneness of man which Marx senses, as a spiritual Being. His vision is a spiritual one."[255]

---

[254] President Ezra Taft Benson, "Strengthening the Family," Conference Report, October, 1970, 22, http://scriptures.byu.edu/#:t6fc:p401.

[255] Creme, *The Reappearance of the Christ and the Masters of Wisdom*, 180-181.

To New Age gurus like Creme, communism is a "spiritual" message and foreshadows the system that will be implemented when Lord Maitreya comes to reign on earth. I recommend that the reader take the time to study this "Lord Maitreya," his Hierarchy, and the Ascended Masters of Wisdom who work with him to influence mankind and lead them into the jaws of a communist world government crowned by a global occult religion.

Bringing our tale back to the United Nations, we should note that the first Secretary-General of the U.N. was none other than Alger Hiss, the Soviet spy and influential advisor to FDR. Literally *every* U.N. Secretary-General since has been either a communist or socialist.[256] The U.N. General Assembly is composed of representatives from primarily socialist nations, including many of the "former" republics of the Soviet Union. Without hesitation, we can say that the United Nations is part of the Beast system described by John in Revelation, the very same which has been identified as communism by our prophets.

President Ezra Taft Benson made this remark about the U.N.:

> "When one stops to consider the degree of communist influence at the U.N., not only from countries that are totally behind the iron curtain, but from many of the non-communist countries as well, it is no wonder that the U.N. has *never* performed a real anti-communist act. How could it? On the other hand, it has helped the forces of communism on many occasions – helped either by direct action, as in the Congo, or by total paralysis, as in Hungary, Tibet and Israel. . . .
>
> "As long as communists are permitted to hold membership in and allowed to help direct the activities of the U.N., it can never keep

---

[256] John F. McManus, "Socialist-in-Chief: a History of the UN Secretaries General," *The New American*, April 26, 2016, accessed March 17, 2018, https://www.thenewamerican.com/reviews/opinion/item/23064-socialist-in-chief-a-history-of-the-un-secretaries-general.

the peace, and it can never promote the high ideals so glibly written into the Charter and the Declaration of Human Rights.

"We should get out of the U.N. and get the U.N. out of the United States."[257]

While any idea or program coming out of the United Nations should be immediately suspect – particularly in light of its vital occult and New Age affiliations – few should make us recoil more than the pagan environmental movement. This Green Communism is not even a good hoax – it is easily discerned as a threat to our way of life owing to its collectivist nature and foundation of lies.

Collectivism in all its forms has no place in America. It is contrary to the U.S. Constitution and to American tradition. Inasmuch as environmentalism helps transfer U.S. sovereignty to the United Nations – a body controlled by a hostile foreign power – it is aiding the enemy and is as treasonous as any philosophy of which I know. And inasmuch as the U.N. partners with occultists, it represents Satan's prototype of world government. Do not go green, for, if you do, you may really be going Red.

The Drugging of America and Organized Crime

Few things have damaged this once great nation as severely as have drugs. Drugs are an evil device used to enslave people to Satan, corrupt morals and values, and soften our society for eventual conquest. They are a scourge to humanity. Drugs are *not* a victimless crime; they destroy innocent lives every day and lower the national morality significantly. And the communists can be found lurking behind many of the organized crime syndicates used to distribute drugs within the United States.

J.R. Nyquist has written of the threat of organized crime wielded by modern Gadiantons:

---

[257] Benson, Newquist, ed., *An Enemy Hath Done This*, 207-208.

"Organized crime, under the control of an enemy power, is a tremendous weapon. The threat of this weapon is yet another dimension of the ongoing Cold War that was never fully appreciated in the West. Again and again, the Western mind separates the criminal sphere from the political sphere. It does not see that the two spheres have been combined in support of a global revolution. The strategic potential of mafias and of drug traffickers has been harnessed by Russia – and has long been used to subvert major institutions in Europe, Latin America, Canada and the United States."[258]

With the benefit of *The Book of Mormon's* account of the Gadianton Robbers, Latter-day Saints should realize that Satan's conspiracies *always* combine underground criminal activity with politics, religion, and every other aspect of life. When we look for the enemy, he can be found in every sphere of existence. And forever and always the Gadiantons seek influence in government, even if it means hooking entire populations on mind-numbing, soul-destroying substances.

According to a very meticulous plan, communists began using organized crime to dispense drugs throughout the United States, beginning with minority populations in the inner cities. It was assumed that if the black and Latino populations could be hooked with drugs, the habit would spill over into the rest of society. That is exactly what has happened.

Drugs have ripped the soul out of America. This is by design. It was not an accidental consequence. The communists knew, from their experience with opium in China, that drugs soften a population and makes them easier to conquer. Beginning with the cities, the communists have corrupted America from the inside out.

---

[258] Kincaid and Nyquist, *Red Jihad*, 83-84.

Author Joseph D. Douglass, Jr., in his preeminent book on the subject of communist drug-pushing titled *Red Cocaine*, wrote of this communist tactic. The information is taken directly from one of their own reports:

> "Racism was to be promoted because it was a destabilizing factor. Efforts were to be directed at the youth, since older blacks were believed to be too intimidated by the white establishment. Narcotics and propaganda were to be employed to "revolutionize" the blacks. Black unemployment was to be promoted. Emphasis was to be placed on the concept of "taking" or making the whites "give," in opposition to the concept of working.

> "This report also emphasized the need to bring Hispanic and black minorities together. The Hispanics were believed to be already well into drugs and by bringing them into closer contact with the U.S. blacks, the use of drugs in the black communities would be accelerated. The principle target of the drugs was the "lumpen proletariat," that is, the unemployed who were concentrated in the inner city ghettos. By pushing drugs into this group, crime and the general erosion of Western moral values would be stimulated because the use of drugs destroyed the judgement and led people into crime, homosexuality, and other immoral activities."[259]

By hooking the inner cities on drugs, the communists created a cancer in the bowels of America. We have not recovered from this cancer, but show more and more signs of illness as the years fly by.

President Russell M. Nelson gave a Conference talk in 1988 titled "Addiction or Freedom." In it, he said:

> "I raise my voice with others throughout the world who warn against abuse of drugs beyond prescribed limits, and the

---

[259] Joseph D. Douglass, Jr., *Red Cocaine: The Drugging of America* (Atlanta, Georgia: Clarion House, first edition, 1990), 89.

recreational or social use of chemical substances so often begun naively by the ill-informed.

". . . Enslaving shackles of habit are too small to be sensed until they are too strong to be broken. Indeed, drugs are the modern "mess of pottage" for which souls are sold. No families are free from risk. . . .

"Drugs such as LSD, marijuana, heroin, and cocaine are also endangering people throughout the earth. The noble attributes of reason, integrity, and dignity, which distinguish men and women from all other forms of life, are often the first to be attacked by these drugs and alcohol."[260]

The position of the Church on drugs is clear – drug use is a deadly scourge that is "endangering people throughout the earth." Those who take drugs sell their souls for a mess of pottage. Those who peddle drugs damn themselves even more.

There is nothing whatsoever good about drugs; no, not even marijuana despite the propaganda to make it appear as a miracle drug.[261] All drugs – yes, even prescription drugs – impair a person's free will and reasoning abilities. As such, drugs are a key weapon in Satan's arsenal.

---

[260] President Russel M. Nelson, "Addiction or Freedom," General Conference, October, 1988, https://www.lds.org/general-conference/1988/10/addiction-or-freedom?lang=eng.

[261] Hemp – as opposed to marijuana which contains high-inducing THC – is indeed a miracle plant offering mankind tens of thousands of practical, beneficial uses including medicines, paper, clothes, building materials, rope, food, health care products, and other industrial supplies. But, in typical fashion, Satan inverts these facts and spreads the lie that marijuana is healthy and good. It is not. Don't be deceived. Know the difference between hemp and marijuana and don't be found on the wrong side of this equation. Do not throw your support behind efforts to legalize marijuana. If you do, you will be aiding and abetting the wicked drug culture that is rapidly rising in the United States.

In the book of Revelation, the Apostle John uses the word "sorcery" to describe one of the ways that Satan's minions will bewitch the world in the latter days. One of the relevant verses, speaking of Babylon, reads:

> "And the light of a candle shall shine no more at all in thee; and the voice of the bridegroom and of the bride shall be heard no more at all in thee: for thy merchants were the great men of the earth; for by thy sorceries were all nations deceived" (Revelation 18:23).

The Greek word translated as sorcery in English is *pharmakeia*. *Pharmakeia* has multiple meanings, one referring to magic and the other implying pharmaceuticals or drugs. Our word pharmacy in fact comes from this word. *Strong's Concordance* defines *pharmakeia* as "the use of medicine, drugs or spells." *HELPS Word-Studies* defines it as "drug-related sorcery, like the practice of magical-arts."[262]

Perhaps both definitions apply simultaneously in this case. At any rate, one of the probable implications is that Satan will use drugs, including legal, over-the-counter drugs, to deceive the nations. Those familiar with the plague of anti-depressants, vaccines, GMO-food, and other items that could fall under the umbrella "drugs," must conclude that this prophecy has come to fruition. Make every effort to wean yourself and your family off of these soul-destroying, conscience-eroding drugs.

Author Robert E. Hales wrote of some of the entities pushing drugs on the streets:

> "Truly, organized crime is a vehicle which helps fulfill Satan's intent to control people's lives and to destroy the souls and happiness of men, thus making them miserable like unto himself. . . .

---

[262] "Pharmakeia," *Bible Hub*, accessed March 17, 2018, http://biblehub.com/greek/5331.htm.

> "In previous decades gangs were only a large-city problem, but gangs have now spread to every part of our society and culture. They are growing greatly in power and influence."[263]

Following the trajectory outlined by the communists, drugs and organized crime have spread from the big cities to every corner of our nation. Through organized crime syndicates, the communist conspiracy has poured drugs into the United States. By the late 1960s – the era of sex, drugs, and rock 'n' roll – the Soviets controlled at least 37% of the illicit drug industry in the United States, and the program showed no signs of slowing.[264]

President M. Russell Ballard once spoke of drugs and secret combinations and their danger to our society. Pay careful attention to his words:

> "The Book of Mormon teaches that secret combinations engaged in crime present a serious challenge, not just to individuals and families but to entire civilizations. Among today's secret combinations are gangs, drug cartels, and organized crime families. The secret combinations of our day function much like the Gadianton robbers of the Book of Mormon times. They have secret signs and code words. They participate in secret rites and initiation ceremonies. Among their purposes are to "murder, and plunder, and steal, and commit whoredoms and all manner of wickedness, contrary to the laws of their country and also the laws of their God."

> "If we are not careful, today's secret combinations can obtain power and influence just as quickly and just as completely as they did in Book of Mormon times. Do you remember the pattern? The secret combinations began among the "more wicked part" of

---

[263] Hales, *Secret Combinations of Today*, 95.

[264] Douglass, *Red Cocaine: The Drugging of America*, 180.

society, but eventually "seduced the more part of the righteous" until the whole society was polluted.

"Today's young people, just as those "of the rising generation" in Book of Mormon times, are the most susceptible to the influence of gangs. Our young men and young women see it all around them. There is an entire subculture that celebrates contemporary gangs and their criminal conduct with music, clothing styles, language, attitudes, and behaviors. Many of you have watched as trendy friends have embraced the style as something that was "fashionable" and "cool," only to be dragged into the subculture because of their identification with gangs. We've all heard the tragic stories of unsuspecting wanna-bes who have been victimized by gangs simply because they were wearing the wrong color in the wrong neighborhood.

"The Book of Mormon teaches that the devil is the "author of all sin" and the founder of these secret combinations. He uses secret combinations, including gangs, "from generation to generation according as he can get hold upon the hearts of the children of men." His purpose is to destroy individuals, families, communities, and nations. To a degree, he was successful during Book of Mormon times. And he is having far too much success today. That's why it is so important for us as priesthood holders to take a firm stand for truth and right by doing what we can to help keep our communities safe."[265]

Truly, a secret combination is behind much of the drug-pushing in the United States and throughout the world. This combination is the communist conspiracy.

---

[265] President M. Russell Ballard, "Standing for Truth and Right," General Conference, October, 1997, https://www.lds.org/general-conference/1997/10/standing-for-truth-and-right?lang=eng.

Drug addiction is a core element in the Adversary's plan to conquer the world. A drug-addicted population is an easily subjected population. The proliferation of drugs is a symptom of our dramatic decline as a once powerful, free, and moral People. If we do not acknowledge the fact that drug abuse is a grave problem and immediately address it by hunting down those who push drugs and punish them as severely as the Nephites punished Gadianton Robbers and king-men (3 Nephi 5:4-5), the "author of all sin" will get his way and his secret combinations will strengthen their already staggering influence over us.

Civil Rights

The next front which I choose to highlight is the Civil Rights movement and the modern manifestations of racial strife. It may surprise you to learn that Martin Luther King, Jr. was a diehard Marxist and that the entire Civil Rights agenda was a communist-inspired drive to create a "Soviet America" through the age-old divide and conquer strategy. I refer you to my book *A Century of Red* and to my article "MLK: Communist Revolutionary, Plagiarizer, Degenerate"[266] for more on this sordid subject.

Communists always seek to stir up strife and cause division. This is most effective if there are preexisting prejudices, animosities, or grievances, such as was the case in America because of the slavery of yesteryear. In these cases, communist agents seek to pour as much salt into the wounds as possible.

In 1920, Lenin drafted a document for the subversive Communist International (Comintern). This document stated:

> "All communist parties must directly support the revolutionary movement among the nations that are dependent and do not

---

[266] Zack Strong, "MLK: Communist Revolutionary, Plagiarizer, Degenerate," *The American Citadel*, January 15, 2008, https://theamericancitadel.com/2018/01/15/mlk-communist-revolutionary-plagiarizer-degenerate/.

have equal rights (for example Ireland, the Negroes in America, and so forth), and in the colonies."[267]

In pursuance to this directive from Moscow, the Comintern began fueling the flames of division on a global scale. The movement progressed slowly in the United States, but, in 1932, William Z. Foster ran for president under the Communist Party ticket with a black vice-presidential candidate named James W. Ford. Together, this communist duo promoted a black uprising, cheered for "equal rights for Negroes everywhere," and gushed about a future "Soviet America."

In 1935, the Communist Party USA followed the same line in a pamphlet titled *The Negroes in a Soviet America*. One of the authors was the aforementioned James Ford. Among other things, Ford and his co-author James S. Allen called for "another revolution in the United States." This revolution would be a result of the black uprising which they predicted. On the coattails of this revolution would come a "Soviet America." In this "Soviet America," whites were to be reeducated with socialism. Through this reeducation, the whites' supposed racism was to be thoroughly beat out of them. Finally, the authors declared: "Only on the basis of socialism is the possibility created for the full and equal development of the Negro people."[268]

J. Edgar Hoover once wrote:

> "The Party's claim that it is working for Negro rights is a deception and a fraud. The Party's sole interest, as most American Negroes know, is to hoodwink the Negro, to exploit him and use him as a tool to build a communist America."[269]

---

[267] John Riddell, "Black liberation and the Communist International," *International Socialist Review*, Issue 81, January, 2012, accessed March 17, 2018, https://isreview.org/issue/81/black-liberation-and-communist-international.

[268] James W. Ford and James S. Allen, *The Negroes in a Soviet America* (1935), 2, 47.

[269] Hoover, *Masters of Deceit*, 229.

Exploitation is the name of the game. The communists seek to convince blacks and other minorities that they are "victims," thereby employing them as cannon fodder for their world revolution.

In his book, *Color, Communism and Common Sense*, ex-communist Manning Johnson, a black man, described the trap the communists have set for America by fueling racial tensions. He said:

> "Little did I realize until I was deeply enmeshed in the *Red Conspiracy,* that just and seeming grievances are exploited to transform idealism into a cold and ruthless weapon against the capitalist system—that this is the end toward which all the communist efforts among Negroes are directed.

> "Indeed, I had entered the red conspiracy in the vain belief that it was the way to a "new, better and superior" world system of society. Ten years later, thoroughly disillusioned, I abandoned communism. The experiences of those years in "outer darkness" are like a horrible nightmare. I saw communism in all its naked cruelty, ruthlessness and utter contempt of Christian attributes and passions. And, too, I saw the low value placed upon human life, the total lack of respect for the dignity of man, the betrayal of trust, the terror of the Secret Police and the bloody hand of the assassin, during and since, those fateful years when I embraced communism."[270]

Johnson was an honest man and realized, after a decade of firsthand experience working with the communists in the United States at a high level, that communism was destroying blacks while claiming to fight for them. He realized that the race issue was being used to divide, rather than heal, America. Referring to his fellow black American communists who

---

[270] Manning Johnson, *Color, Communism and Common Sense* (New York: Alliance, Inc., 1958), chapter 1, accessed March 17, 2018, http://manningjohnson.org/book/CCCS_Contents.html.

collaborated with the Moscow-based communists in their destructive work, he noted:

> "They are the ones that history may well record as the political Uncle Toms who plotted with a diabolical alien power the moral decay, physical slavery and spiritual death of their own race."[271]

Truly, communists have stoked the flames of racial strife in the United States since at least the 1930s. They are also behind the revolting campaign to inculcate whites with "white guilt." The communists want to guilt trip whites into hating their incredible heritage and the free and noble institutions their ancestors established, and to acquiesce to socialistic laws and "reparations" because of events related to slavery that occurred long before they or their grandparents were born. This Soviet-style anti-white racism is an attempt to make whites a minority in the nation their forefathers built. It is, at its core, an effort to create strife and, if possible, a civil war which can be manipulated to bring communist agents into power. Remember, communism thrives on chaos and cannot come fully to power without it. This was true of Gadiantonism and it is true of communism.

Not only were open and avowed communists such as Manning Johnson and James Allen part of the Civil Rights movement, but nearly all major figures within that movement were communists. Even minor figures like Rosa Parks were communists. When Rosa Parks refused to give up her place on the bus in 1955, that was not a spontaneous act of civil disobedience; it was a contrived political stunt designed to further the communist Civil Rights agenda. Parks was a member of the communist front organization the National Association for the Advancement of Colored People (NAACP). Additionally, Parks attended a communist training school known as the Highlander Folk School just prior to her

---

[271] Johnson, *Color, Communism and Common Sense*, chapter 3, http://manningjohnson.org/book/CCCS_Contents.html.

famous incident on the bus.[272] Parks was a subversive agent of the communist conspiracy, *not* an American hero who stood up (or sat down) for "equality."

Malcolm X was also a communist. When communist murderer and dictator Fidel Castro visited the United States in 1960, Malcolm X put him up in a hotel in Harlem. Malcolm X wrote about the wonderful "impression among the Negroes" made by Castro and his communist entourage. Malcolm X fell in love with Castro and later remarked that he was the only white person he ever liked.[273] Needless to say, Malcolm X promoted the communist agenda as it related to black revolutionary activity within the United States.

The arch-communist leader of the Civil Rights movement was Martin Luther King, Jr. MLK famously said that we should judge a man by the "content of his character." I agree. We ought to look past façades and rhetoric to the inner heart of an individual. Having researched the content of MLK's character, it is my estimation that MLK was an all-around terrible person and a subversive communist, regardless of his rhetoric about "equality," "rights," and the like. A few facts may be enlightening.

King was a known adulterer who frequently engaged in drunken sex orgies with prostitutes. FBI records — most of which are still classified and deliberately kept from the American People — overflow with accounts of his sexual exploits. MLK is known to have physically abused prostitutes on occasion. We have record of King coercing female prostitutes into lesbian acts for his viewing pleasure. King was a sadistic degenerate and a thoroughly wicked man possessed of a demonic spirit.

---

[272] Henry Makow, "'Red' Rosa Parks: Fabricating an American Icon," *Rense*, November 5, 2005, accessed March 17, 2018, http://www.rense.com/general68/rosa.htm.

[273] David Smith, "Fidel Castro in the US: cars, cigars and a meeting with Malcolm X," *The Guardian*, November 27, 2016, accessed March 17, 2018, https://www.theguardian.com/world/2016/nov/27/fidel-castro-new-york-malcolm-x.

King often hosted leadership conferences for pastors and aspiring urban leaders. At these conferences, drunken orgies were commonplace. A recently declassified FBI report contains this account from a Christian attendee at one of King's conferences:

> "One Negro minister in attendance later expressed his disgust with the behind-the-scenes drinking, fornication, and homosexuality that went on at the conference. Several Negro and white prostitutes were brought in from the Miami area. An all-night sex orgy was held with these prostitutes and some of the delegates in attendance.
>
> "One room had a large table in it which was filled with whiskey. The two Negro prostitutes were paid $50.00 to put on a sex show for the entertainment of guests. A variety of sex acts deviating from the normal were observed."

As if this was not disturbing enough, the FBI report contains another description of similar perversions:

> "As early as January, 1964, King engaged in another two-day, drunken sex orgy in Washington, D.C. Many of those present engaged in sexual acts, natural as well as unnatural, for the entertainment of onlookers. When one of the females shied away from engaging in an unnatural act, King and other of the males present discussed how she was to be taught and initiated in this respect.
>
> "Throughout the ensuing years and until this date King has continued to carry on his sexual aberrations secretly while holding himself out to public view as a moral leader of religious conviction."[274]

---

[274] "Martin Luther King, Jr., A Current Analysis," Federal Bureau of Investigation, March 12, 1968, accessed March 17, 2018, https://www.archives.gov/files/research/jfk/releases/104-10125-10133.pdf.

Yes, Martin Luther King, Jr. was a degenerate of the highest order. While pretending to be a righteous reverend, he was actually a promiscuous peddler of filth and depravity. He was a hypocrite who deserves not one ounce of our respect and admiration – and certainly not a national holiday.

Apart from his rampant immorality, King was also a prolific plagiarizer. He knowingly plagiarized his speeches, books, and doctoral dissertation. This has even been admitted by sources friendly to King. In truth, King's doctoral and theological degrees should be revoked and the titles reverend and doctor stripped from his name. MLK was a total fraud. Even the name "Martin Luther King, Jr." was a phony. His real name was Michael King.

Furthermore, King's rallies – contrary to public perception – were violent. MLK is touted as the paragon of nonviolence and peaceful civil disobedience, yet he was arrested numerous times for attempting to obstruct lawful arrests, for interfering with police officers in the line of duty, for disobeying injunctions against his rallies, for causing public disorder, etc. King deliberately collaborated with violent black nationalist groups who vowed to cause violence. Preceding his famous march in Washington, D.C., King told reporters: "Jail will be the safest place in Washington this spring."[275]

Finally, we know from various sources that King was a closet communist. Not only did King attend a communist training center, but he surrounded himself almost exclusively with communist advisors and collaborators. One such advisor was the Jewish communist Stanely Levison. It was Levison, not King, who wrote "King's" book *Where Do We Go From Here?* Levison might be described as King's handler. Levison himself wrote to a fellow communist, Clarence Jones, that MLK was such a "slow thinker"

---

[275] Ibid.

that "under no circumstances should King be permitted to say anything without their approving it."[276]

In 1962, Levison wrote to Gus Hall, the General Secretary of the CPUSA, that "King is a whole-hearted Marxist who has studied it (Marxism), believes in it and agrees with it, but because of his being a minister of religion, does not dare espouse it publicly."[277] While espousing communism in secret, MLK held himself up as a man of God, a humble social reformer, and a friend of the American People. Truthfully, King was a traitor to the country, to his own race, and to Freedom-loving people everywhere. Think of how shameful it is that the United States has a national holiday in honor of this communist agent, habitual plagiarizer, and diehard sex addict!

I have demonstrated that the leaders of the Civil Rights movement were subversive communists. But what of the crowing jewel of the movement, the Civil Rights Act of 1964? Sadly, the Civil Rights Act was a piece of communist legislation from start to finish. It did not promote rights but, rather, extended the government's already bloated power and restricted the Liberty of Americans by chipping away at our constitutionally-protected right to discriminate.

By the word "discriminate" I do *not* refer to racism, but to the true sense of the term discriminate, which means to choose. Choosing with whom to associate and do business is a *fundamental right* – a right protected by the First Amendment as well as the unwritten laws of human nature. Yet, the Civil Rights Act mercilessly assaulted this constitutionally-protected right by granting the government power to intervene in private business affairs. The right of discrimination/association was bartered away to the applause of the American People.

---

[276] Ibid.

[277] Ibid.

I stated previously that I favor equality under the law. Every Liberty-loving American patriot does. Indeed, this is the American tradition established by the Founding Fathers – those men so unjustly called "bigots" and "racists" by today's activists. The Declaration of Independence proclaimed man's equality under the law back in 1776. In 1787, the U.S. Constitution canonized this doctrine. The Constitution's supremacy clause meant that no state, or public institution, could legally deny any right to any of its citizens.

Thus, not having "equal" laws and "equal" rights was never the issue. Rather, the problem was one of enforcement. This glorious principle enshrined in our founding documents had not, in some cases, been properly applied and enforced by America's public servants. In the legitimate cases of unjust segregation in public institutions, the officers of government should have invoked their constitutional authority and defended the rights of those being wronged. But to claim new legislation was necessary to make everyone "equal" flew in the face of history and denied the American heritage of Freedom and the Constitution's guarantee of equality under the law.

I repeat: The Civil Rights Act was an abomination that violated the Constitution's protection of individual Liberty in the name of defending Liberty. It is the communist way to declare "peace" when waging war; to "liberate" when enslaving populations; to advocate "rights" while stealing them; and to "fight for equality" by destroying the very document inspired of God to ensure it.

President Ezra Taft Benson was disgusted with the Civil Rights Act and described it as "about 10 percent civil rights and 90 percent a further extension of socialistic Federal controls."[278] And so it was. Yet, how many of us – even members of the Church with the privilege of higher discernment through the gift of the Holy Ghost – blindly accept the Civil

---

[278] Wallace Turner, "For Benson, The Wait Is Nearly Over," *The New York Times*, November 8, 1985, accessed March 17, 2018, http://www.nytimes.com/1985/11/08/us/for-benson-the-wait-is-nearly-over.html.

Rights Act and believe it was a "step forward," true "progress," or a victory for "equality"?

Citing President Benson's remarks about the communist Civil Rights Act in context would be beneficial. In a 1963 speech, as the Civil Rights Act was being drawn up, presented, and debated, President Benson declared:

> "There are three possible methods by which the Communists might take us over. One would be through a sufficient amount of infiltration and propaganda, to disguise Communism as just another political party.

> "The second method would be by fomenting internal civil war in this country, and aiding the communists' side in that war with all necessary military might.

> "The third method would be by a slow insidious infiltration resulting in a takeover without the American people realizing it.

> "The Soviets would not attempt military conquest of so powerful and so extensive a country as the United States without availing themselves of a sufficiently strong fifth column in our midst, a fifth column which would provide the sabotage, the false leadership, and the sudden seizures of power and of means of communication, needed to convert the struggle, from the very beginning, into a civil war rather than clear-cut war with an external enemy.

> "We can foresee a possibility of the Kremlin taking this gamble in time. In fact, it is clear that the Communists long ago made plans to have this method available, in whole or in part, to whatever extent it might be useful. The trouble in our southern states has been fomented almost entirely by the Communists for this purpose. It has been their plan, gradually carried out over a long period with meticulous cunning, to stir up such bitterness between the whites and blacks in the South that small flames of civil disorder would inevitably result. They could then fan and

coalesce these little flames into one great conflagration of civil war, in time, if the need arose.

"The whole slogan of "civil rights" as used to make trouble in the South today, is an exact parallel to the slogan of "Agrarian reform" which they used in China. The pending "civil rights" legislation is, I am convinced, about 10% civil rights and about 90% a further extension of socialistic Federal controls. It is part of the pattern for the Communist takeover of America. The whole "civil rights" program and slogan in America today is just as phony as were the "Agrarian reform" program and slogan of the Communists in China 20 years ago."[279]

As you can see, many of my comments in this section are but a repeat of what President Benson said all those decades ago. The entire Civil Rights movement was a sham from the beginning; a communist front designed to feed the flames of hatred and ultimately split America apart along racial lines. Those who supported the movement were, to one degree or another, communist dupes.

Today, due to decades of communist propagandizing and subversion, over 90% of blacks vote Democrat. From its stance on welfarism to guns to banking to foreign aid to abortion to marriage, the Democratic Party platform is almost straight communism (and there is no substantive difference between the Democratic and the Republican Party when the rhetoric is stripped away and you exam their track record). Consequently, not only are we confronted with racial division, but a very marked ideological struggle.

Minorities have been coopted into the worldwide revolution by smooth-talking communists and their allies who have convinced these groups that they are "victims" who must avenge themselves on their white "oppressors." At the present time, black leaders are *still* calling for

---

[279] Ezra Taft Benson, "We Must Become Alerted and Informed," speech, December 13, 1963, in Newquist, ed., *Prophets, Principles and National Survival*, 271-272.

"reparations" for the evils of slavery – an institution which officially ended 153 years ago.[280] Thus, a ruthless cadre within the black community has become part of the "fifth column" President Benson warned about. President Barack Obama – an all but admitted Marxist revolutionary who championed the communist cause – is the chief representation of what the black community has been twisted into by their Bolshevik taskmasters.

President Benson's above remarks attest that he was very vocal against the Civil Rights movement, correctly recognizing it as a communist agenda of division and hate. President Benson also wrote the foreword to a hard-hitting book by Wes Andrews which I highly recommend titled *The Black Hammer: A Study of Black Power, Red Influence and White Alternatives*. In this work, Andrews wrote:

> "Very frankly, if [the advocates of Black Power] succeed in its implementation, this bloodthirsty philosophy will be relegated to history as the BLACK HAMMER which drove the Communist spikes into the hearts and hands of America. In the words of one of its most vociferous spokesmen – known to the initiated as Brother Lennie, of Watts – "Black Power means the complete and total destruction of the white power structure" by whatever means are necessary. The battle cry is "move on over, or we'll move on over you.""[281]

Today, the "black hammer" is still being used to divide the American People along racial and ideological lines. Over the past few years, the de facto terrorist group Black Lives Matter has dominated news headlines.

---

[280] Donna Owens, "Veteran Congressman Still Pushing for Reparations in a Divided America," *NBC News*, February 20, 2017, accessed April 20, 2018, https://www.nbcnews.com/news/nbcblk/rep-john-conyers-still-pushing-reparations-divided-america-n723151.

[281] Wes Andrews and Clyde Dalton, *The Black Hammer: A Study of Black Power, Red Influence and White Alternatives* (Oakland, California: Desco Press, 1967), 32-33.

Along with other likeminded groups such as the revamped Black Panthers, this racist, communist organization has been at the forefront of the attempt to blame all whites for all the ills of society.

In response to the allegations that whites – including white police – are waging a war against blacks, retired police officer Doug Traubel wrote the following in his all-star book *Red Badge*:

> "The "Hands Up, Don't Shoot" and "Black Lives Matter" dolts ignore this black-on-black holocaust and black-on-police officer violence.

> "Instead, these demonstrators portray all blacks as mere innocents terrorized by a bigoted legal system and its sadistic enforcers. They are part of the Black Liberation Movement. It is a farce; another Marxist revolutionary group calling for social justice.

> ""Police killings of blacks are an extremely rare feature of black life and are a minute fraction of black homicide deaths," argues Manhattan Institute fellow Heather MacDonald.

> ""The police could end all killings of civilians tomorrow and it would have no effect on the black homicide risk, which comes overwhelmingly from other blacks.""[282]

The black community is indeed being attacked – by itself and by the communist traitors it has chosen for its leaders. There is simply *no* white-on-black war going on. Indeed, crime statistics show an appalling, and increasing, trend of black-on-white, racially-motivated violent crime, as well as an ever-steady rate of massive black-on-black crime and violence. I cite but one paragraph from a news report on black crime rates:

---

[282] Doug Traubel, *Red Badge: A Veteran Peace Officer's Commentary on the Marxist Subversion of American Law Enforcement and Culture* (February 14, 2016), 204-205.

> "Despite being outnumbered by whites five to one, blacks commit *eight times* more crimes against whites than vice-versa, according to FBI statistics from 2007. A black male is 40 times as likely to assault a white person as the reverse. These figures also show that interracial rape is almost exclusively black on white."[283]

If there is a race war going on in this country, you can rest assured that it is *not* being instigated by whites. Truth be told, though institutionalized slavery spanned millennia in every corner of the globe, it was the white European races that ended it as an institution throughout the Western hemisphere and much of the world. It was a white man, the great Thomas Jefferson, who attempted to end slavery first through his work in the Virginia House of Burgesses, and later by including a condemnation of the institution in the original draft of the *Declaration of Independence*. That Jefferson draft copy – errors and all – included this hearty rebuke of slavery:

> "[King George] has waged cruel war against human nature itself, violating it's most sacred rights of life & liberty in the persons of a distant people who never offended him, captivating & carrying them into slavery in another hemisphere, or to incur miserable death in their transportation thither. this piratical warfare, the opprobrium of infidel powers, is the warfare of the CHRISTIAN king of Great Britain. determined to keep open a market where MEN should be bought & sold, he has prostituted his negative for suppressing every legislative attempt to prohibit or to restrain this execrable commerce: and that this assemblage of horrors might want no fact of distinguished die, he is now exciting those very people to rise in arms among us, and to purchase that liberty of which he has deprived them, & murdering the people upon whom he also obtruded them; thus paying off former crimes committed

---

[283] Paul Joseph Watson, "Black Crime Facts The White Liberal Media Daren't Talk About," *InfoWars*, May 5, 2015, accessed March 17, 2018, https://www.infowars.com/black-crime-facts-that-the-white-liberal-media-darent-talk-about/.

against the liberties of one people, with crimes which he urges them to commit against the lives of another."[284]

As history would have it, Jefferson's draft was shortened and the paragraph on slavery excised. What we are left with is this simple declaration which has reverberated throughout the Union and which set the stage for the future abolition of slavery:

> "We hold these truths to be self-evident, that all men are created equal, that they are endowed by their Creator with certain unalienable rights, that among these are Life, Liberty, and the pursuit of Happiness."

Elsewhere in his incredible book, Officer Traubel wrote a spot-on description of communism's true intent in using fronts such as the Civil Rights movement:

> "The true goal is the seizure of power through subversion for the benefit of an elite ruling class. To accomplish this America must be discredited in the eyes of the majority. To that end, the Diversity Movement promotes the myth that today even with a "black" president in the White House put there by white votes – the U.S. is a racist, bigoted country with no moral authority that oppresses victim classes made of non-white minorities, women and homosexual/transgender people. This hate and intolerance is said to come from generations of political and cultural dominance by white male conservatives and Christians."[285]

For decades, white, Christian America has been exposed to unrelenting propaganda demonizing us and portraying us as intolerant, racist, homophobic, closedminded, nationalist (as if that is a bad thing), etc. In

---

[284] Julian P. Boyd, ed., *The Papers of Thomas Jefferson*, Vol. 1 (Princeton: Princeton University Press, 1950), 243-247, accessed April 25, 2018, https://www.loc.gov/exhibits/declara/ruffdrft.html.

[285] Traubel, *Red Badge*, 21.

truth, these people – inspired by communist agitators – are the most intolerant, belligerent, and racist group in the country. And when I say "these people," I refer to people of any stripe, race, or creed who have gone along knowingly or unwittingly with the communist subversion, including its victim ideology and anti-white, anti-Christian, anti-constitution smear campaign.

When you recall that our prophets have taught that communism is a *Satanic* philosophy, all of these attempts to divide and conquer come into brighter focus.[286] When you remember that communism is *anti-Christ*, it makes sense that it would attack the traditional Christian institutions our People have cherished for generations.[287] When you understand that the Devil is the father of these lies, it only makes sense that he would play upon the fears and prejudices of minority groups in order to foment a fear-based, hate-driven national crisis designed to fracture the majority white Christian bloc which has held America together all these years.[288]

---

[286] "I say unto you, be one; and if ye are not one ye are not mine. And again, I say unto you that the enemy in the secret chambers seeketh your lives. Ye hear of wars in far countries, and you say that there will soon be great wars in far countries, but ye know not the hearts of men in your own land." – Doctrine and Covenants 38:27-29

[287] "For behold, the Spirit of Christ is given to every man, that he may know good from evil; wherefore, I show unto you the way to judge; for every thing which inviteth to do good, and to persuade to believe in Christ, is sent forth by the power and gift of Christ; wherefore ye may know with a perfect knowledge it is of God. But whatsoever thing persuadeth men to do evil, and believe not in Christ, and deny him, and serve not God, then ye may know with a perfect knowledge it is of the devil; for after this manner doth the devil work, for he persuadeth no man to do good, no, not one; neither do his angels; neither do they who subject themselves unto him." – Moroni 7:16-17

"For I say unto you that whatsoever is good cometh from God, and whatsoever is evil cometh from the devil." – Alma 5:40

"For God is not the author of confusion, but of peace, as in all churches of the saints." – 1 Corinthians 14:33

[288] "For God hath not given us the spirit of fear; but of power, and of love, and of a sound mind." – 2 Timothy 1:7

Unfortunately, this racial thrust by Satan's henchmen has been as successful as it is clever.

Red Terrorism

Terrorism, broadly defined, has existed from the earliest days of humanity's sojourn on earth. The roots of modern terrorism, however, stretch back to the 1800s when the communist revolution was coming into its own. In chapter five, I cited a lengthy article written by President William Budge. President Budge, serving in as a mission president in England at the time, described the communistic terrorism taking root throughout Europe and spreading from there to the rest of the world. Said he:

> "The character of those combinations is well known by their outcroppings, as observable in the sanguinary, murderous history of the French commune; the destructive course of a similar element in the United States, scarce two years since, during the great railroad strikes; the Nihilistic assassinations of government officials in Russia; the socialistic attempts at murder in Germany, and the various late attempts against monarchy, in the efforts to take the lives of several of the crowned heads of Europe. These show the objects to be the possession of gain and power, the necessity of shedding blood to obtain them being considered no obstacle."[289]

"Therefore, whosoever belongeth to my church need not fear, for such shall inherit the kingdom of heaven." – Doctrine and Covenants 10:55

"For none of these iniquities come of the Lord; for he doeth that which is good among the children of men; and he doeth nothing save it be plain unto the children of men; and he inviteth them all to come unto him and partake of his goodness; and he denieth none that come unto him, black and white, bond and free, male and female; and he remembereth the heathen; and all are alike unto God, both Jew and Gentile." – 2 Nephi 26:33

[289] President William Budge, "Secret Combinations," *The Latter-Day Saints' Millennial Star*, Vol. 41, 248-250, April 21, 1879, http://contentdm.lib.byu.edu/cdm/compoundobject/collection/MStar/id/39268/rec/1.

The secret combinations that dotted Europe in the 1800s, you will recall, originated in the amalgam of Illuminati, Freemason, and Jewish conspirators. These groups spawned what came to be known as communism. These communists used every means – including, very prominently, terrorism and assassination – to create the chaotic conditions in which they could bring themselves to power. The ultimate manifestation of this organized terrorism was the 1917 Bolshevik coup and its bloody aftermath.

Communist revolutionary terrorism found fertile ground in the Russian empire, most particularly among the disaffected Jewish population. With few (though rapidly increasing) rights, little (though rapidly increasing) power, and no Christian moral foundation, the Jewish population living in the Pale of Settlement (and beginning to spread throughout the Russian empire) provided a willing pool of revolutionaries for the conspiracy's world revolution. Jewish involvement in communist terrorism and subversion was so conspicuous that a Russian satirist wrote: "Eleven anarchists were executed at the city jail; fifteen of them were Jews."[290]

Anna Geifman, in her superb book *Thou Shalt Kill: Revolutionary Terrorism in Russia, 1894-1917*, observed:

> "In their writings on Jewish involvement in the Russian revolutionary movement, several thinkers, foremost among them Nikolai Berdiaev, noted that the Jewish radicals had emerged from an environment dominated by the profound, centuries-old pride and spiritual burden of being the chosen people. These writers sought to trace the roots of Jewish radicalism to a concept that lies at the heart of the Jewish national and religious identity – the messianic ideal. Connected with the dream of a Jewish homeland and the quest to overcome the tremendous catastrophe of the diaspora and the associated misfortunes and

---

[290] Anna Geifman, *Thou Shalt Kill: Revolutionary Terrorism in Russia, 1894-1917* (Princeton: Princeton University Press, 1993), 34.

injustices that have befallen the Jews throughout history, the messianic tradition encompasses the belief that salvation and glory will ultimately be attained by the entire Jewish nation on earth, rather than by selected individuals following death. . . .

"Indeed, having on the surface broken all ties with religion, Jewish radicals merely reshaped and restated the traditional messianic outlook to conform to the new historical situation and intellectual concepts. The old beliefs verbalized in a new and slightly altered form are particularly notable in the teachings of Karl Marx, whom Berdiaev called "a very typical Jew." A materialist who denied any higher principles, Marx transformed the idea of a messiah leading the Israeli people to an ultimate paradise on earth into a theory envisioning the eventual redemption of the world from oppression and injustice by the new chosen people – the proletariat. This adaptation of familiar assumptions to the atheist perception of reality (which included Marx's emphasis on class, rather than individuals, as the only active agent in the historical process) proved extremely attractive to many Russian Jews, who began to participate in radical politics in large numbers directly proportionate with the degree of dissemination of Marxism in the empire late in the nineteenth century."[291]

So many Jews – instilled with the sense of revolutionary purpose that communism gave them and the hopes of power it promised – filled the communist ranks that when the first Soviet government was formed in 1917, nearly 85% of the officers of that regime were Jewish.[292] Of the 388 members of that first communist government, only 16 were Russians. Most of the rest were Jews.[293] When communist revolutions erupted in

---

[291] Geifman, *Thou Shalt Kill*, 32-33.

[292] "Putin: First Soviet Government Was Mostly Jewish," June 20, 2013, *Haaretz Daily Newspaper Ltd.*, accessed April 21, 2018, https://www.haaretz.com/jewish/news/1.530857.

[293] Denis Fahey, *The Rulers of Russia* (1938; Fitzwilliam, NH: Loreto Publications, 2014), 30.

other nations – Germany, Hungary, Spain, Mexico, etc., – Jews were invariably chosen by Moscow to head up operations. Two notable examples are Bela Kun in Hungary and Rosa Luxemburg in Germany.

This wildly disproportionate Jewish involvement in communism has led some to incorrectly call communism a Jewish conspiracy. Communism is *not* a Jewish conspiracy. Rather, communism is a *Satanic* conspiracy which a disproportionate number of Jews belong to. Having forsaken their religion, or, in fact, having been driven by modern Judaism's apostate and anti-Christ and Kabbalistic elements to the Adversary, Jews have found a home in the counterfeit state religion of communism.

Jews have always been a revolutionary people – both for good and for evil. They have been noted for their violent outburst and proclivity for revolution. It only makes sense, then, that Satan would work hard to seduce them to his side to use them in his revolt against God. And, considering the covenants made with Abraham, Isaac, and Jacob, and their posterity, Satan would see enlisting Jews in his war as a slap in the face to the Eternal Father.

Most of the Jews involved with communism were avowed atheists, but some of the primary leaders of Jewish ethnicity, such as Marx and Lenin, were Satanists. Richard Wurmbrand, in his must-read book *Marx & Satan*, wrote:

> "It is essential at this point to state emphatically that Marx and his comrades, while anti-God, were not atheists, as present-day Marxists claim to be. That is, while they openly denounced and reviled God, *they hated a God in whom they believed*. They challenged not His existence, but His supremacy."[294]

Apart from the Jewish heritage of a large swath of communists, another unifying factor was the penchant for using terrorism. As part of their tribal nature and their ability to hold a grudge indefinitely, Jews made perfect

---

[294] Wurmbrand, *Marx and Satan*, 29.

terrorists once converted to communism. But Gentiles could be just as merciless and cruel once corrupted by communism, as the case of Joseph Stalin evinces. At any rate, it was among these hardhearted communists of Russia that organized terrorism was used as a tactic of revolution.

Lenin was particularly fond of terrorism. He once fumed:

> "When I see Social Democrats proudly and smugly declaring, 'We are not anarchists, thieves, robbers, we are superior to all this, we reject guerrilla warfare' – I ask myself: Do these people realize what they are saying?"[295]

Lenin was continuously chiding his fellow communists for not being cruel enough and for being too slow to use terror and force to get their way. After all, Lenin had taught:

> "The revolutionary army is needed because great historical issues can be resolved only by force."[296]

Lenin was of the same school of thought as Gadianton chief Giddianhi, who believed plunder, murder, and guerrilla warfare were "good" (3 Nephi 3:9). This communist kingpin loved murder and bloodshed so much that he often laughed about it openly. British socialist Bertrand Russell once traveled to Moscow and met Lenin. In their conversation, Russell recorded that Lenin laughed about how he had incited the peasants to murderous violence. Russell recalled: "His guffaw at the thought of those massacred made my blood run cold."[297]

Another gruesome incident gives insight into the communist view of the usefulness of terrorism and brutality. In 1921-1922, Lenin engineered a

---

[295] Claire Sterling, *The Terror Network: The Secret War of International Terrorism* (New York: Reader's Digest Press, 1981), 297.

[296] Ibid.

[297] Richard Pipes, *A Concise History of the Russian Revolution* (New York: Vintage Books, 1996), 209.

famine as a means of cowing the unruly Russians into submission to the Bolshevik regime. At the height of the suffering, Lenin told the Politburo:

> "With the help of all those starving people who are starting to eat each other, who are dying by the millions, and whose bodies litter the roadside all over the country, it is now and only now that we can – and therefore must – confiscate all church property with all the ruthless energy we can still muster . . . this is the moment . . . to act without any mercy at all, with the sort of brutality that they will remember for decades . . . The more representatives from the reactionary clergy and the recalcitrant bourgeoisie we shoot, the better it will be for us. We must teach these people a lesson as quickly as possible, so that the thought of protesting again doesn't occur to them for decades to come."[298]

Such was the dark heart of Vladimir Lenin and the Soviet empire he helped found. To this dictator and his cohorts, murder, terror, fear, and suffering served very specific purposes. First, inside of a communist-controlled country, terror served the purpose of quelling dissent and bringing the people in line with communist dictates. Second, outside of communist-controlled regions, terrorism was a valuable destabilizing agent which created the chaotic conditions required for the spread of communism.

The Russian Federation under "former" KGB agent and mass-murderer Vladimir Putin continues the tradition of employing terrorism to cause bedlam and manipulate world events in its favor. Years ago, before the 9/11 era of terrorism hysteria, Jay Adams predicted:

> "Moscow plans to shift blame for global war onto the West by underhandedly provoking the U.S. and its allies into taking military action against Russian allies-of-old. With the collapse of

---

[298] Stephane Courtois, Nicolas Werth, Jean-Louis Panne, Andrzej Paczkowski, Karel Bartosek, and Jean-Louis Margolin, *The Black Book of Communism: Crimes, Terror, Repression* (Cambridge: Harvard University Press, 1999), 124-126.

communism, the U.S. has taken on the role of "world policeman." This has provided Moscow an opportunity to lure the U.S. and its military allies into a trap, particularly by using the United Nations."[299]

With the 9/11 false flag event, the United States was drawn into a major trap in the Middle East fighting an elusive, ambiguous enemy called "terrorism." While we launched ourselves into a major effort to fight an idea and a tactic (i.e. terrorism), Russia and her allies went to work to bog us down and destroy our image on a global scale. The hoax known as the "War on Terror" was the perfect opportunity for Moscow to turn the tables and present America as the world's enemy and Russia as the world's savior.

Today, most people consider terrorism to be a predominately Islamic venture. This is not so. It is true that many Muslims and Arabs are recruited by communists and other enemies of humanity to do their dirty work, but the real string-pullers should always be kept in mind. We must recognize that there is very little organic, grass-roots Islamic terrorism. Rather, the "Islamic" terrorism that we see is of the contrived sort – the sort inspired and organized by outside entities with a very un-Islamic agenda.

In Cliff Kincaid's and J.R. Nyquist's fantastic book *Red Jihad: Moscow's Final Solution for America and Israel*, Kincaid wrote:

> "Islam as a whole is not the enemy. Islam is an "enemy" only in the sense that it has been hijacked by communists, mostly of the Soviet/Russian variety, to use against the United States. . . .

> ". . . we find many people on the political scene today who want to take on "global Islam" without understanding that the Jihadists have been co-opted as cannon fodder in the world revolution. . . .

---

[299] Jay Adams, in David N. Balmforth, *America's Coming Crisis: Prophetic Warnings, Divine Destiny* (Bountiful, Utah: Horizon Publishers, 1998), 153.

". . . International Marxism has hijacked much of global Islam."[300]

Organic "Islamic terrorism" is mostly a bogeyman – a chimera of the Western mind. The truth is that Arab terrorists have been recruited and trained by outside forces – most importantly Russia. The Soviet Union set up a series of dozens of terrorist training centers throughout its territory, and abroad in nations as diverse as Yemen and Cuba. In Russia, perhaps the most prestigious of such facilities was the Patrice Lumumba University which specialized in training foreign revolutionaries in everything from media manipulation to Marxist ideology to terrorism.

So thoroughly have the communists dominated international terrorism that a Russian defector once told Russia expert J.R. Nyquist: "If you ever hear of Muslims attacking the USA with a nuclear weapon, do not believe it, because it will be the Russians behind it."[301] False flag terrorism is not only a Western or Israeli invention, as I have seen alleged; it is a thoroughly Soviet tactic. Truthfully, the Russians and their like-minded conspirators in Red China, Cuba, and elsewhere are behind most of the terrorism in the world. The laundry list of terrorist attacks attributable to Soviet intelligence agents stretches many pages long. Numerous defectors have testified of this fact.

In his book *Behind the Deseret Storm*, Pavel Stroilov presents evidence from state documents stolen by him upon his defection from Russia which proves that Russia has been meddling in the Middle East and is behind much of the chaos we see there. Stroilov explained:

> "It was the Soviet Empire – not British Empire – that was responsible for the instability in the Middle East. In fairness, the modern history of a country like Iraq begins not from getting its

---

[300] Kincaid and Nyquist, *Red Jihad*, 24-25.

[301] Cliff Kincaid, et al., *Back from the Dead: The Return of the Evil Empire* (Owings, MD: America's Survival, Inc., 2014), 41.

independence from the British, but from losing its independence to the Soviets.

"All major conflicts in the region were caused by the Soviet expansion. The Cold War was not a rivalry between two superpowers, but a ruthless crusade of communist hordes against dwindling oases of freedom. . . .

"The international terrorism, too, was created by the Soviets as a Cold War weapon. The Islamist version only emerged much later. Furthermore, the Islamist threat is also a by-product of the Cold War. Islamists could have never become a serious global force were they not supported by Socialists."[302]

I remind the reader of Moroni's prophecy in Ether 8:25. Moroni foresaw that the latter-day secret combination would seek "to overthrow the freedom of all lands, nations, and countries" through violence and subversion. What is this secret combination? It is communism. And communism has been identified as the "greatest satanical threat" to humanity by the Lord's prophets. Communism, then, *must* be the chief culprit when we examine revolutions, wars, and chaos in recent history and current events. Middle East convulsions are no exception.

Soviet defector Anatoliy Golitsyn explained that the sham "collapse" of communist power hasn't deterred communist aggression in the Middle East. He wrote:

"The longer-term purpose of this manoeuvre is, through the Muslims of the former USSR, to consolidate concealed Russian influence over Islamic fundamentalism to complement that being openly sought by the Chinese Communists.

---

[302] Pavel Stroilov, *Behind the Desert Storm: A Secret Archive Stolen from the Kremlin that Sheds New Light on the Arab Revolutions in the Middle East* (Chicago, IL: Price World Publishing, LLC, 2011), 17.

"This Sino-Soviet strategy is based on the experience of Iran where the Islamic fundamentalists came to power. As an anti-American and anti-Western movement, Islamic fundamentalism offers obvious possibilities for undermining the pro-western regimes in Saudi Arabia and the Gulf. The Chinese Communists are openly supporting and supplying the Iranian Government.

"Under concealed Russian guidance, the Muslims of the former USSR, especially the Azers, will seek to cooperate and ally themselves with Muslims in Iran and the Arab states while Russia maintains its open policy of cooperation and partnership with the West. In this way China openly and Russia secretly will jointly attempt to swing the balance of power in their favour in the highly strategic, oil-producing Arab/Iranian areas of the Middle East."[303]

Considering the soaring hatred for, and resistance to, America sweeping through the Middle East, and the upsurge in love for Russia, the communist strategy has definitely paid off. The new alliances that are forming are all pro-Russia and decidedly anti-America. China is also moving into the Middle East in a very perceptible way, gobbling up oil, transplanting workers, forming alliances, transferring technology and weapons, etc. This is all a part of the communist strategic plan to gain influence over the entire Middle East while isolating the United States.

At this stage, let me digress and fully acknowledge that the United States, Britain, France, Israel, and other world powers not traditionally thought of as "communist" have also been involved in sponsoring and using terrorism. Israel has been highly active in this regard, as has the United States. It is well known that the United States under President Ronald Reagan created Al Qaeda to serve as a counterbalance to the Soviets after the USSR invaded Afghanistan. Osama Bin Laden was on the CIA's payroll,

---

[303] Anatoliy Golitsyn, *The Perestroika Deception: The World's Slide Towards the 'Second October Revolution'* (New York: Edward Harle, 1998), 215.

along with a myriad of other individuals now referred to as "Islamic terrorists," "Islamic fundamentalists," and "jihadists."[304]

More recently, various ISIS organizations – for ISIS is not a monolithic group under one head – have been supplied and funded by the United States, Israel, and additional Western powers, while other groups are supplied by Russia, China, Syria, Iran, Turkey, etc. The U.S.-backed terrorists are called "moderates" by the Western press, whereas those not controlled by the West are considered "extremists."[305] In the business of international terrorism, the United States and her allies are *not* guiltless.

That being said, we must dig deeper to unearth the real story. Let's look at ISIS. While it is undeniable that the United States supports certain ISIS groups, it is also undeniable – albeit underreported – that Russia supports various ISIS factions. A large percentage of ISIS fighters in fact speak Russian and were born within the boundaries of the "former" Soviet Union.[306] Some of these have sided with, and some against, Russia. Most ISIS leaders, with several exceptions who of course capture the headlines, were trained in Soviet terrorist training centers during the Cold War. The majority of ISIS commanders were previously members of the Iraqi Republican Guard – Saddam Hussein's elite troops trained by the

---

[304] Garikai Chengu, "America Created Al-Qaeda and the ISIS Terror Group," *Global Research*, September 19, 2014, accessed April 21, 2018, https://www.globalresearch.ca/america-created-al-qaeda-and-the-isis-terror-group/5402881.

[305] Ron Paul, "Ron Paul: America's Lies Exposed in Syria," *FITSNews, LLC*, October 2, 2017, accessed April, 22, 2018, https://www.fitsnews.com/2017/10/02/ron-paul-americas-lies-exposed-in-syria/.

[306] "Report: Russia, Former Soviet Region Largest Source For Foreign Fighters In Syria, Iraq," *Radio Free Europe/Radio Liberty*, October 24, 2017, accessed April 22, 2018, https://www.rferl.org/a/soufan-report-iraq-syria-russian-fighters/28813611.html.

Soviets.[307] Describing Russian involvement with ISIS, Cliff Kincaid has reported:

> "Writer and researcher Christian Gomez traced the roots of ISIS to the Islamic Revival Party, created by the KGB during the final days of the old Soviet Union.

> "More recently, a defector from the KGB's successor, the FSB, confirmed Russia's role in creating ISIS by recruiting former members of Saddam Hussein's security services. The former FSB officer told Ukrainian journalist Andriy Tsaplienko that "the Russian special services believed that if a terrorist organization was set up as an alternative to Al-Qaeda and it created problems for the United States as Donbas does for Ukraine now, it would be quite good.". . . .

> "The FSB defector said that in order to create ISIS, the Russians selected former officers of the Iraqi army and members of the Arab Socialist Ba'ath Party. All of them had graduated from Moscow-based "educational institutions". . . .

> ". . . ISIS is a Marxist-style organization that uses religious cover."[308]

Is it probable that these Soviet-trained, Soviet-equipped terrorists flipped sides? It is of course possible that some did just that, acting as mercenaries for the highest bidder or out of a sense of tribalistic ire. However, it seems unlikely that the majority of these Soviet-trained figures made a clean break with their past and now work for the Americans or Israelis. Said differently, it is more likely that the "greatest

---

[307] Hamza Hendawi and Qassim Abdul-Zahra, "ISIS Top Brass Is Iraqi Army's Former Best and Brightest," *Haaretz Daily Newspaper Ltd.*, August 8, 2015, accessed April 22, 2018, https://www.haaretz.com/isis-top-brass-is-iraqi-army-s-former-1.5384550.

[308] Kincaid and Nyquist, *Red Jihad*, 28-29.

satanical threat" on earth – communism, whose chief representatives are Russia and China – is also behind most modern acts of terrorism. And this should not be surprising considering the slogans adopted by these various "Islamic" groups. The Iraqi Baath Party's motto, for instance, was: "One Arab nation with a holy message: Unity, liberation, and socialism!"[309]

At this point, let me pose another theory. I have previously referred to the massive subversion of the United States government by communist agents. They infiltrated our government and military by the thousands, as books such as *Stalin's Secret Agents* by M. Stanton Evans and Herbert Romerstein detail. Is it possible that some of the men inside the U.S. government and military establishment who are responsible for using American resources to create, fund, equip, and train Middle East terrorists are actually communist secret agents following Moscow's agenda rather than Washington's? In other words, is it possible that Red Gadianton infiltrators inside our government are sabotaging the United States pursuant to the Bolsheviks' long-range strategy rather than out of a desire to create an American empire?

This question has never been properly researched by those who otherwise investigate conspiracy, the bogus War on Terror, or the Russian threat. Yet, I think it is a pressing question to ask and consider. After all, America's wars in the Middle East have done nothing but poison the world's opinion against the United States and make us a pariah in the eyes of millions who once loved us or looked to us for hope. We have lost thousands of our best men and wasted trillions of dollars. And for what?

Who has stepped in as the savior to "fix" the bad situation caused by the "imperialist" Americans? Russia. Russia, *not* the United States, has been the great beneficiary of American Middle East interventionism. China has also benefited massively and is making tremendous inroads in the region. As the great Roman statesman Cicero once asked, "Cui bono?" Indeed, cui bono – who benefited?

---

[309] Stroilov, *Behind the Desert Storm*, 18.

By riding into the Middle East as a white knight, Russia has gained crucial allies and is now looked upon – even by so-called American "conservatives" – as the only remaining country that can stand up to the New World Order. Of course, such people are ignorant of the fact that communism *is* the agent that will bring about the New World Order, that communism never died, and that Russia is more dangerous now than at the height of the Cold War. Cui bono?

It is no secret that Syria – the hotbed of the current conflict – is a long-time ally of Russia and that Syria was supported and equipped by the Soviet Union all throughout the Cold War; as were Egypt, Iran, Iraq, Libya, Lebanon, and other nations. Russia also maintains important military bases in Syria, such as its naval base located at Tartus on the Mediterranean coast and its airfield at Latakia.[310] Russia is sending ever-increasing amounts of war armaments into the Middle East and is arming its allies to the teeth. China is also contemplating sending its troops into the melee.

In his book *Russia Rising: Tracking the Bear in Bible Prophecy*, Mark Hitchcock has written:

> "Syria is a flashpoint that is aligning Russia, Iran, and Turkey into a fearsome triumvirate. Russia and Iran have seized the chaos in Syria as an opportunity to bring in troops and air power, putting them just north of Israel."[311]

---

[310] Damien Sharkov, "Vladimir Putin Has Big Plans for Russia's Naval Base in Syria – Including Staying Until 2092," *Newsweek*, December 14, 2017, accessed April 22, 2018, http://www.newsweek.com/vladimir-putin-could-expand-russian-navy-syria-despite-announcing-pullback-747815.

[311] Mark Hitchcock, *Russia Rising: Tracking the Bear in Bible Prophecy* (Illinois: Tyndale Momentum, 2017), 143.

Hitchcock summed up the trend of Middle Eastern politics in one ominous line: "Russia is pulling the strings in the Middle East."[312] Again I ask: Cui bono?

These alliances are significant when we realize that these nations match the historical entities mentioned in Ezekiel's prophecy of Gog, Magog, the future siege of Israel, and Battle of Armageddon (Ezekiel 38-39). As they say, the stars are aligning.

A recent article ran the headline: "The Emerging China-Iran-Pakistan Alliance Is Directed Decidedly Against The United States." The article informs the reader:

> "As China expands commercially, the Chinese military, in particular its navy, will advance concomitantly to protect China's growing economic empire, as did the British in an earlier era. Chinese intent is to gain access to a number of harbors and airports to create a chain of mutually-supporting military facilities.

> "China's plans to expand its naval footprint in Pakistan have accompanied signs of increasing military cooperation between Tehran and Beijing over the last several years.

> "In June 2017, Iranian warships joined a Chinese naval flotilla conducting exercises in the Persian Gulf. The Chinese ships also made an official visit to the Iranian port city of Bandar Abbas after having earlier docked in Karachi, Pakistan. One Chinese military affairs expert, speaking at the time, said China was poised to increase its military presence in the Middle East to support BRI and would involve itself more in the affairs of the region.

> "Chinese efforts towards Iran-Pakistan cooperation have also borne fruit. In recent months, there has been a flurry of agreements in trade, defense, weapons development, counter-

---

[312] Hitchcock, *Russia Rising*, 5.

> terrorism, banking, train service, parliamentary cooperation and — most recently — art and literature."[313]

Both Russia and China are strategically positioning themselves in the Middle East and Central Asia and are gaining massive influence throughout the region. Some of prominent nations in the region now allied against the United States include Turkey, Iran, Syria, Pakistan, and, of course, Russia and China. The list of Russian-Chinese allies grows almost by the day while the list of countries friendly to the United States shrinks. Cui bono?

Russia and China are major sponsors of so-called "Islamic" terrorism and of Middle Eastern regimes. The purpose is *not* to achieve victory for Islam – Islam is a red herring – but to seize control for communism. In the preface to Roberta Goren's excellent book *The Soviet Union and Terrorism*, Jillian Becker wrote:

> "The Soviet Union has always had one supreme aim: to establish Communism everywhere on earth, as an unchallengeable orthodoxy, the only Truth and the only Way, and itself as the universal absolute power which enforces and guards and perpetuates it. To realize this awful ambition, it has used without compunction whatever means and methods, however immoral, however dishonourable, however unjust or cruel or bloody or devastating, which have seemed most likely to bring success according to time, place and circumstance. One method it has always used, with varying degrees of intensity, is terrorism. . . .

> "World War Three IS BEING WAGED, and has been waged for decades now, against the West – while most of us in the West, our governments, our press and news analysts remain blind to the

---

[313] Lawrence Sellin, "The Emerging China-Iran-Pakistan Alliance Is Directed Decidedly Against The United States," *The Daily Caller*, May 23, 2018, in Tyler Durden, *ZeroHedge*, May 24, 2018, accessed May 28, 2018, https://www.zerohedge.com/news/2018-05-23/emerging-china-iran-pakistan-alliance-directed-decidedly-against-united-states.

nature of the aggression, and to the intention behind it, while it threatens to destroy our world piecemeal, surreptitiously, by ambush, by attack from behind the camouflage of causes with other names, by the guerrilla stealth of some who live treacherously and often unrecognizably among us."[314]

Through terrorism, subversion, infiltration, propagandizing, and a thousand other methods, the communists have – since World War II ended with the Soviet conquest of much of the globe – waged unrelenting war against what little remains of the "free world."

The following quotation from Chapman Pincher's book *The Secret Offensive* gives an insight into the extensive, global nature of Russian-backed terrorism:

"The Soviet authorities are ingenious in distancing themselves from the terrorism they exploit, so that in the event of exposure their involvement can be denied. This has been confirmed by an extensive study undertaken by the CIA which showed that while there are many camps inside the Soviet Union for the training of terrorists, Soviet citizens are not involved in their operations abroad and so can never be caught with a 'smoking gun'. . . .

"The Cuban intelligence service is being increasingly used to support terrorists, the funds and weapons being supplied by Moscow along with KGB advisers based in Cuba. During the 1960s the United States suffered a serious terrorist campaign from a group calling itself the Weathermen. It was responsible for many bombing outrages and for what it called The Days of Rage, in October 1969, when anti-Vietnam war protesters, urged on by Weathermen agitators, rioted in Chicago, engaging in pitched battles with the police. The Weathermen, assisted by Cubans, were also responsible for terrorist bombings in Quebec, in

---

[314] Roberta Goren, *The Soviet Union and Terrorism* (London: George Allen & Unwin Publishers, 1984), Preface.

support of French Canadian separatists, their aim being to support any movement which would create chaos and uncertainty in true democracies. A former member of the Weathermen, Larry Grathwohl, gave first-hand evidence of the movement's ties with Cuba on Canadian television in June 1982. He described how he was always able to establish contact with other terrorists through Cuban embassies. Using Soviet money, the Cuban intelligence service recruited Weathermen volunteers from radical young Americans visiting Havana and then trained them in bombing techniques. On the same programme a former member of the Cuban intelligence service declared that the Soviets were behind the whole involvement with the Weathermen who were not made aware that they were being used in Soviet active-measures operations. . . .

"In the late 1960s Mexican students recruited by the KGB but trained away from the Soviet Union, in North Korea, were used in an attempt to plunge Mexico into civil war . . . the KGB has tried to manipulate the Red Brigades in Italy through surrogate organizations believed to have included the IRA, the PLO and West Germany's Red Army faction. Soon after the British Government expelled 105 Soviet agents in 1971 the Kremlin persuaded the Eire Government to agree to full embassy status with the Soviet Union, and Soviet-Bloc agents were quickly in Dublin contacting the IRA with a view to supplying weapons.

"In addition to assisting terrorists logistically, the Soviet Union also backs them up with active measures against the governments of the countries where they are operating. From the moment the Russians were expelled from Egypt they made unremitting efforts to disrupt that country's relationship with the US and to undermine the authority and reputation of the Egyptian leader, Anwar Sadat, especially after the Camp David Accords with Israel . . . KGB forgeries purporting to be of American origin and suggesting that Sadat was an American puppet, or could easily be disposed of if he offended Washington, were surfaced in Egyptian publications in ways calculated to enrage ordinary Arabs as well as Islamic fundamentalists. . . .

"Whenever the governments being attacked by terrorists and 'freedom fighters' take steps to defend themselves and their citizens they are vilified in the Communist-controlled and penetrated media as Fascist butchers using brutal force against heroic 'guerillas', and the photographs in the newspapers and on television are far more likely to concentrate on the slain terrorists than on the defenders . . . This manifestation of the upside-down ploy in which those being indiscriminately attacked by car-bombs, booby traps and every other kind of savage device are projected as the villains has been used by the Politburo with stunning effect in the United Nations. Almost unbelievably, this agency of 'peace', which is packed with Soviet client states, has affirmed in solemn session of the General Assembly that 'national liberation movements', even when patently Moscow-inspired revolutionaries, are fully justified in using terrorism and that elected governments which react by using counter-force to protect their citizens and their property are violating 'human rights'."[315]

From Mexico to Italy to Egypt to Japan to the USA, the communists have instigated terrorism, riots, and revolutionary subversion. Through its international press organs, the conspirators downplay Russian and Chinese involvement while painting the United States and her allies as the sole enemies of mankind; the chief instigators of aggression and oppression. The United Nations, an organization founded and directed by communists and called "an open KGB/FSB puppet" by high-ranking Soviet

---

[315] Chapman Pincher, *The Secret Offensive: The Soviet Challenge to Western Freedom* (London: Sidgwick and Jackson, 1986), 288-290.

defector Ion Mihai Pacepa,[316] is also used to deflect attention away from the enemy while demonizing America. This was the pattern during the Cold War. Is it really so different today?

Is it possible that the "greatest satanical threat" in the world is behind much of the terrorism we witness on the nightly news? Is it possible that Russia inherited the Soviet Union's legacy of sponsoring terrorism and revolution on a global scale? Is it possible that President Benson was correct when he told the Saints that communism was as an "unsurpassed" evil which represented, among other things, terrorism? I end this section with that very quote from our dear prophet, President Ezra Taft Benson, and encourage you not to be fooled into believing that all modern terrorism is a product of American, British, or Israeli intrigue. The truth is that modern terrorism was manufactured in mother Russia:

> "The fight against godless communism is a very real part of every man's duty who holds the priesthood. It is the fight against slavery, immorality, atheism, terrorism, cruelty, barbarism, deceit, and the destruction of human life through a kind of tyranny unsurpassed by anything in human history. Here is a struggle against the evil, satanical priestcraft of Lucifer."[317]

Conclusion

We have barely scratched the surface of the known front movements employed by Moscow. The communist conspiracy exists, through its front groups, in every nation on earth. It disseminates its philosophies and principles under names such as "feminism," "democracy," "gay liberation," and "civil rights." Communism is alive in the churches, in the

---

[316] Ion Mihai Pacepa and Ronald J. Rychlak, *Disinformation: Former Spy Chief Reveals Secret Strategies for Undermining Freedom, Attacking Religion, and Promoting Terrorism* (Washington, D.C.: WND Books, 2013), 330.

[317] President Ezra Taft Benson, "The American Heritage of Freedom – A Plan of God," Conference Report, October, 1961, 69-75, http://scriptures.byu.edu/#:t48d:p401.

schools, in the media, in the White House, in the halls of Congress, in the Supreme Court, in your local youth groups, in the military, in Hollywood, on Wall Street, and everywhere else human beings are found. At the end of the day, communism is nothing but a ruthless, Satanic philosophy that lies, cheats, steals, and employs force and terror whenever necessary to advance its agenda.

Communist fronts inevitably undermine faith, families, and Freedom. Through feminism, communists control women and use them as a battering ram to topple the fortress of the home. Through the homosexual and transgender movements, Red agents further twist and confuse all things related to marriage and the traditional home – even confusing what it means to be a man or woman, a son or daughter of the Almighty. Through environmentalism, communist pagans enlist mankind in a tacit earth-worship cult while simultaneously stealing the wealth and sovereignty of the world in order to "save the planet." Through drugs and organized crime, America has been morally softened and made vulnerable to communist machinations. Through the Civil Rights movement and its modern manifestations, the Reds have stoked the flames of racial strife in an effort to foment a civil war in which communists could come to power in the chaos, as they have done in country after country. And, finally, through terrorism, Russia and her allies are able to destabilize and paralyze entire nations, paint the United States as the great oppressor, and position themselves as the saviors who will rescue humanity from the Western imperialists.

President Ezra Taft Benson explained this communist tactic of using fronts to sow discord and then manipulate that resulting chaos in their favor. He said:

> "The Communist method of confusing the issues is to use pseudo-idealistic and pseudo-moral words and phrases in order to trap the unwary into following their designs. The fisherman knows that he cannot entice a fish to bite upon a raw, steel hook on his bait casting fishing reel, so he dresses it up with a nice, juicy worm and

the poor fish bites. In the same way, the pseudo-moral and pseudo-idealistic expressions trap many innocents so that they will follow out the aims of the Communist Conspirators, for example, the false appeals made by the Communists in the name of "peace" and the "brotherhood of man." They know full well that Communism has nothing in common with these expressions as we understand them. Yet, they deliberately misuse them in order to deceive.

"This has been the means by which the Communists, throughout the world, have been able to set class against class, religion against religion, race against race and group against group. The Conspiracy so enflames people against one another that they fight among themselves and thus bring about mutual destruction. The Communists then come in and take over."[318]

With their "pseudo-moral words and phrases" like "peace" and "fraternity," the conspirators trap idealistic and gullible dupes. Once the barbed hook is carefully set in our flesh, the communist fishermen reel us in no matter how hard we fight. Tragically, most of us do not even fight at all. We are so blinded by shiny communist slogans and deceived by doublespeak and emotion-driven propaganda that we allow ourselves to be pulled along down the path of destruction.

Hundreds of other front movements could be listed, such as the pornography industry, the political correctness sickness, the CIA, or the Zionist movement. A word about each of these would be appropriate to round out the picture of the comprehensive nature of the communist conspiracy. I want the reader to understand that communism is everywhere and that its agents have spared no effort to destroy humanity's Liberty and bring us into bondage to Lucifer.

---

[318] President Ezra Taft Benson, "A Race Against Time," BYU address, December 10, 1963, https://www.latterdayconservative.com/ezra-taft-benson/a-race-against-time/.

Zionism

Zionism is one wing of the overall Illuminati/communist conspiracy to conquer the earth. One of the chief founders of this movement was Moses Hess, an evil man influential in the rise of socialism in Europe and the figure who converted Friedrich Engels – coauthor of *The Communist Manifesto* – to communism.[319] Hess had also convinced Karl Marx "to embrace the Socialist ideal" and was "the man who played the most important role in [Marx's] life."[320] According to one account, Hess may have actually been the one who penned the rough draft of *The Communist Manifesto* which was taken and polished by Marx and Engels.[321]

Zionism did not cavort solely with communism, however. Zionism was popular among the Western elites, bankers, and men such as socialist Woodrow Wilson and communist FDR. At the fateful Yalta conference in 1945, Soviet dictator Joseph Stalin was asked by FDR whether he was a Zionist, to which he replied in the affirmative.[322]

Despite the occasional antagonism between communists and Zionists, and Russia and Israel, the goals and principles of Zionism and communism are remarkably similar. I talk about this in more depth in my book *A Century of Red*, but here I will simply cite author Peter Christian who has described the twin evils of communism and Zionism thus:

---

[319] Wurmbrand, *Marx & Satan*, 37.

[320] Wurmbrand, *Marx & Satan*, 24.

[321] Peter Christian, *The Work of All Ages: The Ongoing Plot to Rule the World from Biblical Times to the Present*, (Washington, D.C.: The Barnes Review, 2010), 124.

[322] Griffin, *Descent into Slavery?*, 206.

"Zionism was promoted by infiltrating the highest levels of society in order to gain control from the top down. It was the upper arm of the pincer, of which communism moving from the bottom up, was the lower arm."[323]

While communism is certainly the most destructive and deadly of the two philosophies, Zionism has had an immense influence in the United States and has been at least partially responsible for dragging us into several undeclared, unconstitutional wars that serve foreign interests (and which also, as I pointed out earlier, benefit Russia and bolster her posture as the "defender" of bullied states). The Zionist regime in Israel may yet drag the United States into another quagmire in the Middle East before the final clash between the communist world and the United States occurs. Ultimately, however, communism has been identified by the Lord's anointed as the "greatest satanical threat," and if only one must prevail, it will not be Zionism.

The CIA

The Central Intelligence Agency (CIA) got its start in 1942 when FDR ordered the creation of the Office of Strategic Services (OSS). The OSS was headed by the firebrand "Wild Bill" Donovan. In 1947, the CIA was created and superseded the OSS, adopting its international intelligence functions. Without question, the OSS/CIA has had a significant impact on both national and international affairs.

Researchers have implicated the CIA – sometimes the agency itself and other times shadowy factions operating independently – with complicity in events ranging from the assassination of General George Patton to the overthrow of the Iranian government in 1953 to the assassinations of JFK, MLK, and RFK to the 9/11 false flag attack to drug running in Latin America. Whether you choose to believe they have been involved in all of these occurrences is up to you. However, what is certain is that while

---

[323] Christian, *The Work of All Ages*, 130.

there have been many faithful Americans who have belonged to the agency (including those who have diligently carried out anti-communist operations), there have also been a number of known traitors.

Author M. Stanton Evans has written:

> "[C]lose students of such matters have long regarded OSS as the most heavily infiltrated of the wartime units, with estimates of the number of Communists ranging as high as a hundred staffers. This is, however, an estimate only, so the number was conceivably smaller but might also have been a good deal larger. . . .
>
> "Though its posthumous reputation as a den of Communists and Soviet agents would exceed that of OWI, less was known about the OSS back in the 1940s. The secret nature of the service allowed its employees to roam about the globe at will, engaging in all sorts of actions concealed from Congress and the public."[324]

It is significant that the OSS/CIA was so heavily infested with communists from its earliest days. Is it possible that those CIA agents implicated in terrorism, drug running, revolution, and assassination were in fact agents of the Kremlin and not agents of Washington, D.C.? To this day, there have been so many black operations with off-the-record budgets and slush funds that no one has any idea the true extent of the CIA's operations. What we know, however, is that the CIA has been thoroughly compromised and does not serve the best interests of the United States.

Since OSS days, a number of Soviet spies have been uncovered working in the CIA, and others have been alleged. David Barnett and Philip Agee were two such enemy spies uncovered and positively confirmed as communist agents. Barnett was working for Soviet Russia and Agee was a

---

[324] M. Stanton Evans, *Blacklisted by History: The Untold Story of Senator Joe McCarthy and His Fight Against America's Enemies* (New York: Crown Forum, 2007), 92.

mole for the Cubans at the height of the Cold War. CIA operative Edward Lee Howard, a Soviet spy, defected to the USSR and eventually had books written about his treachery.

Very recently, CIA agents Kevin Mallory and Jerry Chun Shing Lee were arrested for separate espionage charges. They had been feeding information to Red China, proving that communist espionage is still a formidable challenge. As I completed the final edits in this book, another U.S. intelligence operative working for the Defense Intelligence Agency (DIA), Ron Hansen, was arrested by the FBI for attempting to supply communist China with information.[325]

The number of Americans who have betrayed their country and have worked for the communists is legion. They have found employment in the CIA, FBI, DIA, and all other major U.S. intelligence services, just as they have thoroughly infiltrated British intelligence operations and those of other allies. Harold "Kim" Philby, for instance, was a KGB agent working in London. He rose through the ranks of British intelligence and came to head the unit tasked with countering Soviet espionage! As Philby's case suggests, and as we will see herewith, communist agents and sympathizers have not only existed at the ground level; they have reached to the highest echelons of power and influence within Western intelligence agencies.

From 2009 to 2011, Leon Panetta was the director of the CIA and, later, Obama's secretary of defense. Of Panetta's Soviet ties, Aaron Klein and Brenda Elliott have written in their book *Red Army: The Radical Network that Must be Defeated to Save America*:

> "Panetta's concerning ties, meanwhile, do not stop at his oceans initiative. He also keynoted the conference of a pro-Soviet,

---

[325] Bill Gertz, "Ex-DIA Official Charged as Beijing Spy Used Chinese Cell Phones," *The Washington Free Beacon*, June 5, 2918, accessed June 5, 2018, http://freebeacon.com/national-security/ex-dia-official-charged-beijing-spy-used-chinese-cell-phones/.

antiwar group during the height of the Cold War. Panetta also honored the founding member of the group, the Women's International League for Peace and Freedom, or WILPF, which was once named by the State Department as a "Soviet front." . . . .

"Panetta has a larger history of ties to pro-Soviet groups. He has come under newfound scrutiny for his ties to a pro-Marxist think tank accused of anti-CIA activity. The Institute for Policy Studies, or IPS, has long faced criticism for positions some say attempt to undermine U.S. national security and for its cozy relationship with the Soviet Union during the Cold War. A review of the voting record for Panetta, a member of Congress from 1977 to 1993, during the period in question shows an apparent affinity for IPS's agenda. The IPS is currently funded by philanthropist George Soros's Open Society Institute."[326]

Klein and Elliott also document Panetta's public praise of fellow communists like Lucy Haessler, a decidedly pro-Soviet activist. Yet, Panetta was not the first CIA chief to be a communist sympathizer and he wasn't the last. I highlight but one more.

John Brennan, head of the CIA from 2013 to 2017, was also a "former" communist. At least, in 1976 Brennan admittedly voted for the Communist Party USA presidential candidate Gus Hall.[327] Perhaps Brennan is a repentant communist. Or, perhaps, his recent actions relative to undermining our government, colluding with foreign agents, and perjuring

---

[326] Aaron Klein and Benda J. Elliott, *Red Army: The Radical Network that Must be Defeated to Save America* (New York: Broadside Books, 2011), 289-291.

[327] Natalie Johnson, "CIA Director Once Voted for Communist Presidential Candidate," *The Washington Free Beacon*, September 21, 2016, accessed May 24, 2018, http://freebeacon.com/politics/cia-director-once-voted-for-communist-presidential-candidate/.

himself demonstrate that he has always been a communist sympathizer.[328]

It should be noted that both Brennan and Panetta were appointed by President Barack Hussein Obama. President Obama was not, as some have alleged, a Muslim. He was, however, a blatant Marxist; a fanatical anti-white racist and a communist. Overwhelming evidence suggests that Obama was groomed from a young age to ascend to the presidency and push forward the communist agenda.

In his youth, Obama was mentored by Frank Marshall Davis, a pornographer and a member of the Communist Party USA. Like arch-communist Vladimir Lenin, Obama was a full-time activist and agitator from his youth. He surrounded himself with known communists and Marxist terrorists, such as convicted terrorist Bill Ayers, and appointed such men to his cabinet. Obama's admitted role models were all communist revolutionaries, such as Nelson Mandela whom Obama idolized. Per his training and indoctrination, Obama devoted himself to world revolution and his presidency succeeded in dividing and weakening America to levels not seen in generations.

George Soros, a Jewish-Hungarian communist about whom I have hitherto written nothing, was one of Obama's major financial backers. In his own words, Soros is seeking to overthrow the capitalist order and replace it with a "Marxist" version.[329] Indeed, he thinks Red China should be part of the vanguard of the new economic world order.[330] Soros has used his

---

[328] George Neumayr, "Confirmed: John Brennan Colluded With Foreign Spies to Defeat Trump," *The American Spectator*, April 19, 2017, accessed May 20, 2018, https://spectator.org/confirmed-john-brennan-colluded-with-foreign-spies-to-defeat-trump/.

[329] "George Soros, Puppet Master," *YouTube*, uploaded February 20, 2012, accessed June 1, 2018, https://www.youtube.com/watch?v=pPLm0-uAZbs.

[330] "George Soros – Obama's Boss – America's Communist Leader – CommieTunes 13," *YouTube*, uploaded November 29, 2010, accessed June 1, 2018, https://www.youtube.com/watch?v=71NXb-I-06c&t=335s.

billions – filtered through organizations such as the Open Society Institute – to overthrow regimes, disrupt international banking and devalue currency, foment division through groups like Black Lives Matter and the Occupy protests, and create total chaos.

Soros – a man who says he is a god[331] – is one of those men you look at and instantly realize he is hollow and dead inside. He has no light. Rather, he is engulfed in darkness and spreads darkness by catapulting henchmen like Barack Obama to positions of sensitive influence. For more on Soros, see the relevant works listed in the Recommended Reading on Conspiracy section in the back of this book.

I have deliberately not spoken much about President Obama, or George Soros for that matter, because his story is fresh in the public mind and there is not much I can add to the saga that can't be easily uncovered elsewhere. Entire books have been written exposing the detrimental effects Obama has had on our Republic, on American morale, and on our culture. I want the reader to understand, however, that Obama was indeed a communist operative and one of the biggest traitors in U.S. history. His administration gave us nothing but eight years of communist revolution in America.

If the reader wants to know more about Obama and his sordid legacy, he should read relevant books such as the following: *Comrade Obama Unmasked: Marxist Mole in the White House*, by Cliff Kincaid, et al; *Red Star Rising: The Making of Barack Hussein Obama and the Transformation of America*, by Cliff Kincaid; *Barack Obama and the Enemies Within*, by Trevor Loudon and Rodney R. Stubbs; and *Red Army: The Radical Network that Must be Defeated to Save America*, by Aaron Klein and Brenda J. Elliott.

---

[331] Rachel Ehrenfeld and Shawn Macomber, "George Soros: The 'God' Who Carries Around Some Dangerous Demons," *Los Angeles Times*, October 4, 2004, accessed June 1, 2018, http://articles.latimes.com/2004/oct/04/opinion/oe-ehrenfeld4.

Returning to our topic, communist defector Anatoliy Golitsyn relentlessly warned of KGB penetration into nearly every agency and department within our government, military, and intelligence services. He once wrote:

> "The Central Intelligence Agency was already penetrated in 1958 – by both the KGB and Chinese intelligence. In 1958, the Agency lost its most important source, Colonel Popov of Soviet Military Intelligence [GRU], who could have provided strategic information had he not been compromised by KGB penetration, arrested by the KGB, and burned alive in the GRU's crematorium furnace."[332]

Red Chinese penetration of the CIA has been particularly decisive in thwarting American opposition to communist advances. Golitsyn noted:

> "Through penetration, Chinese Communist intelligence destroyed the CIA's sources in China during the 1950s, 1960s and 1970s and prevented the Agency developing reliable sources on the strategic intentions of the Chinese leaders. The National Security Agency cannot help because information on secret Sino-Soviet strategic coordination is not carried on accessible communications channels."[333]

A third time, he wrote:

> "From 1963 onwards I argued that the well advertised Sino-Soviet differences were intended to conceal a common Sino-Soviet strategy, in other words that the 'split' was a joint strategic disinformation operation intended to deceive the West. Between 1963 and 1969 my view of the 'split' was debated within the CIA. I have good reason to believe that information on the existence of this internal debate in the CIA was leaked to the KGB and through

---

[332] Golitsyn, *The Perestroika Deception*, 207.

[333] Golitsyn, *The Perestroika Deception*, 35.

them to the Soviet leadership who took drastic steps to settle the argument within the CIA in their favour."[334]

This is just a smattering of evidence pointing to massive communist infiltration of the CIA. Further research is necessary; however, I want people to be open to the possibility that the CIA is operating against America's best interests not because of orders from Western "globalists," but because of orders from Moscow. It is fair to say that from day one the communists have assiduously infiltrated the CIA, filling the chief posts on more than one occasion and converting it into a mechanism of global subversion.

Political Correctness

Next, it should not be shocking to learn that political correctness is an enterprise established by communist agents. While the term "politically correct" came into existence over two hundred years ago, its meaning was quite different. In its modern usage, references to political correctness came into vogue in 1917 after the Bolsheviks overthrew Russia and established it as their base of operations.

The *Encyclopedia Britannica*, hardly a conspiratorial source, said this of the origin of political correctness:

"The term first appeared in Marxist-Leninist vocabulary following the Russian Revolution of 1917. At that time it was used to describe adherence to the policies and principles of the Communist Party of the Soviet Union (that is, the party line)."[335]

In harmony with this analysis, another writer observed:

---

[334] Golitsyn, *The Perestroika Deception*, 155.

[335] Cynthia Roper, "Political Correctness (PC)," *Encyclopedia Britannica*, accessed May 3, 2018, https://www.britannica.com/topic/political-correctness.

"According to the *International Encyclopedia of the Social Sciences*, Kremlin advisers were the first to widely use the term. They did so without a trace of irony. Calling someone "politically correct" in Soviet Russia meant they toed the party line. A PC Kremlin insider was one who could reflect what Moscow was thinking—exactly the sort of person who would go far."[336]

Finally, in his brilliant book on the Soviet origins of political correctness titled *Willing Accomplices*, Kent Clizbe stated:

"PC was created as an attitude and point-of-view in the early 1920s. It was inserted into American culture by selected agents of influence. The agents of influence, whether witting of communist intelligence guidance, or unwitting, were all Willing Accomplices in propagating the attitudes that became PC."[337]

Elsewhere in his book, Clizbe informed the reader:

"Covert influence is the classic example of a Soviet Active Measure that has no expiry date. As we'll see, the KGB . . . ran a brilliant covert influence operations designed to destroy America's self-pride and sense of exceptionalism. . . .

"Using experienced operatives and highly compartmentalized operations, the KGB sought to insert covert influence "payloads" designed to call into question the fundamental bases on which American society and culture had been built. Many progressives eagerly carried out these covert operations for the Communists.

---

[336] Admin, "The Unlikely Origins of the Phrase 'Politically Correct'," *KnowledgeNuts*, May 28, 2015, accessed April 23, 2018, https://knowledgenuts.com/2015/05/28/the-unlikely-origins-of-the-phrase-politically-correct/.

[337] Kent Clizbe, *Willing Accomplices: How KGB Covert Influence Agents Created political Correctness, Obama's Hate-America-First Political Platform, and Destroyed America* (USA: Andemca Publishing, 2011), 54.

Others not involved in the operations received the covert messages and accepted them as gospel.

"The agents of influence denigrated American patriotism, capitalism, and individualism, and called into question American foreign policy, all of which seemed to form the philosophical bases of an elite attitude, which coalesced during the Great Depression and was nurtured and strengthened by the American transmitters of the KGB's covert influence operations: journalists, screenwriters, and professors, among others A Willing Accomplice in Hollywood, in the 1950s, commented that by participating in the anti-anti-communist groups, "I would be spared the agony of thinking my way through difficult issues: all the thinking would be done for me by an elite core of trained [thinkers]. . ."

"The goal of the KGB's covert influence operations was to make Americans feel that their country was bad. The KGB utilized Willing Accomplices to spread the message that America was an evil, racist, imperialist war-monger and that Communism was a benign, noble experiment designed to rid the world of corruption, oppression and injustice."[338]

Political correctness was a sham from the start – a conformist ideology that has dealt a severe blow to the constitutionally-protected notions of free speech, free expression, and individuality.

Under the aegis of covert KGB agents, political correctness battered the American psyche and convinced large swaths of the population that their own country was an evil, misogynist, racist, bigoted, imperialist, intolerant, closed-minded, prudish, backward, oppressive, exploitative nation. Political correctness is the ultimate in anti-American thought and the epitome of all that is amiss and defective in the souls and minds of Americans today.

---

[338] Clizbe, *Willing Accomplices*, 105.

The mouthpieces of PC have aimed their venomous concepts at Christian values, America-first nationalism, individuality, constitutional republicanism, traditional gender roles, true love, law and order, and everything else sacred, moral, and good. And in their place they have promoted everything vile, detrimental, and wrong, such as the gamut of LGBT psychoses, feminism, multiculturalism, internationalism and a "community of nations," so-called "tolerance," lust, mobocracy/democracy, and brutally enforced collectivism. These political correctors are the gatekeepers of the communist conspiracy's assault on humanity.

Our once praiseworthy culture has become so polluted with communist ideas, politically correct jargon, and an infusion of degrading values that it has become thoroughly Soviet in nature. Even the beloved children's fable the Little Red Hen promotes the Communist Party line of conformity and collectivism. Under communist-inspired political correctness, individuality dies and people are swallowed up in the "formless mass of the state," as Elder McConkie warned. Freedom of speech crumbles under the crushing hammer blow of PC censorship. And because of this rampant social disorder, Freedom of thought languishes in an intellectual GULAG.

Pornography Industry

Lastly, the pornography industry is a multi-billion dollar global trade which rests in the hands of the Satanic conspiracy. Pornography is a scourge of international proportions; a curse foreseen and warned against by ancient prophets. President Boyd K. Packer taught:

> "In our day the dreadful influence of pornography is like unto a plague sweeping across the world, infecting one here and one there, relentlessly trying to invade every home, most frequently

through the husband and father. The effect of this plague can be, unfortunately often is, spiritually fatal."[339]

Because of my own run-ins with this plague, I understand how vile and vicious it truly is. And what I have also learned over time is that the pornography industry is a secret combination in its own right. In the outstanding book *The Sex Industrial Complex: America's Secret Combination*, LDS authors John Harmer and James B. Smith wrote:

"This secret combination of enormously powerful business and financial entities have engaged in a conspiracy of mutual protection and deception. The Sex Industrial Complex has co-opted a variety of technologies which have made it possible to produce and then distribute directly into the home every conceivable graphic obscenity. . . .

"The Sex Industrial Complex that advanced the moral crisis that we now face were fed by greed and personal carnality. Greed led them to create the strategy by which millions of Americans have been exploited financially and emotionally through the deceitfulness of pornography. Personal carnality has destroyed any sense of shame for the incalculable suffering, misery, torture and death that the pornographers have brought into the lives of millions. Their carnality allowed them to deceive themselves, and then, when conscience was past all feeling, they skillfully deceived an entire generation by labeling their products as those of "personal pleasure" instead of the venomous poisons that they actually are."[340]

---

[339] President Boyd K. Packer, "Cleansing the Inner Vessel," General Conference, October, 2010, https://www.lds.org/general-conference/2010/10/cleansing-the-inner-vessel?lang=eng.

[340] John L. Harmer and James Bradford Smith, *The Sex Industrial Complex: America's Secret Combination: Pornographic Culture, Addiction and the Human Brain* (Salt Lake City, Utah: The Lighted Candle Society, 2007), 11.

Whether through pornography, drugs, terrorism, or any of the other isms, schemes, or tactics used by the communists, Satan's agenda is making stunning headway on every front. While temple building continues and Church growth ticks steadily upward, politically, the people of God are *not* pushing back the conspiracy in any perceptible way. We are rapidly losing the battle for Freedom against the forces of darkness because we have not been wise enough to notice their carefully organized deception – particularly in matters of culture. And in the few instances where we have identified a ruse, we have not been bold enough to step forward and resist the influx of evil. Like President Clark, I fear we will wade through much persecution and bloodshed as Saints for our lack of attention in this all-important fight for Liberty.

This overview of deception via front movements segues nicely into a discussion of the greatest deception of them all; namely, the myth that communism is "dead" and that the Soviet Union "fell."

Chapter 8

The Fall that Wasn't

Some readers may now be thinking: "This is all well and good, but how is it relevant today? Isn't communism dead? Didn't the USSR collapse? Isn't the Cold War over?" Unfortunately, no, the war between the anti-Christ forces of communism and the remaining soldiers of Christ is *not* over. The Soviet Union did *not* collapse. And communism is most certainly *not* dead.

Let me explain the truth about present-day communism in as clear and concise terms as I can:

Communism is not dead. In fact, communism has never been more powerful and pervasive than it is today. Communism is the dominant factor in modern life. Furthermore, the Soviet Union did *not* collapse. Rather, it faked its demise. It was political theater. It was a stage production put on to fool the West and lull us to sleep in preparation for the final stage of our destruction. The Communist Party simply went underground and the Soviet Union was branded the Russian Federation.

Truthfully, nothing substantial has changed since Cold War days when we openly acknowledged the communist threat. In fact, communism's subversive activities have *intensified* under the cloak of "peace," "openness," and "friendship" that the fake "fall" of communism provided. With the Western monetary aid that poured into Russia after communism's "collapse," the communist kingpins built a state-of-the-art military which rivals and, in numerous key respects, surpasses the U.S. military. Other funds graciously given by Western nations have been used to finance international mafia operations and a host of subversive movements in our country. In a word, we have been conned by the "masters of deceit."

The ancient Chinese strategist Sun Tzu wrote:

"All warfare is based on deception.

"Hence, when able to attack, we must seem unable; when using our forces, we must seem inactive; when we are near, we must make the enemy believe we are far away; when far away, we must make him believe we are near.

"Hold out baits to entice the enemy. Feign disorder, and crush him.

"If he is secure at all points, be prepared for him. If he is in superior strength, evade him.

"If your opponent is of choleric temper, seek to irritate him. Pretend to be weak, that he may grow arrogant. . . .

"Attack him where he is unprepared, appear where you are not expected. . . .

"Now the general who wins a battle makes many calculations in his temple ere the battle is fought.

"The general who loses a battle makes but few calculations beforehand. Thus do many calculations lead to victory, and few calculations to defeat: how much more no calculation at all! It is by attention to this point that I can foresee who is likely to win or lose."[341]

The communist conspirators understand these timeless principles perfectly. Communism is, as I stated earlier, organized deception. Communism was instituted by the very Father of Lies. No one deceives as effectively and completely as a committed communist.

If communism must feign weakness in order to gain advantage, it does. If it must get rid of the name "USSR" in order to appease its critics, it will. If

---

[341] Lionel Giles, translator, *Sun Tzu on the Art of War: The Oldest Military Treatise in the World* (1910), 36, http://www.idph.com.br/conteudos/ebooks/suntzu10.pdf.

it must fall down and play dead to fool its foolish enemies, it does not hesitate to drop to the dirt and lie lifeless. Communism is forever and always a secret society that thrives underground and operates best in the dark.

The Red Gadiantons have "pretended to be weak" that their enemy, the United States, "may grow arrogant." Pride and arrogance are the hallmarks of official U.S. government policy towards Russia and China. Only very recently have certain leaders within our military and government realized that Russia and China have "suddenly" become very grave threats. By and large, however, the United States exhibits a stunning arrogance in relation to other nations.

Whereas the United States *is* the greatest nation on earth, occupies the Promised Land, and is the inheritor of the richest blessings God has ever bestowed upon any people, "nevertheless the strength of the Lord [is] not with us; yea, we [are] left to ourselves, that the Spirit of the Lord [does] not abide in us; therefore we [have] become weak like unto our brethren" (Mormon 2:26). As Mormon lamented in a letter to his son Moroni: "Behold, the pride of this nation, or the people of the Nephites, hath proven their destruction except they should repent" (Moroni 8:27). I sense we are in the same situation today.

Furthermore, as Sun Tzu advised, the communists plotted and planned in their Moscow temple – the Kremlin. They coordinated their planned "fall" with their agents abroad in the major centers of the world – Beijing, London, Washington, D.C., Paris, etc. In their secret chambers, they laid a trap for the unsuspecting nations. They harnessed all of their resources to spread the lie that communism was dead, that the evil empire was gone, and that a new age of "democracy," "restructuring," and "openness" had dawned in Russia. But it was all a lie.

The Lord warned the Saints through the Prophet Joseph Smith that "the enemy in the secret chambers seeketh your lives" (D&C 32:28). He warned of "conspiring men in the last days" (D&C 89:4). He told converts to His Church to flee to the West to Zion "in consequence of that which is coming on the earth, and of secret combinations" (D&C 42:64). The warnings of the prophets about communism agree fully with these instructions from the Lord. In their secret temples and chambers, conspiring communists and their sympathizers crafted the most incredible deception in history – the death of communism.

Early on, the communists recognized that the American People were, by nature, gullible and naïve and always hopeful for the best. They knew that America would leap at a chance to be friends and end hostilities. What normal person would not want an end to the pending threat of nuclear holocaust? What normal person would not want peace and tranquility?

Not only did communists sense our gullibility, but they understood that America had become a prideful nation. Americans, they knew, could never believe that they were not #1. Therefore, the conspirators sought to exploit our pride, arrogance, and gullibility by kow-towing – at least on the surface – to the United States and pretending to be weak. They patted our egos and made us feel powerful and strong. They made sure we knew that we were the "lone" superpower in the world and that Russia no longer posed any threat to the free world.

The Soviets made a grand spectacle of their "weakness," tore down the Berlin Wall, and withdrew military forces from Eastern Europe. They took down many Soviet symbols, such as the hammer and sickle flag, and began preaching about "reform" and "democracy." These seemingly subservient actions fed America's pride and made us complacent. After all, who could stand against us now that the Soviets had caved? We didn't even need to fight a war in order to defeat the "evil empire" – we beat them using simple American will power! Now we could, as "victors," extend the hand of friendship to "defeated" Russia and work together for world peace.

Unfortunately, that was our attitude in 1991 and it is still our attitude today. The problem is that this attitude is based on a carefully calculated and masterfully presented lie. Our misguided hope and wishful thinking overrode our objective reasoning ability and we gave into our emotions.

We *wanted* peace, so we grasped at the first hint of it in spite of the mountain of evidence screaming at us that the communist conspiracy was as active, dangerous, and malicious as ever. Our foolish approach to the Soviet Union's deceptive ruse has been exploited to the maximum by the modern communist Sun Tzus.

The cold, hard reality suggests that the communist conspiracy was so thrilled with the overwhelming strength of its global position by the late 1980s that it decided to shed its Soviet skins in order to carry out the final phase of softening up America before dealing her the ultimate death blow. In part, I base this opinion on the two statements of President Ezra Taft Benson quoted in chapter four. In 1979 he warned:

> "The truth is, we have to a great extent accommodated ourselves to Communism—and we have permitted ourselves to become encircled by its tentacles. . . .
>
> "Never before has the land of Zion appeared so vulnerable to so powerful an enemy as the Americas do at present."

And again, in 1988 he lamented:

> "I testify that wickedness is rapidly expanding in every segment of our society. (See D&C 1:14–16; D&C 84:49–53.) It is more highly organized, more cleverly disguised, and more powerfully promoted than ever before. Secret combinations lusting for power, gain, and glory are flourishing. A secret combination that seeks to overthrow the freedom of all lands, nations, and countries is increasing its evil influence and control over America and the entire world. (See Ether 8:18–25.)"

If the communist conspiracy had the United States totally encircled and on the verge of defeat in 1979, and by 1988 it was still growing and entrenching itself more rapidly than before, there is little doubt that by 1991 its position was equally strong if not stronger. Certainly, there was no moral or religious revival during the 1980s. The American family continued its decline. Media continued to deteriorate and produce more filth and greater lies. Tens of millions were indoctrinated with socialism in public schools and universities. The national debt grew massively. American interventionism continued, wasting American blood and treasure. And so forth.

Fortunately, we do not have to rely upon conjecture or supposition. We have several statements by leading communists telling us outright that the USSR planned to feign weakness and fake its death in order to trick the West.

In 1920, as the Bolshevik regime was just beginning to consolidate its power within Russia, Lenin said:

> "It is necessary to bribe capitalism with extra profit . . . and we will get the basics with the aid of which we will strengthen ourselves, will finally get up on our feet and then defeat it."[342]

In the same year, Lenin also stated:

> "All the capitalist countries of the world, which were united in the war against us, against our terror and our system, are forced against their will to enter into trade agreements with us, knowing full well that in this way they are helping us to strengthen and secure our system."[343]

Even in the earliest days of the communist conspiracy, its leaders were preparing to play friends with the West in order to secure the aid, technology, funds, and recognition with which it would eventually betray and destroy them. Communism is a parasite that feeds off its host until it is strong and the host is weak enough to be eliminated.

---

[342] Gussack, *Red Dawn In Retrospect*, 138.

[343] Ibid.

In his 1924 book *The Foundations of Leninism*, Soviet tyrant Joseph Stalin referred to the long struggle and strategic maneuvering that would be necessary before communism could triumph. He wrote:

> "It scarcely needs proof that there is not the slightest possibility of carrying out these tasks in a short period, of accomplishing all this in a few years. Therefore, the dictatorship of the proletariat, the transition from capitalism to communism, must not be regarded as a fleeting period of "super-revolutionary" acts and decrees, but as an entire historical era, replete with civil wars and external conflicts, with persistent organisational work and economic construction, with advances and retreats, victories and defeats. The historical era is needed not only to create the economic and cultural prerequisites for the complete victory of socialism, but also to enable the proletariat, firstly, to educate itself and become steeled as a force capable of governing the country, and, secondly, to re-educate and remould the petty-bourgeois strata along such lines as will assure the organisation of socialist production."[344]

Stalin and his fellow oligarchs knew that communism was a conspiracy with a long-range plan for taking over the world. It would not happen all at once and it would not all be achieved through force. Gradual cultural subversion, feigning "defeat," reeducating the opposition, and ushering in a socialistic economy were all prerequisites for the "complete victory of socialism." The cabal was fully prepared to make strategic retreats and stage "defeats" in order to advance its interests. The key takeaway from this quotation, then, is that the communist scheme is a long-range plan that anticipates events generations in advance, and therefore moves and acts in a way that will secure not an immediate, but an eventual, victory.

---

[344] Joseph Stalin, *The Foundations of Leninism* (1924), chapter 4, https://www.marxists.org/reference/archive/stalin/works/1924/foundations-leninism/ch04.htm.

In the early 1930s, a prominent Soviet politician and theoretician named Dmitri Z. Manuilski gave a speech at the Lenin School of Political Warfare where he informed his listeners of the conspiracy's long-range goal. He declared:

> "War to the hilt between communism and capitalism is inevitable. Today, of course, we are not strong enough to attack. Our time will come in thirty or forty years. To win, we shall need the element of surprise. The bourgeoisie will have to be put to sleep. So we shall begin by launching the most spectacular and unheard of concessions. The capitalist countries, stupid and decadent, will rejoice to cooperate in their own destruction. They will leap at another chance to be friends. As soon as their guard is down, we shall smash them with our clenched fist."[345]

Read that statement again and let it sink in. The communists have planned their endgame *at least* forty years in advance. The Lord warned us clear back in 1831 that the enemy already sat "in secret chambers" plotting our demise (D&C 38:28). Their long-term goal is the destruction of all opposition to their seizure of world power, which means, above all, the destruction of the United States. In order to achieve this goal, the communists would feign weakness and hold out an olive branch to the West. They would give "spectacular" and "unheard of concessions" to the "stupid and decadent" bourgeoisie. Through these extravagant concessions and the ploy of friendship, the West would be "put to sleep." Once asleep, the Beast would rise and smash its unsuspecting enemy.

As you may have noted, Manuilski's timeline was off by a few years. It is my observation that World War II delayed the timetable for this "unheard of" propaganda campaign. Though Stalin was instrumental in bringing about World War II, the war did not go exactly as planned. He had planned, as detailed by authors such as ex-Soviet intelligence officer

---

[345] Balmforth, *America's Coming Crisis*, 131-132.

Viktor Suvorov in his books *Icebreaker* and *The Chief Culprit*, to launch a massive surprise invasion of Western Europe in 1941.

As history would have it, Hitler knew of Stalin's ungodly plot and therefore preempted his invasion by attacking the Soviet Union. The attack threw Stalin's plans out the window and, instead of launching his own swift invasion and engulfing the whole of Europe in Bolshevik slavery, Stalin's Red Army was forced to battle the Germans for every inch of ground. It was only through Western (primarily American) aid to the Soviet Union that the communists survived.

Yes, the Western "Allies" saved the communists at the very time that Hitler – the supposed Devil incarnate – was desperately attempting to rid the world of the Red Plague of Bolshevism. We can thank the Germans, *not* the Allies, that Stalin did not conquer *all* of Europe. It was German blood, and German blood alone, that staved off the entire conquest and enslavement of mainland Europe.

In the end, with the willing express acquiescence of the United States, the Soviet Union was openly allowed to march to Berlin and consume half of Europe. Yet, this was only half of Stalin's original goal. This temporary setback and the resulting Cold War further delayed the Soviets' master plan.

When additional Cold War advances had set things on track again, the communists dusted off their old plan and began launching "spectacular" peace overtures and "détentes." When everything was in place, the Red Gadiantons tore down the Berlin Wall and very publicly converted from diehard communists to "democrats" who only wanted "peace."

Soviet defector Viktor Suvorov, whose words will be quoted more in the next chapter, wrote of the Bolshevik's false peace campaigns dating all the way back to Lenin's façade of peace during World War I. He wrote:

> "Lenin's party was not only the most militaristic in the world, but also the most peace-loving. . . .

"Lenin's party began an unprecedented campaign for peace. By September-October of 1917, the Bolshevik party had seventy-five newspapers and magazines, with a total daily run estimated as high as 600,000 copies. All these publications advocated for immediate peace. The Communists distributed their publications free of charge in city streets, in factories, in military barracks, and in the trenches at the front. On top of the newspapers and magazines, Lenin's party printed millions of books, brochures, pamphlets, and proclamations. Soldiers were told to try to establish friendly relations with the enemy, instead of shooting at them. Communist slogans urged the troops: "Put down your rifles!" "Go home!" "Let's transform the Imperialist War into a Civil War!". . . .

"Communists are proud of their love of peace. However, the stubbornness with which they fought for peace far surpasses common sense, to the point of suspicion."[346]

At first glance, one might think, "Isn't that good to advocate peace?" Yes, Latter-day Saints are instructed to "renounce war and proclaim peace" (D&C 98:16). However, the context and motivations must be taken into account.

What was Lenin's motivation for crying peace? As we have documented, Lenin was one of the most bloodthirsty tyrants to ever stalk this planet. He is responsible for the deaths of millions. He helped establish the worst system of slavery and oppression ever known to man. His motives were *never* "glory to God in the highest, and on earth peace, good will toward men" (Luke 2:14). So, why did he publicly proclaim peace so vociferously?

The answer is simple, yet conspiratorial. Lenin wanted Russian troops to stop fighting the Germans during World War I so that they could be used in his private revolution against the Russian imperial government. He

---

[346] Suvorov, *The Chief Culprit*, 2-3.

wanted to create a condition of desperation, confusion, and mutiny. He wanted to divide allegiances. He knew that communism can only gain power in a condition of complete chaos, and he sought to create those conditions to facilitate his long dreamed of Bolshevik coup.

Furthermore, Lenin's subsequent actions once his clique of conspirators had stormed the Winter Palace and usurped political power in Russia betray his true intentions. Immediately, Moscow began sponsoring revolts and uprisings in nations throughout the world. Moscow-backed insurrections occurred in Hungary and Germany, to name only two. In 1920, the Soviet Union's Red Army invaded Poland. Within its own borders, the Bolshevik cabal used its secret police and military units to hunt down and exterminate its opposition by every ruthless means imaginable.

No, the Bolsheviks *never* wanted peace. They did not want it during World War I when they campaigned on "Peace! Land! Bread!" yet delivered the Soviet State with its nameless horrors. They did not desire peace when they instigated World War II and, during that conflict, invaded the Baltics, Ukraine, Manchuria, Korea, and Finland, and occupied all of Eastern Europe and parts of Western Europe. They did not wish peace when their international press organs chanted "peaceful coexistence," "disarmament," and "détente" like religious mantras. And Red Gadiantons like Vladimir Putin certainly do not want peace today despite the myth of Russian religious revival and the ridiculous ruse of communism's "death."

In order to cement the ruse in the minds of Westerners, Mikhail Gorbachev inaugurated two programs – Perestroika and Glasnost. Glasnost means openness and Perestroika means restructuring. American history books gush with praise for these programs and hold them up as a sign of the death of communism, the end of the Cold War, and the peaceful intentions of Russia. As usual, the reality is 180 degrees different than the perception.

Gorbachev, who is treated as a savior of sorts in the West, told his collaborators in the Soviet Politburo the following in late 1987 – a full two years *before* the "fall" began:

> "Gentlemen, comrades, do not be concerned about all you hear about Glasnost and Perestroika and democracy in the coming years. They are primarily for outward consumption. There will be no significant internal changes in the Soviet Union, other than for cosmetic purposes. Our purpose is to disarm the Americans and let them fall asleep. We want to accomplish three things:
>
> "One, we want the Americans to withdraw conventional forces from Europe. Two, we want them to withdraw nuclear forces from Europe. Three, we want the Americans to stop proceeding with Strategic Defense Initiative."[347]

Can we believe this dictator? We certainly cannot believe him when he promises peace, but we most definitely can believe his threats, for the communists have proven their savagery and duplicity over the course of many decades. In every corner of the globe the communists have instigated revolutions, armed terrorists, assassinated opposition, stole state secrets, and trained agents in the art of subversion.

Glasnost and Perestroika were fake programs. They were designed to both appease the West and fail domestically, thus ensuring indefinite communist rule in Russia. Only superficial, or "cosmetic," changes were allowed. For instance, no longer would Russia fly the Soviet flag or call itself the Union of Soviet Socialist Republics. But we should remember that a change of name does *not* imply a change of substance, content, or character. The same mass-murderers, liars, spies, and conmen who ruled the Soviet Union were the same men who retained power in the new Russian Federation. Yet, when the Soviet Union "fell," Americans exhaled a collective sigh of relief, forgot all about the communist threat, and

---

[347] Balmforth, *America's Coming Crisis*, 132.

moved forward with their lives not knowing they were walking into the communist trap.

In his book *Perestroika: New Thinking for Our Country and the World*, Gorbachev again admitted, this time publicly, that the "fall" of the USSR was a sham. Please pay close attention to his words and what they really mean:

> "There are different interpretations of perestroika in the West, including the United States. There is the view that it has been necessitated by the disastrous state of the Soviet economy and that it signifies disenchantment with socialism and a crisis for its ideals and ultimate goals. Nothing could be further from the truth than such interpretations. . . .

> ". . . [Perestroika] has to a far greater extent been prompted by an awareness that the potential of socialism had been underutilized. . . .

> "The works of Lenin and his ideals of socialism remained for us an inexhaustible source of dialectical creative thought, theoretical wealth and political sagacity. His very image is an undying example of lofty moral strength, all-round spiritual culture and selfless devotion to the cause of the people and to socialism. Lenin lives on in the minds and hearts of millions of people. . . .

> "Turning to Lenin has greatly stimulated the Party and society in their search to find explanations and answers to the questions that have arisen. . . .

> "The essence of perestroika lies in the fact that *it unites socialism with democracy* and revives the Leninist concept of socialist construction both in theory and in practice. Such is the essence of perestroika, which accounts for its genuine revolutionary spirit and its all-embracing scope. . . .

> "Perestroika is closely connected with socialism as a system. . . .

"Does perestroika mean that we are giving up socialism or at least some of its foundations? Some ask this question with hope, others with misgiving. . . .

"To put an end to all the rumors and speculations that abound in the West about this, I would like to point out once again that we are conducting all our reforms in accordance with the socialist choice. We are looking within socialism, rather than outside it, for the answers to all the questions that arise. We assess our successes and errors alike by socialist standards. Those who hope that we shall move away from the socialist path will be greatly disappointed. Every part of our program of perestroika—and the program as a whole, for that matter—is fully based on the principle of more socialism and more democracy."[348]

What a stunning revelation! There you have it, straight from the horse's mouth – Perestroika is nothing but a drive to revive Leninism and to entrench "more socialism" throughout Russia. Gorbachev is emphatic that Russia was *not* abandoning socialism or the principles of Lenin (which were the principles of Stalin, Khrushchev, and the rest of the gang), but, rather, that it was developing a more effective way to implement them. It was evolving into a more lethal and vigorous entity. I summarize Gorbachev's words with a popular Russian saying: "Lenin lived, Lenin lives, Lenin will live!"

After reviewing many of the same facts just cited, Latter-day Saint author David Balmforth concluded in his truly fantastic book *America's Coming Crisis*:

"This treacherous ploy of Gorbachev and the Soviet/Russian hierarchy has been accomplished and the so-called "collapse" of Communism, around the world, is nothing more than a continuation of a clever stage production, possum-act strategy

---

[348] Mikhail Gorbachev, *Perestroika: New Thinking for Our Country and the World* (New York: A Cornelia and Michael Bessie Book, 1987), 10, 25, 35-36.

that was created to promote the unilateral disarmament of the United States."[349]

Concurring with Balmforth, Ken Bowers, LDS author of *Hiding in Plain Sight* – possibly the best overview of secret combinations available – wrote:

> "[D]on't be fooled into thinking that communism is dead because of glasnost or perestroika. The communists, including Gorbachev and Putin, still believe they will take over the world with their own brand of the New World Order. The members of the worldwide conspiracy think that they control communism, or at least are able to influence it, but the communists think differently. It's kind of like trying to control a tiger by putting a leash around its neck. The Frankenstein monster of communism created by the international conspiracy could easily turn on them. For that reason, there is an excellent chance that communism could attack the West and start World War III."[350]

Communism *is* the international conspiracy, and it is alive and well. While certain factions within the Western sphere of the cabal may desire to be at the helm of the conspiracy rather than the Moscow or Beijing-based conspirators (and neither Moscow nor Beijing fully trust each other and may very well fight once America is dealt with), it is nonetheless true that *communism* is the "greatest satanical threat" to mankind.

In his tome *The New Underworld Order*, Christopher Story has written:

> "Given that the 'collapse of Communism' was orchestrated by Soviet intelligence, with extensive clandestine financial engineering assistance from the West, it follows that the Communist dimension of the World Revolution dialectic, including

---

[349] Balmforth, *America's Coming Crisis*, 133.

[350] Bowers, *Hiding in Plain Sight*, 184,

its drug-trafficking and organised criminal operations, have remained not just intact, but hugely invigorated by the predicted realisation that the West has remained fast asleep while this strategic deception proceeds in accordance with the Soviet revolutionary blueprint initially formulated by the Comintern in 1928 and upgraded after the death of Stalin."[351]

All is going according to plan. It is communism that subverted the West and promoted secret combinations within its ranks. It is communism that fueled cultural rot through feminism, homosexuality, and other disorders of the soul. It is communism that pushes drugs and pornography. It is Karl Marx's destructive policies that have ruined our national economy and made us slaves to the privately-owned Federal Reserve monstrosity.[352] Satanic communism is the ideology that animates the elites in Moscow, Washington, Beijing, London, Paris, Berlin, Pyongyang, Tel Aviv, Tehran, and every other enemy outpost in battleground earth.

In recent years, the scarlet Beast has noticeably stirred and only sloppily continues the propaganda that the Soviet Union is gone. Instead, Soviet Russia and Red China are openly arming at breakneck speed and Russian leaders constantly threaten the West with nuclear war.

During the writing of this book, yet another Russian spokesperson reminded Britain of its nuclear strength – the implication being that Russia will use those nuclear weapons if pushed too far. The incident that sparked the threat was the double homicide of a Russian spy named Sergei Skripal and his daughter living in Britain. They were murdered with

---

[351] Christopher Story, *The New Underworld Order* (Edward Harle Limited, 2006), 87.

[352] Remember, *The Communist Manifesto* calls for the establishment of a national bank in order to complete its agenda. Wall Street does *not* represent "capitalism." Wall Street embodies communism and fights for a socialistic monopoly – or, said differently, a state monopoly – over the "means of production" and the money supply. The Federal Reserve, then, is a communist device for conquest of the United States. Let's never allow our knowledge of the Federal Reserve's intrigues distract us from the true masters behind this evil plan – the Luciferian communists.

a Russian nerve agent Novichok – a nerve agent, we should note, that was illegally developed by Russia in contravention of its international treaties against such weapons.

Simultaneous with these slayings, another Britain-based Russian was found strangled. Russia has carried out numerous hits against dissidents, defectors, and agents within Britain in the past, and it appears it is continuing to thumb its nose at Britain by openly murdering people within their territory. Once the incident became public, Britain expelled 23 Russian spies, threatened to close the KGB-created Russia Today (RT) news station, and gave Russia 24 hours to respond to its allegations. In response, Russian spokeswoman Maria Zakharova said: "One does not give 24 hours notice to a nuclear power."[353] Again, this is a thinly veiled threat of nuclear war in the Soviet tradition. It goes right along with what Putin himself has said that "a bear will not ask anyone for permission,"[354] referring, of course, to the symbolism of Russia as the bear.

Again, during the final editing of this book, two Russian nuclear-capable bombers flew precariously close to the Aleutian Islands in Alaska and were intercepted by U.S. F-22s. In an article about the incident, a Pentagon weapons expert, Mark Schneider, is quoted as saying these provocative bomber routes are a deliberate attempt by Russia to intimidate the West. He also said: "Threatening people with nuclear weapons is Russia's national sport."[355] From the dozens of Russian threats

---

[353] Tyler Durden, "Russia Threatens UK: "One Does Not Give 24Hrs Notice To A Nuclear Power,"" *ZeroHedge*, March 14, 2018, accessed March 16, 2018, https://www.zerohedge.com/news/2018-03-13/russia-threatens-uk-one-does-not-give-24hrs-notice-nuclear-power.

[354] "Putin: Russian bear won't ask for permission," *Russia Today*, October 24, 2014, accessed May 24, 2018, https://www.rt.com/news/199000-putin-bear-ask-permission/.

[355] Bill Gertz, "Russian Nuclear Bombers Intercepted Near Alaska," *The Washington Free Beacon*, May 11, 2018, accessed May 11, 2018, http://freebeacon.com/national-security/russian-nuclear-bombers-intercepted-near-alaska/.

I've seen just during my own lifetime in the supposed "post-Soviet" era, I have to concur with Schneider's analysis.

More importantly, we can closely observe the past whenever we want a clear vision of the future. If the Soviet Union was a serious threat during the Cold War, it remains a serious threat today because it is dominated by the same communist ideology. In 1957, J. Edgar Hoover gave us something important to consider. He wrote:

> "Communism – the scourge of our generation – has not weakened. Its philosophy has not changed. The danger from it has not lessened. At this very moment, the same old communist crowd is doing business at the same old communist stand in the same old subversive way! And we are letting them do it! . . . .
>
> "Communism cannot change. Should it change, it would cease to be communism."[356]

Communism has *not* changed and it has *not* ceased to be the conspiracy Moroni foresaw in ancient times. Communist Russia is as belligerent as it was at the height of the Cold War. And this is to be expected, for, as Hoover reminded us, the philosophy, ideals, and principles of communism have not changed. If communism has changed, then Satan, the father of this hellish conspiracy, has changed. And we know that will never happen.

It is well to ask ourselves a few questions: Has a single evil empire in world history ever given up its power voluntarily? Has a wicked regime ever abdicated control without the shedding of blood? Have Satanic conspirators ever forsaken their oaths and covenants while at the height of their power and influence? The answer to each of these questions is a resounding *no*. Yet, this is what the mainstream media, university professors, court historians, and public school teachers would have us believe.

---

[356] J. Edgar Hoover, *American Legion Magazine*, November, 1957, in Jerreld L. Newquist, *Prophets, Principles and National Survival*, 297.

The truth is that *never* in all of human history has an evil regime voluntarily, without bloodshed, uprisings, or fighting, given up its power and control over its subjects. It has never happened and it will never happen. Communism cannot relinquish its power because communism is Satan's sword, and Satan's duel with Christ is not complete.

The sole exception to this millennia's-old pattern of tyrannical regimes maintaining control at all costs, if the media propagandists are to be believed, is the "fall" of the USSR. Yet, I submit to every rational mind the truth that communism is *not* dead and that the tyrants in the Kremlin did *not* relinquish their power over the largest and most globally-expansive empire in world history. If our prophets said communism is the "greatest satanical threat" to the Church and to mankind in the past, then it must be so today as well because *nothing* has changed and the same occultist oligarchs rule in Moscow. And in China, North Korea, and Cuba, the communists have not even pretended to give up their power, but still maintain an iron grip over their enslaved societies.

Again, in order for this Soviet "fall" to have happened the way we have been told, we would have to believe the lie that Lucifer has had a change of heart and voluntarily gave up his control over the billions of God's children enslaved in vast Soviet empire. We would have to believe that the initiates of Satan's communist secret combination suddenly patted each other on the back, called it a day, disbanded, and forsook their carefully laid plans, their oaths, and their covenants.

In a 1963 BYU address titled "A Race Against Time," President Benson lamented that his countrymen were being lulled to sleep regarding the expanding communist threat. He observed:

> "We are now – this very day – at war with the Socialist-Communist Conspiracy. This is a point that a lot of people do not seem to realize. They think that just because we are not shooting at each other with bullets that it isn't a real war. But, we are really at war and we must win this war if we expect to survive as a free people. . . .

"The Communists are winning the war and building their empire largely with the help of non-communists – fellow travelers, sympathizers, dupes, liberals, etc.

"Some people foolishly believe that the communists are changing, that they are "mellowing." This is not true."[357]

The communists have never mellowed. Their tactics may have evolved at various times, and differing slogans may have been employed to deceive, but the goal of world domination remains the same. The conspirators are "winning the war" – and we are helping them by remaining oblivious to their machinations and by keeping silent even when we do understand them. In a word, we are complicit in our own enslavement.

Czech communist defector, General Jan Sejna, warned that the communists have one eternal goal: The absolute victory of communism over all opposition. He said:

"The ultimate victory of the Communist revolution is the red thread that runs through all Soviet policy, no matter what new chieftains rise or fall. It is a precise, long-term commitment to which all planning, whether economic, military, cultural or whatever, is harnessed, just as are all activities in the intelligence and propaganda fields."[358]

The "red thread" of communist conquest runs through everything undertaken by the Russians, Chinese, and their allies today just as it did during the Cold War. The communists have never mellowed. Communist are incapable of mellowing; it goes against their intrinsic nature. Communism is incapable of change – it is everlastingly evil and single-minded in its objective of world domination and the destruction of

---

[357] President Ezra Taft Benson, "A Race Against Time," BYU address, December 10, 1963, https://www.latterdayconservative.com/ezra-taft-benson/a-race-against-time/.

[358] Pincher, *The Secret Offensive*, 84.

Christianity with its natural endowments of happiness, peace, and Freedom. It frequently adapts, evolves, and updates its tactics, but its goal is the same.

Unfortunately, the communists are winning on all fronts. In his recent book *Russia Rising*, Mark Hitchcock has written:

> "Putin's grand goals are to destroy the West by breaking up the European Union, dividing NATO, frustrating and unnerving the United States, and expanding Russia's global influence. On all fronts Russia seems to be succeeding."[359]

Again, he wrote:

> "Putin's success in his raw expansionist aggression has emboldened him to keep moving forward. Putin invaded Georgia and "took Crimea with barely a shot fired. He flooded Eastern Ukraine with agents and weaponry." When he annexed Crimea, protests in Russia against him stopped, and his personal approval ratings shot up from 60 percent to 80 percent. Putin seems to have a sense of invincibility and destiny. In September 2014, Putin boasted, "If I wanted, in two days I could have Russian troops not only in Kiev, but also in Riga, Vilnius, Tallinn, Warsaw and Bucharest.""[360]

If the U.S. president nonchalantly boasted that American forces could be in Mexico City, Ottawa, Panama City, or Havana in two days, the world would suffer a collective coronary from outrage and shock. The United States would be denounced as an "imperialist" nation preying on its poor neighbors and seeking world hegemony. Yet, when the Russian dictator makes the same remarks, no one bats an eye or even seems to notice.

---

[359] Hitchcock, *Russia Rising*, 5.

[360] Hitchcock, *Russia Rising*, 91.

Why? Perhaps it is because the conspiracy controls the world's major press organs and, thus, dominates public opinion.

Steadily, gradually, yet quite strategically, Russia and her allies are carving up the world, breaking down the few bastions of resistance, and pouring cold water on the dying embers of Freedom. In the past, their tactic was to use force and more militant subversion alongside ideological subversion and cultural rot. Today, the former tactics have been temporarily sidelined while the Russian bear pretends to hibernate. Yet, the revolution moves forward; and all options are still on the table for achieving the final victory over the West.

In a secret 1973 speech to his co-conspirators gathered in Prague, Soviet oligarch Leonid Brezhnev boasted of the stunning success of the ruse of détente. He beamed:

> "We are achieving with détente what our predecessors have been unable to achieve using the mailed fist. . . . We have been able to accomplish more in a short time with détente than was done for years pursuing a confrontation policy. . . . Trust us, comrades. For by 1985, as a consequence of what we are now achieving with détente, we will have achieved most of our objectives."[361]

Yes, by the "end" of the Cold War, the Soviets had achieved nearly all of their objectives and had consolidated their global position. Using outright force in some instances, and other times using "détente" and massive "peace" campaigns, the Red conspirators marched toward their goal of world conquest. At the opportune time, the communists donned the mask of peace, held out the hand of friendship, and feigned weakness and defeat for all to see. What America did not notice, however, was the dagger of betrayal carefully hidden in Russia's other hand.

---

[361] Paul Kengor, *Dupes: How America's Adversaries Have Manipulated Progressives for a Century* (Wilmington, Delaware: ISI Books, 2010), 359.

J.R. Nyquist has described what happened behind the façade of "collapse" presented to the West on their TV screens:

> "But as we watched our television screens, and heard the summaries of the news anchormen, the Soviet Union was still there. It only seemed to disappear. The ruling elite of the USSR did not step down. A partial replacement of Soviet symbols with Russian symbols took place. But the apparatus of power, the military complex and KGB took on new names and struck a new pose. Yet these people were Soviet beneath the skin."[362]

Yes, beneath the skin the Moscow-based Gadianton Robbers remained the same. The Soviet "collapse" was a sham from day one; a planned deception foisted upon a hopeful world. Yet, this deception had been foretold by Soviet defectors anxious to prevent the West from falling into the trap they had once helped lay.

One of the preeminent spies to defect from Soviet Russia to the West was Anatoliy Golitsyn. The Kremlin and its worldwide allies undertook to discredit Golitsyn, but his words not only withstood their lies but became eerily prophetic. In his book *New Lies for Old*, originally published in 1984, Golitsyn predicted, based on his insider knowledge of Soviet long-range strategy, that the USSR would formally dissolve and feign weakness in order to put the West to sleep. He wrote:

> "The conclusion was reached that, if the factors that had previously served to forge a degree of Western cohesion – that is, communist ideological militancy and monolithic unity – were to be perceived by the West, respectively, as moderating and disintegrating and if, despite an increase in the bloc's actual strength, an image was to be successfully projected of a bloc weakened by economic, political, and ideological disarray, then the Western response to communist policy would be feebler and

---

[362] Kincaid and Nyquist, *Red Jihad*, 110.

less coordinated; actual Western tendencies toward disintegration might be provoked and encouraged, thereby creating conditions for a change in the balance of power in favor of the communist bloc.

"In other words, common logic suggested that the bloc should proceed towards its aim of worldwide victory for communism by forging its own unity and coordinating its own policies as far as possible in secret while at the same time undermining the unity and resistance of the noncommunist world by projecting a misleading image of its own evolution, disunity, and weakness. This was in fact the hidden essence of the long-range bloc policy adopted in 1958-60 and the basis of the various strategies developed from then onward in the execution of that policy."[363]

From Golitsyn's information, the Soviets were planning to strategically deceive the West by simulating weakness and disunity. This would diffuse much of the tension and concern about communism throughout the Western world. In the absence of Western pressure and unity of purpose, communism – forever unified in its Satanic goals – could carry out its agenda in secret.

Please also note when this policy was adopted – 1958-1960. Recall the words of Dmitri Manuilski who said in "thirty or forty years" the communists would feign peace and weakness. Thirty years after Golitsyn said the old policy had been brushed off and finalized, it was carried out like clockwork and the USSR "fell."

Elsewhere in the book, Golitsyn similarly explained:

"The impressions that the influence of ideology is declining, that the Soviet Union is evolving from an ideological into a conventional national state, that there is a struggle between the

---

[363] Anatoliy Golitsyn, *New Lies for Old: The Communist Strategy of Deception and Disinformation* (Atlanta, Georgia: Clarion House, 1990), 38.

Soviet Union and Communist China, and that the communist bloc is disintegrating are all false. These impressions are the product of [Soviet] bloc disinformation operations that have successfully hidden the true situation. Since 1958-60, communist ideology in the communist countries has been revived, restored, and intensified; the communist bureaucracy has been given a new, constructive purpose; real and effective, but secret, coordination between the communist countries, especially between the Soviet Union and China, has been practiced on the basis of the long-range policy. Whether intended to do so or not, Western convergence theories effectively contribute to the successful fulfillment of this policy. They promote détente, and hereby help the communist bloc to acquire advanced technology from the West and to shift the balance of power in communist favor. They provide an unsound basis for a rational Western response to the increasing communist political and military threat. They promote the political and ideological disarmament of the West. They divert Western diplomatic effort from the reinforcement of Western anticommunist alliances toward illusory and unrealistic realignments with one or another communist state. They create exaggerated expectations in the West about the possibilities of accommodation with the communist world. They are laying the basis for destroying Western morale and public confidence in those Western statesmen, diplomats, and academics who have expounded theories based on common interests and convergence and who will be exposed as bankrupt prophets when the notion of convergence is exploded."[364]

As noted, Golitsyn's words were prophetic. Russia and China did *not* split – they are stronger allies than ever. The Eastern Bloc did *not* push away from Moscow, but ran into its arms. Western diplomats and "experts" diverted their attention away from Russia to focus on fake or secondary

---

[364] Golitsyn, *New Lies for Old*, 240-241.

threats like Islam, Syria, Iran, etc. In accordance with their long-range policy, the Russians pretended to project weakness and disorder when in reality they were strong, coordinated, and growing rapidly.

During and after the so-called "collapse" of communism, Golitsyn wrote memoranda to the CIA which were compiled into a book titled *The Perestroika Deception*. If anyone wishes to understand this ruse more fully, he should get a copy of this book. It is unsurpassed in its prescience. In that superb text, Golitsyn wrote:

> "The central domestic purpose of the strategy and the final phase of 'perestroika' is to renew the regimes in the Soviet Union and other Communist countries, and to convert them into states of 'mature socialism with a human face' in order to promote the external strategy of 'convergence'. These regimes must be 'acceptable' to the West for 'convergence' purposes. Thus the strategy goes far beyond domestic political restructuring, since it is aimed at the 'restructuring' or 're-shoeing' *of the West* – the 'reform' of *Western* attitudes and policies – and ultimately at the peaceful conquest of the United States and Western Europe from within.

> "The essence of the special manoeuvre within this strategy is the creation of secretly controlled opposition movements and the use and manipulation of them in a transition to a spectrum of new 'democratic' or 'democratist', 'non-Communist' and 'nationalist' power structures which will remain Communist-controlled in practice. It is these renewed regimes which are intended to achieve the global hegemony of Communism by means of 'convergence' on Communist terms of the 'former' Communist and non-Communist systems.

> "The West has failed to comprehend the deceptive, controlled nature of the new 'democratic' and 'non-Communist' structures which have been introduced in the USSR and Eastern Europe. The West is jubilant that former so-called 'dissidents', seen as

members of the 'persecuted political opposition', are now becoming presidents, premiers, members of government and parliament, and ambassadors in these new structures. For the Communists have succeeded in concealing from the West that this so-called 'political opposition' of 'dissidents' has been created, brought up and guided by the Bloc's Communist Parties and security services during the long period of preparation for *'perestroika'*. The Bloc's political and security potential have been fully deployed in the interests of the strategy.

"Gorbachev and his strategists are not true democrats and never will be. They remain committed to socialism and Communism. They are a new, smoother generation of revolutionaries who are using 'democratic' reforms as a new method, based on Leninist principles, of achieving final victory.

"The Communist strategists appreciated that they could not implement their strategy of 'convergence' using the old, obsolete, Stalinist, Communist Party structure and dormant institutions like the old Soviet parliament. But they do believe that they can carry it out using new, revitalised, 'democratic' structures.

"They are therefore reorganising the party system, the Presidency and the legislature to give them more power and prestige and at the same time greater likeness to their American counterparts. Meanwhile the Communist Party appears to be taking a backseat, relegated to the shadows.

"However in reality, the Communist Party has not surrendered its real monopoly of power. On the contrary, it has broadened it by handing power to its members in the Presidency and the legislative organs, for the purpose of executing the strategy of 'perestroika' and 'convergence'. Greater presidential powers are needed in order to carry this strategy throughout the world. . . .

". . . 'perestroika' amounted in fact to a broad strategic assault on the Western mindset- to a Leninist 'reshoeing' of the West designed to alter Western attitudes, to facilitate the abolition of the 'image' of the enemy, and to inveigle the West into signing bilateral treaties, supporting broad inter-bloc 'collective security' arrangements (despite the 'abolition of the image of the enemy'), the entry of East European and CIS states into the European Union and other devices intended to establish 'irreversible' Soviet hegemony through 'convergence' with the West on Communist terms."[365]

Golitsyn also suggested that the Western "globalists" who are collaborating in bringing about a New World Order are in for a rude awakening when this world government actually arrives. They will not be in charge, but the Red Gadiantons will instead be at the head. He predicted:

"This 'convergence' is to take place not on the West's terms – as elite Western globalists surely imagine – but rather on the terms intended by the Leninist strategic planners. The resulting 'one world' will be Marxist-Leninist-Gramscian-Communist – hardly what unwitting Western collaborators truly want to see established."[366]

So many more quotations could be drawn from *The Perestroika Deception*. However, these should be sufficient. According to the communists' long-range strategy, the outward forms of Soviet power were dismantled in order to fool the West and change the perception of the average American. They wanted to deprive America of an "enemy." By feigning weakness, they were able to consolidate their position and actually increased the likelihood of conquering the last bastions of the free world.

---

[365] Golitsyn, *The Perestroika Deception*, 205-208.

[366] Golitsyn, *The Perestroika Deception*, 153.

To Golitsyn, the "restructuring" of Perestroika was actually designed as a restructuring of Western perceptions and ideas. Instead of thinking in terms of East vs West, good vs evil, or the American Republic vs the Evil Empire, Westerners suddenly began thinking in terms of "global community" and "cooperation." This was exactly the cover the Soviets needed to carry out the final phase of their diabolical scheme of world domination.

So strong and confident has Russia grown in the absence of Western pressure and scrutiny that its official state propaganda organ *Pravda* published an article in November 2014 titled "Russia takes complete advantage of castrated armed forces of the West." In the piece, *Pravda* boasted:

> "The West, having discarded Russia, had been cutting its tanks and destroying tactical nuclear weapons. Russia, feeling its own weakness, kept all tanks and tactical nuclear weapons.
>
> "As a result, Russia overcame the inertia of collapse and started reviving its power, while the West, being lulled by sweet day-dreams of the liberal "end of history," castrated its armed forces to the point, when they could be good for leading colonial wars with weak and technically backward enemies. The balance of forces in Europe has thus changed in Russia's favor.
>
> "When the Americans realized that, it was too late."[367]

While we have been sidetracked chasing the Islamic bogeyman and policing the globe, Russia has been arming to the teeth, subverting our culture, placing its agents of influence in our government, and continuing the old communist strategy to the letter. And Red China is likewise sabotaging the West, stealing Western technology, secrets, and patents,

---

[367] Dmitry Sudakov, "Russia takes complete advantage of castrated armed forces of the West," Part 2, *Pravda*, November 13, 2014, accessed March 14, 2018, http://www.pravdareport.com/russia/politics/13-11-2014/129021-russia_usa_nuclear_weapons-0/.

engaging in cyber and economic warfare, and rapidly arming for war and expansion.

In Part 1 of the article just cited, *Pravda* again boasted of Russia's military superiority over NATO in both nuclear weapons and tank forces:

> "It just so happens that today, Russia's strategic nuclear forces (SNF) are even more advanced in comparison with those of the US, as they ensure parity on warheads with a significantly smaller number of carriers of strategic nuclear weapons. This gap between Russia and the United States may only grow in the future, given the fact that Russian defense officials promised to rearm Russia's SNF with new generation missiles.

> "The progress was made possible thanks to the treaty on the limitation of nuclear weapons, also known as START-3. The treaty was signed by Dmitry Medvedev and Barack Obama on 8 April 2010 in Prague. . . .

> "Having written off Moscow as a serious geopolitical rival, flying on the wings of inaccessible military and technological superiority, Washington drove itself into a trap, from which it does not see a way out even in a medium-term perspective.

> "Recently, a lot has been said about so-called "sixth-generation wars" and high-precision long-range weapons that should ensure victory over enemy without coming into direct contact with its armed forces. This concept is highly questionable (The US failed to achieve victory in such a way both in Iraq and Afghanistan). Yet, this is the point, where Russia enters the parity line as well. . . .

> "In today's Russia, many find this hard to believe. This is a common belief for many of those, who still enthusiastically remain in captivity of the myths about the absolute "weakness" of Russia and the absolute "superiority" of the West. The myth was made up in the 90's under the influence of Boris Yeltsin and his

betrayal of Russian national interests. One has to admit that during that time, the myth was real, if one may say so.

"Times have changed. One can easily understand the new state of affairs. . . .

"In early 2013, the Americans withdrew the last group of heavy Abrams tanks from Europe. In NATO countries, over the last 20 years, one new tank would replace 10-15 old, yet still capable, tanks. At the same time, Russia was not decommissioning its tanks.

"As a result, today Russia is the absolute leader in this regard. . . .

"Therefore, the decisive superiority of Russian tanks has not gone anywhere since the times of the USSR.

"Here is another surprise. As for tactical nuclear weapons, the superiority of modern-day Russia over NATO is even stronger.

"The Americans are well aware of this. They were convinced before that Russia would never rise again. Now it's too late."[368]

Let this information sink in. It is not fiction. It is not fantasy. It is not "fake news." It is reality. Since the phony "collapse" of communism, the West has lost its military superiority (if it ever had any) over Soviet Russia. The Russians understand this. And they understand that their position is so powerful that even if America wakes up, it is "too late." The scale has tipped. We are in a grave situation.

During the writing of this book, Russian dictator Vladimir Putin – who unfortunately, though not surprisingly, won reelection as president –

---

[368] Dmitry Sudakov, "Russia prepares nuclear surprise for NATO," Part 1, *Pravda*, November 12, 2014, accessed March 14, 2018, http://www.pravdareport.com/russia/politics/12-11-2014/129015-russia_nato_nuclear_surprise-0/.

boasted of Russia's military superiority over the United States. In speaking of Russia's new state-of-the-art nuclear missiles, he said:

> "No anti-missile system – even in the future – has a hope of getting in its way . . . Their ability to move around missile shield intercepts make them invincible for all current and projected anti-missile and anti-aircraft systems."[369]

Not to be outdone, Red China's military has achieved "parity" with many U.S. capabilities according to Admiral Harry Harris of U.S. Pacific Command. In February, he gave this brief but alarming testimony:

> "China's impressive military buildup could soon challenge the United States across almost every domain."[370]

In a more recent article, Bill Gertz explained China's rapid expansion into the field of high-tech weaponry. He wrote:

> "Anti-satellite missiles and orbiting killer satellites, swarms of attack drones, hypersonic missiles, maneuvering warheads, lasers, and high-speed rail guns are key systems China is fielding in the coming years in a bid to leap ahead of the U.S. military supremacy."

Across the board, Red China is gaining on us and, in a number of key aspects, either equals or surpasses us. Certainly, in terms of manpower and the number of men-under-arms China holds a monopoly, but now these hordes are being outfitted with the best weapons and equipment.

---

[369] Oliver Carroll, "Russia has 'unstoppable' supersonic nuclear missile that cannot be traced by Western defence systems, says Putin," *Independent*, March 1, 2018, accessed March 4, 2018, https://www.independent.co.uk/news/world/europe/russia-nuclear-weapon-tests-drones-west-nato-defence-systems-putin-presidential-address-a8234296.html.

[370] "China Approaches Parity With US Military in All Domains – PACOM Chief," *Sputnik*, February 14, 2018, accessed February 15, 2018, https://sputniknews.com/asia/201802141061665418-china-approach-parity-us/.

The People's Liberation Army is a ruthless, communist-controlled entity whose threat should not be taken lightly.

While we like to think of ourselves as the world's superpower, Russian and Chinese Gadiantons know better. They are content to let us think we are powerful and strong. They are happy to see us waste our strength, wealth, and blood in pointless and immoral wars in the Middle East (and our involvement in these wars only strengthens their anti-American propaganda and drives smaller nations into their outstretched arms). They are pleased to see our unity fracture and our power dissipate.

The truth is, we are weak and our national institutions have all but crumbled under the withering barrage of communist subversion. If we were morally strong, as our forefathers were, no power could ever defeat us. If we clung to God as did the American Founders, we would never slip and falter. But we have spiritually fallen and are left to our own worldly strength. And in terms of worldly strength, the communists have outstripped us. Unless we repent, turn back to God, and resurrect our traditional Christian institutions, we will face down the communist sickle in a death match.

In 1963, Chairman Mao of China stated what the communists' duty is:

> "In the fight for complete liberation the oppressed people rely first of all on their own struggle and then, and only then, on international assistance. The people who have triumphed in their own revolution should help those still struggling for liberation. This is our internationalist duty."[371]

In reality, all communist revolutions rely on outside assistance – they are never organic, grass-roots, or spontaneous. However, the second half of this quotation is where our attention should be riveted.

---

[371] Mao Tse-Tung, *Quotations from Mao Tse-Tung* (1966), Chapter 18, https://www.marxists.org/reference/archive/mao/works/red-book/ch18.htm.

The Chinese communists, as the Russians, have "triumphed in their own revolution." Their focus has consequently shifted to the international stage. Russia since 1917 and China since 1949 have been aiding the worldwide revolt against humanity. From these two enemy strongholds, the communist virus has been strategically and deliberately disseminated into the world. But the communists understand that, ultimately, only force and violence can impose communism. Therefore, the Russians and Chinese have never ceased preparing for international war.

When the time is right, the Red Army of Russia, the People's Liberation Army of China, and the lesser militaries of North Korea, Iran, Turkey, Pakistan, and numerous other states will be given the long-awaited green light to eliminate the "Main Enemy" once and for all. After all, it is a communist's "internationalist duty."

Russian defector Sergei Tretyakov understands full well that an active war is being waged against the United States by the communists. He once commented on the devastating effectiveness of the "communism is dead" ruse and counseled:

> "I want to warn America as a people, you are very naïve about Russia and its intentions. You believe because the Soviet Union no longer exists, Russia now is your friend. It isn't, and I can show you how the SVR [Russian intelligence agency] is trying to destroy the U.S. even today and even more than the KGB did during the Cold War."[372]

The SVR, KGB, GRU and other foreign intelligence services have been so successful in their work that America's moral compass has gone haywire. We have come to resemble the Soviets in many particulars. Soviet defector Vladimir Bukovsky defected to the West in high hopes that he would witness the Soviet system crumble. His hopes were swiftly dashed,

---

[372] Sergei Tretyakov, 2007, in Kincaid and Nyquist, *Red Jihad*, 95.

however, after meeting the average voter. He was appalled at how Soviet-like the average Westerner had become and said:

> "[A]fter spending some time in the West and seeing the voters' attitude toward elections, nothing surprises me any more. Almost half of the voters don't go to the polls at all: they don't dare. A certain proportion votes out of a sense of obligation to their party, just like in the Soviet Union. The rest generally vote not for what they desire but against that which they fear. For the right, so that the left does not come to power, or vice versa. . . .

> "The voters are discouraged and can see no reason for going to the polls: nothing will change anyway. But is it not true that these same voters have brought about the situation by acting on the principle of the lesser evil? Do they not have the right (and the duty, I would add) as citizens of their country to pave the way for a government that corresponds to their convictions? The answer I got to these questions frightens me by its similarity to the reasoning of a Soviet man: "What can one individual do all by himself? What can even a small group do? The majority will go right on as before, no matter what I do.""

Bukovsky was right – we have allowed our enemy to overcome us through our inattention, our ignorance, and our lack of moral courage to do what is right rather than merely what is popular. Nowhere is this more apparent than in elections where Americans continue to vote for Republicans and Democrats despite the verifiable fact that there is not a dime's worth of difference (other than rhetoric and talking points) between the Republican and Democratic Parties.

The Republicans and Democrats are two sides of the same coin of counterfeit currency. They are two wings of the same bird of prey – and the American People are the prey. As long as we continue to vote Republican and Democrat, *absolutely nothing will change*. If you vote Republican or Democrat, you need only look in the mirror to discover who is ultimately to blame for the havoc caused by Satan's secret combinations.

Additionally, Bukovsky noted when he defected that:

> "the countries of the West had become more socialist, and had in some respects begun to resemble the Soviet Union. Communism and Marxism ceased being the ideology of rebels, having been absorbed by the establishment."[373]

As sad as it is to recount, *communism has become the predominant ideology in this country*, and more especially among the elite. The American People have adopted all ten planks of *The Communist Manifesto*, including our love for "free" public schooling, our acceptance of a national bank (i.e. the Federal Reserve), our reception of a graduated income tax, our endorsement of wealth redistribution under various guises including welfare programs, and so forth. We live in a de facto communist nation.

The only things holding back the Red tide are the battered and bruised U.S. Constitution, the armed segment of the American People, and the dwindling group of righteous inhabitants of this Promised Land. Like the Jaredites and Nephites, however, the Americans will also be swept off this land if they uphold secret combinations and persist in their wickedness until they are fully ripe (see Ether chapters 2 and 8).

This downward spiral into the hellish communist abyss did not happen by accident, however; it was planned. High-ranking communist defector Jan Sejna, in his book *We Will Bury You*, highlighted the existence of a plan designed to demoralize the West and lull us to sleep with the pipedream of "friendship" with the communist world. He wrote:

---

[373] Vladimir Bukovsky, *To Choose Freedom* (Stanford, California: Hoover Institution Press, 1987), 22, 88-89.

"By fostering belief in our policy of friendship and co-operation with America, we planned to receive the greatest possible economic and technological help from the West, and at the same time convince the Capitalist countries that they had no need of military alliances. The erosion of N.A.T.O. . . . would be completed by the withdrawal of the United States from its commitment to the defence of Europe, and by European hostility to military expenditure, generated by economic recession and fanned by the efforts of the 'progressive' movements. To this end we envisaged that it might be necessary to dissolve the Warsaw Pact, in which event we had already prepared a web of bilateral defence arrangements, to be supervised by secret committees of Comercon."[374]

To reiterate, the communist strategy is flexible – the ends justify the means forever and always. If dissolving the Warsaw Pact (the communist version of NATO), or the Soviet Union itself, is required to achieve the agenda and hoodwink the West, so be it. The Soviet Bloc did not need the Warsaw Pact – it already had secret alliances and covert plans in place. As an underground secret society, the communists had a global network of organized crime syndicates, spy rings, etc., through which to carry out their operations.

In his book *Red Dawn In Retrospect*, Nevin Gussack has written of the continuing communist plan to conquer the United States:

"The final prize in the eyes of the Soviets (after 1991, the Russian Federation), Red China, and their allies is the ultimate conquest of the United States . . . The United States has always played the role of the Main Enemy in the eyes of the of the Politburos and oligarchs ruling the USSR, China, and their allies. Defector information and the historical precedents of previous Soviet

---

[374] Jan Sejna, *We Will Bury You* (London: Sidgwick and Jackson Limited, 1982), 107-108.

occupations of other nations also indicated that Moscow intended to co-opt elements of the native leftist forces and opportunists in all walks of life to govern a defeated United States and run day-to-day affairs such as communications, the economy, law enforcement, and education. Currently, there is some convincing empirical evidence which proves that the Soviets and their allies possessed a conscious intention to conquer the United States either through subversion during an economic collapse, limited nuclear strike, or nuclear blackmail."

What form might a Russian-Chinese strike on the United States take? No one can know for sure, but there are several probable theories, depending on the circumstances at the time. One theory is described by Gussack:

"It appears that a massive military attack on the United States by the Soviets (later Russian Federation) and China would be presaged by costly, sabotage operations that were difficult to trace. After the "*collapse*" of the USSR in December 1991, leaked secret speeches and defector information indicated that the Russians and Chinese sought to occupy the United States and Canada through a selective nuclear attack, with the Chinese eliminating the resident populations in an effort to attain Nazi-style Lebensraum (living space). There is also clear evidence that the territory of the United States would be dismembered and handed over to Russia and a revanchist, anti-American Mexico. The Soviets/Russians and Chinese also sought to surround the United States with leftist allies in Latin America, which would then choke America economically through control of strategic assets, such as the Panama Canal.

"A collapse of the Republic would ensue under the pressure of enemy military power. The framework and political culture of the constitutional republic would in all likelihood collapse. Either an extreme leftist puppet or a transitional government headed by the current President and Congress would attempt to maintain a façade of legitimacy for a Russian and/or Chinese occupation."[375]

While many analysts debate whether Russia and Chinese will attempt to physically invade and occupy the United States, no serious researcher denies that Russia and China have developed and coordinated extensive plans to open any major war against us with a nuclear barrage against strategic (mostly military) targets. All of their planning points toward this disaster scenario not as a mere possibility, but as an inevitability.

To give themselves the upper hand, the Soviets covertly launched a massive "peace" campaign in the West. The Russians in fact originated the utterly absurd myth of "nuclear winter" and were the impetus behind the worldwide movement to reduce nuclear armaments. A KGB agent revealed Moscow's hand in orchestrating these "peace" movements for strategic purposes. He said:

> "Do you know that all those well-meaning people in the Netherlands are being taken for a ride? They believe that the anti-neutron bomb movement and the reaction against the cruise missiles and other NATO activities have grown out of a pure idealism based on compassion for and concern with the fate of one's fellow man and his children. Oh, if those people just knew that everything is taking place according to a blueprint in Moscow, how they are being manipulated by a small group of communist ideologues who receive their instructions through me. If Moscow decides that 50,000 demonstrators must take to the streets in the Netherlands, then they take to the streets."[376]

While believing that Moscow can snap its fingers and 50,000 people in another country will suddenly protest this or that without knowing they are following her orders surely stretches the credulity of some readers, it

---

[375] Gussack, *Red Dawn In Retrospect*, 6.

[376] Gussack, *Red Dawn In Retrospect*, 19-20.

is nonetheless true. The communists have the most massive and elaborate subversion operation known to man. Its tentacles span the globe. The global narrative on everything from war to climate change to homosexuality to economics emanates from Moscow, Beijing, and other communist centers.

For instance, Russian intelligence defector, Sergei Tretyakov, made this comment about the "nuclear winter" propaganda:

> "There was an incident in recent times where Soviet intelligence managed not only to deceive the US, but the entire Western world, with propaganda. It created the myth of nuclear winter."[377]

Nevin Gussack explained how this propaganda originated and how it spread to the West where it became the dominant, albeit false, belief among the public:

> "Andropov, according to Tretayakov, funneled money into European and anti-nuclear organizations that opposed the presence of US military bases in West Germany. The KGB used the Soviet Peace Committee to fund these demonstrations in Europe against the American military installations in West Germany. Andropov also ordered the Soviet Academy of Sciences to prepare a doomsday report that would highlight the environmental dangers of nuclear weapons fired on a German battlefield. This was intended to stall the stationing of Pershing II missiles in West Germany. The USSR news agencies released a "study" performed by Dr. Kirill Kondrayev which allegedly showed the phenomenon of nuclear winter. This story was picked up by the BBC and Tretayakov revealed that the whole *"study"* was KGB disinformation. He noted "I was told the Soviet scientists knew this theory was completely ridiculous. There were no legitimate scientific facts to support it. But it was exactly what Andropov

---

[377] Gussack, *Red Dawn In Retrospect*, 20.

needed to cause terror in the West." . . . the Russians/Soviets engage in disinformation efforts to stoke mass fears of nuclear war in an effort to cripple all Western defensive and offensive weapons systems specifically conceived to effectively counter the threat of Moscow. The *"nuclear winter"* Active Measures operation clearly was an example of Soviet exploitation of the legitimate fears of nuclear war for the greater strategic purpose of terrifying the Western public to completely disarm their strategic forces."[378]

The United States has been crippled by this unrelenting Russian and Chinese propaganda. The American People has become paralyzed by fear. Moscow's lackeys in Washington, D.C. have acquiesced to communist desires and have severely limited American nuclear capabilities by decommissioning and dismantling our best missiles while firing hundreds of others off into the ocean.

On this issue, W. Cleon Skousen wrote:

"The Communists have created the illusion in free men's minds that "the way to peace is through disarmament." We must not forget that this originated as a *Communist* slogan. Now free men have adopted it as their own and are even setting up special commissions to explore ways and means to carry it out. In this action we are deliberately closing our eyes to everything we promised ourselves at the end of World War II and again at the end of the Korean War. Experts tell us that to disarm in the face of an obvious and present danger is an *immoral* act. It is an act of self-destruction."[379]

Truly, to disarm and give up our defensive capabilities is an immoral act. This can be done without building up an army designed for aggression or

---

[378] Gussack, *Red Dawn In Retrospect*, 20-21.

[379] Skousen, *The Naked Communist*, 263.

overseas adventurism. We must build up our home defenses against the day the communists attack – and make no mistake, the communists have never given up their aggressive plans.

President Benson once called out those who would, out of fear of nuclear war, make concessions to the communists. He said:

> "There are some Americans who have been so effectively frightened by the extensive A-bomb propaganda that they have become convinced that it is "better Red than dead." Perhaps they wouldn't want to express it quite that bluntly, but that's what it boils down to. . . .
>
> ". . . If we should ever come to place mere survival above all else, if we should now make our national slogan "Better Red than dead," we shall end up Red and only wish that we were dead."[380]

I, for one, would rather die or go down fighting than become a communist or even live under their tyrannical rule. But these are the options the enemy has given us: 1) Join their cause; 2) live under their rule as slaves; or 3) die. When faced with such a choice, true Americans will repeat Patrick Henry's immortal words:

> "Gentlemen may cry, Peace, Peace – but there is no peace. The war is actually begun! The next gale that sweeps from the north will bring to our ears the clash of resounding arms! Our brethren are already in the field! Why stand we here idle? What is it that gentlemen wish? What would they have? Is life so dear, or peace so sweet, as to be purchased at the price of chains and slavery? Forbid it, Almighty God! I know not what course others may take; but as for me, give me liberty or give me death!"[381]

---

[380] Benson, Newquist, ed., *An Enemy Hath Done This*, 172.

[381] Patrick Henry, "Give Me Liberty Or Give Me Death," March 23, 1775, http://avalon.law.yale.edu/18th_century/patrick.asp.

On another occasion, President Ezra Taft Benson spoke of the insanity of disarmament in the face of communist aggression, and of our waning military might. He lamented:

"The first step toward formulating an intelligent attitude toward current disarmament proposals is to examine what the word "disarmament" really means. As it is used today by those who are its foremost advocates, the word "disarmament" can be defined simply as "the transfer of our national military apparatus to the control of the U.N." . . . .

"Most Americans find it hard to believe that our leaders in Washington would make such a fantastic proposal. This is merely part of the overall plan to resolve our conflict with communism, not by victory over it, but by merging with it into a world body, since it will have superior military force at its disposal, will become by definition a one-world government.

"This plan is not new. It has been developed and gradually moved forward ever since the end of World War II and the creation of the U.N. President Kennedy described the "beneficial effects" [of disarmament]. . . .

"In 1961, Adlai Stevenson spelled it out for even the most thick-headed to understand when, describing our proposals for disarmament, he said: "In short, the U.S. program calls for total elimination of national capacity to make international war." . . . .

"There is yet another grim aspect to our disarmament proposals. While the major long-range thrust is the transfer of our military might to the U.N., the secondary short-range thrust is to weaken our military might so that, even if real anti-communists should somehow regain control of our government before the transfer is complete, they would not be able to pose any real threat to the communist empire. . . .

". . . it is generally acknowledged that the Soviets very well may be better equipped than we in nuclear hardware that can be relied upon. Whether they really are, is beside the point. The mere fact that there can be speculation on the matter is serious enough. Don't let anyone say that there are a "miscalculation," though. The record is quite clear that our sagging nuclear defense was calculated as part of our proposals for general and complete disarmament!"[382]

With this statement, President Benson proved himself a prophet yet again. Since this testimony was given, the United States has forfeited its ability to fight a multi-front international war. In fact, it is now the official Pentagon program to *not* be able to fight a two-front war! Marine General James Cartwright even called such a notion "extreme."[383]

Under President Obama, this decades-old doctrine was retired in favor of a limited, one-front war strategy – a strategy that is nothing short of national suicide. While certain leaders are attempting to reboot the military, the fact is that our capabilities have been severely diminished and we are at a disadvantage to an enemy that has unceasingly prepared for major world war for a full century.

Today, Moscow's nuclear armaments outstrip anything the United States has deployed. And you can be sure that Russia will *never* disarm its weapons despite expecting the West to do just that in accordance with propaganda originating from the dark halls of the Kremlin.

Nevin Gussack has observed:

---

[382] Benson, Newquist ed., *An Enemy Hath Done This*, 174-177.

[383] Paul Bedard, "Pentagon to Change Two-Front War-Fighting Strategy," *U.S. News and World Report*, July 29, 2009, accessed May 25, 2018, https://www.usnews.com/news/blogs/washington-whispers/2009/07/29/pentagon-to-change-two-front-war-fighting-strategy.

"In the eyes of the Soviet leadership, détente and peaceful coexistence proved to be a huge joke. While Moscow rhapsodized about peace, the Reds prepared for war. Such Soviet-led peace offensives also served to embolden the pro-Soviet Left in the Western nations, which in turn mobilized popular and elite support in the campaigns to neutralize anti-communist policies. [Jan] Senja reported that Khrushchev retorted to a member of the Czech Central Committee concerned about Khrushchev's policy of peaceful coexistence being interpreted as surrender to capitalism: "Shut up! By peaceful coexistence I do not mean pacifism. I mean a policy that will destroy imperialism and make the Soviet Union and her allies the strongest economic and military power in the world . . . It is essential to understand that this new diplomacy will be successful only as long as there is a Soviet Marshal behind every diplomat. Peaceful coexistence is not 'class peace.' There can never be world peace while one imperialist lives."[384]

In reality, "peaceful coexistence" means absolute communist victory over the forces of Freedom. There is no middle ground — no possibility of coming to terms with communism. President Benson reminded us that it is futile "talking "peace" with the very communists who blaspheme the Prince of Peace."[385] Communism and the Gospel of the Lord — including His plan for the agency and Liberty of mankind — are diametrically opposed to one another. Only one can survive this death struggle.

In 1959, President Ezra Taft Benson, then serving as the U.S. Secretary of Agriculture in the Eisenhower administration, had the unpleasant task, which he vigorously protested, of taking Soviet dictator Nikita Khrushchev on a tour of American agricultural sights. President Benson recorded a verbal exchange he had with the communist kingpin thus:

---

[384] Gussack, *Red Dawn In Retrospect*, 16.

[385] Benson, Newquist, ed., *An Enemy Hath Done This*, 98.

"I have talked face-to-face with the godless Communist leaders. It may surprise you to learn that I was host to Mr. Khrushchev for a half day, when he visited the United States. Not that I'm proud of it – I opposed his coming then and I still feel it was a mistake to welcome this atheistic murderer as a state visitor. But according to President Eisenhower, Khrushchev had expressed a desire to learn something of American agriculture, and after seeing Russian agriculture I can understand why.

"As we talked face-to-face, he indicated that my grandchildren would live under Communism. After assuring him that I expected to do all in my power to assure that his, and all other grandchildren, would live under freedom, he arrogantly declared, in substance:

"You Americans are so gullible. No you won't accept Communism outright, but we'll keep feeding you small doses of socialism until you'll finally wake up and you find you already have Communism. We won't have to fight you. We'll so weaken your economy until you fall like over-ripe fruit into our hands.

"And they are ahead of schedule in their devilish scheme."[386]

I will repeat something I stated previously; namely, that we cannot declare communism dead if socialism still exists, for socialism *is* communism. The Red Gadiantons knew that implementing full communism would be a process spanning generations. They therefore devised a scheme by which communism would be instituted piece by piece, a little here and a little there, by force one day and in "peace" the next. By employing these creeping tactics, the Luciferian conspiracy has consumed most of the globe. Even in President Benson's day the

---

[386] President Ezra Taft Benson, "Our Immediate Responsibility," BYU devotional, October 25, 1966, https://www.latterdayconservative.com/ezra-taft-benson/our-immediate-responsibility/ or https://speeches.byu.edu/talks/ezra-taft-benson_immediate-responsibility/.

communists were "ahead of schedule in their devilish scheme" of world conquest. And this conquest has proceeded with hardly a word of protest from those being enslaved.

Apart from tricking the West into letting down its guard, getting rid of its greatest offensive and defensive capabilities, and participating in its own subjugation, communism reaped an additional benefit of faking its suicide: Western aid. Through simulating a process of "democratizing," the communists swindled wishful-thinking Westerners into pouring money and technology into the new "peace-loving" Russian Federation. Nearly all of it went straight to the Russian military. In essence, the West built a gallows and then tied its own noose and handed it to the executioner.

In his incredible book *America's Coming Crisis*, LDS author David Balmforth spoke of the planned "collapse" of communism as a ruse designed to, among other things, extract funds from the West. While Russia would feign weakness, it would secretly maintain the Communist Party apparatus below ground. Balmforth recounted that Russian dissident Lev Timofeyev had obtained an official Communist Party document dated August 23, 1990 which "provides evidence that the Communists were preparing to go underground." Balmforth recorded:

> "The leadership of the Communist Party realized that they could not modernize the nation without a massive amount of Western capital. They also realized that Western businessmen would be very unwilling to invest vast sums of money into an economy as heavily indebted as theirs. To overcome this they began to speak publicly about privatization and covertly started to seize as much for themselves as possible and turn it into private property. Timofeyev stated that "long before the collapse of above-ground Communist Party structures in August, 1991, apparatchiks were carefully planning political action to preserve the maximum of power in secret Party structures. Timofeyev then went on to explain how "the old Party apparatus has deeply concealed its

underground structure. Criminal prosecutors who were involved in beginning an investigation in October of 1991, "found more than a hundred commercial Communist Party enterprises in Moscow and about six hundred all told throughout Russia. Among the direction of these shadowy Party firms are people who have substantial influence in the current legitimate government."

"Russia feels that the West, particularly America, has been completely deceived by their overtures of peace. They feel that they have succeeded in instilling into the West a huge false sense of security, and the stage is now set for Russia and her allies to successfully launch a war when the West is least prepared and least expects it."[387]

You will recall that Engels admitted that communism began as a "secret society." As such, the Communist Party *always* concealed itself from prying eyes. Like an iceberg, only a small portion of the communist apparatus was visible above the surface while the true bulk of this modern Gadianton society was invisible.

Though it reigns from the shadows, the Communist Party maintains its stranglehold on the Russian culture, including its religious life. One of the big myths circulating these days is that there is a "religious revival" occurring in Russia. The internet is abuzz with talk of Russia as the "last bastion of Christianity." Some Latter-day Saints might even be convinced of this myth because of the recent announcement of the future construction of a temple in Russia. Yet, the truth is that our numbers are so low and that the Russian government is actively persecuting true Christians.

In July 2016, Vladimir Putin signed an anti-terrorism law severely restricting the activities of Christian denominations. As a consequence of the pressure, the Church has cut down the number of its missionaries

---

[387] Balmforth, *America's Coming Crisis*, 142-143.

(now called "volunteers") being called to Russia, and their ability to teach and proselytize has been severely curtailed. Nearly all other churches with foreign missionaries have been kicked out of Russia, and domestic denominations other than the Russian Orthodox Church are under constant attack.

The Russian Orthodox Church is, truthfully, a shell of its former self – an organization devoid of spiritual life. Few Russians actively attend their church and those who do are led by KGB agents posing as priests. Thorough study into the matter convinces the honest student that the main reason the communist regime allows the Russian Orthodox Church to exist is because they control it and it serves as an effective tool to keep the people in spiritual bondage. It also serves as a tool to promote nationalism in Russia and pro-Russian sentiment abroad, such as in the United States through the Russian Orthodox Church Outside of Russia (ROCOR) – an organization that pledged total fealty to Moscow in 2007.

When the Bolsheviks came to power, the Russian Orthodox Church was severely persecuted, its priests murdered, its nuns raped, and its buildings looted then demolished. The beautiful Temple of Christ Our Savior cathedral, headquarters of Russian Orthodoxy in Moscow, was demolished on Stalin's orders and the grounds turned into the world's largest swimming pool.

In 1943, Soviet dictator Joseph Stalin created the Moscow Patriarchate and staffed the newly reconstituted Russian Orthodox Church with KGB agents adorned in priestly robes. After the alleged "collapse" of the USSR, the Temple of Christ Our Savior was rebuilt and Russian government leaders put on a big show of attending ceremonies on major holidays.

This phony show of religiosity should not fool anyone. In June 1992, a report presented to the U.S. House of Representatives made a list of known KGB operatives posing as high authorities within the Russian Orthodox Church, men such as Metropolitan Filaret of Kiev and the famous Metropolitan Pitirim. The report stated:

> "[T]he atheist Soviet authorities exploited the Russian Orthodox Church and other official religious institutions in the USSR in order to bolster Soviet foreign policy by appealing to religious sentiments in the noncommunist world."[388]

Truly, the sham "religious revival" in Russia is nothing but a stage production performed to bewitch naïve Western audiences into developing a soft spot for Russia. Elder Hans Verlan Andersen warned of this type of priestcraft. In referring to Roman leaders during the early days of Christ's Church, Elder Andersen may as well have been referring to our own day:

> "Sensing the depth and power of religious conviction, political leaders cunningly used it for their own despotic ends. By combining church and state they added the force of religious prejudice steeped in ignorance to that of patriotic fervor, thus creating powerful support for themselves and the organizations through which they imposed servitude. Pretending to share the religious beliefs of their people, these tyrants demonstrated their zeal and maintained control over religious and political thinking by using the police power to physically suppress all religious denominations except the favored one. By taxation and outright confiscation they supported the priestly class of the state church and financed the erection of state church buildings, proselyting, and "religious" instruction."[389]

Priestcraft runs amok in our own era. To wit, Vladimir Putin – the "former" KGB officer, known adulterer, and mass murderer – parades around pretending to be a true Christian while his regime props up the Russian Orthodox Church for purely political purposes. Putin has cleverly

---

[388] "Soviet Active Measures in the "Post-Cold War" Era 1988-1991," June 1992, accessed May 14, 2018, http://intellit.muskingum.edu/russia_folder/pcw_era/index.htm.

[389] Andersen, *The Great and Abominable Church of the Devil*, 120.

incorporated the Russian Orthodox Church into the Russian military and now a special unit of paratrooper priests has been formed who will parachute into a warzone with a mobile confessional.[390] All of this is done to legitimize the Russian regime in the eyes of the world.

On Easter 2008, I stood about a hundred yards away watching as police formed a protective ring around the Temple of Christ our Savior to guard Vladimir Putin's entourage while they went through the motions of worshipping. Putin makes a big show of his supposed Christian faith and has a close working relationship with the puppet patriarch of the Russian Orthodox Church, Patriarch Kirill. Despite what Russophiles and apologists claim, I hope no reader is fooled; Putin is no true Christian and the Russian Orthodox Church is controlled by Russian state intelligence services.

On December 15, 1987, Mikhail Gorbachev reiterated that the war against religion was still fundamental to the Russian regime. He told a group of fellow conspirators in Uzbekistan:

> "There must be no let-up in the war against religion because as long as religion exists Communism cannot prevail. We must intensify the obliteration of all religions wherever they are being practiced or taught."[391]

After the fake "fall" of communism, the communists resorted to destroying religion from the inside rather than by a full frontal assault. The communists have always infiltrated churches, most prominently the Roman Catholic Church, but from 1991 onwards, these soft methods kicked into overdrive. While there are no doubt dark days ahead where nuns will again be defiled and churches demolished, for now we must be on the lookout for wolves in sheep's clothing in our congregations; smooth-faced hypocrites who work for the Adversary.

---

[390] "Russian Priests to Get Military Training," *Sputnik*, September 29, 2013, accessed May 13, 2018, https://sputniknews.com/military/20130927183772300-Russian-Priests-to-Train-at-Moscow-Military-University/.

[391] Golitsyn, *The Perestroika Deception*, 116.

In a May 20, 1989 article titled "Religion and Perestroika," Konstantin Kharchev, head of the Soviet Council for Religious Affairs (CRA), wrote of the future of religion in Russia. He gloated:

> "Whether by our will or against, religion is entering into socialism, and not just walking into socialism, but entering on rails. But since power belongs entirely to us, I believe that we can direct these rails in any direction that suits our interests."[392]

Again, please do not be fooled into believing that a Christian revival is happening in Russia or that the "former" KGB agent Vladimir Putin is a true Christian as he claims. All of this is contrived. "Religion is entering into socialism," and the Red Gadiantons are directing it "in any direction that suits [their] interests." Just like the ancient Roman despots adopted the trappings of Christianity to consolidate their power and spread their pernicious influence, so, too, have the communists in Russia draped themselves in Orthodox robes to perpetuate their ruse.

In the United States, by contrast, secularism is being promoted by the Brotherhood of darkness. God once enjoyed a prominent place in American society, but He has been systematically removed from schools, the military, the halls of government, the media, and the public discourse. Marxist materialism is fast becoming the dominant life philosophy. Everyone chases the almighty dollar and the dollar sign has become the de facto American symbol. Promoting crass materialism is one of the surest ways to prepare a populace to embrace communism.

Writing in his book *Origins of the Fourth World War*, J.R. Nyquist, one of the foremost experts on communism, made numerous fascinating observations not only about communism but about life and human nature. Speaking of the decadent influence of materialism and how it ill-equips us to fight our enemies, he wrote:

---

[392] Kent R. Hill, *The Puzzle of the Soviet Church: An Inside Look at Christianity and Glasnost* (Portland, Oregon: Multnomah Press, 1989), 256.

"America refuses to understand the intercontinental rocket, the H-bomb, poison gas, and bioweapons . . . We are without bomb shelters. We refuse to make adequate preparations, to accept a military draft, to require greater economic sacrifices from our citizens.

"In additions, Americans believe that economic power *is* military power. For us it is not a question of diminishing the one for the sake of the other. The economy is viewed as the basis of national security. We expect Mammon, at whose temple we worship, to marshal our military forces. But Mammon is not a god of war. He is a corrupter who confiscates the concrete of the nation and diverts it from fallout shelters to freeways. At every turn he cries butter and not guns. He makes us eager to accept the friendship of Mr. Yeltsin or Mr. Gorbachev who talk smoothly and flatter; communists who say, "We represent the primacy of economics in Russia." And so we rush headlong to embrace these play-actors, even while the strategic rockets stand ready, hundreds upon hundreds of them, capped with fire, poison, and pestilence. Behind these rockets, the atomic Napoleons are waiting. "You cannot escape us," they whisper. "Our day is coming." . . . .

"The liberal capitalist state, though it can build a greater war machine, is disinclined to do so during its last and most decadent phase of existence, and often fails to produce great military leaders because of its conformism and bureaucratism, its clerkish effeminacy and democratic pretensions. Latter-day bourgeois society is a society which prefers the joys of consumerism to the thrill of battle. It is a society made up of economic men, all other types being excluded from respectability. Military man has now shrunk to a thin idiot shadow of his former self . . . Therefore, in practice, a non-bourgeois society, laboring under every kind of economic difficulty and theoretical misapprehension, will alone have the wherewithal to build the mightiest of military machines because it is not inhibited by the logic of economics; because it views war as inevitable and victory as the highest prize. Thus what follows, in practice, is that socialist states, which are deeply confused on the subject of economics, shall alone strive for victorious means. For they have no faith whatever in peace and free trade, but all their faith is in armaments."[393]

If any of these assertions seem strange at first glance, consider them in the context of human history and you will arrive at the conclusion that they are correct. In particular, a society focused on Mammon and hooked by materialism is a society ripe for destruction. It is a society that produces effeminate men, selfish women, weak families, bloated bureaucracies, and decaying militaries. This pattern played out in the old Roman Empire and it is repeating itself today, thus giving the brutish, violent, diabolically-minded communists a massive advantage in the event of an all-out war of annihilation where hard sacrifices must be made to achieve total victory.

In the United States, nothing exemplifies the domination of money quite like the Federal Reserve. This privately-owned central bank is integral to the communist plot and it was Karl Marx who wrote in his *Manifesto* that establishing a national bank was essential to establishing communism. Not only does the unconstitutional Federal Reserve manipulate the American currency, incur debts in the name of the United States, and print money out of thin air thus causing inflation which serves as a hidden tax on the American People, but it is used to funnel trillions of dollars to other nations. The Federal Reserve is essentially a blank check or open tab on which the communist world subsists.

Billions, if not trillions, of dollars have been given to both Russia and China by Washington and the traitors who own and operate the private entity deceptively called the Federal Reserve. Concerning the aid being given to communist China, Texe Marrs has written:

---

[393] Nyquist, *Origins of the Fourth World War*, 77-79.

"Red China has been chosen to be the poster child and role model for the Illuminati's Hegelian synthesis of Communism and Capitalism. The United States, meanwhile, is being purposely beat down and suppressed. Alien philosophies and a wave of immorality are being used to destroy peoples' minds while Wall Street operators continue their Ponzi scheme manipulation. The Federal Reserve, under Jewish banker Ben Bernanke's direction, is regularly transmitting boatloads of electronic cash to foreign banks in China. Thanks to this infusion of dollars, along with the trillions of dollars brought in from stolen Iraqi oil use and sales, the Chinese economy is galloping ahead, roaring at 10% annually."[394]

American aid to the communists has been one of the most underreported elements of the communist saga. I devote a chapter to this East-West collusion in my book *A Century of Red*. Here it will suffice to quote from Congressman Carroll Reece who headed the 1950s Reece Commission which investigated the major American foundations and corporations for their anti-Americanism. He marveled:

"Here lies the story of how communism and socialism are financed in the United States, where they get their money. It is the story of who pays the bills.

"There is evidence to show there is a diabolical conspiracy back of all this. Its aim is the furtherance of socialism in the United States.
. . .

"The method by which this is done seems fantastic to reasonable men, for these Communists and Socialists seize control of

---

[394] Texe Marrs, *Conspiracy of the Six-Pointed Star: Eye-Opening Revelations and Forbidden Knowledge About Israel, the Jews, Zionism, and the Rothschilds* (Austin, Texas: RiverCrest Publishing, 2011), 202.

fortunes left behind by capitalists when they die, and turn these fortunes around to finance the destruction of capitalism."[395]

Fantastic, yet true. Modern Gadiantons are masters of infiltration and subterfuge. They disguise themselves and, chameleon-like, pose as capitalists in order to use American dollars to finance the death of America.

The biggest "monopoly capitalists" are actually the biggest fans of socialism/communism. Remember, communism is *not* a philosophy of the downtrodden working class, but the ideology of the elite to consolidate their power on a global scale. The New World Order the Rothschilds, Rockefellers, and other big-name "globalists" seek to bring about is a *communist* order. Never forget that. The communist conspiracy doesn't play second fiddle to anyone.

In this work I have focused primarily on Russia, but it is well to keep Red China in mind, too. China plays an integral part in the communist conspiracy. China has not even pretended to shed its communist skins, but is an avowedly communist state openly ruled by the Chinese Communist Party. The Red Gadiantons have set up China as another base of operations from which to carry out their crusade against the United States.

China's history since the communist ascent to power in 1949 has been one of bloodshed, savagery, and forced conformity. Mao's Great Leap Forward and the subsequent Cultural Revolution constitute the zenith in communist treachery in China. Of the Great Leap Forward, Harun Yahya has written:

> "In the mid-fifties, Mao designed a system similar to Stalin's collectivization and put it into effect in 1958. This was called the

---

[395] Robert Henry Goldsborough, *Lines of Credit: Ropes of Bondage - The Story of the Financiers, Their Fellow Conspirators, and the Plot to Destroy Western Christian Civilization* (Baltimore, Maryland: Washington Dateline Publishers, 1989), 27.

"Great Leap Forward," but all it succeeded in doing was to bring torture and a great famine upon the Chinese people. . . .

"Within a short time, the Great Leap disintegrated into a great famine. Like the famine that Stalin fabricated in the Ukraine, this famine was also man-made. . . .

"In the years between 1958 and 1961, as a result of Mao's Great Leap policy, all of China suffered what's accepted as the greatest, most deadly famine in history. It is estimated that as a result, as many as 40 million died. . . .

"The "Great Leap" was actually a kind of experiment in natural selection. Mao forced the Chinese into the most difficult conditions in order to eliminate the weak and those opposed to Communism. On the one hand, he tried to brainwash the peasants by starving them so as to make them dependent on him and the Communist organization. [The] basis of this attempt was Darwinism."[396]

And of the Cultural Revolution, Yahya has written:

"The Cultural Revolution was a mass folly never before seen in the history of the world. The Red Guards arrested, tortured and executed tens of thousands for praying, just listening to music, or feeding a domestic animal. People were sent into a trance in which they supported every manner of savagery; they would shout their support as they watched people being murdered."[397]

During the Great Leap Forward and the Cultural Revolution, tens of millions perished in Chinese labor camps, during stents of backbreaking forced labor, in the massive famines caused by Mao's policies, in vicious purges, and for thousands of other reasons. Mao Tse-tung was the worst

---

[396] Yahya, *Communism in Ambush*, 122-123, 126, 130.

[397] Yahya, *Communism in Ambush*, 138.

butcher in human history. Mao and his associates killed, depending on the numbers you believe, anywhere from 60-100 million Chinese.

The oppression continues, however, with the 1989 Tiananmen Square massacres claiming the lives of some 5,000-6,000 unarmed protestors and bystanders, and routine purges of Christians and other dissidents. And those who aren't being purged have no conception of Freedom because the Chinese Communist Party boasts a totalitarian hold over its subjects. China's tradition of totalitarianism dates back millennia to the Legalists, but even the Legalists never enjoyed the universal domination of mind, body, and spirit the Red communists do today.

Recently, China has taken their ironclad control to the next level with a social credit system designed to compel obedience and punish dissent. In this system, each subject receives points based on their level of obedience to the regime. If one does not receive the requisite number of points, he may be denied access to government services, public transportation, etc.[398] The system has an eerie resemblance to the Anti-Christ scheme described in the Book of Revelation (Revelation 13:16-17). Truly, communism has unleashed a deluge of blood-soaked insanity in China.

With Moscow's support, and aid given by naïve and treasonous entities in the West, Red China has become a formidable foe. Her espionage and subversion apparatus equals Russia's, and her economic warfare efforts against the West are unrivaled. China's People's Liberation Army (PLA) has caught the U.S. military in many respects and is swiftly closing the gap in others. The largest population in the world – one seventh of Heavenly Father's children – is kept in chains by the conspirators in Beijing while the United States continues to court and depend on Chinese leaders, businesses, and products. Without hesitation, we can declare that Red China has become a very severe threat.

---

[398] "China Assigns Every Citizen A 'Social Credit Score' To Identify Who Is And Isn't Trustworthy," *CBS New York*, April 24, 2018, accessed May 1, 2018, http://newyork.cbslocal.com/2018/04/24/china-assigns-every-citizen-a-social-credit-score-to-identify-who-is-and-isnt-trustworthy/.

China expert Bill Gertz gave us this observation of China's mentality and goals in his book *The China Threat*:

> "China's communists believe world socialism is inevitable . . . When Chinese tanks rolled through Beijing's Tiananmen Square to crush democratic protests, they did so under the watchful gaze of a large portrait of Mao Zedong above the main building in the square. It is Mao's communism that justifies, sustains, and guides China's government even as it enriches itself with Western investment.

> "In a December 1998 speech, Jiang Zemin affirmed that "without Comrade Mao Zedong's leadership, there would not be New China; and without Comrade Deng Xiaoping's leadership, there would not be the path of building socialism with Chinese characteristics!"

> "Such socialism "with Chinese characteristics" means a communism that fulfills China's sense of its own superiority. China considers its culture to be the oldest in the world. It refers to itself as the Middle Kingdom – the place between heaven and earth. And to restore its former grandeur through modernizing communism, it will pay any human price."[399]

The spirit of the Dragon is alive in China. This demonic essence has animated revolutionaries such as Mao Tse-tung, Deng Xiaoping, and China's current dictator Xi Jinping in their murderous task. This evil spirit flows from the Chinese Communist Party which rules China with an iron fist. The goal is world domination – to become the global hegemon and restore China's former glory as the center of the universe.

---

[399] Bill Gertz, *The China Threat: How the People's Republic Targets America* (Washington, D.C.: Regnery Publishing, Inc., 2000), 10-11.

In their book *Red Dragon Rising*, Edward Timperlake and William C. Triplett II described China as "a brutal expansionist regime that will go to any length to fulfill its territorial ambitions." They continued:

> "The PLA's fifty years of armed aggression and subversion against China's neighbors have accounted for the deaths of millions and for devastation throughout Asia. And today, the Tiananmen Square killers infest the highest ranks of the Chinese military establishment. Having butchered young Chinese people without hesitation, they would have no reluctance to do the same to foreigners."[400]

Elsewhere in their book, the duo said:

> "Communist China poses an extraordinary military threat to the United States and the rest of the world.
>
> ". . . The democratic countries are about to be unpleasantly surprised by the emergence of a hostile, expansionist, nondemocratic superpower armed with the most modern weapons . . . and it will be our fault."[401]

This hostile superpower has been extremely aggressive since it came into existence in 1949. Since that time, Red China has invaded, attacked, or stolen land from the following nations: India; Tibet (this nation is still occupied by China); Vietnam; Burma; Laos; Cambodia; Malaysia; Singapore; Indonesia; Thailand; the Philippines; Japan; and South Korea.

Furthermore, China constantly threatens and bullies the island nation of Taiwan where the legitimate Chinese government fled in exile when Mao Tse-tung's communists conquered China. They have declared that Taiwan

---

[400] Edward Timperlake and William C. Triplett II, *Red Dragon Rising: Communist China's military threat to America* (Washington, D.C.: Regnery Publishing, Inc., 2002), 15.

[401] Timperlake and Triplett, *Red Dragon Rising*, 12.

will be theirs one way or another – and through force if necessary. And let us never forget that Chinese forces fought directly against American troops during the Korean War, killing thousands of our men, and that China greatly aided the Vietnamese who killed Americans during the Vietnam War debacle. Anyone who claims China is a peaceful nation that means us no harm is either ignorant or lying.

It is impossible for the Chinese Red Army *not* to wage aggressive struggle against its enemies. Chairman Mao once stated:

> "The Chinese Red Army is an armed body for carrying out the political tasks of the revolution. Especially at present, the Red Army should certainly not confine itself to fighting; besides fighting to destroy the enemy's military strength, it should shoulder such important tasks as doing propaganda among the masses, organizing the masses, arming them, helping them to establish revolutionary political power and setting up Party organizations . . . Without these objectives, fighting loses its meaning and the Red Army loses the reason for its existence."[402]

Yes, as long as communism exists, and as long as the Chinese Communist Party rules that oppressed empire, the Red Army will be used to carry out "Party" objectives, the supreme objective being to maintain "revolutionary political power" in China and to establish it across Asia and the globe.

Additionally, Timperlake and Triplett describe China's hostility towards Christians and people of faith. They reported:

> "Christianity was declared an "evil cult" by Communist judges, and two leaders of an underground Protestant church were sentenced to the firing squad for their religious activity. Hundreds of religious believers have died in police custody or labor camps in the past two years. The Washington Post reported widespread

---

[402] Mao, *Quotations from Chairman Mao Tse-Tung*, 39.

use of officially sanctioned torture and brainwashing directed against the Falun Gong spiritual movement. Twelve Chinse Christians were sent to the PRC's slave labor camps for three years each, charged with holding private religious services."[403]

While millions of Chinese are secretly converting to Christianity despite communist persecution – an effort the Lord is no doubt directing in order to prepare the ground for the future preaching of the Restored Gospel in that beleaguered nation – the fact remains that Christianity is the official enemy of the communist state.

Despite its egregious abuses, China was viewed during the Cold War as a counterweight to the Soviet Union. Western leaders believed the nonsense about a Sino-Soviet split – an alleged break in unity between the two communist titans. As a handful of Soviet defectors and political analysts have detailed, the Sino-Soviet split was a sham. Soviet defector Anatoliy Golitsyn has written about the outstanding benefits this deception has yielded to both Russia and China:

> "As the 1970s wore on and as Soviet aggressiveness became more apparent in Europe, Africa, and finally Afghanistan, China began to look attractive as a potential ally for the West. The common interest between the Soviet Union and the West in resisting Chinese militancy in the 1960s had been superseded by a common interest between China and the West in resisting Soviet expansionism in the 1970s. West European and Japanese capitalists tumbled over one another to build up China's economic and military potential, egged on by anti-Soviet conservative Western politicians and experts on defense. Alliance with China seemed to offer the best hope of redressing the growing military imbalance between the Soviet Union and the West, especially in Europe. The United States has been more and more disposed to "play the China card." The relationship with Communist China,

---

[403] Timperlake and Triplett, *Red Dragon Rising*, 7.

initiated under Nixon and Kissinger and developed under Carter and Brzezinski, was carried to the point of military cooperation, under Reagan and Haig, with the intention of building up China as a counterweight to the Soviet Union. Both in relation so the Soviets in the 1960s and to the Chinese in the 1970s and 1980s, the West has forgotten the error of the German General Staff in helping to rearm the Soviet Union after the Treaty of Rapallo in 1922. The Sino-Soviet scissors strategy has not been recognized for what it is.

"In short, first the Soviet Union and then China carried out the classical strategic precept of seeking to enter the enemy's camp unopposed and, if possible, welcomed by him. As Sun Tzu said: "To subdue the enemy without fighting is the acme of skill."

"Fighting between communist states is generally regarded as conclusive evidence of a split between them. But it should be remembered that the conflicts in the Sino-Soviet and Sino-Vietnamese border areas have taken place in the presence of few, if any, Western observers. Border incidents are easily staged and open radio communication about them can be used in support of their authenticity. Joint exercises can be made to look very much like battles. Even if genuine damage and casualties are caused, incidents are still open to more than one interpretation. Apparent fighting between communist states can contribute to such specific communist strategic objectives as promoting agreements and false alignments between communist and noncommunist states. For example, the Sino-Vietnamese "war" – and fears that it might spread – intensified Western pressure on the United States to conclude the SALT II agreement with the Soviet Union and helped make China look attractive as a potential Western ally against the Soviet Union."[404]

---

[404] Golitsyn, *New Lies for Old*, 278-279.

The communist strategy is based on deception just as ancient Gadiantonism rose or fell according to its ability to deceive. The Red Chinese are full partners in the communist plot and have played their role to near perfection. The Chinese have convinced many in the West that China is a valuable ally in the fight against communism, and against seemingly "rogue" states like North Korea. By accepting Western aid and pretending to allow capitalistic ventures inside China (companies and ventures actually controlled by the Chinese Communist Party), China has ingratiated itself into the Western psyche and has been catapulted to the forefront in world politics.

Never forget that Red China is an integral part of that system which President Benson described in 1988 as "increasing its evil influence and control over America and the entire world." There was no Sino-Soviet split, except that which was presented to the West by communist-controlled press. For all their alleged Cold War hostility, Red China and the Russian Federation have never been more closely allied and have never been in such a dominant position to extend their Devilish influence. By strategically ushering in periods of détente, "peace," "cooperation," and pretend infighting, the Russians and Chinese conspirators have thoroughly confused and dazed the West. We are now bound tight in a Gordian knot tied by communist hands.

As a brief aside, do *not* be fooled by the hype about "peace" on the Korean Peninsula. As of this writing, North Korean dictator Kim Jong-un (a puppet of Red China) has met with South Korean leaders and American diplomats. The North Korean oligarch is even planning to meet with President Donald Trump in an upcoming summit. While there have been some hazy, back-and-forth reports that the summit has been called off, it appears that some form of high-level diplomatic conference will occur.

Coinciding with their announcement that they will come to the table, North Korea is allegedly shutting down its nuclear plants and claiming that it will denuclearize. Both North and South Korean leaders are speaking of some form of unity between the two enemy nations. The controlled

Western media are lauding these moves and heralding "peace" in Asia. But there will be no real peace. Remember that – there will be no *real* peace in Asia.

To be sure, there may be summits held, peace accords signed, agreements entered into, or good words and promises uttered. But it will be a gargantuan lie – another deception like Soviet "détente" during the Cold War or the phony "fall" of communism. Every treaty and agreement entered into by a communist nation should be at once suspect. Communism, being the brainchild of the Father of Lies, cannot help but lie, deceive, mislead, trick, and betray. It's in their nature.[405]

The communists are notorious for breaking their promises and violating their treaties. There hasn't been one arms treaty the Russians have ever signed, for instance, that they haven't broken. *Not one.* Are we to believe that Kim Jong-un, a madman who keeps his own people in chains and at a starvation level of existence, will abide by a treaty aimed at reducing his power? Of course not! No matter what the press may say, no matter what South Korea claims, and no matter what President Trump may tweet, don't believe it if "peace" is proclaimed.

Keep in mind President Marion G. Romney's words and you won't be deceived:

> "Liberty loving people can no more expect to secure cooperation from communism in the establishment of peace than Christ could secure such cooperation from Satan. Communism being what it is, will never voluntarily yield in its evil purposes. Every time it negotiates, it advances its own cause or it does not deal."[406]

---

[405] I recommend the reader familiarize himself with the old fable of the scorpion and the frog. It illustrates a principle that we must always bear in mind when dealing with communism (the scorpion). Read the fable here: http://www.aesopfables.com/cgi/aesop1.cgi?4&TheScorpionandtheFrog.

[406] President Marion G. Romney, BYU devotional, March 1, 1955.

The North Korean communists will never deal – at least, they will never deal honestly. Any deal they may pretend to make will only benefit them. Even if a genuine desire to deal ever truly swept North Korea, we must never forget that North Korea is a puppet state of Red China. And Red China will *never* relinquish its hegemony over the Korean peninsula.

Finally, Nevin Gussack recorded the following. Though I disagree that China is the standard bearer of the communist movement – I believe it is Russia – this statement is highly relevant:

> "Presently, China appears to be the lead power carrying the red flag towards the goal of world communism. Wang Huning is a secretary to the CCP Central Committee Secretariat who drafted the document "Great Nation Diplomacy Strategy." Wang wrote: "The ideal of global communism is very likely to be achieved by the Chinese communists.""[407]

China's goal, like Russia's, is the demolition of the few remaining strongholds of Liberty in the Western world. Communism's eternal aim, no matter whether espoused by a Chinaman, a Russian, or a North Korean, is to install Lucifer's throne over the whole earth. In order to do that, the United States – the only nation with a semblance of Freedom remaining – must first be eliminated. Christianity must also be obliterated and man's agency must be subjected to communist dictates.

Ultimately, it matters little whether Satan achieves world domination through his agents in Russia, China, or elsewhere. He may very well sacrifice one or the other in order to achieve the greater goal of global primacy. But he understands that his greatest chance for victory – albeit a temporary one – is through his communist legions that stand at the ready in Russia and China.

By pretending to cooperate with the West for "world peace," the Russian and Chinese master deceivers successfully pulled off the most colossal

---

[407] Gussack, *Red Dawn In Retrospect*, 182.

ruse in history – and have raked in trillions of American dollars and vital technology in the process. Courtesy of the deception created in the Western mind by the "fall" of communism, the conspiracy has now moved to within a hair's breadth of triumph. And the worst part is that the average American has no clue the enemy is within the gates.

In a June 21, 1968 speech, President Ezra Taft Benson admonished us to not ignore, but, rather, admit, the reality of our "awful situation." He asserted:

> "We must put off our rose-colored glasses, quit repeating these soothing but entirely false statements about world unity and brotherhood, and look at the world as it is, not as we would like it to become. Such an objective, and perhaps painful, survey leads to but one conclusion. We would be committing national suicide to surrender any of our independence, and chain ourselves to other nations in such a sick and turbulent world. . . .

> "The world is smaller, you say? True, it is, but if one finds himself locked in a house with maniacs, thieves and murderers – even a small house – he does not increase his chances of survival by entering into alliances with his potential attackers and becoming dependent upon them for protection to the point where he is unable to defend himself. Perhaps the analogy between nations and maniacs is a little strong for some to accept. But if we put aside our squeamishness over strong language, and look hard at the real world in which we live, the analogy is quite sound in all but the rarest exceptions."[408]

We are trapped in a room full of maniacs – communist maniacs and those unwittingly manipulated into championing their cause. But whether or not the majority of people know they are furthering a demonic agenda is irrelevant – the fact is they are aiding and abetting the enemy of us all.

---

[408] Benson, Newquist, ed., *An Enemy Hath Done This*, 154-155.

A multitude of additional witnesses could be called forward to testify of the Soviet "collapse" myth, the ploy of peace propagated by the propagandists, and of Russia's and China's current threat to humanity. However, those already cited should be sufficient to obliterate the lies regarding communism's bogus "death." Communism is *not* dead; it is alive and seething and "seeketh to overthrow the freedom of all lands, nations, and countries." If we do not wake up, recognize the communist threat, and aggressively check its advances in our precious country, "it bringeth to pass the destruction of all people, for it is built up by the devil, who is the father of all lies" (Ether 8:25).

To close this chapter, I quote from President Benson who stated simply:

> "To the socialist-communist conspiracy there is no such thing as "peaceful coexistence" except as a tool for further conquest. Their stated objective is to "bury" us."[409]

---

[409] President Ezra Taft Benson, "A Race Against Time," BYU address, December 10, 1963, https://www.latterdayconservative.com/ezra-taft-benson/a-race-against-time/.

Chapter 9

Additional Testimonies against the Communist Conspiracy

Communism is the greatest threat to have ever faced mankind. More people have been murdered, raped, abused, humiliated, plundered, tortured, enslaved, and corrupted by communism than by the actions of any other system – or combination of systems – in all of world history. There is no limit to the evil in the communist heart.

In his book *Freedom and Foreign Policy*, former Senator Thomas J. Dodd wrote, as if echoing the 1942 First Presidency message cited earlier, this stunningly precise description of the Devilish nature and intent of communism:

> "Let's get communism in true focus.
>
> "Communism is total evil. It is all black. There is nothing gray about it. There is nothing good about it. Its ends are evil. Its means to those ends are evil.
>
> "If, by force of circumstance, Communists are for something right, it is only as an expedient to advance their evil ends. . . .
>
> "There is no evil so appalling that Communists would shrink from it, if it would effectively advance their ends. There is no atrocity so hideous that they would not willingly commit it if it served their purpose. . . .
>
> "Communism is at war with the whole human race. It is based on the blasphemy that a human being is just a particle of matter, without independent mind or spirit. It seeks to destroy the family as an institution. It seeks to blot out the human conscience and to

distort all concepts of right and wrong. It seeks to reduce man to a mere beast of burden, without a will, without a personality, without a home, without personal property, without knowledge of God, without hope of eternal life. . . .

". . . Communism is fundamentally dedicated to the destruction of the Free World and of the ethical and rational bases of that world. Its fixed and unswerving objective is to destroy us. The Communists may have to postpone this destruction, they may have to adopt new approaches to it, but it remains their central objective in foreign affairs."[410]

What can be added other than "Amen!" Senator Dodd's words hit the nail on the head. Communism's everlasting goal – like that of its founder, Lucifer – is our enslavement and the destruction of our souls. If we embrace or aid communism, under any of its names, we face the very real risk of losing our exaltation and eternal life – let alone our temporal Freedom here on earth. It therefore behooves us to study and understand communism so that we might know how to resist it and protect our families.

Bolshevik ruler Joseph Stalin once boasted that the Soviet system would, as Senator Dodd warned, destroy the free world. He said that communism is inherently international in nature and that its goal was a worldwide "state union." He wrote:

"In that Soviet power is the most internationalist of all state organisations in class society, for, by destroying every kind of national oppression and resting on the collaboration of the labouring masses of the various nationalities, it facilitates the uniting of these masses into a single state union. . . .

---

[410] Thomas J. Dodd, *Freedom and Foreign Policy* (New York: MacFadden-Bartell Corporation, 1962), 14-16.

"The Republic of Soviets is thus the political form, so long sought and finally discovered, within the framework of which the economic emancipation of the proletariat, the complete victory of socialism, must be accomplished."[411]

Remember, the Soviet Union was never restricted by national boundaries. It always envisioned a global union, a one-world order, under the Party's command. The state symbol of the USSR was, in fact, a hammer and cycle superimposed over the globe, representing Soviet aspirations for world dominion.

A former Soviet intelligence officer who defected to the West in 1978, the provocative Viktor Suvorov, is famous for spearheading the theory – an accurate theory, I might add, with which President Benson was in full agreement – that Stalin and the communists were responsible for starting World War II. In his book *The Chief Culprit: Stalin's Grand Design to Start World War II*, Suvorov wrote of his conversion from committed communist to anti-communist while a student in the military academy. In his treatise, he wrote:

"The head of my country told Americans: "We will bury you!" That was the essence of the Soviet Union's foreign policy at the time. We were digging a grave for the United States and all the other countries of the world. Our foreign policy was the top priority. We had more nuclear submarines than all of the countries of the world combined. We also had more airborne divisions, tanks, and field artillery. We filled the world with Kalashnikovs. . . .

". . . I consider the Soviet Union a criminal conglomerate. The Soviet leaders have committed uncountable acts of atrocity against their own people and against neighboring nations."[412]

---

[411] Joseph Stalin, *The Foundations of Leninism* (1924), chapter 4, https://www.marxists.org/reference/archive/stalin/works/1924/foundations-leninism/ch04.htm.

[412] Suvorov, *The Chief Culprit*, Introduction, xvi-xvii, xxi.

Suvorov said that in order to truly understand the communists, one must "seek what is hidden" and use "methods of criminology and intelligence" to dissect their motives and actions. Additionally, Suvorov described what he learned through his secretive studies in Soviet archives about the true criminal origins of the Bolsheviks and their intent to fill the world with blood in order to bring about the final communist conquest:

> "[A] small group of people existed in Russia, who dreamed that a second world war would be crueler, that the bloodshed would encompass not only Europe and part of Asia but all the other continents as well. These people called themselves Bolsheviks, or Communists. Vladimir Lenin headed the group, and called their organization a political party. However, the infrastructure, tactics, and strategies of Lenin's group did not resemble those of a political party, but of a small, well-organized, conspiratorial cult. Lenin's party had a perceptible structure, parallel to which ran a secret, invisible organization. Just like a mafia organization, Lenin's party had open and entirely legal associations and undertakings, along with a secret unifying force that always remained in the shadows. On the one hand, representatives from Lenin's party sat in the Russian parliament (the Duma). On the other hand, Lenin and his followers believed the party's funds could be enhanced by any means, including bank robbery . . . Lenin's cult must be called an organized crime gang, not a political party of a new sort.

> "The leaders of this cult concealed their real names. Lenin, Trotsky, Stalin, Zinoviev, Kamenev, Molotov, and Kirov: these are all aliases. . . .

> "Lenin and his gang worked hard to draw out World War I as much as possible. As early as September 1916, during the peak of the war, Lenin declared that one world war might be insufficient, and humanity might need another one of the same or even greater destructive scale. He reasoned that war is the mother of

revolution, and world war is the mother of world revolution. The longer the war lasts, the more bloodshed and destruction it brings, the sooner revolution takes place. If a world revolution did not arise as a result of the first world war, a second world war becomes necessary."[413]

Soviet defector Stanislav Lunev recorded his conversion from communist to dissident in his book *Through the Eyes of the Enemy*. Of his time studying at the military academy, he wrote:

"I lost my ideological virginity in the walls of this fortress of communism, paradoxically because of the privileges I had as a student there. I was allowed to visit the closed archives of the Central State Lenin Library, and to view many original documents that had handwritten notes and the signatures of Lenin, Bukharin, Sverdlov, and other communist leaders. As I read their notes, it became obvious that not only were these people not saints, as depicted in Soviet history books, but many of them were mentally and morally deranged. They had ordered the deaths of millions of ordinary persons whose only crime was their dissatisfaction with the political ambitions of the Soviet leaders. I was horrified when I read a paper signed by Lenin, ordering intelligence officers to go into small towns and stir up civilian uprisings – after which the military would arrive and kill everyone in sight. After my research, I no longer believed in communist dogmas and principles. I was sickened by the sight of the pervasive huge portraits of Lenin and other Soviet leaders, with their hypocritical and psychopathic smiles. Everything that I had been taught was sacred was a lie."[414]

From my time as a missionary walking the backstreets of Russia, I can attest that portraits and statues of Lenin dominate the Soviet landscape.

---

[413] Suvorov, The Chief Culprit, 1-2.

[414] Stanislav Lunev, *Through the Eyes of the Enemy* (Washington, D.C.: Regnery Publishing, Inc., 1998), 65-66.

His hypocritical and psychopathic smile follows you wherever you go. Nearly every town has giant statues of this despicable, mass-murdering tyrant. While many Russians acknowledge the dastardly legacy of Stalin, most still revere Lenin. Most Russians — including many members of the Church — consider Lenin a noble figure who tried to help and uplift Russia. The truth, however, is quite the opposite. Anyone who takes the time to study the records, as Colonel Lunev did, comes away with a feeling of disgust and contempt for Lenin and the murderous Bolshevik conspiracy he led.

In *Red Badge*, a book I sincerely wish everyone would read, Officer Doug Traubel was blunt about the depraved character and conduct of communism. He stated:

> "Marxism is a philosophy that uses the worst of human nature to enslave the best of human nature. It is a lie and a threat to man's God-given, unalienable rights."[415]

Communism is indeed a vicious lie. It is a mammoth hoax — a counterfeit gospel of death and corruption. It is organized gangsterism. It is professional cronyism and institutionalized exploitation of everything innocent, good, and holy. Yet, so many Americans falls for communism's deliberate lies, embrace its spoils, or simply stand idly by not knowing what to do. J. Edgar Hoover famously remarked:

> "The truth is that the global tyranny of the Twentieth Century has never been more deadly because it has never before been camouflaged with such shrewd effectiveness. . . .

> ". . . we must now face the harsh truth that the objectives of communism are being steadily advanced because many of us do not readily recognize the means used to advance them. The communist, meanwhile, does not allow himself the luxury of inertia. He is intensely active. Because of him, the menace of

---

[415] Traubel, *Red Badge*, 22.

communism in this country will remain a menace until the American people make themselves aware of the techniques of communism. No one who truly understands what it really is can he taken in by it. The individual is handicapped by coming face-to-face with a conspiracy so monstrous he cannot believe it exists. The American mind simply has not come to a realization of the evil which has been introduced into our midst. It rejects even the assumption that human creatures could espouse a philosophy which must ultimately destroy all that is good and decent."[416]

With some 6,000 years of experience under his belt, Satan is an expert in his craft of deception and trickery. He knows every trick because he is the Father of Lies. His followers in the modern secret combination that we know exists are camouflaged and blend into our society just as the Gadianton conspirators did in the Nephites' day. We are dealing with a highly organized and dedicated band of robbers and murderers who want nothing more than to conquer political power and give the throne to their god, the Devil himself.

Because of the implications of having organized evil in our midst, the individual – and, indeed, society at large – is paralyzed into inaction and mass denial. The United States has developed cognitive dissonance and has diverted its attention to pleasure seeking, sports, gossip, fashion, social justice, etc. – anything but tackle the problems head on. And, of course, *anything* is preferable to admitting that a global Satanic conspiracy exists and that *you* have been supporting it and sanctioning its treachery each time you have stepped inside the voting booth!

In 1964, just days prior to the presidential election, Ronald Reagan gave the speech of his life titled "A Time for Choosing." I urge everyone to watch or read that inspiring sermon. President Reagan understood the communist threat. He understood that America was the last hope for

---

[416] J. Edgar Hoover, "Communist "New Look:" A Study in Duplicity," *Elks Magazine*, August, 1956, 45, 47-48.

humanity to thwart the communist menace. He knew that if America fell, there was no place left to flee. Reagan stated:

> "Not too long ago two friends of mine were talking to a Cuban refugee, a businessman who had escaped from Castro, and in the midst of his story one of my friends turned to the other and said, "We don't know how lucky we are." And the Cuban stopped and said, "How lucky you are! I had someplace to escape to." In that sentence he told us the entire story. If we lose freedom here, there is no place to escape to. This is the last stand on Earth. And this idea that government is beholden to the people, that it has no other source of power except to sovereign people, is still the newest and most unique idea in all the long history of man's relation to man. This is the issue of this election. Whether we believe in our capacity for self-government or whether we abandon the American revolution and confess that a little intellectual elite in a far-distant capital can plan our lives for us better than we can plan them ourselves."

That really is the core issue of eternity – whether man will be free to choose or whether he will be a puppet on a string. We will uphold God's perfect Plan of agency or will we betray Him and seek to establish Satan's plan which exterminates agency? Will we be a self-governing Republic that takes the Lord's Constitution as our guide or will we allow a group of Gadianton Robbers in Moscow, Beijing, or elsewhere to dictate to us and micromanage our lives?

In closing his momentous address, Ronald Reagan warned the American People. He testified:

> "You and I have a rendezvous with destiny. We will preserve for our children this, the last best hope of man on Earth, or we will

sentence them to take the last step into a thousand years of darkness."[417]

What will it be? Whom will we serve? Whose side will we stand on? Whose team will we join? Which cause will we champion? The time is late; far too late. We are in the eleventh hour. We must recall General George Washington's 1776 call to action:

> "The Enemy have now landed, . . . and the hour is fast approaching, on which the Honor and Success of this army, and the safety of our bleeding Country depend. Remember officers and Soldiers, that you are Freemen, fighting for the blessings of Liberty—that slavery will be your portion, and that of your posterity, if you do not acquit yourselves like men . . . every one for himself resolving to conquer, or die, and trusting to the smiles of heaven upon so just a cause, will behave with Bravery and Resolution."[418]

Our forefathers heeded General Washington's words and stood up like real men. They won for us our precious Freedom. It was purchased with their blood according to Heaven's will. It is our duty, therefore, to *never* relinquish our Liberty. You elders of the Priesthood, it is your special duty to "acquit yourselves like men" and rise up against your enemies – to contend against the great and abominable church of the Devil (D&C 18:20).

The American patriots who forged this nation envisioned her as a shining city on a hill, a beacon of hope to the world. President Benson testified that we can yet realize this vision *if* we change our ways, become

---

[417] Ronald Reagan, "Address on Behalf of Senator Barry Goldwater: "A Time for Choosing,"" October 27, 1964, *The American Presidency Project*, accessed May 28, 2018, http://www.presidency.ucsb.edu/ws/index.php?pid=76121.

[418] George Washington, General Orders, August 23, 1776, *Founders Online*, National Archives, accessed, May 28, 2018, https://founders.archives.gov/documents/Washington/03-06-02-0100.

educated, and take steps to promote Americanism while fighting communism. He declared:

> "God grant that the United States of America may become alerted and informed and provide the courageous leadership so desperately needed in the world today. Then the enslaved people everywhere would start throwing off their shackles. And God grant that the restoration of freedom and honor and sanity to the conduct of human affairs will begin before the godless communist conspiracy destroys our civilization.
>
> "What a glorious day it would be to see America, a land choice above all other lands, exert her power and leadership. America, the greatest nation under heaven, is the hope of the free world, and the hope for the slaves of despotism. This nation can be the only effective deterrent to total communist slavery. We can stop communism. We can restore and preserve freedom."[419]

America has the greatest potential for good and for exerting positive power and godly leadership of any nation on earth. Yet, we have forgotten our heritage. We do not remember the lessons of history. And we have not followed President Brigham Young's admonition to study evil so that we might recognize and thwart the Adversary.

Though many of us possess the spirit of 1776 – the spirit of Liberty that animated us in the pre-earth councils – a large number do not correctly understand the enemy or his tactics and, thus, their resistance is ineffective. And some do not fathom that we are presently in a war to the death. Yet, the prophets have emphatically declared that we *are* in a struggle and that Satan is temporarily winning and gaining ground because we do not recognize him.

---

[419] Benson, Newquist, ed., *An Enemy Hath Done This*, 112.

In his classic talk "The Great Imitator," President James E. Faust warned of the sophisticated barrage the Adversary will level against us in these last days:

> "I think we will witness increasing evidence of Satan's power as the kingdom of God grows stronger. I believe Satan's ever-expanding efforts are some proof of the truthfulness of this work. In the future the opposition will be both more subtle and more open. It will be masked in greater sophistication and cunning, but it will also be more blatant. We will need greater spirituality to perceive all of the forms of evil and greater strength to resist it. But the disappointments and setbacks to the work of God will be temporary, for the work will go forward (see D&C 65:2)."[420]

Though we know the final score of this galactic game, *the stakes have never been higher*. Our individual souls hang in the balance. Our Freedom and right to worship God are at stake. Satan's machinations are "ever-expanding" and the "evidence of Satan's power" is increasing. The Devil's deeds are more blatant and, yet, more subtle and sophisticated than ever before. He has perfected his craft.

Communist subversion is the epitome of Satan's handiwork. It is the ultimate manifestation of his effort to undermine Christ's Kingdom and destroy human kind. Unless we develop "greater spirituality to perceive all of the forms of evil," we will fall.

I can imagine few things more horrifying than appearing before the bar of God in the next life only to learn that I had supported, even inadvertently, Satan's cleverly camouflaged conspiracy during my mortal probation. We *must* make a stronger attempt to stand on the right side of the line and never be seduced to cross it by Satan's flattery, temptations, or shrewd snares.

---

[420] President James E. Faust, "The Great Imitator," General Conference, October, 1987, https://www.lds.org/general-conference/1987/10/the-great-imitator?lang=eng.

Our day is that which Moroni called "awful." He plainly told us that our "awful situation" would be brought about "because of this secret combination which shall be among you" (Ether 8:24). President Dallin H. Oaks described the deplorable conditions our planet finds itself in. Said he:

> "Viewing our surroundings through the lens of faith and with an eternal perspective, we see all around us a fulfillment of the prophecy that "the devil shall have power over his own dominion" (D&C 1:35). Our hymn describes "the foe in countless numbers, / Marshaled in the ranks of sin" ("Hope of Israel," *Hymns,* no. 259), and so it is.

> "Evil that used to be localized and covered like a boil is now legalized and paraded like a banner. The most fundamental roots and bulwarks of civilization are questioned or attacked. Nations disavow their religious heritage. Marriage and family responsibilities are discarded as impediments to personal indulgence. The movies and magazines and television that shape our attitudes are filled with stories or images that portray the children of God as predatory beasts or, at best, as trivial creations pursuing little more than personal pleasure. And too many of us accept this as entertainment.

> "The men and women who made epic sacrifices to combat evil regimes in the past were shaped by values that are disappearing from our public teaching. The good, the true, and the beautiful are being replaced by the no-good, the "whatever," and the valueless fodder of personal whim. Not surprisingly, many of our youth and adults are caught up in pornography, pagan piercing of body parts, self-serving pleasure pursuits, dishonest behavior, revealing attire, foul language, and degrading sexual indulgence.

> "An increasing number of opinion leaders and followers deny the existence of the God of Abraham, Isaac, and Jacob and revere only the gods of secularism. Many in positions of power and

influence deny the right and wrong defined by divine decree. Even among those who profess to believe in right and wrong, there are "them that call evil good, and good evil" (Isa. 5:20; 2 Ne. 15:20). Many also deny individual responsibility and practice dependence on others, seeking, like the foolish virgins, to live on borrowed substance and borrowed light.

"All of this is grievous in the sight of our Heavenly Father, who loves all of His children and forbids every practice that keeps any from returning to His presence."[421]

We must recognize that the perversion, disbelief, idolatry, pride, pornography, secularism, and all the other evils being "paraded like a banner" are the result of organized, calculated, deliberate evil. Satan is the arch mastermind. He divulges his plan to the initiates of his secret combinations. These Luciferian high priests then use their influence to nudge mankind into dark paths wherein they become "carefully" ensnared by the evil one (2 Nephi 28:21).

Once this virulent virus infected the population, reaching a watershed moment in the 1960s though beginning much earlier, a very pagan culture emerged. Remember, President Clark dubbed communism "organized paganism." All that is grievous, self-serving, and rebellious stems from these Red Gadiantons.

Anti-communist analyst Fred Schwarz explained part of the reason why the communists are so successful and why our resistance is so ineffective. He wrote:

"[W]e are confronted with a movement which is frightening in its superb organization, strategic mobility and universal program, but

---

[421] President Dallin H. Oaks, "Preparation for the Second Coming," General Conference, April, 2004, https://www.lds.org/general-conference/2004/04/preparation-for-the-second-coming?lang=eng.

which is perfectly understandable and almost mathematically predictable.

"In the battle against Communism, there is no substitute for accurate, specific knowledge. Ignorance is evil and paralytic. The best intentions allied with the most sincere motives are ineffective and futile if they are divorced from adequate knowledge. . . .

"[Communists] are extremely trustworthy. You can trust a cancer cell to obey the laws of its lawless growth. You can trust an armed bank robber to take the money and try to escape. Similarly, you can trust the Communists to act in accordance with the laws of their being. . . .

"The weapons of this warfare are not merely the classical weapons of guns, tanks, bombs, and aircraft. The weapons are universal. Education is a weapon; language is a weapon; trade is a weapon; diplomacy is a weapon; religion is a weapon; cultural interchange is a weapon. The Communists view every act and judge every situation as part of the class war. When the Bolshoi Ballet performs in the United States, that is an action in the class war; when a group of American clergymen visits Russia, that is an action in the class war; when the Soviet participates in negotiations for "peace," they fight a battle in the class war. Their participation in the United Nations is part of this warfare. The basic Communist doctrine is: "We are at war!" This is the frame of reference within which every action and thought must be assessed and judged.

"It does not take two to make a fight. An idea in the mind of one is enough. . . .

"The Communists believe that they are at war with us. This conviction will never be changed in the slightest degree by any action in the Free World . . . We must either recognize this and defend against it, or ignore it and be destroyed. We have no other choice."[422]

Recapitulating and expounding on Schwarz's observations, we can say that communists succeed for several reasons:

1) Communists are highly organized. They have a strict hierarchy and incredibly severe discipline. Communists follow the identical plan passed down from Lucifer to Cain. It is an ancient plan with secret words, secret handshakes, and secret oaths to keep its members in line and promote unity of purpose in carrying out the cult's objectives. The objective – subjugating the world – takes precedence at all times and all methods of achieving it are valid. America is factionalized and divided along racial, gender, ethnic, economic, political, and religious lines. They are, in essence, one. Our resistance to communist attacks upon our way of life is pitifully ineffective because it is not equally unified. A small, organized, unified force will *always* conquer a larger, divided opponent.

2) Communism provides a "universal" life plan much the way Christianity or other major religions do. Everything from family relationships to marriage to education to economics to spirituality is encompassed and touched by communism. Christianity, in its apostate condition, no longer offers such a universal life plan, but has been reduced to a Sunday social club. This has caused many people to grope in the dark for some higher purpose – and often that purpose is found in the communist Brotherhood which offers immediate action and involvement.

3) Communists are devoted and committed. If communists can be admired for anything, it is their utter dedication to their principles and worldview. Communists will die for their cause if need be. They will break any law, tell any lie, and commit any atrocity to

---

[422] Fred Schwarz, *You Can Trust the Communists (to be Communists)* (Long Beach, California: Christian Anti-Communism Crusade, 1972), 1-6.

further their ends. Ordinary people lack this level of sincerity and devotion to whatever principles they espouse. Unfortunately, Satan is able to capitalize on this Jesuitical zealousness and has created profound chaos with a handful of dedicated revolutionaries.

4) Communists possess a much broader view of what constitutes "warfare." To a communist, anything and everything is a form of warfare and the struggle is perpetual. Music, entertainment, legal battles, environmentalism, New Age spirituality with its energy healing, yoga, and sham holistic techniques, the homosexual agenda, presidential elections, drugs, cyber hacking, diplomatic pressure, CNN/FOX/MSNBC broadcasts, public school indoctrination, socialist economics, terrorism – all of these are communist battle tactics. Like Gadianton Robbers, communists are not afraid to use organized crime to carry on clandestine warfare against its enemies. At all times, a communist considers himself at war. By contrast, the average American goes about his life oblivious to the fact that he is in a life-and-death struggle. Americans do not comprehend that when they watch a Hollywood movie containing anti-American, feminist, or pro-collectivism messages, they are really being assaulted by their enemy. And a nation that does not understand it is at war can never win that war no matter how superior it might be.

As should be gathered, Satan's scheme is comprehensive. It is a universal life plan. It is being carried out by a small yet highly zealous and organized cadre of Satanic gangsters. They believe in their ultimate victory because they know they are in a war and are pursuing active measures to ensure that their side wins. We have no option but to suffer defeat and destruction if we do not wake up, recognize the enemy, admit we are in a war (and that we are losing), and take every necessary step to regain and maintain our rights.

It must be remembered that Lucifer presented an alternative plan to Heavenly Father's children during the pre-earth life. In this amended version of the Father's Plan of Salvation, Satan proposed to strip man of his agency. The scriptural record does not indicate that he proposed to do this through force, but, rather, through permissiveness. In other words, Lucifer likely told us we could do whatever we wanted and that he would save us in our sins. He no doubt called this permissiveness "love" and "compassion," and dismissed the Father's Plan as devoid of love and compassion inasmuch as people could choose to kick themselves out of the Kingdom through an improper use of their agency.

In a highly interesting encounter, an LDS missionary named Marion Law met a high leader of the Communist Party in Australia while knocking doors in 1947. If true, this account sheds light on the ideology Satan teaches his followers. Elder Law explained that this man, whom he dubbed "the Melbourne man," dismissed the Gospel because it is not based on true love. He said that Elder Law did not love his own mother because:

> "Under your plan, she can either choose to go to hell, or make a mistake and fall through the cracks into hell. If you really loved your mother, you'd be eager to guarantee that she would go to heaven. With our plan, it is guaranteed. In fact, no one will he lost; they will all go to heaven. Of course, we don't believe in heaven or hell, anyway. But if you really love your fellow man, our plan is the only way to show it."

Even more curious are the methods which the Melbourne man proposed to implement in order to "save" every soul and show true "love." Several methods of bringing mankind into conformity included rock music (which had not yet been invented), "behavior modification conditioning" through public school indoctrination, placing additives and chemicals in food and water to desensitize people after prolonged use, drug addiction, propaganda in television and movies, etc. The Melbourne man called this plan "spiritual communism" and boasted that two-thirds of the world's governments were then firmly under communist control and that the United States was the "last hurdle" to world domination.

It is not coincidence that the Melbourne man's predictions have come true. Each of these things, from the introduction of raucous music to the tainting of food with chemicals to the social engineering via public education and media, has come to fruition in accordance with a plan concocted decades ago. Indeed, a plan invented by Lucifer before this world was. It has been carried out step-by-step by the illumined communists and their dupes throughout the world.

Elder Law further recounted:

> "He said they controlled all major conditioning instruments in America now: the entertainment industry, the news media, the education system, the courts, the financial system, political parties. Where they don't have full control, they have infiltrated and have embedded their agents into all important decision-making bodies. He said they control every agency that affects daily living in America. Their agents were everywhere, doing their jobs."

Not only were communist agents in politics, the news, business, and education, but they had infiltrated the churches. The Melbourne man told Elder Law:

> "We know all about your church. We control every church in the world, except yours, and we will infiltrate that."[423]

Satan and his followers are very aware of everything that goes on in the Lord's Church. Their agents have even infiltrated our Church and pose as faithful members. Remember, after Cain converted to Satan's side, he retained his position as high priest in the Church and continued to make sacrifices to the Lord on Lucifer's orders. Do you think that does not happen today? You had better believe it happens.

---

[423] Marion Albert Law, "Secrets of the Melbourne Man," 2010, https://www.latterdayconservative.com/articles/the-brother-law-fireside/.

There is clear evidence – which will be saved for a future study – that there are organized groups of Satanists, and those who perform Satanic Ritual Abuse (SRA), operating in our Church and posing as normal Latter-day Saints. I have personally talked with two LDS victims of SRA and I have read enough other material to know that it is a massive, albeit little publicized, problem.

And members of the Church who believe in the principles of socialism/communism (though they would never call them that) are a dime a dozen. One cannot attend BYU, for instance, without running into these deceived Church members on a daily basis. And it almost goes without saying that most BYU professors are socialists and honor the dictates of communist-inspired political correctness.

Though it may rankle some people, my opinion, based on my personal experience, is that the average Latter-day Saint is a communist in principle, or, at minimum, holds many socialistic principles without even realizing they are such. These otherwise decent, well-meaning people have never been properly educated. President Benson referred to such individuals in an April 1968 Conference address titled "Americans Are Destroying America." He said *they* are the ones who will ultimately be responsible for America's demise. He taught:

> "If American freedom is lost, if America is destroyed, if our blood-bought freedom is surrendered, it will be because of Americans. What's more, it will probably not be only the work of subversive and criminal Americans. The Benedict Arnolds will not be the only ones to forfeit our freedom. . . .

> "If America is destroyed, it may be by Americans who salute the flag, sing the national anthem, march in patriotic parades, cheer Fourth of July speakers—normally good Americans, but Americans who fail to comprehend what is required to keep our

country strong and free—Americans who have been lulled away into a false security."[424]

Everyday Americans are ultimately to blame for what happens in this once great country because they have the privilege of electing their own representatives, changing their laws, and directing their own affairs. Their forefathers gave them the right of self-rule and an unsurpassed heritage of republicanism in action. They can't blame others.

In a similar vein, Elder John A. Widtsoe once said:

> "The troubles of the world may largely be laid at the doors of those who are neither hot nor cold; who always follow the line of least resistance; whose timid hearts flutter at taking sides for truth. As in the great Council in the heaven, so in the Church of Christ on earth, there can be no neutrality."[425]

If Americans are too afraid to ride the wild wave of Liberty, they will never remain free, for, as the great Thomas Jefferson stated: "The boisterous sea of liberty is never without a wave."[426] And again the Sage of Monticello affirmed the truth that "timid men . . . prefer the calm of despotism to the boisterous sea of liberty."[427]

Only the timid would pass up the opportunity to declare their allegiance to the Lord and step forward to boldly defend their faith, families, and Freedom like the sons of Helaman (Alma 53:16-19). President Benson taught that we have a chance for "eternal glory" if we stand up to Satan now and fight in the Lord's Royal Army:

---

[424] President Ezra Taft Benson, "Americans Are Destroying America," Conference Report, April, 1968, 49-54, http://scriptures.byu.edu/#:t649:p401.

[425] Elder John A. Widtsoe, in Benson, Newquist, ed., *An Enemy Hath Done This*, 276.

[426] Thomas Jefferson to Richard Rush, October 20, 1820.

[427] Thomas Jefferson to Philip Mazzei, April 24, 1796.

"Many of us are here today because our forefathers loved truth enough that they fought at Valley Forge or crossed the plains in spite of the price it cost them or their families. We had better take our small pain now than our greater loss later. There were souls who wished afterwards that they had stood and fought with Washington and the founding fathers, but they waited too long—they passed up eternal glory. There has never been a greater time than now to stand up against entrenched evil."[428]

It is a striking indictment that many of us have *not* stepped forward to defend our Liberty, but have remained on the sidelines. In truth, however, *there is no neutrality in this war for Freedom*. If we are not actively engaged in preserving Liberty, we are, by default, acquiescing to its destruction. Silence is complicity. Inaction is criminal. And this is exactly what the Adversary is counting on. In order to win, he must convince the majority to remain "neutral" while his small clique of initiated disciples take over society and install his throne over the earth.

The Red Gadiantons in Moscow and Beijing could *never* hope to subjugate the United States were it not for the inward rot caused by everyday Americans who don't have a clue what their rights are, who don't understand their history, who have never studied the U.S. Constitution, who can't identify communism as their mortal enemy, or who simply do not care enough to sacrifice and take the time to do what is right and what is necessary.

The American People, once fiercely independent, manly, and strong, now act like sheep. They are led by the Republican and Democrat pied pipers who themselves are being led by the nose by communist Gadianton Robbers. After observing the peoples of Europe, Thomas Jefferson noted that they were divided into two classes – wolves and sheep. He warned how this could happen in the United States and how it could be avoided:

---

[428] President Ezra Taft Benson, "Not Commanded in All Things," Conference Report, April, 1965, 121-125, http://scriptures.byu.edu/#:t585:p401.

"Cherish therefore the spirit of our people, and keep alive their attention. Do not be too severe upon their errors, but reclaim them by enlightening them. If once they become inattentive to the public affairs, you and I, and Congress, and Assemblies, judges and governors shall all become wolves."[429]

By proper education, keeping alive the unique American spirit of Liberty and the tradition self-rule, and by keeping the public involved, the United States could avoid the pitfalls of decadent and oppressed Europe. If the American People did not remain attentive enough — if they were neither hot nor cold or simply ceased caring — their leaders would become ravenous wolves, warned Jefferson. Once in this situation, the sheep would be easy prey for the wolves.

Quoting again from the 1968 Conference address just noted, President Benson asserted:

"Great nations are never conquered from outside unless they are rotten inside. Our greatest national problem today is erosion, not the erosion of the soil, but erosion of the national morality—erosion of traditional enforcement of law and order. . . .

"In this blessed land we have exalted security, comfort, and ease above freedom. . . .

"The facts are clear. Our problem centers in Washington, D.C. And this applies to the administration of both political parties. . . .

"If America is to withstand these influences and trends, there must be a renewal of the spirit of our forefathers, an appreciation of the American way of life, a strengthening of muscle and sinew

---

[429] Thomas Jefferson to Edward Carrington, January 16, 1787.

and the character of the nation. America needs guts as well as guns. National character is the core of national defense."[430]

The reason Americans have gone so wildly off course is because of the small cadre of communist elitists we have been discussing. They have captured the levers of power over the intellectual and spiritual life of our nation. Through deceit, indoctrination, and systematized conditioning the conspiracy has caused Americans to forget their own heritage of Freedom, or, worse, to see it as bigoted, racist, intolerant, misogynistic, or oppressive. A People that does not understand its history is easily led astray. And a People – as well as an individual – that does not understand Liberty cannot claim to truly love it; nor can it claim to defend Freedom.

Founding Father James Wilson observed that "law and liberty cannot rationally become the objects of our love, unless they first become the objects of our knowledge."[431] That is true. If we are not aware of our rights, we *cannot* defend them. If we don't understand the Constitution, we can't possibly know when it is being violated. If we don't know the Constitution, we can't possibly elect true constitutionalists to office. If we do not know the principles of communism, we cannot truthfully claim we aren't supporting them.

This "awful situation" of profound ignorance has been brought about because the American People have blindly heeded and followed America's "leaders." I do not necessarily refer to elected representatives in Washington, D.C. Rather, more important to the conspiracy are local agents of influence, from media personalities to "educators" to pastors. Public school teachers are especially valuable to the Adversary. The public school system has been used as a tool of Lucifer to destroy the minds and souls of Americans from sea to shining sea. I recommend every Latter-day

---

[430] President Ezra Taft Benson, "Americans Are Destroying America," Conference Report, April, 1968, 49-54, http://scriptures.byu.edu/#:t649:p401.

[431] James Wilson, *Lectures on Law*, 1790, chapter 1, accessed May 28, 2018, http://www.nlnrac.org/node/241.

Saint read Elder Hans Verlan Andersen's book *The Great and Abominable Church of the Devil* to learn more about the evils of socialized education and why our prophets have traditionally opposed it.

As noted, these deceivers not only exist in the community, but they exist within our own Church as well. In fact, I encounter them and their pupils on an almost daily basis as I go about my business of spreading unpopular truth. It pains me to say, but it seems clear that a great many of the members of this Church are being carefully led astray by wolves in sheep's clothing. They may be perfectly well-meaning, but they are nonetheless supporting the Adversary's system.

Many years ago, President J. Reuben Clark, Jr. warned the Church of wolves in sheep's clothing. These ravening wolves, said he, were in our midst. We are largely blind to their existence, however, because they pose as faithful Priesthood holders. He admonished:

> "Now, our enemies are seeking to attack and are attacking our Church. . . .
>
> "The ravening wolves are amongst us, from our own membership, and they, more than any others, are clothed in sheep's clothing, because they wear the habiliments of the priesthood; they are they to whom Brother Widtsoe referred, as distorting the truth. We should be careful of them."[432]

These shady figures lurk in our wards and stakes, in our quorums and councils. They gossip, spread discord, encourage pettiness, and subtly teach false doctrine. These false teachers water down our doctrine to infantile levels and have almost entirely stripped the meat from the Gospel bones. These wolves are not only male Priesthood holders, but seemingly honorable women, too. They go around secretly, like Alma and the Sons of Mosiah before their conversion, "seeking to destroy the

---

[432] President J. Reuben Clark, Jr., "Beware of False Prophets," Conference Report, April, 1949, 161-165, http://scriptures.byu.edu/#:t191:p527.

church, and to lead astray the people of the Lord" (Mosiah 27:10). They are those whom Moroni chastised for polluting the holy Church of God (Moroni 8:38-40).

Yes, the agents of Satan's secret combinations are *everywhere*. In a 1946 speech, President J. Reuben Clark, Jr. further warned:

> "There are amongst us agents of an alien communistic ideology, and probably these agents are also, in considerable proportion, the paid agents of a foreign government. The purpose of these is to foment dissatisfaction, then disputes, then strikes and violence, then bloodshed, to the end of creating a condition of chaotic disorder, and then taking over our government and making us a member of a Sovietized world. It is the duty of every free citizen to do his utmost to see that this perversion of our free institutions, and this destruction of our national welfare, with its blessings to our citizenry – blessings unequalled anywhere else in the world, and, among western powers, unequaled least of all in sovietized Russia – shall not come to pass."[433]

If the communist secret combination is successful in its attempt to bring the United States into its world order, our Freedom will be crushed. Once our Liberty is demolished, our right to worship the Lord as we please will be snuffed out. Satan cannot allow those under his control to worship the true Christ since *he* holds himself up as the "savior" of mankind.

In an "Encyclical on Atheistic Communism" produced in 1937, Pope Pius XI spoke of the counterfeit anti-Christ nature of communism. He wrote:

> "The Communism of today, more emphatically than similar movements in the past, conceals in itself a false messianic idea. A pseudo-ideal of justice, of equality and fraternity in labor

---

[433] President J. Reuben Clark, Jr., speech, December 6, 1946, in J. Reuben Clark, Jr., *Stand Fast by Our Constitution* (Salt Lake City, Utah: Deseret Book Company, 1973), 54-55.

impregnates all its doctrine and activity with a deceptive mysticism, which communicates a zealous and contagious enthusiasm to the multitudes entrapped by delusive promises. . . .

"There is another explanation for the rapid diffusion of the Communistic ideas now seeping into every nation, great and small, advanced and backward, so that no corner of the earth is free from them. This explanation is to be found in a propaganda so truly diabolical that the world has perhaps never witnessed its like before. It is directed from one common center. It is shrewdly adapted to the varying conditions of diverse peoples. It has at its disposal great financial resources, gigantic organizations, international congresses, and countless trained workers. It makes use of pamphlets and reviews, of cinema, theater and radio, of schools and even universities. Little by little it penetrates into all classes of the people and even reaches the better-minded groups of the community, with the result that few are aware of the poison which increasingly pervades their minds and hearts."[434]

With missionary zeal, these Red Gadiantons have spread their "messianic" message around the globe until it has penetrated every corner. Communism – the "greatest satanical threat" to mankind – is a false religion inducting its adherents into a fraternity of wickedness. Its sacraments are heretical and its ordinances are wicked. Its high priests and false prophets are devoted to enthroning their lord as supreme master over the earth, and his priestcraft as the only creed. Blasphemy drips from every communist utterance as from the lips of Baal himself. Every means are used to corrupt the minds and hearts of human beings until they either join, willingly or unwillingly, the communist cause or are brought into Bolshevik bondage.

---

[434] Pope Pius XI, Divini Redemptoris, "Encyclical on Atheistic Communism," March 19, 1937, accessed March 19, 2018,

https://w2.vatican.va/content/pius-xi/en/encyclicals/documents/hf_p-xi_enc_19370319_divini-redemptoris.html.

J. Edgar Hoover described the ultimate consequence of tolerating the spread of this communist religion. Said he:

> "Communism is more than an economic, political, social, or philosophical doctrine. It is a way of life; a false, materialistic "religion." It would strip man of his belief in God, his heritage of freedom, his trust in love, justice, and mercy. Under communism, all would become, as so many already have, twentieth-century slaves."[435]

Those who come into the communist orbit become slaves. They become slaves both temporally *and* spiritually. Those who worship at the altar of the Dragon – the same who gives power to the scarlet Beast – mark themselves as enemies of Christ. Those who look to communism for salvation from the woes of earth life embrace Satan, the father of this cosmic conspiracy against God.

The famous author Simon Sebag Montefiore, who has written some of the most well-documented books on mass murderer Joseph Stalin, observed:

> "Bolshevism may not have been a religion, but it was close enough. Stalin told Beria the Bolsheviks were a "sort of military-religious order." . . . Stalin's "order of the sword-bearers" resembled the Knights Templars, or even the theocracy of the Iranian Ayatollahs, more than any traditional secular movement."[436]

Isn't it fascinating that some of the most well-versed students of communism – Montefiore, Hoover, Wurmbrand, the Soviet defectors, etc. – agree with what our prophets have revealed about the counterfeit religious nature of communism? They have discovered through secular research and first-hand experience what *The Book of Mormon* revealed

---

[435] Hoover, *Masters of Deceit*, Foreword, VI.

[436] Simon Sebag Montefiore, *Stalin: The Court of the Red Tsar* (New York: Alfred A. Knopf, 2004), 85.

prophetically to the world many generations previous; namely, that the latter-day conspiracy to overthrow the Freedom of all lands would be a secret society founded and directed by Lucifer. And so it is that communism began as a secret conspiracy, or, more accurately, an amalgam of several secret societies with the same object of overthrowing Christ and enthroning Lucifer.

It is paramount to understand – and I have attempted to emphasize this point repeatedly throughout this book – that the leading communists were not and are not atheists; they are Satanists. They are initiates in the Adversary's latter-day secret combination. They are Illuminists who belong to a secret worldwide Brotherhood that employs the oaths, handshakes, signs, and tokens of old. They are members of a fanatical Satanic cult. They are the high priests of this organized paganism.

The world conspiracy is a Luciferian conspiracy. This occult Luciferian conspiracy is *the* conspiracy, the mysterious woman riding the scarlet Beast (Revelation 17:3-6). And communism – likely the scarlet Beast foreseen by John – is the symbolic woman's chief weapon.

In his phenomenal book *Marx and Satan*, a book I wish everyone would own, the Reverend Richard Wurmbrand lays out the evidence suggesting that Marx and his fellow communist kingpins were avowed Satanists. In one particularly illuminating line quoted earlier, but repeated here for added emphasis, Wurmbrand stated:

> "It is essential at this point to state emphatically that Marx and his comrades, while anti-God, were not atheists, as present-day Marxists claim to be. That is, while they openly denounced and reviled God, they hated a God in whom they believed. They challenged not His existence, but His supremacy."[437]

In like fashion, Cain and his companions, the Gadianton Robbers, the members of Akish's household, the idolatrous priests of ancient Egypt,

---

[437] Wurmbrand, *Marx and Satan*, 29.

Adam Weishaupt and his Illuminists, Marx and his Communist League, Lenin and his Bolsheviks, and all other secret conspirators of past generations, swore blasphemous oaths to one another and to Lucifer "by their everlasting maker" (Helaman 1:11) and "by the God of heaven" (Ether 8:14). They believed in God, but they rejected His rule. They loved Satan more than their Eternal Father (Moses 5:18, 28) and hated their own blood (Moses 7:33). Instead of serving the Lord Jesus Christ and building up His Kingdom, they attempted to tear it down and establish Lucifer's throne atop the heap of rubble.

A former Soviet military specialist named Igor Shafhid, who dealt with biological/chemical and nuclear weapons, wrote of communism's relentless attack on the spirit, dignity, and faith of man. He explained how Satan is using the communists to establish an earthly kingdom with himself as king:

> "Anti-Christian regimes know that faith can protect a free will and a sound mind. That is why Lenin feared religious belief. Religion was not an opposition to his communist ideology; locking up a church door was effective enough, but faith rooted in the heart spread like wildfire, and that worried him. How could he get a society to worship him if they loved God more? This is why he called them "believers" and strove hard to stop those who preached the true Gospel of Jesus Christ. Religion is never a threat, but relationship is. Lenin knew that people's minds founded in faith and dedicated to Christ Jesus would be hard to conquer.   .   .   .

> "Mind control is a great terror weapon bludgeoning today's churches . . . Phony religious leaders use similar tactics to control assemblages within churches, as did . . . Stalin.

> "The worst mistake a Christian can make is in believing that all churches are safe zones. Not so. In Soviet Russia the government used churches to validate their constitution's "freedom of

religion," using pastors hired by the KGB as a guise to fool the people. True believers were beaten and imprisoned, and few citizens were made aware of this.

"The numerous false doctrines spreading across the world, and the extra-biblical, esoteric experiences that are introduced with these "new" revelations are a great preparatory tool for mass mind manipulation. This kind of seduction works well because feelings are involved. Forming an anti-christ government cannot be accomplished without mind control, and the church is the first to be targeted. . . .

". . . When the nations fight against the antichrist army, they won't be reverting to outdated sabers and cannons. Nuclear, biological, and chemical warfare are the advanced weapons of this age, and it would not seem plausible that these weapons would be ignored during the great tribulation time. . . .

"We should never become complacent. There are enough WMDs developed now to destroy this world, but Satan has not yet succeeded in his mission. There is unfinished business between him and God, and he plans on taking as many onto his side as he can.

"How can he effectively get humankind to bow before him? Force and bullying hasn't worked too well in the past, but he knows his most ingenious plan will work, and he has been perfecting it and bringing it to completion for hundreds of years. Deceptive love, false promises of peace, and mind control are his greatest tools in this plan. How does he accomplish this deception? By fooling people, of course, into thinking they can live in a good and peaceful world without wars or famine or terrorism. His devoted followers have pushed his deceptive agenda by participating in elite societies, clubs and orders — all of these different groups united secretly to bring about this socialistic new world order. . . .

"When Satan's real mask is removed at the end of time, then he will be exposed for what he is, the father of lies. Many nations will become confused and start fighting against him during the Battle of Armageddon. Satan's evil that prompted humankind to develop the WMD will come in handy for him to destroy God's creation. He knows that an ungodly nation that harbors nuclear/biological/chemical weapons, such as Russia, China, and North Korea, are excellent candidates for using this weaponry as a "power" to horsewhip other nations under their submission. I remember all too well in the Soviet army how I reveled in the fact that my country had so much power over all the other nations. Let us not be naïve; those thoughts are still alive in the Russian Federation. That is why the Russian military recently started refreshing its new generation of ICBMs (Intercontinental Ballistic Missiles), which have been lying in stockpiles for years, and have been placing them inside strategic controlled areas. Those that fight to do away with weapons of mass destruction will not succeed, because no one nation will give up its place for power – and the Day of Wrath will come, and nuclear war will be inevitable."[438]

If a Russian defector can correctly identify communism as an anti-Christ system and a Satanic counterfeit that seeks to destroy the world and consolidate humanity in a "socialistic new world order," Latter-day Saints who have the luxury of living prophets and the gift of the Holy Ghost ought to be able to as well.

Latter-day Saints also should not be "naïve," but should recognize the very grave threat posed by Russia, China, and their allies. We should not be lured astray by the incessant cry of "fake news" used to discount as rumors, or "liberal" lies, true reports about Russia's brutality and

---

[438] Igor V. Shafhid, *Inside the Red Zone: Physical and Spiritual Preparedness Against Weapons of Mass Destruction* (Las Vegas, NV: Global Strategic Resources, 2004), 83-85, 160-163.

intrigues. We should understand, as President Joseph Fielding Smith taught, that Satan is *personally* "governing the nations" of the world. We should realize as President McKay warned, that "a third World War is inevitable unless communism is soon subdued."

I close this chapter with one additional quote by a modern seer who saw the mortal threats facing mankind and warned about them to his last breath. In 1963, President Ezra Taft Benson stated:

> "Now we should all be opposed to Socialistic-Communism, for it is our mortal and spiritual enemy – the greatest evil in the world today. But the reason many liberals don't want the American people to form study groups to really understand and then fight Socialistic-Communism is that once the American people get the facts they will begin to realize that much of what these liberals advocate is actually helping the enemy.
>
> "The liberals hope you'll believe them when they tell you how anti-Communist they are. But they become alarmed if you really inform yourself on the subject of Socialistic-Communism. For after you inform yourself you might begin to study the liberal voting record. And this study would show you how much the liberals are giving aid and comfort to the enemy and how much the liberals are actually leading America towards Socialism itself.
>
> "Communism is just another form of socialism, as is fascism.
>
> "So now you can see the picture. These liberals want you to know how much they are doing for you – with your tax money of course. But they don't want you to realize that the path they are pursuing is socialistic, and that socialism is the same as communism in its ultimate effect on our liberties. When you point this out they want to shut you up – they accuse you of maligning them, of casting aspersions, of being political. No matter whether they label their bottle as liberalism, progressivism, or social

> reform – I know the contents of the bottle is poison to this Republic and I'm going to call it poison.

> "We do not need to question the motive of these liberals. They could be most sincere. But sincerity or supposed benevolence or even cleverness is not the question. The question is: "Are we going to save this country from the hands of the enemy and the deceived?""[439]

Are we prepared to step forward and save our country from the machinations of the enemy and the suicidal actions of our deceived countrymen? Are we careful not to imbibe one drop of communist philosophy, understanding that it is a deadly poison, a Satanic sarin to the soul? Do we truly recognize the mortal danger not only to our Liberty, but to our spirits, that communism and its cousin philosophies socialism, fascism[440], and liberalism pose?

And I would also underscore the fact that it is not only "liberals" who are aiding the communist enemy, but a good many so-called "conservatives." Indeed, careful research shows that the entire neo-conservative movement is infested by dedicated communists and their dupes – a fact which ought to be obvious when we examine its warmongering, anti-Constitution track record. Yes, Republicans are just as responsible for

---

[439] Ezra Taft Benson, "An Internal Threat Today," December 19, 1963, in Newquist, ed., *Prophets, Principles and National Survival*, 287-288.

[440] Fascism is not nearly as evil, tyrannical, or corrupt as communism, despite all the popular hype to the contrary. On the surface, there is a resemblance between socialism and fascism. However, when we dig deeper, we find many key, even fundamental, differences. Fascism is certainly *not* "Marxian socialism." For instance, fascism actually protects, to a great extent, the all-important right of private property, whereas communism/socialism abolishes the right completely, making men slaves. Human rights, wealth, health, education levels, gun ownership, private property rights, and general happiness actually *increased* dramatically in 1930s Germany under Hitler as opposed to the deplorable despotism, depression, and misery Germans suffered while the Marxian socialist Weimar Republic ruled Germany. However, at the end of the day, the Lord has said that any political system that is "more or less" than the U.S. Constitution is uninspired and "cometh of evil" (D&C 98:5-7).

aiding and abetting the communist conspiracy as the Democrats are. Be exceedingly careful who you choose to support. Examine their principles, *not* merely the R or D next to their name.

The world is in the grip of a malignant anti-Christ conspiracy known as communism. Communism deceives many by slapping misleading labels on its principles and operating through fronts such as the Women's Liberation or LGBT movements. But *always* the cabal drives humanity into the outstretched arms of Satan. *Always* it steals human dignity and makes men miserable. *Always* it leaves people broken and enslaved. Communism is global tyranny on an unprecedented scale both in terms of pervasiveness and wickedness. It is Satan's favorite tool to blind minds, corrupt hearts, and erode people's faith in their true Redeemer, the Lord Jesus Christ.

We have a very distinct choice. The lines of demarcation are clearly drawn between Christ's Kingdom, Freedom, and the U.S. Constitution on one hand and Lucifer's fiefdom, slavery, and Satanic communism on the other. The prophets, ancient and modern, have stood united in their opposition to Satan's conspiracies. They beckon all to join them on the Lord's side of the line.

"Who's on the Lord's side? Who?

"Now is the time to show.

"We ask it fearlessly:

"Who's on the Lord's side? Who?"

Chapter 10

Final Words of Warning

It is my prayer that this book has touched your heart in some way. I pray that you now have a deeper understanding of the communist secret combination that threatens your faith, your family, and your Freedom. I hope that you recognize the Satanic character of communism and feel the same urgency I feel to warn people about this looming threat to all that is good and to all we hold dear.

This book is not intended to frighten you or give you a sense of hopelessness. It is not meant to overwhelm or depress you. It is meant, rather, to inform and alert you to the very real danger so that you might be inspired to act swiftly to save your families from the Adversary.

To be frank, I have no hope for the United States in the short term. We have become so infected by the Red Plague of communism that our odds of recovery are slim to none. Our illness is exacerbated by the fact that we do not even realize we're sick. Having the odds stacked against us does not mean we shouldn't persevere and try our hardest to reverse the tide, but I believe it will not happen and that things will continue to deteriorate until the Lord returns to set in order His House. As we are told, in our day "all things shall be in commotion; and surely, men's hearts shall fail them; for fear shall come upon all people" (D&C 88:91).

However, notwithstanding my "pessimism" for the short term, and the threat of calamities and judgments being poured out upon us "without measure" (D&C 1:9), I have a burning and vibrant testimony that *the Lord Jesus Christ has already won the victory*! He won it two millennia ago when He suffered in Gethsemane, died on the Cross, and rose in glory from the tomb on Resurrection morning. Jesus Christ has subdued all things and is the King of kings and Lord of lords. The final outcome is *not* in doubt. We can rejoice because *we are on the winning side*.

On that first Easter morning, the clock began ticking and Satan's days were officially numbered. In the time he has remaining before his kingdom is hurled down and obliterated, the Father of Lies is prophesied to make a mighty mess of this world one last time, dragging millions of souls into the abyss with him and reigning with blood, fire, and cruelty over a global empire created in his image. Lucifer's Red Gadiantonism is a universal cancer afflicting all peoples under the sun.

President Ezra Taft Benson proclaimed:

> "We live today in a wicked world. Never in our memory have the forces of evil been arrayed in such a deadly formation. The devil is well organized and has many emissaries working for him. His satanic majesty has proclaimed his intention to destroy our young people, to weaken the home and family, and to defeat the purposes of the Lord Jesus Christ through his great church.
>
> "As Latter-day Saints, we know the adversary will not succeed. The Church stands stronger today than ever before in its history . . . Today we have the fullest and richest program for the blessing of our Father's children to be found anywhere upon the face of the earth. I know this is true.
>
> "But we live in a day of wickedness. It seems that almost everything that is good, pure, uplifting, and strengthening is being challenged as never before – yes, almost discarded by many. . . .
>
> "As Christian people, as members of the true church of Jesus Christ, we face difficult days. But they are also days filled with challenge, hope, and assurance. We have clearly before us the answers to the problems facing mankind. We know what the Lord expects of us. He said that we should all "arise and shine forth" and "be a standard for the nations." (D&C 115:5.) We know the

course we should follow. Do we have the faith and courage to follow that course? I hope and pray we do."[441]

Truly, as Latter-day Saints we have been blessed above all the peoples of the earth. We know the truth. We know the will of the Lord for these last days. We have scriptures promulgating the teachings of our all-powerful Master. We are led by living prophets who declare the current will of the Lord. But do we have the courage and faith to do what we know is expected of us; to do what the prophets have counseled?

It has been the burden of Christ's disciples in all ages to preach the truth no matter the consequence. Frequently, they have been forced to preach against secret combinations, secret murders, and secret abominations. Their testimony has often sparked outrage, reviling, and persecution. Yet, they faithfully spoke what the Spirit put into their hearts.

We will certainly face persecution when we tell the truth, but it is a duty nonetheless. The very Son of God was taken by His own people and crucified for telling the truth, condemning their wickedness, and spreading the good news of His Gospel. Should we, then, expect to be treated kindly for our testimony of the Savior and His truth?

In challenging times, people feel overwhelmed and want a "plan of action." They ask: "What can we do?" They want to be told what to do to stop corruption and restore sanity to the world. While there are a number of practical steps that could be mentioned, they all pale in comparison to the importance of the first step – education. I do not refer to public schooling or formal education – these are little more than enemy indoctrination. Rather, I refer to true education and the learning of correct principles and truths, such as those taught in the scriptures, by the prophets, and by our inspired Founding Fathers. President Benson stated:

---

[441] Ezra Taft Benson, *God, Family, Country: Our Three Great Loyalties* (Salt Lake City, Utah: Deseret Book Company, 1975), 90-91.

"Once you get the facts about our American Constitutional Republic and the threats to it – then you are going to want to do something. Certainly those who are organized and have a plan and are dedicated, though they be few, will always defeat the many who are not organized and have no plan or dedication. . . .

"Yes, the Fabian Socialists are as busy as bees rolling out the red carpet which leads inevitably to Communism. Faced with this situation our first duty is that of education. Starting with ourselves we must become familiar with the broad outlines of our movement toward destruction. We must, as President McKay has urged, become alerted and informed. After becoming informed ourselves, we must carry the word to all within hearing or seeing range, so that they, too, can become awakened. Take every opportunity to pass sound literature and books around so that your neighbors and their neighbors will awaken before it is too late. We are literally in a race against time and we must take every opportunity to spread the word."[442]

Beginning with ourselves, *we must become informed*. This *is* our plan of action. We must obey the Lord's command to "awake to a sense of your awful situation" (Ether 8:24). Once awake and informed, we must climb to the top of our personal watchtower and sound the alarm – and keep sounding it until the Lord says His work is finished. We must pass around "sound literature and books" to our neighbors and friends. I pray that you will share this book with those you love so that they, too, may know the truth about the threats to their family.

An analogy might be useful to illustrate why it is so important to spread the word once informed. If you woke up in the middle of the night and saw that your neighbor's house was on fire, what would you do? You surely would not shrug your shoulders and go back to sleep. Rather, you

---

[442] President Ezra Taft Benson, "A Race Against Time," BYU address, December 10, 1963, https://www.latterdayconservative.com/ezra-taft-benson/a-race-against-time/.

would rush outside and pound on your neighbor's door to wake him up. He might not like being woken up, but the moment he realized his house was on fire, he would be grateful and, more importantly, he would act quickly to save his family from the flames.

In similar fashion, our warnings about spiritual and political dangers might be instrumental in helping to save our neighbors. Our sleepy neighbors might be angry at being awakened at first, but once they are intellectually awake, they will thank you. Our efforts might not save our country, but they just might save our own souls and those of our families and friends. Sometimes all it takes is for one person to open his mouth and share a simple testimony of truth.

On another occasion, President Benson simplified his message and said:

> "The only thing which can possibly stop the Communists is for the American people to learn the truth in time – to become alerted and informed."[443]

Anti-communist author Fred Schwarz agreed and affirmed:

> "A knowledge of the true program of Communism and its strategy and tactics is the only protection good people of every sort have against the Communist snare."[444]

And, finally, J. Edgar Hoover taught and urged:

> "Communism can exist only where it is protected and hidden. The spotlight of public exposure is the most effective means we have to use in destroying the communist conspiracy. Drag that

---

[443] Ezra Taft Benson, "We Must Become Alerted and Informed," December 13, 1963, in Newquist, ed., *Prophets, Principles and National Survival*, 274.

[444] Schwarz, *You Can Trust the Communists (to be Communists)*, 56.

conspiracy into the light! Tear it apart. Reveal the flaws in its philosophy. Keep the pressure on it. Force it into retreat."[445]

When a person knows that communism is *the* greatest threat to the world, he is enabled to focus his full attention on the enemy, and his resistance will be an hundred times stronger and more effective. When he truly knows this, he will drag the conspiracy into the light and tear it apart. He will not stop or rest until he forces communism into retreat. So, I repeat: "Drag that conspiracy into the light! Tear it apart."

Education is the key. It always has been and always will be. Think of the automatic and natural results of being properly informed. When a person understands the real threat, he will never again vote for a candidate who espouses communistic views – no matter how bad the opposing candidate seems. When a person comprehends the prophetic warnings, he will no longer call people "conspiracy theorists" or dismiss their counsel without proper investigation. When a man understands that a Satanic conspiracy exists in our midst and that its camouflaged agents are everywhere, he will not naively trust his rights, or abdicate his duties of self-rule and self-defense, to the "experts" or to his "representatives." The inherent benefits of waking up and becoming informed are too many to list, and too precious to disregard.

Truth is of God. Everything naturally falls into place when you educate and enlighten your mind to the truth. *Truth is the foundation stone of every good and positive change that occurs in life.* Attaining truth is a prerequisite to becoming free. After all, our Master taught, "the truth shall make you free" (John 8:32).

While there is not much good news regarding communism, being armed with the truth about this conspiracy is inherently empowering. *Knowledge is power!* All light is uplifting, even when it must cover such seedy topics as secret combinations. We must not become discouraged as we see the

---

[445] J. Edgar Hoover, *The Lion*, October, 1957, in Newquist, ed., *Prophets, Principles and National Survival*, 251.

world go from bad to worse to awful. Instead, we must thank the Lord for revealing the truth to us in time, shoulder our burden faithfully, and stand on the Lord's side against Satan and his armies of darkness.

After referring to numerous prophecies foretelling destruction in our day unless the people of the world repent, President Marion G. Romney made this relevant comment:

> "Now I am not calling attention to these things to frighten, stampede, or discourage anyone. I refer to them because I know they are true, and I am persuaded that if we are to "conquer Satan, and . . . escape the hands of the servants of Satan that do uphold his work" (D&C 10:5), we must understand and recognize the situation as it is. This is no time for Latter-day Saints to equivocate.

> "Nor is it a time for us to panic. The difficulties of our times have not come upon us unawares. A hundred and forty years ago the Lord clearly revealed the tenor of our times. We know that as the second coming of the Savior approaches, the tempo of Satan's campaign for the souls of men is being and will continue to be accelerated. We know that the experiences of the intervening years will try men's souls.

> "We also know that God lives; that his "eternal purposes . . . shall roll on" (Morm. 8:22). We know that to qualify us to prevail against Satan and his wicked hosts, we have been given the gospel of Jesus Christ. We know that the Spirit of Christ and the power of his priesthood are ample shields to the power of Satan. We know that there is available to each of us the gift of the Holy Ghost—the power of revelation which embraces the gift of discernment by which we may unerringly detect the devil and the counterfeits he is so successfully foisting upon this gullible generation. Our course is clear and certain. It is to strictly obey

the commandments of the Lord, as they are recorded in the scriptures and as they are being given by the living prophets."[446]

Yes, our only sure course lies in strict obedience to the Gospel, including obedience to the counsel and direction given to us by our prophets. On few subjects have our prophets been as emphatic as they have on the subject of communism and secret combinations. If we have testimonies of the truthfulness of this work and know that the Lord calls and inspires His prophets, then we will have no misgivings about heeding the prophetic warnings regarding the Satanic communist conspiracy and our obligation to resist its machinations and to be politically active in the cause of Freedom.

In his emphatic way, President Benson warned the world of the high stakes war we are engaged in. He declared:

> "Let's get one thing straight at the very beginning. International communism is the self-avowed enemy of every loyal American. It has declared war against us and fully intends to win. The war in which we are engaged is total. Although its main battlefields are psychological, political and economic, it also encompasses revolution, violence, terror and limited military skirmishes. If we should lose this war, the conquering enemy's wrath against our people and our institutions will result in one of the greatest blood-baths of all history. Call it a "cold war" if it makes you feel better, but our freedom and our very lives are the stakes of this contest.
>
> "We didn't start this war, and we don't want to be in it. But, we have no choice. True, we can pretend that it doesn't exist. We can hope that, somehow, if we just don't fight back, if we keep smiling at the enemy and show him that we intend no harm, then maybe he will call off his war, and we can all live in peace. But the

---

[446] President Marion G. Romney, "Satan – the Great Deceiver," General Conference, April, 1971, http://scriptures.byu.edu/#:t7d8:p4cb.

communists merely laugh at our naivete, take advantage of concessions, consolidate their gains and press toward ultimate victory."[447]

We are at war whether we want to be or not. Wishing the enemy didn't want to kill you does not protect you and your family. Hoping for sunny skies and peace on earth won't put an end to Satan's secret combinations. In fact, Nephi denounced those who say "all is well" and ignore Satan's efforts to drag them "carefully down to hell" (2 Nephi 28:18-28). If we lose this war, our nation will be baptized in blood. "If we lose freedom here, there is no place to escape to. This is the last stand on earth."[448] And have no doubt, we *will* lose this war in the short term unless we wake up immediately and take action.

Some might ask, "If all of this is really so important, why don't the prophets talk about it today?" My only response is: Good question. I honestly do not know. I have two primary theories.

First, it is quite possible that the day of warning is past and that the Lord is now trying the faith of the Saints to see if they will heed the warnings they had been given year in and year out for many decades. Not always, but often the scriptures record that the Lord silences His prophets' mouths for a season before sending them to warn the people one final time. I do not know if we will get another round of warnings or if the final full-force warnings ended approximately with President Benson. However, even if the prophets never again sound the warning voice against conspiracy and communism, we can't say we have not been warned. *We have been warned over and over and over again.*

Alternatively, the Lord may have silenced our seers because we have been so negligent in following their counsel. Truthfully, the Saints' record of

---

[447] Benson, Newquist, ed., *An Enemy Hath Done This*, 165-166.

[448] Ronald Reagan, "A Time for Choosing," October 27, 1964, http://www.presidency.ucsb.edu/ws/index.php?pid=76121.

obedience to prophetic counsel is utterly abysmal – particularly when "politics" are involved. Anciently, Alma gave us an important insight. He taught:

> "It is given unto many to know the mysteries of God; nevertheless they are laid under a strict command that they shall not impart only according to the portion of his word which he doth grant unto the children of men, according to the heed and diligence which they give unto him.

> "And therefore, he that will harden his heart, the same receiveth the lesser portion of the word; and he that will not harden his heart, to him is given the greater portion of the word, until it is given unto him to know the mysteries of God until he know them in full.

> "And they that will harden their hearts, to them is given the lesser portion of the word until they know nothing concerning his mysteries; and then they are taken captive by the devil, and led by his will down to destruction. Now this is what is meant by the chains of hell" (Alma 12:9-11).

To reiterate, the Lord gives His children knowledge "according to the heed and diligence which they give unto [it]." Those who are negligent or hardhearted receive "the lesser portion of the word." These people are described as being wrapped in the chains of hell and being taken captive by Satan. When Satan successfully tempts us and causes us to disobey, a natural consequence is that we lose light and knowledge (D&C 93:39).

Furthermore, Nephi warned us that we would be cut off from revelation unless we paid diligent heed to our prophets' words. He wrote:

> "For behold, the Lord hath poured out upon you the spirit of deep sleep. For behold, ye have closed your eyes, and ye have rejected the prophets; and your rulers, and the seers hath he covered because of your iniquity" (2 Nephi 27:5).

Is it possible that the Lord is displeased that we have, collectively, failed to listen to our prophets' counsel to contend against the Devil's church (D&C 18:20), and, thus, has closed His servants' mouths so that they do not warn us as they used to? Unfortunately, this may be the precise reason communism and secret combinations are so rarely mentioned today and why the prophets have reverted back to teaching the basic, primary-level fundamentals that we should have learned generations ago.

From the time of the Prophet Joseph Smith to the ministry of President Benson, the prophets warned the Saints constantly regarding Satan's conspiracies. Every Church prophet from Joseph Smith to President Benson spoke of the threat socialism and communism. And each of those men who have been called to lead the Church since then have, if you read their past talks, likewise denounced communism. Indeed, our prophets have consistently identified communism as *the* secret combination foreseen by Moroni, Nephi, and others. They wrote books and delivered talks during Conference, at BYU, and elsewhere. They endlessly warned the Church and the world. Yet, it seems we have not listened.

Even today our leaders throw a word or two in their addresses which let the spiritually attuned know the Lord is aware of the "awful situation" we are in. For instance, in the April 2008 General Conference, President Thomas S. Monson observed:

> "Political machinations ruin the stability of nations, despots grasp for power, and segments of society seem forever downtrodden, deprived of opportunity, and left with a feeling of failure."[449]

More recently, President Russell M. Nelson, whom I unequivocally sustain as the Lord's inspired mouthpiece on earth, gave his hallmark talk titled "Becoming True Millennials." In it, he gently warned of the modern Gadiantons who infest our society. Said he:

---

[449] President Thomas S. Monson, "Examples of Righteousness," General Conference, April, 2008, https://www.lds.org/general-conference/2008/04/examples-of-righteousness?lang=eng.

"Around 41 b.c., many Nephites joined the Church, and the Church prospered. But secret combinations also began to grow, and many of their cunning leaders hid among the people and were difficult to detect. As the people became more and more prideful, many of the Nephites made "a mock of that which was sacred, denying the spirit of prophecy and of revelation."

"Those same threats are among us today. The somber reality is that there are "servants of Satan" embedded throughout society. So be very careful about whose counsel you follow."[450]

I underscore, highlight, and emphasize President Nelson's line: "Those same threats are among us today." Indeed, the *exact same* Gadianton conspiracy is among us today! The same conspiracy with the same Satanic oaths and covenants and the same murderous disposition exists today. Its agents – the "servants of Satan" – are truly "embedded throughout society." Consequently, we must be "very careful" whose counsel we follow.

In October 2017, President Nelson gave an incredible Conference talk titled "The Book of Mormon: What Would Your Life Be Like without It?" In the written version of his remarks, President Nelson supplemented his remarks with several lists of things we know because of that sacred volume of scripture. The very last point on President Nelson's final list – a list documenting information "previously unknown" but revealed by *The Book of Mormon* – stated simply: "Warnings about "secret combinations.""[451]

---

[450] President Russell M. Nelson, "Becoming True Millennials," Worldwide Devotional for Young Adults, BYU-H, January 10, 2016, https://www.lds.org/broadcasts/article/worldwide-devotionals/2016/01/becoming-true-millennials?lang=eng.

[451] President Russell M. Nelson, "The Book of Mormon: What Would Your Life Be Like without It?" General Conference, October, 2017, https://www.lds.org/general-conference/2017/10/the-book-of-mormon-what-would-your-life-be-like-without-it?lang=eng&country=mx.

Yes, *The Book of Mormon* revealed the existence of secret combinations to the world. No other book of scripture available before the Restoration contained this crucial intelligence. Our living prophet, President Russell M. Nelson, is well aware of secret combinations. It is time the general body of Saints caught up and became aware of them as well.

Communism besieges us on all sides every day while hiding behind names and slogans such as feminism, civil rights, equality, and tolerance. The communist virus has infected our nation and we are dying a cruel, agonizing death just as Moroni foretold we would if we built up this secret combination (Ether 8:25). Despite the warnings of prophets throughout the entirety of this dispensation, the Saints have been lulled to sleep by the Devil's siren song.

In his classic Conference talk "Not Commanded in All Things," President Benson exposed the communist secret combination. He also warned the men of the Church that the Devil has largely neutralized them. Listen to this great apostle's cautioning voice:

> "Now, the Lord knew that before the gospel could flourish there must first be an atmosphere of freedom. This is why he first established the Constitution of this land through gentiles whom he raised up (D&C 101:80) before he restored the gospel. In how many communist countries today are we doing missionary work,

building chapels, etc.?[452] And yet practically every one of those countries have been pushed into communism and kept under communism with the great assistance of evil forces which have and are operating within our own country and neighboring lands.

"Yes, were it not for the tragic policies of governments—including our own—tens of millions of people murdered and hundreds of millions enslaved since World War II would be alive and free today to receive the restored gospel. . . .

"Now where do we stand in this struggle, and what are we doing about it?

"The devil knows that if the elders of Israel should ever wake up, they could step forth and help preserve freedom and extend the gospel. Therefore the devil has concentrated, and to a large extent successfully, in neutralizing much of the priesthood. He has reduced them to sleeping giants. . . .

"For our day President David O. McKay has called communism the greatest threat to the Church, and it is certainly the greatest mortal threat this country has ever faced. What are you doing to fight it?

---

[452] As detailed earlier, the Soviet Union faked its "collapse" in order to fool the West. Yet, the Lord God is omnipotent and has shown the communists to be the real fools. He foresaw this ruse and used it against Satan. In opening their nations to the West, the communists have inadvertently allowed the Lord's missionaries in to establish wards, stakes, and temples. I shed tears of joy at the recent announcement in General Conference of a future temple to be built in Russia, the nation in which I served my mission and tried so hard to spread the Gospel to a largely unreceptive people. Missionaries called to Russia are no longer allowed to proselytize and are now called "volunteers." Putin's regime has placed severe restrictions on missionary work in Russia, yet the Lord's work rolls on. However, President Benson's words are still valid when we consider that Red China – home to over 1.3 billion of Heavenly Father's children – does not have the blessing of the Restored Gospel of Christ. Neither do other hostile nations such as North Korea, Israel, and Saudi Arabia. The elders of the Church have a lot of work left to do. And we could do it much more effectively if we realized who our enemy is and how the "servants of Satan" embedded throughout our society operate.

"Brethren, if we had done our homework and were faithful, we could step forward at this time and help save this country. The fact that most of us are unprepared to do it is an indictment we will have to bear. The longer we wait, the heavier the chains, the deeper the blood, the more the persecution, and the less we can carry out our God-given mandate and worldwide mission. The war in heaven is raging on earth today. Are you being neutralized in the battle?"[453]

If you can answer President Benson's piercing question with a clear conscience, I commend you. If you cannot, and you have either not fully awakened or have sat idly by not knowing what to do, I urge you to be up and doing. Educate yourself and spread the word in order to alert your family members and neighbors. Take to social media and trumpet the word of the Lord. Vote properly and in accordance with the principles revealed by the Lord (D&C 98:5-10), and never out of fear of a "worse candidate," or in blind support of your political party. The longer we wait to push back, the more blood and effort will be required to defeat Satan's communist conspiracy.

In addition to informing yourself, President M. Russell Ballard encouraged the Saints to be directly involved in the political process. In the April 2018 General Conference, he advised:

"Church members—both men and women—should not hesitate, if they desire, to run for public office at any level of government wherever they live. Our voices are essential today and important in our schools, our cities, and our countries. Where democracy exists, it is our duty as members to vote for honorable men and women who are willing to serve."[454]

---

[453] President Ezra Taft Benson, "Not Commanded in All Things," Conference Report, April, 1965, 121-125, http://scriptures.byu.edu/#:t585:p401.

[454] President M. Russell Ballard, "Precious Gifts from God," General Conference, April, 2018, https://www.lds.org/general-conference/2018/04/precious-gifts-from-god?lang=eng.

Democracy, as I have noted, is nothing but mobocracy and is anathema to our God-given rights. It is antithetical to the Lord's Constitution. It is often a tool of communists to pave the way for socialism and, finally, communism. Yet, the point is well taken and correct. We must let our unique voices be heard. We must stand up for revealed principles by running for office or supporting only "honorable" candidates – that is, righteous individuals whose principles conform to those given by Jehovah. We *must* become involved. We must distinguish ourselves now more than ever before as "a chosen generation, a royal priesthood, an holy nation, a peculiar people" (1 Peter 2:9).

There are many conflicting voices in the world today. While admitting my weakness and taking full responsibility for every word in this book, I have sincerely tried to present the voice of the prophets as they have warned the Saints these many years. I have a rock-solid testimony of their prophetic call and of their inspired teachings. I wholeheartedly believe their warnings and know they are men of God. I know from personal research, my time in Russia, and the whisperings of the Holy Ghost that what our prophets have taught about communism is the honest truth. I have an absolutely unmovable testimony of the truth that communism is the "greatest satanical threat" to mankind.

I also know that the Lord has used men not of our faith to spread the truth about the communist conspiracy. One such individual was J. Edgar Hoover. Hoover gave this antidote to communism:

> "If communism is to be defeated, the task must rest largely upon the theologians and the ministers of the Gospel. . . .
>
> "In the final analysis, the Communist world view must be met and defeated by the Christian world view."[455]

---

[455] J. Edgar Hoover, *Christianity Today*, October 10, 1960, in Newquist, ed., *Prophets, Principles and National Survival*, 255, footnote.

Only light dispels darkness. Said differently, only Christ – the Light of the world – dispels Satan. As members of the Lord's only true and living Church – those with the greatest measure of light – Latter-day Saints have a special responsibility to be Gospel warriors and slay the Dragon with the mighty sword of the Spirit (D&C 27:15-18).

As the Lord's shock troops, we have a tall order to fill. The Kingdom rests on our shoulders. Our wives and children rely upon us. Our country depends on us. The world needs us.

President Benson painted a dreary picture of our "awful situation" – a picture designed to impress upon us the seriousness of our situation and inspire us to valiant action. As you read his description, remember that stars shine brightest in the dark:

> "Our prestige as a nation is at an all-time low. When will we act like men of courage? When will we stand up to the Godless leaders of the communist conspiracy – the greatest evil in this world? What has happened to our leadership – including the leadership of the Republican Party? There seems to be little moral courage and statesmanship left.
>
> "The hour is late. God help us to wake up and act before it is too late."[456]

Yes, the hour is late. But is it too late? Are we consigned to destruction? Certainly in the long term God's victory is assured and we know that righteousness, happiness, and Freedom will triumph. However, you and I are liable to fall or be swept away in the maelstrom. President Benson feared for the Saints in his day and his remarks are applicable today:

> "What in heaven's name does it take to wake up the slumbering American spirit of resistance? . . . It is too late for mere gestures

---

[456] Andrews, *The Black Hammer*, Foreword, 21.

and admonitions. The hour calls for men of action to step forward and turn our ship away from the treacherous reef dead ahead!"[457]

Yes, it is time for drastic, committed action. Education is the first and most important step, but once we are educated, we must *act*. Knowledge not acted upon is worthless. It is therefore time to be men of courage – men like our forefathers – and stand up for our Freedom against the Red Gadiantons.

We must stand up like the Nephite Freedom Fighters and hoist our own Title of Liberty above our nation. We must come "running together" to rally around our standard. We must declare our heartfelt intention to fight: "In memory of our God, our religion, and freedom, and our peace, our wives, and our children" (Alma 46:12).

Perhaps President Brigham Young's advice is worth our consideration. In his endearing, colorful way, President Young recommended:

> "Let the people make a whip . . . and walk into the temple of the nation, and cleanse it thoroughly out, and put in men who will legislate for their good."[458]

Are you armed with your spiritual and ideological whip? Are you helping to cleanse the temple of our nation? Are you at least attempting to drive out the Red moneychangers?

On Independence Day 1966, President Benson roused us to action and explained the eternal consequences of inaction. He affirmed:

> "[T[he fight for freedom is God's fight. For free agency is an eternal principle. It existed before the world was formed – it will exist forever. Some men may succeed in denying some aspects of

---

[457] Benson, Newquist, ed., *An Enemy Hath Done This*, 180.

[458] President Brigham Young, *Journal of Discourses*, Vol. 7, 13-14, July 4, 1854, http://jod.mrm.org/7/9.

this God-given freedom to their fellow men, but their success is temporary. For freedom is a law of God, a permanent law. And, like any of God's laws, men cannot really break it with impunity. They can only break themselves upon it. So when a man stands for freedom he stands with God. And as long as he stands for freedom he stands with God. And were he to stand alone he would still stand with God – the best company and the greatest power in or out of this world. Where the Spirit of the Lord is, there is liberty; and because truth is eternal, any man will be eternally vindicated and rewarded for his stand for freedom.

"Now being assured that freedom is a God-given principle that will triumph finally and eternally, there yet remains the crucial question: Can freedom triumph now? But the answer to that hangs on the answer to a yet more crucial question: What are we doing to keep freedom alive? For the answer to that first question – Can freedom triumph now? – you see, is speculative. But the answer to the second question – What are we doing to keep freedom alive? – has riding on it matters which will have eternal consequence to every soul, no matter what the temporary outcome; for the Lord has endowed this matter of freedom with such everlasting repercussions that it sifted the spirits of men before this world in the Great War in heaven. And it seems today to be the central issue that is sifting those who are left in the world."[459]

One third of our brothers and sisters rebelled against our Father and the Savior, and against us, in the pre-earth life. The central issue in that struggle was Freedom – the free will, agency, and accountability of mankind. Lucifer's followers opposed this eternal law, but you and I supported the Father's plan of perfect Liberty. The opposition was ultimately banished from God's presence for opposing Freedom. Can you and I expect to escape eternal banishment from our Holy Father's

---

[459] Benson, Newquist, ed., *An Enemy Hath Done This*, 54-55.

presence in the next life if we change our former position and reject Liberty in this life?

When we consider what momentous days we live in, and the steep challenges we face, we tend to make more time for introspection. I suggest each of us ask ourselves these questions: What have *I* done to resist the communist conspiracy? What have *I* done to safeguard my family and home? What have *I* done to warn my neighbor about secret combinations?

Far more importantly than what you have or have not done in the past is what you will do now. So, I ask you, what will you do *now* that you have taken the time to inform yourself by reading this book? What will you do now that you know communism is the "greatest satanical threat" to society and is the cause of our "awful situation"? I hope you will leave this experience a changed person or, at least, more committed to resisting Satan and better equipped to do so.

If you have reached the end of this book, you are now responsible for this information. Not only are you responsible for your personal conduct relative to this material, but you now have a solemn duty to warn your neighbor (D&C 88:81). If you do not act upon these warnings and use this information to help you "throw [your] support on the side of freedom," I fear you may fall and your family may suffer terrible consequences both here and in the hereafter.

You must dig down deep inside you and rekindle your testimony of the Lord's Gospel of Liberty and everything worthy and good which has come because of it. The Gospel really is about Freedom – Freedom from sin, Freedom from sorrow, Freedom from pain, Freedom from death, Freedom from the Devil. Repentance is the remedy to repel Satan's influence in your own life. And faith in the Lord Jesus Christ, our marvelous Redeemer and King, is a prerequisite to true repentance and positive change.

As we have all heard before, faith is an action word. Faith in Jesus Christ activates our lives. Faith is the first step to healing and personal revival. If we have the faith to follow Jesus, we have what it takes to oppose any enemy, conquer any challenge, and soar over every strategically-placed obstacle. We must develop this enlivening faith in our Savior and use it to propel us forward in our battle against the Devil's great and abominable church.

After communist defector Yuri Bezmenov abandoned his KGB post and fled to North America, he devoted himself to exposing the Red conspiracy and teaching the ins and outs of subversion. Bezmenov said that, ultimately, there is only one thing the American People can do to avoid being conquered by the communists. With a gentle smile, he explained:

> "So the answer to ideological subversion, strangely enough, is very simple. You don't have to shoot people. You don't have to aim missiles – Pershings and cruise missiles – at Andropov's headquarters. You simply have to have faith . . . Strike with the power of your spirit and moral superiority. If you don't have that power, it's high time to develop it. And that's the only answer."[460]

Truly, faith in the Savior Jesus Christ – including the vital repentance process which brings God's power rushing into your life – is the *only answer*. "Righteousness exalteth a nation" (Proverbs 14:34). "Blessed is the nation whose God is the Lord" (Psalms 33:12). If we repent and return to the Lord as a People, He will "hear from heaven, and will forgive [our] sin, and will heal [our] land" (2 Chronicles 7:14).

Our nation's scarlet sins will become as "white as snow" if we turn to Jesus the Christ (Isaiah 1:4-18). We have the Lord's promise, His oath and covenant, that "this is a choice land, and whatsoever nation shall possess it shall be free from bondage, and from captivity, and from all other

---

[460] "Yuri Bezmenov: Psychological Warfare Subversion & Control of Western Society (Complete)," *YouTube*, uploaded February 23, 2011, accessed April 10, 2018, https://www.youtube.com/watch?v=5gnpCqsXE8g.

nations under heaven, if they will but serve the God of the land, who is Jesus Christ" (Ether 2:12). Whom do we serve?

We must remember that this is the Lord's fight. We are not alone, our Master goes before us. Let's keep these encouraging lyrics always in our hearts:

> "Onward, Christian soldiers!
>
> Marching as to war,
>
> With the cross of Jesus
>
> Going on before.
>
> Christ, the royal Master,
>
> Leads against the foe;
>
> Forward into battle,
>
> See his banners go!"[461]

At the end of the day, President Benson's words ring true:

> "If we lose our freedom it will be because we did not care enough – because we were not alert enough – because we were too apathetic to take note while the precious waters of our God-given freedom slipped away – drop by drop – down the drain."[462]

Will President Benson's words be prophetic, or will we step forward and wave our own Title of Liberty in the air for all to see? Will we follow our Master into battle and carry His banner or will we brandish the Red flag of the Adversary? Will we allow the communist current to sweep us away, or

---

[461] "Onward Christian Soldiers," LDS Hymn #246, https://www.lds.org/music/library/hymns/onward-christian-soldiers?lang=eng&_r=1.

[462] Benson, The Red Carpet, 63.

will we stand firm in holy places? Will we be overcome by the Red Gadiantons, or will we, like Lachoneus, Captain Moroni, Helaman, Mormon, Teancum, and the other Nephite Freedom Fighters, take the initiative and defend our children, our wives, our peace, our Freedom, our religion, and our God?

To repeat: *The Lord has already won the victory!* He conquered death and hell when He burst forth from the tomb on Resurrection morning. His Atonement vanquished the eternal consequences of sin for all who will repent and follow Him. His brilliant light will ultimately repel Satan and his works of darkness. The Lord is our King – the only rightful Ruler of this earth.

The Savior marches before us. He leads us into battle. You and I fought with Him in the pre-earth clash for our agency. We fought together to uphold the Father's Plan of Happiness and we acknowledge the Savior as our General, the Lord of Hosts, the God of Heavenly Armies. In that titanic struggle, we fought and we won. Take courage; we will win here, too, so long as we plant ourselves on the Lord's side.

The Lord Jesus promised the Prophet Joseph Smith that the Devil's church *will* fall. He declared:

> "And the great and abominable church, which is the whore of all the earth, shall be cast down by devouring fire, according as it is spoken by the mouth of Ezekiel the prophet, who spoke of these things, which have not come to pass but surely must, as I live, for abominations shall not reign" (D&C 29:21).

And Nephi, who walked this earth some 2,600 years ago, was also aware of the final outcome of the struggle and likewise promised:

> "[T]hat great and abominable church, the whore of all the earth, must tumble to the earth, and great must be the fall thereof" (2 Nephi 28:18).

No, the result of this spiritual war is *not* in question. From the day that the Father banished Lucifer and his hosts from the pre-mortal councils, Satan's fate was sealed. The Atonement was the death nail in Lucifer's gloomy coffin. However, the short-term outcomes, your personal fate, and the safety of your family, *are* up for grabs and depend upon how you use your agency.

Agency relies upon knowledge and correct information. The Holy Ghost confirms truth to the human soul, making a man stalwart and firm in the face of all worldly opposition. But this gift does not come for free – there is a price to be paid. Will you pay the price of repentance, obedience, and sincerity of soul so that you can join Nephi and the righteous at the tree of life, or will you be caught in Lucifer's red fog of lies and throw your lot in with the multitudes in the great and spacious building?

After having read this book, you have the necessary knowledge to make correct decisions regarding Satan's assault on humanity. You now know that there are modern Gadianton Robbers in our midst – the Satanic communists and their allies. You can now identify this enemy and, therefore, you have the ability to choose to resist him and to serve the Lord Jesus Christ in His Kingdom instead. You can now carry out your "imperative duty" to your brothers and sisters because you now see the enemy who lies in wait to deceive and destroy (D&C 123:11-15).

Yes, you have the great honor of showing that *you* are on the Lord's side. You have the privilege of declaring your allegiance to that humble Man of Nazareth, the Prince of Righteousness, the Lord God of Heaven and earth. You now have the power, and the sacred duty, to stand fearlessly against the communist conspiracy, because now you have been warned.

In the name of Jesus Christ, Amen.

Recommended Reading on Communism:

100 Things You Should Know About Communism in the USA; Religion; Education; Labor and Government, by the U.S. House of Representatives, Committee on UnAmerican Activities

A Century of Red, by Zack Strong

A Concise History of the Russian Revolution, by Richard Pipes

A People's Tragedy: The Russian Revolution 1891-1924, by Orlando Figes

A Riddle Wrapped Up in an Enigma: The Gorbachev-Yeltsin-Putin Deception, by Nevin Gussack

Again, May God Forgive Us, by Robert Welch

An Enemy Hath Done This, by Ezra Taft Benson

Back from the Dead: The Return of the Evil Empire, by Cliff Kincaid, Konstantin Preobrazhensky, J.R. Nyquist, and Toby Westerman

Behind Communism: Updated, Revised and Expanded 1917-2010, by Frank L. Britton

Behind the Desert Storm: A Secret Archive Stolen from the Kremlin that Sheds New Light on the Arab Revolutions in the Middle East, by Pavel Stroilov

Blacklisted by History: The Untold Story of Senator Joe McCarthy and His Fight Against America's Enemies, by M. Stanton Evans

Blowing Up Russia: The Secret Plot to Bring Back KGB Terror, by Alexander Litvinenko

Clash of Kingdoms: What the Bible Says About Russia, ISIS, Iran, and the End Times, by Charles Dyer and Mark Tobey

Communism in Ambush: How the Scourge of the 20th Century is Preparing for Fresh Savagery, by Harun Yahya

Communism in Germany: The Truth about the Communist Conspiracy on the Eve of the National Revolution, by Adolf Ehrt

Communism with the Mask off and Bolshevism in Theory and Practice, by Joseph Goebbels

Comrade Obama Unmasked: Marxist Mole in the White House, by Cliff Kincaid

Death of a Dissident: The Poisoning of Alexander Litvinenko and the Return of the KGB, by Alex Goldfarb

Disinformation: Former Spy Chief Reveals Secret Strategies for Undermining Freedom, Attacking Religion, and Promoting Terrorism, by Ion Mihai Pacepa

Double Lives: Spies and Writers in the Secret Soviet War of Ideas Against the West, by Stephen Koch

Dupes: How America's Adversaries Have Manipulated Progressives for a Century, by Paul Kengor

Freedom and Foreign Policy, by Thomas J. Dodd

From the Gulag to the Killing Fields: Personal Accounts of Political Violence and Repression in Communist States, edited by Paul Hollander

Golitsyn Vindicated? A Second Look at "Splits" in the Communist World During the Cold War, by Nevin Gussack

Hegemon: China's Plan to Dominate Asia and the World, by Steven W. Mosher

I Saw Poland Betrayed: An American Ambassador Reports to the American People, by Arthur Bliss Lane

In Denial: Historians, Communism, and Espionage, by John Earl Haynes and Harvey Klerh

Inside the Red Zone: Physical and Spiritual Preparedness Against Weapons of Mass Destruction, by Igor V. Shafhid

Jewish-Run Concentration Camps in the Soviet Union, by Herman Greife

Khrushchev's "Mein Kampf", by Nikita Khrushchev, with introduction by Harrison E. Salisbury

Lenin: A Biography, by Robert Service

Lenin: Life and Legacy, by Dmitri Volkogonov

Lines of Credit: Ropes of Bondage: The Story of the Financiers, Their Fellow Conspirators and the Plot to Destroy Western Christian Civilization, by Robert Henry Goldsborough

Marxism and the National-Colonial Question, by Joseph Stalin

Mao's Great Famine: The History of China's Most Devastating Catastrophe, 1958-1962, by Frank Dikotter

Mao: The Unknown Story, by Jung Chang and Jon Halliday

Marx and Satan, by Richard Wurmbrand

Marxist Madrassas: The Hostile Takeover of Higher Education in America, by Cliff Kincaid

Masters of Deceit: What the communist bosses are doing now to bring America to its knees, by J. Edgar Hoover

Men Without Faces: The Communist Conspiracy in the U.S.A., by Louis Francis Budenz

New Lies for Old, by Anatoliy Golitsyn

On a Field of Red: The Communist International and the Coming of World War II, by Anthony Cave Brown and Charles B. MacDonald

One World Order: Socialist Dictatorship, by John Coleman

Operation Snow: How a Soviet Mole in FDR's White House Triggered Pearl Harbor, by John Koster

Origins of the Fourth World War, by J.R. Nyquist

Prophets, Principles and National Survival, edited by Jerreld L. Newquist

Putin's Kleptocracy: Who Owns Russia? by Karen Dawisha

Putin's Labyrinth: Spies, Murder, and the Dark Heart of the New Russia, by Steve LeVine

Putin's Russia, by Anna Politkovskaya

Red Army: The Radical Network That Must Be Defeated To Save America, by Aaron Klein and Brenda J. Elliott

Red Badge: A Veteran Peace Officer's Commentary on the Marxist Subversion of American Law Enforcement and Culture, by Doug Traubel

Red Cocaine: The Drugging of America, by Joseph D. Douglass, Jr.

Red Dawn in Retrospect: Soviet-Chinese Intentions for Conquest of the United States, by Nevin Gussack

Red Dragon Rising: Communist China's military threat to America, by Edward Timperlake and William C. Triplett II

Red Jihad: Moscow's Final Solution for America and Israel, by Cliff Kincaid and J.R. Nyquist

Red Star Rising: The Making of Barack Hussein Obama and the Transformation of America, by Cliff Kincaid

Russia Rising: Tracking the Bear in Bible Prophecy, by Mark Hitchcock

Russia's Agony: An Eyewitness of the Russian Revolution, by Robert Wilton

Soviet Impregnational Propaganda, by Baruch Hazan

Stalin: A Biography, by Robert Service

Stalin: The Court of the Red Tsar, by Simon Sebag Montefiore

Stalin's Secret Agents: The Subversion of Roosevelt's Government, by M. Stanton Evans and Herbert Romerstein

Survival is Not Enough: Soviet Realities and America's Future, by Richard Pipes

Takedown: From Communists to Progressives, How the Left Has Sabotaged Family and Marriage, by Paul Kengor

The Arms Control Delusion: How Twenty-Five Years of Arms Control Has Made the World Less Safe, by Senator Malcolm Wallop and Angelo Codevilla

The Bamboo Cross: The Witness of Christian Martyrs in Communist-Ridden Jungles of Viet Nam, by Homer E. Dowdy

The Black Book of Communism: Crimes, Terror, Repression, by Stephane Courtois, et al.

The Black Hammer: A Study of Black Power, Red Influence and White Alternatives, by Wes Andrews

The Bolshevik Invasion of the West, by Louis Francis Budenz

The Book of Mormon and the Constitution, by Hans Verlan Andersen

The Chief Culprit: Stalin's Grand Design to Start World War II, by Viktor Suvorov

The China Threat: How the People's Republic Targets America, by Bill Gertz

The Fabians, by Norman MacKenzie

The Forsaken: An American Tragedy in Stalin's Russia, Tim Tzouliadis

The Great and Abominable Church of the Devil, by Hans Verlan Andersen

The Gulag Archipelago, by Aleksandr Solzhenitsyn

The Harvest of Sorrow: Soviet Collectivization and the Terror-Famine, by Robert Conquest

The Hundred-Year Marathon: China's Secret Strategy to Replace America as the Global Superpower, by Michael Pillsbury

The KGB and Soviet Disinformation: An Insider's View, by Ladislav Bittman

The Less You Know, the Better You Sleep: Russia's Road to Terror and Dictatorship under Yeltsin and Putin, by David Satter

The Long Walk: The True Story of a Trek to Freedom, by Slavomir Rawicz

The Myth of German Villainy, by Benton L. Bradberry

The Naked Communist, by W. Cleon Skousen

The Naked Socialist, by Paul B. Skousen

The Party: The Secret World of China's Communist Rulers, by Richard McGregor

The Party Forever: Inside China's Modern Communist Elite, by Rowan Callick

The Perestroika Deception, by Anatoliy Golitsyn

The Politically Incorrect Guide to Communism, by Paul Kengor

The Puzzle of the Soviet Church: An Inside Look at Christianity & Glasnost, by Kent R. Hill

The Red Carpet: Socialism - the Royal Road to Communism, by Ezra Taft Benson

The Red China Papers: What Americans Deserve to Know About U.S.-Chinese Relations, by Anthony Kubek

The Road Ahead: America's Creeping Revolution, by John T. Flynn

The Rulers of Russia, by Denis Fahey

The Russian View of U.S. Strategy: Its Past, Its Future, by Jonathan Samuel Lockwood and Kathleen O'Brien Lockwood

The Secret Behind Communism: The Ethnic Origins of the Russian Revolution and the Greatest Holocaust in the History of Mankind, by David Duke

The Soviet Experiment: Russia, the USSR, and the Successor States, by Ronald Grigor Suny

The Soviet Offensive: The Soviet Challenge to Western Freedom, by Chapman Pincher

The Soviet Union and Terrorism, by Roberta Goren

The Soviet World of American Communism, by Harvey Klehr, John Earl Haynes, and Kyrill M. Anderson

The Sword and the Shield: The Mitrokhin Archive and the Secret History of the KGB, by Christopher Andrew and Vasili Mitrokhin

The Sword of Revolution and the Communist Apocalypse, by Cliff Kincaid

The Terror Network: The Secret War of International Terrorism, by Claire Sterling

The Web of Subversion, by James Burnham

The World Conquerors: The Real War Criminals, by Louis Marschalko

The Whisperers: Private Life in Stalin's Russia, by Orlando Figes

This is My Story, by Louis Francis Budenz

Thou Shalt Kill: Revolutionary Terrorism in Russia, 1894-1917, by Anna Geifman

Through the Eyes of the Enemy, by Stanislav Lunev

Title of Liberty: A Voice of Warming, by Ezra Taft Benson, compiled by Mark A. Benson

To Choose Freedom, by Vladimir Bukovsky

Toward Socialist America: An Analysis of America's Slide into Collectivism, by Robert Gorgoglione, Sr.

Trotsky: A Biography, by Robert Service

Unrestricted Warfare: China's Master Plan to Destroy America, by Qiao Liang and Wang Xiangsui

We Will Bury You, by Jan Sejna

What to Do When the Russians Come: A Survivor's Guide, by Robert Conquest and Jon Manchip White

Willing Accomplices: How KGB Covert Influence Agents Created Political Correctness, Obama's Hate-America-First Political Platform, and Destroyed America, by Kent Clizbe

Winter Is Coming: Why Vladimir Putin and the Enemies of the Free World Must Be Stopped, by Garry Kasparov

Witness, by Whittaker Chambers

World Revolution: The Plot Against Civilisation, by Nesta H. Webster

You Can Still Trust the Communists. . . to be Communists (Socialists and Progressives too), by David A. Noebel

You Can Trust the Communists (to be Communists), by Fred Schwarz

Young Stalin, by Simon Sebag Montefiore

Recommended Reading on Conspiracy:

Against Our Better Judgement: The Hidden History of How the U.S. Was Used to Create Israel, by Alison Weir

America's Secret Establishment: An Introduction to the Order of Skull & Bones, by Antony C. Sutton

America's Defense Line: The Justice Department's Battle to Register the Israel Lobby as Agents of a Foreign Government, by Grant F. Smith

Architects of the Culture of Death, by Donald De Marco and Benjamin Wiker

Awakening to Our Awful Situation: Warnings From the Nephite Prophets, by Jack Monnett

Behind the Green Mask: U.N. Agenda 21, by Rosa Koire

Behind the Lodge Door: Church, State and Freemasonry in America, by Paul A. Fisher

Behold a Pale Horse, by William Cooper

Conspiracy of the Six-Pointed Star: Eye-Opening Revelations and Forbidden Knowledge About Israel, the Jews, Zionism, and the Rothschilds, by Texe Marrs

Cruel Hoax: Feminism and the New World Order, by Henry Makow

Cults that Kill: Probing the Underworld of Occult Crime, by Larry Kahaner

Descent into Slavery? by Des Griffin

Egyptian Magic: A History of Ancient Egyptian Magical Practices Including Amulets, Names, Spells, Enchantments, Figures, Formulae, Supernatural Ceremonies, and Words of Power, E.A. Wallis Budge

End Feminism; Save the World, by Danelle Malchus and Kylie Malchus

Foundations: Their Power and Influence, by Rene A. Wormser

Fourth Reich of the Rich, by Des Griffin

Freemasonry and Its Ancient Mystic Rites, by C.W. Leadbeater

Global Bondage: The U.N. Plan to Rule the World, by Cliff Kincaid

Global Greens: Inside the International Environmental Establishment, by James M. Sheehan

Gods of the New Age, by Caryl Matrisciana

Grand Deceptions: Zionist Intrigue in the 20th and 21st Centuries, by Brandon Martinez

Hiding in Plain Sight: Unmasking the Secret Combinations of the Last Days, by Ken Bowers

Hope of the Wicked: The Master Plan to Rule the World, by Ted Flynn

Human Sacrifice: A Shocking Exposé of Ritual Killings Worldwide, by Jimmy Lee Shreeve

Illuminati: The Cult that Hijacked the World, by Henry Makow

Inside the Illuminati: Evidence, Objectives, and Methods of Operation, by Mark Dice

It's Not Easy Being God: The Real George Soros, by Joy Tiz

Kabbalah: A Definitive History of the Evolution, Ideas, Leading Figures and Extraordinary Influence of Jewish Mysticism, by Gershom Scholem

Memoirs Illustrating the History of Jacobinism, vol. 1-4, by the Abbe Barruel

Mind Control, World Control: The Encyclopedia of Mind Control, by Jim Keith

Morals and Dogma of the Ancient and Accepted Scottish Rite of Freemasonry, Albert Pike

New Age Menace: The Secret War Against the Followers of Christ, by David N. Balmforth

None Dare Call It Education, by John A. Stormer

None Dare Call It Conspiracy, by Gary Allen

None Dare Call It Treason, by John A. Stormer

Occult Science in India and Among the Ancients, by Louis Jacolloit

Occult Theocrasy, vol. 1 & 2, by Edith Starr Miller

On the Jews and Their Lies, by Martin Luther

One Nation Under Israel, by Andrew Hurley

Pawns in the Game, by William Guy Carr

Planet Rothschild: The Forbidden History of the New World Order, vol. 1 & 2, by M.S. King

Prince of Darkness: Antichrist and the New World Order, by Grant R. Jeffrey

Proofs of a Conspiracy, by John Robison

Propaganda, by Edward Bernays

Psychic Dictatorship in the U.S.A., by Alex Constantine

Rules for Radicals: A Pragmatic Primer for Realistic Radicals, by Saul D. Alinsky

Secret Combinations Today: A Voice of Warning, by Robert E. Hales

Secret Societies and Subversive Movements, by Nesta H. Webster

Secrets of the Mahdi: Unlocking the Mystery of Revelation and the Antichrist, by Michael Youssef

Strategic Relocation: North American Guide to Safe Places, by Joel Skousen and Andrew Skousen

The Anglo-American Establishment, by Carroll Quigley

The Arcana of Freemasonry: A History of Masonic Signs and Symbols, by Albert Churchward

The Blazing Star and the Jewish Kabbalah, by William B. Greene

The Conspirators' Hierarchy: The Committee of 300, by John Coleman

The Creature from Jekyll Island: A Second Look at the Federal Reserve, by G. Edward Griffin

The Empire of the City, by E.C. Knuth

The Essential Kabbalah: The Heart of Jewish Mysticism, by Daniel C. Matt

The Federal Reserve Conspiracy, by Antony C. Sutton

The High Priests of War: The Secret History of How America's "Neo-Conservative" Trotskyites Came to Power and Orchestrated the War Against Iraq as the First Step in Their Drive for Global Empire, by Michael Collins Piper

The International Jew – The World's Foremost Problem, vol. 1 & 2, by Henry Ford

The Jesuits: The Society of Jesus and the Betrayal of the Roman Catholic Church, by Malachi Martin

The Jewish 1960s: An American Sourcebook, edited by Michael E. Staub

The Leipzig Connection, by Paolo Lionni

The Meaning of Masonry, by W.L. Wilmshurst

The Naked Capitalist: A Review and Commentary on Dr. Carroll Quigley's book Tragedy and Hope, by W. Cleon Skousen

The New Underworld Order, by Christopher Story

The New World Order, by A. Ralph Epperson

The Occult Conspiracy: Secret Societies – Their Influence and Power in World History, by Michael Howard

The Restoration of Our Republic: How to declare independence from Party Politics, Special Interests, Mob Democracy an Money-Power to Re-establish Freedom and Liberty in America, by Farley Anderson

The Ruling Elite: A Study in Imperialism, Genocide and Emancipation, by Deanna Spingola

The Ruling Elite: Death, Destruction, and Domination, by Deanna Spingola

The Ruling Elite: The Zionist Seizure of World Power, by Deanna Spingola

The Satanic Bible, by Anton LaVey

The Secret Societies of All Ages and Countries, vol. 1 & 2, by Charles William Heckethorn

The Secret Teachings of the Masonic Lodge: A Christian Perspective, by John Ankerberg and John Weldon

The Shadow Party: How George Soros, Hillary Clinton, and Sixties Radicals Seized Control of the Democratic Party, by David Horowitz and Richard Poe

The Shadows of Power: The Council on Foreign Relations and the American Decline, by James Perloff

The Tavistock Institute of Human Relations: Shaping the Moral, Spiritual, Cultural, Political, and Economic Decline of the United States of America, by John Coleman

The Ugly Truth About the Anti-Defamation League, by Executive Intelligence Review

The Work of All Ages: The Ongoing Plot to Rule the World from Biblical Times to the Present, by Peter Christian

The World's Last Dictator, Dwight L. Kinman

There Are Save Two Churches Only, vol. 1: Be Ye Not Deceived: God Creates, Satan Imitates, by D. Christian Markham

Tragedy and Hope: A History of the World in Our Time, by Carroll Quigley

Transcendental Magic, by Elphias Levi

Truth is a Lonely Warrior: Unmasking the Forces Behind Global Destruction, by James Perloff

Trilaterals Over Washington, by Antony C. Sutton and Patrick M. Wood

World Freemasonry Unveiled, translated by V.K. Clark

Yoga and the Body of Christ: What Position Should Christians Hold? by Dave Hunt

Zionism, Militarism, and the Decline of US Power, by James Petras

Recommended Reading on Gospel Topics:

A New Witness for the Articles of Faith, by Bruce R. McConkie

Answers to Gospel Questions, by Joseph Fielding Smith

Apostasy from the Divine Church, James L. Barker

Apostasy to Restoration, by T. Edgar Lyon

Bad Guys of the Book of Mormon, by Dennis Gaunt

Doctrines of Salvation, three volumes, by Joseph Fielding Smith

Exploring the Book of Mormon in the Heartland, by Rod Meldrum

Finding Light in a Dark World, by James E. Faust

Gospel Doctrine, by Joseph F. Smith

Hearing the Voice of the Lord: Principles and Patterns of Personal Revelation, by Gerald N. Lund

If Men Were Angels: The Book of Mormon, Christ, and the Constitution, by Brad E. Hainsworth

Joseph Smith: Presidential Candidate – Setting the Record Straight, by Arnold K. Garr

Just and Holy Principles: Latter-day Saint Reading on America and the Constitution, edited by Ralph C. Hancock

Leadership, three volumes, by Sterling W. Sill

Man – His Origin and Destiny, by Joseph Fielding Smith

Many Are Called But Few Are Chosen, by Hans Verlan Andersen

Mormon Doctrine, by Bruce R. McConkie

Motherhood: A Partnership with God, edited by Harold Lundstrom

Prophecies and Promises – The Book of Mormon and the United States of America, by Bruce H. Meldrum and Rod Meldrum

Quotes from Prophets on Mothers & Families, edited by Laura M. Hawkes

Satan's War on Free Agency, by Greg Wright

Stand Fast By Our Constitution, by J. Reuben Clark, Jr.

Take Heed to Yourselves! by Joseph Fielding Smith

The Birth We Call Death, by Paul H. Dunn

The Book of Revelation Today: The Last of the Last Days – Who, What, Where, When, Why and How, by Farley Anderson

The Elders of Israel and the Constitution, by Jerome Horowitz

The Falling Away, by B. H. Roberts

The First 2,000 Years: From Adam to Abraham, by W. Cleon Skousen

The Fourth Thousand Years: From David to Christ, by W. Cleon Skousen

The Gospel through the Ages, by Milton R. Hunter

The Great Prologue, by Mark E. Petersen

The Incomparable Christ: Our Master and Model, by Vaughn J. Featherstone

The Life Before: How Our Premortal Existence Affects Our Mortal Life, by Brent L. Top

The Majesty of God's Law, by W. Cleon Skousen

The Master Deceiver: Understanding Satan's Lies and How to Resist Them, by David J. Stitt

The Millennial Messiah, by Bruce R. McConkie

The Moral Basis of a Free Society, by Hans Verlan Andersen

The Mortal Messiah, three volumes, by Bruce R. McConkie

The Promised Messiah, by Bruce R. McConkie

The Prophet Joseph Smith's Views on the Powers and Policy of the Government of the United States, by Joseph Smith

The Spirit of America: Patriotic Addresses from America's Freedom Festival, by Bookcraft

The Third Thousand Years: From Abraham to David, by W. Cleon Skousen

This Land: They Came from the East, by Wayne N. May

This Nation Shall Endure, by Ezra Taft Benson

Using the Book of Mormon to Combat Falsehoods in Organic Evolution, by Clark A. Peterson

Woman and the Priesthood, by Rodney Turner

You and Your Marriage, by Hugh B. Brown

Contact/Find Author

zackstrongbooks@outlook.com

amazon.com/author/zackstrong

https://theamericancitadel.com

https://www.facebook.com/TheRedPlague/

https://www.facebook.com/LuciferianismTheConspiracy/

https://www.facebook.com/feminismisadisease/

https://www.facebook.com/ReformersOfError/

https://www.facebook.com/ProphetsInTheLandAgain/